Lecture Notes in Artificial Intelligence (LNAI)

Vol. 345: R. T. Nossum (Ed.), Advanced Topics in Artificial Intelligence. VII, 233 pages. 1988.

Vol. 346: M. Reinfrank, J. de Kleer, M. L. Ginsberg, E.Sandewall (Eds.), Non-Monotonic Reasoning. Proceedings, 1988. XIV, 237 pages. 1989.

Vol. 347: K. Morik (Ed.), Knowledge Representation and Organization in Machine Learning. XV, 319 pages. 1989.

Vol. 353: S. Hölldobler, Foundations of Equational Logic Programming. X, 250 pages. 1989.

Vol. 383: K. Furukawa, H. Tanaka, T. Fujisaki (Eds.), Logic Programming '88. Proceedings, 1988. IX, 251 pages. 1989.

Vol. 390: J. P. Martins, E. M. Morgado (Eds.), EPIA 89. Proceedings, 1989. XII, 400 pages. 1989.

Vol. 395: M. Schmidt-Schauß, Computational Aspects of an Order-Sorted Logic with Term Declarations. VIII, 171 pages. 1989.

Vol. 397: K. P. Jantke (Ed.), Analogical and Inductive Inference. X, 338 pages. 1989.

Other volumes of the Lecture Notes in Computer Science relevant to Artificial Intelligence:

Vol. 170: R. E. Shostak (Ed.), Seventh International Conference on Automated Deduction. IV, 508 pages. 1984.

Vol. 202: J.-P. Jouannaud (Ed.), Rewriting Techniques and Applications. VI, 441 pages. 1985.

Vol. 215: W. Bibel, K. P. Jantke (Eds.), Mathematical Methods of Specification and Synthesis of Software Systems '85. Proceedings, 1985. 245 pages. 1986.

Vol. 221: E. Wada (Ed.), Logic Programming '85. Proceedings, 1985. IX, 311 pages. 1986.

Vol. 225: E. Shapiro (Ed.), Third International Conference on Logic Programming. Proceedings, 1986. IX, 720 pages. 1986.

Vol. 230: J. H. Siekmann (Ed.), 8th International Conference on Automated Deduction. Proceedings, 1986. X, 708 pages. 1986.

Vol. 231: R. Hausser, NEWCAT: Parsing Natural Language Using Left-Associative Grammar. II, 540 pages. 1986.

Vol. 232: W. Bibel, Ph. Jorrand (Eds.), Fundamentals of Artificial Intelligence. VII, 313 pages. 1986. Reprint as Springer Study Edition 1987.

Vol. 238: L. Naish, Negation and Control in Prolog. IX, 119 pages. 1986.

Vol. 256: P. Lescanne (Ed.), Rewriting Techniques and Applications. Proceedings, 1987. VI, 285 pages. 1987.

Vol. 264: E. Wada (Ed.), Logic Programming '86. Proceedings, 1986. VI, 179 pages. 1987.

Vol. 265: K. P. Jantke (Ed.), Analogical and Inductive Inference. Proceedings, 1986. VI, 227 pages. 1987.

Vol. 271: D. Snyers, A. Thayse, From Logic Design to Logic Programming. IV, 125 pages. 1987.

Vol. 306: M. Boscarol, L. Carlucci Aiello, G. Levi (Eds.), Foundations of Logic and Functional Programming. Proceedings, 1986. V, 218 pages. 1988.

Vol. 308: S. Kaplan, J.-P. Jouannaud (Eds.), Conditional Term Rewriting Systems. Proceedings, 1987. VI, 278 pages. 1988.

Vol. 310: E. Lusk, R. Overbeek (Eds.), 9th International Conference on Automated Deduction. Proceedings, 1988. X, 775 pages. 1988.

Vol. 315: K. Furukawa, H. Tanaka, T. Fujisaki (Eds.), Logic Programming '87. Proceedings, 1987. VI, 327 pages. 1988.

Vol. 320: A. Blaser (Ed.), Natural Language at the Computer. Proceedings, 1988. III, 176 pages. 1988.

Vol. 336: B. R. Donald, Error Detection and Recovery in Robotics. XXIV, 314 pages. 1989.

Lecture Notes in Artificial Intelligence

Subseries of Lecture Notes in Computer Science
Edited by J. Siekmann

Lecture Notes in Computer Science

Edited by G. Goos and J. Hartmanis

Editorial

Artificial Intelligence has become a major discipline under the roof of Computer Science. This is also reflected by a growing number of titles devoted to this fast developing field to be published in our Lecture Notes in Computer Science. To make these volumes immediately visible we have decided to distinguish them by a special cover as Lecture Notes in Artificial Intelligence, constituting a subseries of the Lecture Notes in Computer Science. This subseries is edited by an Editorial Board of experts from all areas of AI, chaired by Jörg Siekmann, who are looking forward to consider further AI monographs and proceedings of high scientific quality for publication.

We hope that the constitution of this subseries will be well accepted by the audience of the Lecture Notes in Computer Science, and we feel confident that the subseries will be recognized as an outstanding opportunity for publication by authors and editors of the AI community.

Editors and publisher

Lecture Notes in Artificial Intelligence

Subseries of Lecture Notes in Computer Science
Edited by J. Siekmann

390

J.P. Martins   E.M. Morgado   (Eds.)

EPIA 89

4th Portuguese Conference on Artificial Intelligence
Lisbon, Portugal, September 26–29, 1989
Proceedings

Springer-Verlag

Berlin Heidelberg New York London Paris Tokyo Hong Kong

Editors

João Pavão Martins
Ernesto Marques Morgado
Departamento de Engenharia Mêcanica, Instituto Superior Técnico
Avenida Rovisco Pais, P-1000 Lisboa, Portugal

CR Subject Classification (1987): I.2

ISBN 3-540-51665-4 Springer-Verlag Berlin Heidelberg New York
ISBN 0-387-51665-4 Springer-Verlag New York Berlin Heidelberg

© Springer-Verlag Berlin Heidelberg 1989
Printed in Germany

Printing and binding: Druckhaus Beltz, Hemsbach/Bergstr.
2145/3140-543210 – Printed on acid-free paper

PREFACE

The Fourth Portuguese Conference on Artificial Intelligence (EPIA89) was organized under the auspices of the Portuguese Association for Artificial Intelligence (Associação Portuguesa para a Inteligência Artificial - APPIA). The previous Portuguese conferences, held in 1985, 1986, and 1987 had the goal of communication among the Portuguese AI community. For that reason, the standards of acceptance were low and acceptance was based on abstracts only. The goal of the first three conferences was successfully met as they helped the Portuguese AI community to grow and mature. In the 1987 conference the standards and themes of some presentations reached an international level.

It was decided in 1987 that future conferences would be held every two years, that the participation should be broadened to an international audience, and that the quality of the technical contributions should increase. The 1989 conference is the first edition conducted under such orientation. We received 62 contributions, and each contribution was refereed by at least two members of the Program Committee. Out of those, 28 were selected for publication in the present Proceedings. The papers of the five invited lecturers were accepted without refereeing. The paper "On the Classification and Existence of Structures in Default Logic", by Aidong Zhang and Wiktor Marek received the prize of the most outstanding paper in the Conference.

EPIA89 is devoted to all areas of AI and covers theoretical and foundatioñal aspects as well as applications. Submissions were encouraged in the following areas: Knowledge Representation, Automatic Deduction, Non-standard Logics, Logic Programming, Natural Language Understanding, Learning, Planning, Architectures and Languages, Knowledge Engineering, and Applications.

We thank the other Program Committee members Pavel Brazdil, Helder Coelho, Ernesto Costa, Miguel Filgueiras, Luis Monteiro, Fernando Pereira, Luis Moniz Pereira, and António Porto for their contribution to the technical quality of the Conference.

We thank our invited speakers Robert C. Moore, António G. Portela, Michael Reinfrank, Stuart C. Shapiro, and John F. Sowa for increasing the interest and quality of our Conference with their presentations.

We also thank the following institutions that contributed (financially or otherwise) to the organization of the conference:

BESCL, Banco Espírito Santo & Comercial de Lisboa supplied the participants with folders and note pads;

CONTROL DATA Portuguesa, SA supplied general financial support during the Conference;

CTT/TLP supported the publication of these Proceedings;

DIGITAL Equipment Portugal supported the participation of Robert C. Moore;

Fundação Calouste Gulbenkian allowed us to use their auditoriums for the Conference;

IBM Portuguesa supported the participation of John F. Sowa;

INIC, Instituto Nacional de Investigação Científica supplied general financial support during the Conference;

INTERLOG supplied financial support for the best paper award;

IST, Instituto Superior Técnico supported all the communications (electronic and otherwise) needed for the organization of the Conference;

NIXDORF supported the participation of Michael Reinfrank;

SISCOG supplied secretarial work;

UNISYS supported the participation of Stuart C. Shapiro.

We hope that this first international conference will be a seed for future AI conferences in Portugal and for the development of Artificial Intelligence.

Lisbon, July 1989

João P. Martins
Ernesto M. Morgado

CONTENTS

Knowledge Representation

A Pragmatic Look at Artificial Intelligence
  Jacob L. Mey 1

An Original Object-Oriented Approach for Relation Management
  Mireille Fornarino, Anne-Marie Pinna, and Brigitte Trousse ... 13

Conceptual Representation Techniques in the Framework of
Large   Knowledge Based Systems
  Gian Piero Zarri 27

Efficient Frame Systems
  Dario Giuse 39

First Order Theories of Quantification
  Arkady Rabinov 51

A Horn Clause Theory of Inheritance and Temporal Reasoning
  Stephen G. Pimentel and John L. Cuadrado 63

Automated Deduction

Explicit Context-Based Blackboards Enhancing Blackboard
Systems Performance
  Cheng-Seen Ho 73

Reasoning With the Unknown
  Nuno J. Mamede, Carlos Pinto-Ferreira, and João P. Martins ... 85

Path-Based Inference in SNeBR
  Maria R. Cravo and João P. Martins 97

Relevant Counterfactuals
    Luís Moniz Pereira and Joaquim Nunes Aparício 107

Non-Standard Logics

Non-monotonic Reasoning with the ATMS
    F. Zetzsche 119

On the Classification and Existence of Structures in Default Logic
    Aidong Zhang and Wiktor Marek 129

Inscription - A Rule of Conjecture
    Carlos Pinto-Ferreira and João P. Martins 141

Logic Programming

Algorithmic Debugging of Prolog Side-Effects
    Luís Moniz Pereira and Miguel Calejo 151

Natural Language Understanding

Cooperating Rewrite Processes Revisited
    Miguel Filgueiras 163

CLG: A Grammar Formalism Based on Constraint Resolution
    Luís Damas and Giovanni B. Varile 175

Some Comments on a Logic Programming Approach to
Natural Language Semantics
    Ana Paula Tomás and Miguel Filgueiras 187

Semantic Analysis of Time and Tense in Natural Language:
An Implementation
    Nelma Moreira 198

Extra-sentential Dependencies, Meaning Representation,
and Generics
  Tomek Strzalkowski 210

Enhancing Text Quality in a Question-Answering System
  *Clarisse Sieckenius de Souza, Donia R. Scott, and
  Maria das Graças Volpe Nunes* 222

Learning

A Knowledge-Based System to Synthesize FP Programs
from Examples
  Zhu Hong and Jin Lingzi 234

Planning

A Path Planner for the Cutting of Nested Irregular Layouts
  José Távora and Helder Coelho 246

Architectures and Languages

Reasoning Objects with Dynamic Knowledge Bases
  Christoph Welsch and Gerhard Barth 257

PROSE: A Constraint Language with Control Structures
  Pierre Berlandier 269

An External Database for Prolog
  José Paulo Leal 276

Knowledge Engineering

Non Exact Matching
  Harald Kjellin and Bassam Michel El-Khouri 286

RDA: The Risk Advisor Expert System
  George C. McGregor 297

Applications

Run-Through Algorithms for Applications of
Autonomous Mobile Robots
  Weiqing Tian 308

Invited Talks

Events, Situations, and Adverbs
  Robert C. Moore 320

LING2: A System for Induction
  António G. Portela 333

Logical Foundations of Nonmonotonic Truth Maintenance
  Michael Reinfrank 348

The CASSIE Projects: An Approach to Natural Language
Competence
  Stuart C. Shapiro 362

Knowledge Acquisition by Teachable Systems
  John F. Sowa 381

List of Contributors 397

A PRAGMATIC LOOK AT ARTIFICIAL INTELLIGENCE or:
The proper proper treatment of connectionism [1]

Jacob L. Mey

The Rasmus Rask Institute of Linguistics, Odense University

Campusvej 55, DK-5230 Odense M, Denmark

ABSTRACT

Based on recent claims and counter-claims about the nature of human mental processing, this article reviews some of the evidence presented, and tries to dispel some myths surrounding the 'new' cognitive science (also called 'PDP', 'connectionism', 'neural network theory', and so on).

In particular, the question of the so-called 'subsymbolic' level of representation is raised, and some of the implications of implementing fully connectionist machines in a human surrounding are discussed.

0. Introduction: A new deal in AI

Recently, a new development has struck the field of AI (and in general, of computational data processing, 'Informatik', as the Germans call it.) The development is called <u>connectionism</u> (sometimes, and more or less equivalently in certain dialects of AI-ese, also known as <u>PDP</u> (for 'parallel distributed processing') or referred to as '<u>neural network</u>' theory -- the distinctions between the different terms are not trivial, but need not occupy us here).

What is important about connectionism, and why does it have such an impact on AI? Recently, I came across a strong formulation of the link between AI and connectionism: "Konnektionismus ist Künstliche Intelligenz", i.e. 'Connectionism is AI' (Diederich 1988:28, as quoted by Hoeppner 1988:27). Implying that, as Hoeppner seems to do, the two are simply identical (which indeed is one possible reading of the copula <u>is</u>), seems an unreasonable interpretation of what, in the context, could have been no more than a programmatic statement, or maybe even better, a wishful thought.[2] But that there is a

---

[1] Parts of section 3 of this paper were presented at the Annual Meeting of the Linguistic Association of Finland, Helsinki, 13 January 1989. I want to thank Hartmut Haberland and Kristiina Jokinen for useful comments.

[2] Quite apart from the fact that Diederich's dictum apparently should be read as an 'isa' statement; cf. his opening phrase: "Konnektionismus ist eine Form der Künstlichen Intelligenz..." (1988:28).

strong link between connectionism (as a way of looking at, and practicing, electronic data processing, to take a rather weak interpretation of the term) and artificial intelligence, seen as an endeavor to unite different areas of human research in a computational environment and philosophy, is beyond doubt (as also Hoeppner has noted (ibid.)).

What I would like to do in the following is: first, characterize connectionism as a 'program of research' (Lakatos' term; cf. Winograd & Flores 1986:24) within (or even encompassing) AI; then, talk about some of the difficulties that arise when one tries to incorporate the traditionally accepted notions of the human sciences (such as psychology, linguistics, human learning theory, etc.) into what some have called a new 'paradigm' of understanding (in the sense of Kuhn 1962), but what to others is no more than a novel way of implementing on the computer (albeit not always successfully) earlier acquired knowledge and insights.[3]

1. The Black Box and Other Myths

Ever since the days of Chomsky (1957), the idea of a 'Black Box', i.e. a device that was able to perform certain operations without caring about their content (and without knowing either, for that matter) has been popular among linguists. And even though Chomsky himself has always (and rather vigorously) protested against the notion that his grammatical model was influenced by the computer, or even directly inspired by computational methods, it seems clear, in retrospect, that that was exactly what was happening in the early days of TG. And furthermore, that the computer connection has been responsible for much of the early success and popular appeal of TG.

A variant of the 'Black Box' is the 'Chinese Room', made famous in discussions on AI inspired by Searle's seminal lectures from 1984 ('Minds, brains and science'; originally a series of BBC radio talks, 'The Reith Lectures'). This particular version of the 'black box' is distinguished by the fact that its (Chinese) input and output are manipulated by a robot inside the box ('the Chinese Room'); that the robot doesn't know anything about the semantics of the language ('Chinese') it is manipulating; and that it strictly executes certain reshuffling operations (equivalent to syntactic rules) only on the symbols of the language, or their equivalents within the room (their representations).

What is important here is that within the box, we can talk about symbols or representations indiscriminately: it doesn't make the slightest difference to the robot whether the things it does within the 'Chinese Room' have to do with Chinese characters, or some constellations of 'room-units' (e.g. blinking lights, blocks with names on them, and so on), as long as the output is right in relation to the input. In other words, the robot doesn't have to understand Chinese in order to be able to manipulate the rules for Chinese 'correctly', i.e. according to the syntax of Chinese. As to the semantics of Chinese, or the content of those symbols, it couldn't care less anyway.

---

3   Perusing the literature, one often gets the impression that the 'new' cognitive science (including connectionism) is all a North American invention and exploit.

     However, as early as 1977, the Finnish researcher Teuvo Kohonen published a book in which connectionist hypotheses are clearly stated and accounted for in mathematical and computational terms. Unfortunately, only recently references to Kohonen's work (now in second printing (1984)) are beginning to emerge in the relevant literature (i.a. Smolensky's (1988) review article).

However, in this kind of reasoning, once you've said A, you have to say B as well. For, why stop at symbols? Underneath the symbolic level, we have that of the 'subsymbolic', for instance what Hjelmslev (1943) has called the level of 'glossemes' (units of linguistic analysis below the sign boundary), or what in phonology has become known as the set of 'distinctive features', units of analysis that (within certain limits) could be combined freely across traditional, symbolic boundaries, such as those between vowels and consonants, and so on. If the 'Black Box' is all about operations and manipulations, and if the Chinese robot doesn't care what the units of manipulation look like, or 'are about', then why should we care, as long as the outcome is right? All's well that ends well, and the proof of the pudding is in the eating -- not in its making.

There is, of course, a traditional rub. How are we going to deal with those subsymbolic units? In the case of phonology, despite the 'universal', abstract character of the distinctive features, we still have some 'feel' for the quality denotated ('represented') by features such as [strident] or [grave]. (For example, in the case of the former, we would have some trouble assigning it to a vocalic, rather than to a consonantal member of the phonetic inventory.) So, in a way, we play it both sides: we pretend to be an ignorant robot, obeying only formal rules, but at the same time we know damn well why we are doing what we're doing, and can also remember what we're doing, so we can repeat it time after time. And suppose we pretend to stand wholly aside, leaving everything to the robot or the machine on the subsymbolic level, there is still the problem of sequencing: Which of the features (or other subsymbolic items) goes with what other(s), and in what order?

So, what we're dealing with is not only the Black Box itself, but a whole series of connected notions, of which that of the subsymbolic is an important, but by no means unique exemplar. Like in the case of the 'Black Box', one has to distinguish between what is real and what is not, with regard to those notions and their associated claims. In the following, I will deal mostly with what I will call the 'myth' part: myths about AI that are revived, highlighted, and reinforced in and through recent 'connectionist' forms of thinking. For each of these, I will argue as follows: Admitting that there is some truth and usefulness in some of these notions, it still is important to separate out the real part from the ideal or idealized one (and, a fortiori, from the 'myth'). As to the claims made, in many cases, these belong more to the mythical than to the real; and besides, they may not even be necessary, from a pragmatic point of view. The notions (or myths) I will discuss below are: the subsymbolic vs. the symbolic; the brain and its 'architecture'; parallel (distributed) processing; and finally, implementational performance.

2. The subsymbolic

In some exposés of connectionist theory (e.g. Smolensky 1988), the point is made that the main difference between what could be called 'old AI' and 'new AI' (Hoeppner 1988:28) is the introduction of the 'subsymbolic' level. Whereas in the classical account (see, e.g., Fodor & Pylyshyn 1988), computation is thought of as a manipulation of symbols on a (digital) machine, the '(counter-)revolutionary' view ascribed to the Connectionists[4] is that we do not need any independent level of symbolic representation, or indeed any

---

[4] From an ad blurb for a reissue of Minsky & Papert's (1969) book Perceptrons: "...required reading for anyone who wants to understand the connectionist counterrevolution that is going on today." (MIT Press publicity release)

representation at all: everything can be dealt with at the level of the subsymbolic (if indeed we need to speak of 'level' here). Rather than dealing with traditional macro-units (such as, e.g. in phonology, the phonemes of a language), a connectionist account defines low-level, subsymbolic features that cannot strictly be said to represent any symbol at all, at least not directly. Building up those (after all, indispensable) higher units (symbols) happens through associative connections between the subsymbolic 'nodes', in accordance with the weight of the input, distributed over the entire network. (I will not go into details here; for a clear description of how these subsymbolic features ('Wickel- features') work, see Pinker & Prince (1988)).

So, in a way one could say that networks with distributed, weighted associative connections have come to replace the old, hierarchically organized, constituency-defined structures. Under this interpretation, the difference between the two approaches would be one of architecture, of building blocks of different kinds, some larger, some smaller, and of the way to put them together: on top of each other, or in a randomly organized jumble that is retrievable only by means of a computer program. The things that both the symbols and the subsymbolic units represent, would be the same: "both the conceptual and the sub- symbolic levels postulate representational states, but sub-symbolic theories slice them thinner" (Fodor & Pylyshyn 1988:9).

However, as Dietrich & Fields have pointed out (1988:30), the debate is not so much about architecture as about the interpretation of the structures generated by the different architectural models. In other words, we are dealing with a _semantic_ controversy: What do the symbols, respectively the subsymbols, represent? For mentalists, such as Fodor or Pylyshyn, there is no doubt: the symbols belong to a language of the mind, a 'mentalese' (Fodor 1975), whereas subsymbolic entities don't, which is why they're useless in describing and explaining human activity. For Smolensky, on the other hand, _symbols_ are useless (or too complicated to deal with; see his diatribe against symbolism (1988:4-6)); subsymbolic units only are able to provide the precision, formality, and completeness that is needed to simulate human 'intuitive processing' of mental data.

But not only do we not need a 'conceptual' (read: symbolic) level of description, the 'subsymbolic hypothesis' that is said to be "the cornerstone of the subsymbolic [read: connectionist] paradigm" (ibid.) is stated negatively as:

"The intuitive [human] processor is a subconceptual connectionist dynamical system that does not admit a complete, formal, and precise conceptual-level description." (Smolensky 1988:7).

However, if we take Dietrich & Fields' remark (1988:30), quoted above, about the semantics seriously, and at the same time recall that Smolensky operates within a physicist paradigm, it may be tempting to try and reconcile the two 'levels' (as also suggested by Dietrich & Fields, in continuation of Smolensky's own proposal (1988:12)) by assuming that there is a smooth transition between the subsymbolic and the symbolic, and that connectionism is nothing but a "microtheory of cognition that stands to macroscopic cognitive science as quantum mechanics stands to classical mechanics" (Dietrich & Fields 1988:30). This would, in fact, amount to interpreting lower-level units as in some sense assignable to higher-level ones. The representation relation may not be a one-to-one mapping or a strict, hierarchical constituency (as claimed by Fodor & Pylyshyn); however (to continue the physics example), everybody will agree that quarks, e.g., belong to the sub- atomic level, yet, there is some sense in which they are assigned to the atom: the two levels are not incompatible, and their respective representations are determined by the 'semantics' of each level. As Dietrich & Fields remark: "The only restriction on the semantics of the interpretations used to describe the system are those imposed by intra- level coherence, and by the explanatory goals with which the interpretation is constructed. One can, if one wants, interpret neurons as representing grandmothers; if this interpretation does not prove to be useful, it can always be revised." (Ibid.:31)

Still, on Smolensky's and other connectionists' views, such an 'ecumenical' interpretation cannot be tolerated. The reason is that the symbolic and subsymbolic paradigms are basically and irrevocably incompatible: one cannot be reduced to the other, and they are mutually inconsistent, not in the sense that there couldn't be a way of implementing one program in terms of the other, syntactically, but because of 'real' differences.

According to Smolensky, there is something which the subsymbolic level provides that cannot be captured at the symbolic level, viz. "a complete formal account of cognition" (1988:7). However, the vexing problem still is with us how to map that formal account onto everyday concepts of cognition, i.e. the concepts humans use to deal with their world. While mentalists claim that there is a conceptual (symbolic) level that describes human cognitive activities satisfactorily, or even necessarily, connectionists claim that this is not the case, at least not in the sense of a formal, precise, and complete description. But (pace Fodor) how are we to know that the precise, formal, and complete account that we have obtained on the subconceptual level, thanks to connectionist methods, indeed represents human cognitive activities at the symbolic level? Or (to turn the argument in the other direction, as suggested by Dietrich & Fields (1988:30)), how are we to know that the subconceptual level postulated by the connectionists indeed is a formal, etc. representation of what is going on at lower levels, such as the neural, the biochemical, etc.? And I quote: "If there is something to the claim that concept-level descriptions are fuzzy in principle, what prevents us from using the same argument to show that subsymbolic descriptions are only fuzzy approximations of biochemical descriptions, and so forth?" (Ibid.:30) Isn't being a conceptualist or a mentalist just as bad as being a 'sub-conceptualist' or 'sub-mentalist' -- if indeed, there are no other weighty arguments around than the ones suggested by the respective protagonists of those schools?

In the following, I will examine precisely such an argument. It revolves around the old question of the workings of the brain, and how to explain them.

3. Connectionism and 'brainware'

> "If the human brain were so simple that we could
> understand its workings, then we would be so dumb
> that we couldn't".
>
> (Graffito (Rees 1983))

Being no expert on neurophysiology or on 'brainware', in what follows, I will try to avoid the pitfalls alluded to in the above quote. That is to say, I accept prima facie the evidence about the relative slowness of the human brain, as compared with digital computers, and the ensuing need for some kind of parallel computing in the brain (cf. the 'hundred step' constraint as defined by Feldman et al. (1981, 1982)).

What is at stake here, however, is not the factual implementation of human neurological activity in the brain, but the conclusions that some have drawn from this activity, and the arguments that are built around those conclusions in order to prop up certain connectionist claims.

Connectionism, it is often said, is descriptively more correct than the 'classical' theory (whatever is meant by that), because it "as it were, sneaks up on the brain itself and cribs its tricks" (thus, more or less, Hoeppner 1988:28). Others (e.g. Fodor & Pylyshyn 1988:62) talk about 'brain-style modeling', which, in a very wide sense, may be taken to mean that "theories of cognitive processing should be influenced by the facts of biology" (a tenet with which most of us would agree, presumably); alternatively, and in a more (or even very) narrow sense, 'brain style modeling' can be taken to comprise the explicit modeling of human cognitive activities on "properties of neurons and neural organizations" (cf. 1988:62).

Whatever interpretation of this 'modeling style' is chosen, for a mentalist it seems a priori and intuitively clear that cognitive activity is more than circuits opening and closing, be they neural in character or electronic. The connectionist, of course, is not willing to admit such intentions as evidence, but surely the mentalist is entitled to evidence for the connectionists' claim that indeed the connectionist models are better because they emulate the structure of the human 'brainware', as postulated, and in part corroborated, by neurophysiological research? After all, the debate is not about hardware (inclusive 'brainware'): what we're interested in, is the way that hardware (or 'brainware') is put to work, is 'programmed', to use a computer metaphor.

The point here is not whether or not the brain is structured 'like' a computer (serial or parallel). The facts of the 'brainware' and its organizational patterns can provide interesting and important information about the way we go about our business using that brain. Yet, brain activity is not exhaustively limited to, or described as, the way the neurons 'fire' or the synapses are activated. In any case, a postulate to that effect (such as subscribed to by many connectionists) is no more than that, until concrete evidence has been put forth excluding all other possible interpretations. In particular, it seems doubtful whether the neuronal organizational level should be incorporated in toto, and as such, into the organization of our thoughts and our concept-forming activities. There is no a priori motivation for assuming any one-to-one correspondence between the two, and (as Fodor and Pylyshyn remark), "the structure of 'higher levels' of a system are [sic] rarely isomorphic, or even similar, to the structure of 'lower levels' of a system" (1988:63).

Notice that I'm not saying that it is impossible to imagine a 'brainware'-oriented model of the mind; neither can it be denied that for some areas of neuronal activities, there are structured correspondences or even analogies (and who knows, perhaps isomorphisms) between the two levels of organization (vision and motor control may be such areas; cf. Fodor & Pylyshyn, ibid.) What I am saying is that there is neither an a priori guarantee that this is so, nor a logical or psychological necessity that it must be so; and that, therefore, the brain-mind analogy cannot be used as a supportive argument for the theory that precisely presupposes such an analogical, or even isomorphic, structure. To use a somewhat trite analogy: the fact that the knee-jerk reflex is sufficiently explained by referring to sensori- motoric connections in the spinal cortex does not necessarily entail that all human nerve-activity should preferably or uniquely be explained without reference to the 'higher' processing level of the brain itself. The question whether or not "neural networks offer a 'reasonable basis for modeling cognitive processes'" (Rumelhart

& McClelland 1986:110; cf. Fodor & Pylyshyn 1988:68) is clearly an empirical one and cannot be decided a priori either by mentalists or by connectionists.

4. PDP and neural networks

In discussion on connectionism, much has been made of the distinction between 'old' style computers (also called 'sequential' or 'serial' machines) and 'new'-style ones (parallel or 'Non-Von' machines, as different from the classical 'Von' (Neumann) ones). What seems beyond doubt is that a model of the brain that wants to come close to the latter's actual 'architecture' will have to be based on parallel, distributed processing ('PDP': I'll leave out the technicalities).[5] Connectionist machines do nothing but implement this new architecture, in which knowledge representation no longer is a matter of devising the right symbolic framework, and then inputting the symbols by means of classical (e.g. LISP-style) programming, but rather, by activating a network of highly interconnected units whose total patterning is said to 'represent' (in some weak, and specifically non-retrievable way) the original input.

It has been shown that such networks have been remarkable (and indeed, surprising) properties when it comes to learning, reasoning, and in general, computing at advanced levels. What is more doubtful, however, are the generalized claims about those networks (especially in their 'neural' variety), according to which they should be able to imitate and emulate human cognitive performance tout court.

Looking at the available evidence, one is struck by the fact that learning in a connectionist environment mostly has to do with the acquisition of properties for which relatively simple rules (e.g. of a syntactical nature) are available. Such is the case for the widely publicized abilities of the connectionist program due to Rumelhart & McClelland (1986b), purported to be superior to a traditional model, both insofar as the program gives a formal computational description of the correct forms of the English past tense, and as it provides an explanation of the process of acquisition of those forms by human learners (in particular, developing speakers).

On balance, it seems that the claims made by the connectionists, viz., that their model provides a superior account compared to the traditional, rule-based approach, and that developing speakers' acquisition of a particular linguistic competence, such as knowing how to inflect strong and irregular verbs in English, is more realistically modeled in their framework that in any previous, non-connectionist one, are not entirely borne out by the empirical facts. As Pinker & Prince note (1988:164), the PDP model is at best no better than, and in a number of cases inferior to, the traditional one as far as the actual account is concerned. As to the developmental aspect, one could imagine an equally explicit, rule-based account that would work at least as well. In fact, Pinker & Prince provide such an account in a sketch-like, but still rather detailed form (1988:128-165), incorporating two of the main features of the PDP model: sensitivity to frequency of occurrence (computed on the type, not on the token of the verb form, and combined with stronger weighting of more likely forms), along with a competition among various candidates, resulting in the right

---

5   'Distributed' used to be the opposite of 'local' and has to do with the amount of information that is encoded in each single unit of the parallel-processing network. Lately, the distinction seems to have been overtaken by the factual developments: PDP simply is connectionism, and vice versa.

form being preferred. Pinker & Prince note that these properties by no means are unique to PDP models, and in fact are independent of them (ibid.:130). To this, compare Hoeppner's comment: "...we are dealing here with typical pattern recognition problems, viz. the recognition of syntactically describable regularities in the input data ... a syntactic or pragmatic level cannot be detected in these [PDP] systems." (1988:30).

In my opinion, connectionists and other researchers will profit by taking comments and criticism such as those quoted above seriously. The ultimate test of any interpretive process, be it symbolic or non- symbolic, must be its descriptive adequacy (not to speak of explanation). Pinker & Prince have gone to great lengths to evaluate the PDP proposal "in terms of its concrete technical properties rather than bland generalities or recycled statements of hopes or prejudices" (ibid.); the same holds for another criticism of the past tense learning program, that by Lachter and Bever (1988). In particular, these authors raise the issue of to what extent the amazing results of the connectionist learning program are due to special effects that are introduced ad hoc, such as the sharpening of boundaries between the individual Wickelphones (1988:209)[6], and they generalize this observation to something they humorously, but not entirely without malice, dub 'TRICS', viz., "The Representations It [the PDP model] Crucially Supposes'" (ibid.:208).

Lachter and Bever conclude their discussion of three PDP models of learning (including Rumelhart & McClelland's) by stating: "... we have shown that both the learning and adult behavior models contain devices that emphasize the information which carries the rule-based representations that explain the behavior." (1988:233). In other words, if you need rules anyway (and by implication, a symbolic or conceptual level of explanation and description), then why go to all the bother to avoid them explicitly? And surely such non-rule based models cannot claim to be a sufficient and necessary replacement for older, rule-based approaches.

5. Performance and the pragmatic view

The ultimate test of any model must, of course, be its applicability to serious problems or issues of human life and existence. In this sense, the claims made by the connectionist school purport to deal with real-life matters: How do we, for instance, explain language learning? And more generally: How well can the model explain the workings of the human mind -- the overall issue in cognitive science? Or, put in other words: what kind of human mind are we envisioning, using connectionist models, and can we deal also with other, broader issues such as human responsibility, the realities of societal life, and so on? How well can the PDP model be supposed to perform from a pragmatic point of view?

In this section, I will first deal with some of the problems that have to do with successful implementation of the connectionist proposals, seen as models of the human mind. Fodor & Pylyshyn remark that connectionist models, like the older associationist ones, are not sensitive to structure, but only to frequency. Thus, the strengthening of the network connections that explain the learning process is operated in accordance with a statistical metric of co-occurrence of certain stimuli and certain responses (Fodor & Pylyshyn 1988:31). Similarly, Hoeppner remarks that connectionism, as other behaviorisms, relies on "associative atomism" (1988:29). A model of the human mind that

---

6   A complete set of 200 Wickelfeatures is created separately to characterize phones at word-boundaries (cf. Lachter & Bever 1988: 209-210).

is based on this philosophy, no matter how implemented, will have to deal with the classical objection against behaviorism, viz., its lack of cognitive adequacy (for instance, as formulated in Chomsky's critique of Skinner (Chomsky 1959)). We are left with "a gnawing sense of deja vu [sic]", as Fodor & Pylyshyn conclude their article on 'Connectionism and cognitive architecture' (1988:69).

A more general line of reasoning about cognitive adequacy would incorporate aspects that are usually referred to as pragmatic, i.e. having to do with the users of an implemented model, connectionist or otherwise. First of all, it should be clear that the main goal of cognitive research (and AI as a specific instance) should be to get to know the human mind and understand its workings, not to produce a working replica of what humans are supposed to be at their best. Why have a robot compose a symphony that is just as good as Beethoven's Third, as long as we have (or have had) Beethovens around that are (or were) perfectly capable of taking care of such tasks?

Current fantasies about AI and its 'applied' offshoot, Expert Systems, tend to focus on the role of computerized technological systems that will be able to take over a large part of humans' traditional tasks in engineering, planning, diagnosing, repairing, and so on, in the most varied realms of human activities. In particular, the military's interest in automated weapons systems is well known, its latest manifestation being the notorious Strategic Defense Initiative, also known as 'Star Wars'. All these systems pose questions of implementability and practicality; and they force us to rethink familiar notions such as reliability, decision procedures, and so on.

In a recent book, Stuart Dreyfus tells a refreshing anecdote, illustrating the gap between dreams and realities in this domain: When asked to explain the principles along which expert systems work, he used to come up with the example of buying a car. Suppose, he said, you want to buy a new car. Wouldn't it be nice to have all the necessary information stored in a system that would tell you not only what kind of automobiles were available that corresponded to your specifications, but also all the technical details: repair costs and availability of parts, road performance, supposed or allowed depreciation, and so on? A system that, in addition to all that, suggested a scheme for financing the operation, complete with competitive bids from several money providers, specifying the details of credit, repayment of loan, and so on? A system that you, after having considered all this evidence, could ask to make the decision, and actually buy your car?

Usually, Stuart's story went down well at parties and other social gatherings where one inevitably is confronted with the question: "And what do you do?" -- a question we all know and dread, and to which Stuart thought he had a standard, satisfactory answer. Until one day a young woman asked him: "Dr. Dreyfus, and is this the way you decide when to replace **your** car?" To which Dreyfus replied that he couldn't dream of such a thing -- buying a new car to him was much too important to be left to a mathematical model or a machine! (Dreyfus & Dreyfus 1986:9-10)

In connection with the 'new' trends in AI, the innocuous question of Dreyfus' party conversationalist takes on a wholly new aspect, too. One of the main differences between the 'old' and the 'new' model is that the latter does not respect, or recognize, the level of symbolic structures at input, and that subsequent activations throughout the network at no point resemble those structures, as they are represented in the mind. That means (and connectionists make a point of stressing this as the hallmark of their system) that the path of the activation through the network is basically not recoverable. Thus, the system may be performing correctly, but we don't know how it got at its correct results. While the program is learning, the weightings of its internal connections are changed, but since there are, in principle, no connections that we can trace to the original input, we don't exactly know what it is learning, and how and where it is modifying itself. In other words, "even if a connectionist system manifests intelligent behavior, it provides no understanding of the mind because its workings remain as inscrutable as the mind itself" (Shepard 1988:52). And this lack of understanding means, concretely, that we are unable to correct the system from the 'inside', so to speak, locating the error by inspection. For a connectionist, the system's only mode of interaction is 'take it or leave it': you can't fight statistics, the 'Black Box' reigns supreme. As Lehnert has put it, quite to the point, in my opinion: "If the connectionists ever should come to dominate AI, we will have to deal with the very real possibility that we might be able to simulate something without understanding it very well." (1987:3; cf. Hoeppner 1988:28) [7]

The localization problem alluded to here is by no means unfamiliar to connectionists such as Smolensky; cp.:

"... failures of the system to meet goal conditions cannot in general be localized to any particular state or state component. In symbolic systems, this assignment of blame (Minsky 1963) is a difficult one, and it makes programming subsymbolic systems by hand very tricky." (1988:15)

By the same token, however, if anything goes wrong, it will be difficult to deal with a potential emergency, invoking traditional concepts of diagnosis and repair. This may not be too much of a problem as long as we are at the level of the laboratory experiment and try to teach the computer the past tenses of the English verb or some other, undangerous knowledge, but what could happen if the program were trained (or better: had trained itself) to intercept an enemy airplane and -- upon due recognition but failing somehow to pick up on the necessary and sufficient clues -- shoot it down? With the recent Iranian airliner tragedy in mind, this kind of danger is not at all illusory.[8]

Here, Hoeppner's thoughtful remarks about 'Connectionism and social reality' (1988:2.5) deserve attention, when it comes to assigning the responsibility for the proper functioning of connectionist systems:

"Connectionist systems are self-organizing systems, i.e. systems that adopt to their environment in ways that are not predictable from the outside; neither can they be steered intentionally. ... in the last instance, there is nobody who could be held responsible for the system's actions (with the exception perhaps of the person who pulled the switch...)". In regular programming, Hoeppner continues, "there is a causal chain between the elements of the program and its results, at least initially and in principle; here, it is still possible to discuss matters of responsibility. When it comes to connectionism in its extreme variety, however, such an embedding in existing social and ethical contexts is hardly possible, unless one were to redefine those contexts, and by implication, ourselves." (1988:30)

Indeed, a lot has still to be said on 'The Proper Treatment of Connectionism'.

---

[7] To vary an old joke: Q: What is the mafia's proper treatment of connectionism?
A: Give them an offer they cannot locate.
(But compare footnote 4, above).

[8] The reference is to the cruel and unjustifiable downing of an Iranian civilian Boeing 727 on August 26, 1988 in the Persian Gulf by the USS Vincennes. All 288 passengers were killed in the incident, along with the plane's crew.

REFERENCES

Chomsky, Noam. 1957. Syntactic Structures. The Hague: Mouton.

Chomsky, Noam. 1959. Review of B.F. Skinner, Verbal Behavior. Language 35:26-58.

Diderich, Joachim. 1988. Trends im Konnektionismus. Künstliche Intelligenz 1/88:28-32.

Dietrich, Eric & Chris Fields. 1988. Some assumptions underlying Smolensky's treatment of connectionism. Behavioral and Brain Sciences 11(1):29-31.

Dreyfus, Hubert L. & Stuart E. Dreyfus. 1986. Mind over machine: The power of human intuition and expertise in the era of the computer. Oxford: Blackwell.

Feldman, Jerry A. 1981. A connectionist model of visual memory. In: G.A. Hinton & J.A. Anderson (eds.), Parallel models of associative memory. Hillsdale, NJ: Erlbaum.

Feldman, Jerry A. & David H. Ballard. 1982. Connectionist models and their properties. Cognitive Science 6:205-254.

Fodor, Jerry A. 1975. The language of thought. New York: Crowell.

Fodor, Jerry A. & Zenon W. Pylyshyn. 1988. Connectionism and cognitive architecture: A critical analysis. Cognition 28:3-71.

Hjelmslev, Louis. 1943. Omkring sprogteoriens grundlæggelse. Copenhagen: Munksgaard. [Engl. tr. Prolegomena to a theory of language. Bloomington, IN: Indiana University Press (1954).]

Hoeppner, Wolfgang. 1988. Konnektionismus, Künstliche Intelligenz und Informatik -- Beziehungen und Bedenken. Künstliche Intelligenz 4/88:27-31.

Kohonen, Teuvo. 1988. Self-organization and associative memory. Berlin: Springer [1977].

Kuhn, Thomas. 1962. The structure of scientific revolutions. Chicago, IL: University of Chicago Press.

Lachter, Joel & Thomas G. Bever. 1988. The relation between linguistic structure and associative theories of language learning: A constructive critique of some connectionist learning models. Cognition 28: 195-247.

Lakatos, Imre. 1970. Falsification and the methodology of scientific research programmes. In: I. Lakatos & A. Musgrave (eds.), Criticism and the growth of knowledge. Cambridge, UK: Cambridge University Press.

Lehnert, Wendy. 1987. Possible implications of connectionism. In: Wilks, ed. 1987.

McClelland, James L., David E. Rumelhart & the PDP Research Group. 1986. Parallel distributed processing: Explorations in the microstructure of cognition. Vol. 2: Psychological and biological models. Cambridge, MA: MIT Press.

Minsky, Marvin. 1963. Steps toward artificial intelligence. In: Edward A. Feigenbaum & Jerry A. Feldman, eds., Computers and thought. New York: McGraw-Hill.

Minsky, Marvin & Seymour L. Papert. 1969. Perceptrons. Cambridge, MA: MIT Press.

Pinker, Steven & Alan Prince. 1988. On language and connectionism: Analysis of a parallel distributed and processing model of language acquisition. Cognition 28:73-193.

Rees, Nigel. 1983. Graffiti. [Danish tr.]. Copenhagen: Apostrof.

Rumelhart, David E., James McClelland and the PDP Research Group. 1986. Parallel distributed processing: Explorations in the microstructure of processing. Vol. 1: Foundations. Cambridge, MA: MIT Press.

Rumelhart, David E. & James L. McClellan. 1986a. PDP models and general issues in cognitive science. In: Rumelhart et al. 1986.

Rumelhart, David E. & James McClelland. 1986b. On learning the past tenses of English verbs. In: McClelland et al.1986.

Searle, John. 1984. Minds, brains and science. London: BBC (The Reith Lectures; The Listener, Nov.-Dec. 1984).

Shepard, Roger N. 1988. How fully should connectionism be activated? Two sources of excitation and one of inhibition. Behavioral and Brain Sciences 11(1):52.

Smolensky, Paul. 1988. On the proper treatment of connectionism.Behavioral and Brain Sciences 11(1):1-74.

Wilks, Yorick, ed. 1987. TINLAP-3: Theoretical issues in natural language processing. Las Cruces, NM: New Mexico State University, Computer Research Laboratory.

Winograd, Terry & Fernando Flores. 1986. Understanding computers and cognition: Toward a new foundation of design. Norwood, NJ: Ablex.

AN ORIGINAL OBJECT-ORIENTED APPROACH FOR RELATION MANAGEMENT

Mireille Fornarino - Anne-Marie Pinna - Brigitte Trousse
INRIA, Sophia-Antipolis
2004, route des Lucioles
06565 Valbonne Cedex, France

Abstract

In this paper, we deal with the integration of *slave-master* relations in an object oriented language. The chosen approach consists of implementing relations in a hierarchy of classes. So, we stress a main class which specifies relation semantics and manages the relation consistency. The proposed relational model offers a high-level language to express relations between objects. Our originality is to gather all the semantic information relative to a given relation in a unique entity and to introduce the activation point notion for consistency incremental management. The effective relation integration in an object-oriented language remains consistent with data encapsulation, uniformity and extensibility of such languages. Due to our model, we have implemented a consistent graphical interface and introduced several inheritance links in our language. The link concept issued from this approach appears to be very powerful to express formally dependency links and more precisely inheritance links.

Keywords: relation, consistency management, object-oriented language, knowledge representation.

1 Introduction

The constraint-based systems whose ancestor is SKETCHPAD [Sutherland 63] have appeared very early in order to manage automatically the consistency between a graphical representation and a set of objects. Other various applications need the use of symbolic constraints or relations: spatial reasoning [Brooks 81], computer aided design ([Maher 85], [Cholvy 83], [Trousse 88]) , typesetting graphics [VanWyck 80] and so on ... So the ability to define and manage relations between objects is more and more needed in object-oriented languages [Stefik 86]. Generally, the proposed predefined relations are inheritance relations (is-a, sort-of ...) [Brachman 83] and hierarchical relations (is-part-of [Blake 87], deduction [Herin-Aime 87], is-electrically-tied ...). First we shall present and comment on different ways to express relations, implicitly with object attributes and active values and explicitly with the concept of relation or link.

Our approach concerns oriented relations between objects, which imply *slave-master* relations. Our model offers a high-level language to express relations between objects.

Moreover, we offer an easy way to express all the semantic information relative to a given relation in a unique entity. Our system also provides a powerful relation-management by introducing a very important notion of a relation called *activation point*: its originality lies on the expression of the modification nature concerning this link and on the definition of various actions to activate. The nature of these modifications may be a particular assignment of an object attribute, a specific translation for an object and so on ... These activation points are activated by message reception. The user is offered a great flexibility to set off the relations by using messages like selectors of our activation points.

According to these principles, relations are integrated to an object oriented language called Othelo[1]. The relation integration in such a language is consistent with data encapsulation and with uniformity and extensibility of languages such as Clos [Demichiel 87].

2 How to integrate relations into an object-oriented language?

Traditional object-oriented languages have built-in mechanisms, allowing to link objects together. In this paragraph, we present the advantages and drawbacks of describing relations by means of attributes, active values or classes.

Relationships between two given objects will be called *individual relations* and the corresponding concept will be called *relation* or *link*. For example, we can consider the *is-on* relation and the individual relation *the glass is-on the table*.

2.1 Object attributes are a way to support relations

It is possible to simulate relations by using object attributes when an attribute value may be an object or a list of objects; this attribute defines an implicit relation between the corresponding objects.

The daemons attached to attributes (for example, the *if-modified* daemon...) manage the relation consistency. So, no new concept is needed and the knowledge representation is uniform. But this implementation leads to some drawbacks, such as:

- The information about a relation is divided among different classes of objects, that can be linked by this relation. Indeed, the relation semantics must be described in all the classes, the instances of which can be linked by this relation. So, the whole knowledge about a relation is not gathered and its access is difficult.

- To implement the relation, the user has to define the concerned attributes and to manage the relation consistency. When a large number of relations must be represented, the user has also to prevent cycles between objects, even though the overall structure of the system is not readily apparent: interactions are hidden behind object attributes and daemons.

- The re-establishment of objects, referencing one another, is complex and requires to take unknown objects into account.

---

[1] Othelo [Fornarino 88] has been implemented in Prolog and is a frame language with logical features as well as Lap [Iline 87]. Its implementation carries on research as [Gallaire 86].

- A relation addition or retraction implies to modify structure of the concerned classes or to rewrite some of their daemons. Such a behavior is not always authorized dynamically.

- Procedural attachments have various functions (type validation, display, track, initiation...). One procedural attachment could have several functions, as, for example, relation consistency maintenance. So, relation control is not localized inside one object.

The language modularity and flexibility are altered. Relationships are not explicit and it is difficult to express clearly semantics and properties (inverse, reflection, ..) about such relations.

2.2 Active values are hidden relationships

Some object oriented languages [Bobrow 83] and expert system shells (SMECI [Smeci 88], KEE [KEE 85]) propose an access oriented programming by means of active value or, more rarely, annotations. In access programming, fetching or storing data can cause procedure to be invoked: when an object changes its data a message may be sent in side effect. Active values are objects, installed on the value of any object attribute. They convert a variable reference to a method invocation. The class of the active value determines its behavior on access (putting or getting values). This mecanism can be compared with relations between an object attribute and an active value object. Applications of access oriented programming are gauges, checking data types and constraints, trapps for variables [Stefik 86a]... In the case of gauges [Dery 87], this mechanism links an attribute object to its graphical representation and manages the relation consistency by message sending. Due to attributes and daemons, active value mechanism allows to link two objects. But this mechanism does not specify clearly any kind of relation. An attribute is linked to an object: its representation, for example. The consistency control is activated only at access time. The possibility to control consistency when adding information, object creation or destruction is not proposed.

[Murata 87] proposes to manage consistency between two objects in a more general way than active value by using the *daemon* concept. But they don't emphasize the relational aspect and so they don't isolate the relation notion and not gather all the information concerning the relation in one object. The consistency mecanism is in the related object. On the contrary, we propose to emphasize the relation semantics and the dependancy relation mechanism which associates the consistency mechanism to a relation. Our proposition is more general and aims to offer a clearer relation mechanism specification.

2.3 Relationships designed by classes

Another approach consists of implementing relations in a hierarchy of classes. Research around relation representation by objects has been developed in various domains like expert-systems and data-bases. We can notice

Inheritance relations in Art [Clayton 85]: they are specified by means of schemata and allow users to create their own inheritance links.

Data base relations: some studies [Blaha 88,Elmasri 85,Rumbaugh 87] concern object-oriented representation of these relations, expressing only "natural" relations and no dependencies[Iline 87].

Constraint integration in expert system

Constraints are represented by means of an object called *linker* that relates object attributes [Berlandier 88].

Our approach follows the same track as these different studies. Our originality is to propose to specify relation semantics at the class level and to introduce the activation point notion for consistency incremental management. The dependency nature is explicit at the relation level (class), even though the dependency is effective only for the individual relations (instances).

Let us give some examples of individual relations:

- Dog *sort-of* Mammal, Human *sort-of* Mammal
- window-0 *represents* object-0
- hand *a-part-of* arm
- the square S1 *has-same-center-as* the circle C1.

In the class, all specific information on a relation is regrouped. So the consistency mechanism is totally realized by a set of methods defined at the relation level. Among them, let us note three important methods: creation, destruction and activation of an individual relation .

This kind of representation for relations offers a lot of advantages:

- Any information relative to a link is gathered at the link class level. Then, understanding and extensibility are facilitated.

- A same relation can link objects of different classes. Such a freedom can be limited, since fact the concerned object class can be specified in the relation declaration.

- The relation representation by means of classes follows the fundamental encapsulation principle. A relation is an interface between the linked objects and sending message is the unique communication mode between objects.

- The re-establishment problem of related objects is easily resolved because the knowledge is structured and modular, actual objects in one side and relational objects in another side.

- The cycle detection can be directly managed by means of counter or interruption at the relation level. This mechanism will be developped in the section 3.3.

- When the user adds or destructs a relation, he needs not to modify the object structure but he has to use the class dynamical creation.

- If an attribute is an object, attributes can also be linked one to another.

Notice that if individual relations are numerous, problems of memory space and access to relations must be considered.

Automatic management of opposite links or composed links is not always directly taken into account by this representation. We will develop this point in 3.5.2.

3 The proposed link system

3.1 Introduction: Relation mechanism

In this paper, we are interested in oriented relations, which imply slave-master relationships. In an individual relation, the slave is called *dependent object* and the master is called *influential object*.

Here, we deal only with binary relations. Relations between more objects could be simulated by this design.

When two objects are linked by a relation, the dependent object must sometimes be modified in order to satisfy the relation between both objects , i.e. in order to enforce the individual relation *consistency*.

The dependency relations are not necessarily functional relations [Cholvy 83]. Indeed, the influential object does not always determine completely the dependent object.

When an influential object of an individual relation is modified, the dependent object must sometimes be adjusted in order to reenforce the relation consistency. Then three behaviors are possible:

- The influential object modification does not make the individual relation consistency irrelevant.

  For example, let us consider two objects a square S1 and a circle C1 and the *has-same-center-as* relation and the individual relation *S1 has-same-center-as C1*. If S1 receives the message "increase (S1)", the circle C1 is not concerned by this modification.

- The influential object modification makes the individual relation consistency totally irrelevant.

  If S1 receives the message "move(S1, 10, 20, 45))", the individual relation "S1 has-same-center-as C1" is irrelevant and the center of C1 must be modified.

- The influential object modification makes the individual relation consistency partially irrelevant. In this case, the consistency is reenforced in an incremental way, and the dependent object is readjusted consequently.

  If S1 receives the message "translate-Axis-X(S1, 20)", the relation "S1 has-same-center-as C1" is irrelevant and only the abscissa of the C1 center must be recalculated.

3.2 Link class

The *link class* defines mechanisms needed to enforce an individual relation consistency, while its metaclass *metalink* defines the methods for creating or destroying individual relations... This decomposition presents advantages detailed in [Cointe 86]. All classes describing a relation are direct or indirect subclasses of *link* and instances of *metalink*. So we will call these classes *links*, and their instances *individual links*. An individual link is characterized by its class, an influential object and a dependent object.

The structure defined for a link is given below (for a complete description, see appendix A):

Instance-attributes:
    influential-object, dependent-object
Class-attributes:
    activation-points
Instance-Methods:
    coherence, activate,
Class-Methods:
    create, destroy

So, for a given relation the user must define the following points [2]:

coherence(Individual-Link): What is the relation semantics ?
The body of this method will be executed when an instance of this link is created.
It specifies "what to do " to enforce the individual relation consistency.
The coherence method of the *has-same-center-as* link is defined by:
coherence(Individual-Link) :-
    value(Individual-Link,influential-object,A-square),
    value(Individual-Link,dependent-object,A-Circle),
    calculate-center(A-square,X,Y),
    assign(A-Circle,abscissa,X),
    assign(A-Circle,ordinate,Y).

activation-points: When must the relation be reenforced and how to do that?
A method selector list [3] (when must the relation consistency be reenforced?) and
an update procedure (how to do that?) constitute an activation point. This update
procedure is called *action*, and takes an individual link and a message as arguments.
Let us describe now some activation-points:
move-ap =
    selectors :
        [move(square,dX,dY,Angle),
        translate(square,dX,dY),
        rotate(square,Angle)]
    action : recalculate-center
translate-Axis-X-ap =
    selectors : [translate-Axis-X(S1, dX)]
    action : recalculate-abscissa

Let us describe briefly other predefined methods:

activate(Individual-Link, Message) :
The activation of an individual link consists of executing the *activate* method associated
to the link class. This method arguments are an individual link and the message that
caused the activation of the specialized link.

---

[2]method bodies are given in Prolog because links are implemented in Othelo
[3]A method selector is constituted of the method name, its arity and possibly the argument types.

create(Link-Class, Influential-object, Dependent-object) :
This method creates an instance of *Link-Class*. Thus it enforces a relation between the Influential-object and the Dependent-object, and sets off the *consistency* method.

3.2.1 Hierarchy of links

Different predefined links are offered in our model (see figure 1).

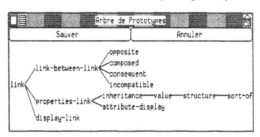

Figure 1 : Hierarchy of links

3.3 Link management

In short, how does our link system maintain the link consistency ? We can distinguish two stages: the individual link creation and the individual link consistency maintenance.

The individual link creation triggers the *coherence* method, defined in its class, in order to enforce the represented individual relation consistency. When the coherence method body is empty, the dependency of both objects is always supposed relevant, which is the case of relational database relations [Elmasri 85]. Any modification of the coherence method implies to reenforce consistency of all its instances, according to the new coherence method.

> Let us assume that the *has-same-center-as* link is defined. Whenever an instance of this link is created between a square and a circle, the circle position is calculated according to the square.

When an object is modified, the individual links in which it plays the role of the influential object must be activated in order to reenforce their consistency. According to the message, that modified the influential object, the actions will be different. The activation predefined function compares each activation point associated to the link with the message. When a selector of activation point corresponds (can be "unified") to the message, the action associated to this activation point is executed.

> If the square S1 is modified by execution of *translate-Axis-X(S1,20)* method, the consistency of *S1 has-same-center-as C1* individual link is reenforced by executing recalculate-abscissa(*S1 has-same-center-as C1*,translate-Axis-X(S1,20)).

A skilled user could modify the *activation* method to get different behaviors such as discriminating actions according to the message argument value.

We assume that the activation points specified by the user for a given link are consistent with its semantics expressed by the *coherence* method of this link. So if no action is precised, the default action is the execution of the coherence method.

3.4   Implementation

3.4.1   Individual link

The number of links used in an application becomes rapidly very large. So, the link activation is very frequent. The chosen object representation must be optimum regarding memory space and access to methods. We have hence chosen a restricted internal representation for individual relations based on Prolog relational aspect.

3.4.2   Link activation

When an influential object method is performed, the concerned individual link must be automatically activated. We provide two kinds of implementation for that purpose:

- To set the link activation: when an individual link is created, all the methods which can activate this link are modified by adding the code required for this individual link activation. In this case, it is not necessary to search all the links to trigger. This solution is hence efficient, but hardly allows link destruction.

- To trigger a daemon after a method execution: this daemon has to search all the concerned individual links and then to activate them. This process is invisible for the user and allows to add and remove individual relations.
  Notice that this solution could be easily adapted to languages which have access to objects by means of primitives or procedures rather than by means of methods. It is sufficient to end the concerned primitives by a call to a procedure that would be equivalent to the daemon and would activate the links. This primitive becomes then an activation point of these links.

3.4.3   Cycle detections

The links used in an application can provide cycles. In order to solve this problem, we propose to add to the link activation, a test that avoids the cycle execution based on the interruption principle. When a cycle is detected, the link warns the user of its presence and stops its evolution. The cycle detection, presented here, is based on the following hypothesis: a link during its activation can not be reactivated by the same activation point, but it could be reactivated by another activation point. However, in some cases, the cycle is intentional and can be controlled by a counter. So this test is optional.

We consider here dynamical cycle-detection. Very often, the possible existence of a cycle can be determine by a knowledge compilation. In this case, the detection is realized by link class inspection and by an analysis of individual links that could be created [Deransart 83].

3.5   Other features

3.5.1   Properties link

The dependency between two objects can concern only some properties of such objects. So it is interesting to specify these properties in the link. The activation of such an individual link will be realized only if the influential object modification concerns these properties. In some cases, the corresponding properties are the same for all individual links and activation points can be shared by all these properties. Another case, usual in inheritance links, is the dynamic detection of the concerned properties. (Properties concerned by a *sort-of* link advance according to the properties addition or withdrawal in the influential object).

3.5.2 Links between links

It is often useful to express dependencies between links. Indeed, the individual link existence can depend on or implies the existence of other individual links. For example, the possibility to define links between links allows to create automatically opposite and composed links.

Expression of such knowledge and its control at run-time allow the immediate detection of new information and of possible errors. Generally, the individual link creation and destruction are link activation points. We can notice, that such a behavior is distinct from inference rules, which infer such a link existence only when they are asked for it, and not as soon as possible [Koseki 87].

opposite link: The *opposite* class allows to express that two links are opposite each other. When an instance of such a link is created, the opposite individual link is automatically created.

> The opposite of the *has-same-center-as* link is the *has-same-center-as* link. When the link individual *S1 has-same-center-as C1* is created, the individual link *C1 has-same-center-as S1* is then created and the consistency of these two individual links is enforced.

composed link: If a link l is declared as a *composed link* of the sequence of links $l_1, ..., l_n$, as soon as such an individual link sequence exists, an instance of the link l is created, connecting the two extreme objects of this sequence.

> The *aunt* link is the link composed of the [sister,parent] links sequence. Any creation of the *parent* (resp. *sister*) link can involve the *aunt* link creation.

A composed individual link is automatically destroyed if one of the link component is destroyed. The transitivity of relations such as equality can be thus expressed.

incompatible link: Two objects cannot be connected by two incompatible links.

> The *be-parallel* and *be-perpendicular* links are incompatible.

4 Applications

The implementation of two large applications allowed us to validate what we call the *link concept*. These two applications are:

1. An inheritance representation in an object oriented language by dependency relations.

2. The realization of a consistent graphical interface for Othelo

These apparently divergent applications have a common point: they link objects by slave-master relations.

- *Inheritance links*

  When two objects are linked by an inheritance link, these two objects are effectively related. In the case of inheritance, an object sends information to another object. When this information is modified, it must automatically be transmitted to the object that inherits it. In Othelo, inheritance is implemented by dependency links. This kind of links allows us to specify the semantics of structure inheritance and value inheritance. So the selective inheritance aspect and the horizontal inheritance are taken into account by the links [Dugerdil 87]. A sub-tree of the link hierarchy, more precisely of *properties-links*, represents inheritance relations. The inheritance along the *sort-of* link is predefined in the language but the user can also simply define different links such as *part-of* and simulate *class variables* of Loops [Bobrow 83] or *own* slots of [KEE 85] by selective inheritance.

- *A consistent graphical interface for Othelo.*

  When a user realizes a graphical interface for an object-oriented language, he ties objects or object attributes to their graphical representation. This kind of relation is a strong constraint, since the representation must always reflect the represented object state. When an object is modified by program (method execution), its representation must be automatically updated. When basic relations of such applications are specified by dependency links, the interfaces are simply feasible by the creation of individual relations.

  > If the user defines, by a link class, the *represented by* relation that binds an object to a window object, he only needs to create instances of this class such that *object1 represented by window1* and so the consistency of the two objects is automatically managed.

  The interface consistency is hence automatically managed and the interface is easily extensible.

5 Conclusion

The relation implementation, in Othelo, valids the link model presented in this paper. The user can use the most of the proposed link class hierarchy. To define new relations, he creates new subclasses and then generates individual relations corresponding to the problem to handle. Our language is composed by a main kernel (system metaclasses and classes) and it is thus user extensible. This relation representation choice guarantees an uniform and reflexive language for Othelo in the way of [Briot 87]. In our model, the individual relation consistency is managed by the relations themselves. Its control is hence neither centralized in a consistency manager, neither scattered in the objects. It is specified at the level of the relations, which clarifies the relation semantics and allows different types of consistency management.

This model is not only the basis of an implementation tool. We are studying the formal foundations of this link model. This one modelizes a concept that describes the relation mechanism in a theoretical way. Some studies on this concept could carry on with writing a dependency mechanism formalization. In an other way, it would be interesting to work on a proposal of the formalization of oriented object language inheritance and situate our approach relatively to [Brewka 87,Ducournau 87] for the inheritance semantics and [America 87,Cardelli 84,Halbert 87] for the comparison between typing and inheritance.

In analogy with the research relative to attributed grammars, mathematical properties could be deduced from such a formalization and thus would give an additional dimension to our approach. Indeed, it would be interesting to study the advantages of compiling the dependency graph and deducting some link properties and detecting cycles.

References

[America 87] P. America, Inheritance and Subtyping in a parallel Object-Oriented Language, in *ECOOP'87, European Conference on Object-Oriented Programming*, p281-289, Paris, 15-17 June 1987.

[Berlandier 88] P. Berlandier. Reflexive constraints for dynamic knowledge-bases. In *International Computer Science Conference '88, Artificial Intelligence: Theory and Applications*, Hong Kong, Décembre 1988.

[Blaha 88] M.R. Blaha, W.J. Premerlani, and J.E. Rumbaugh. Relationnal database design using an object-oriented methodology. *Communications of the ACM*, 31(4):414–427, Avril 1988.

[Blake 87] E. Blake and S. Cook. On including part hierarchies in object-oriented languages, with an implementation in smalltalk. In *ECOOP'87, European Conference on Object-Oriented Programming*, pages 45–54, Juin 1987.

[Bobrow 83] D.G. Bobrow, M. Stefik, The LOOPS Manual, Xerox PARC , 1983.

[Brachman 83] R. Brachman. What is-a is and isn't : An analysis of taxonomic links in semantic networks. In *Computer Knowledge Representation, IEEE*, pages 37–41, Octobre 1983.

[Brewka 87] G. Brewka, The logic of inheritance in frame systems, in *Proceedings of the tenth international joint Conference on Artificial Intelligence IJCAI'87*, Milan p243-488, 23-28 August 1987.

[Briot 87] J.P. Briot and P. Cointe. The objvlisp model : Definition of a uniform, reflexive, and extensible object-oriented language. In *Advances in Artificial Intelligence II*, pages 225–232. Elsevier Science (North-Holland), 1987.

[Brooks 81] R.A. Brooks, Symbolic reasoning among 3-D models and 2-D images, in *Artificial Intelligence*, 1981.

[Cardelli 84] L. Cardelli. A semantic of multiple inheritance. In *Lectures Notes in Computers Science, Semantics of data types*, volume 173. Springer-Verlag, New-York, 1984.

[Cholvy 83] L. Cholvy, Structuration et intégrité des informations dans les BD de CAO. Définition d'un modèle de données et réalisation d'une maquette, Thèse de l'ENSAE, Toulouse, France, 1983.

[Clayton 85] B.D. Clayton. *Art, Programming tutorial*, Mars 1985.

[Cointe 86] P. Cointe. The objvlisp kernel: A reflective lisp architecture to define a uniform object-oriented system. In *Proc. of the workshop on Meta-Level Architectures and Reflection*, Alghero, Italie, October 1986.

[Demichiel 87] L.G. Demichiel and R.P. Gabriel. The common lisp object system : An overview. In *ECOOP'87, European Conference on Object-Oriented Programming*, pages 201–222, Paris, June 1987.

[Deransart 83] R. Deransart, M.Jourdan, and B. Lohro. Speeding up circularity tests for attribute grammars. Research Report 211, INRIA, Rocquencourt, FRANCE, May 1983.

[Dery 87] F.Dery and A.M. Pinna. Intégration à un système-expert d'outils graphiques pour la visualisation et le pilotage. In *Journées AFCET, Reconnaissance des Formes et Intelligence Artificielle*, Antibes, France, Novembre 1987.

[Ducournau 87] R. Ducournau and M. Habib. On some algorithms for multiple inheritance in object-oriented programming. In *ECOOP'87, European Conference on Object-Oriented Programming*, pages 291–302, Paris, 1987.

[Dugerdil 87] P. Dugerdil. Les mécanismes d'héritage d'objlog : vertical et sélectif multiple avec point-de-vue. In *Reconnaissance des formes et intelligence artificielle*, Antibes, France, November 1987.

[Elmasri 85] R. Elmasri, J. Weeldreyer, and A. Hevner. The category concept : An extension to the entity-relationship model. In *Data and Knowledge Engineering*, pages 75–116, 1985.

[Fornarino 88] M. Fornarino and A.M. Pinna. Integration de concepts de la programmation en logique à un langage de schémas paramétrés. In *Actes du séminaire Programmation en Logique*, pages 143–170, Mai 1988.

[Gallaire 86] H. Gallaire, Merging objects and logic programming- Providing relationnal semantics, E.C.R.C. Report,1986.

[Halbert 87] D.C. Halbert, P.D. O'Brien, Using Types and Inheritance in Object Oriented Languages, in *ECOOP'87, European Conference on Object-Oriented Programming*,p23-34, Paris, 15-17 June 1987.

[Herin-Aime 87] D. Herin-Aime, O. Massiot,, DEMSI: Un prototype de système expert orienté objet pour l'évolution des systèmes d'information, in *Proceedings Cognitiva*, Tome 1, p237-241, La-Vilette Paris France, 18-22 May 1987.

[Iline 87] H. Iline and H. Kanoui. Extending logic programming to object programming : The system lap. In *Proceedings of the tenth international joint Conference on Artificial Intelligence IJCAI'87*, pages 34–39, Milan, Italie, August 1987. tome 1.

[KEE 85] Intellicorp. *KEE v.2. Software Development System, User's Manual*, 1985.

[Koseki 87] Y. Koseki. Amalgamating multiple programming paradigms in prolog. In *Proceedings of IJCAI*, pages 76–82, Milan, Italie, August 1987. Tome 1.

[Maher 85] M. Maher, HI-RISE: a knowledge-based expert system for the preliminary design of high rise building, *Technical report R-85-146*, Dept of Civil Engeneering, Carnegie Institute of Technology, CMU, January 1986

[Murata 87] Makoto Murata and Koji Kusumoto. Daemon: A mediator that keeps wholes consistent with their parts. Technical report, Fuji Xerox, 1987.

[Rumbaugh 87] J. Rumbaugh. Relations as semantic construct in an object-oriented language. In *OOPSLA '87 Procedings*, pages 466–481, Octobre 1987.

[Smeci 88] Ilog. *SMECI Manuel de référence*, 1.4 edition, 1988.

[Stefik 86a] M. Stefik, D. Bobrow, and K. Kahn. Integrating access-oriented programming into a multiparadigm environment. *IEEE Software (USA)*, 3(1):10–18, jan. 1986.

[Stefik 86] M. Stefik and D.G. Bobrow. Object oriented programming : Themes and variations. *AI Magazine*, 6(4):40–62, 1986.

[Sutherland 63] I. Sutherland, Sketchpad: A Man Machine Graphical Communication System, *Technical report 296*, MIT Lincoln Laboratory, 1963.

[Trousse 88] B. Trousse. Bénéfices d'une approche orientée objet pour un environnement de cao. In *Proceedings of the MICAD 88*, pages 313–328, Paris, Mars 1988.

[VanWyck 80] , C. Van Wyck, A language for typesetting graphics, PHD Thesis, Stanford University, June, 1980.

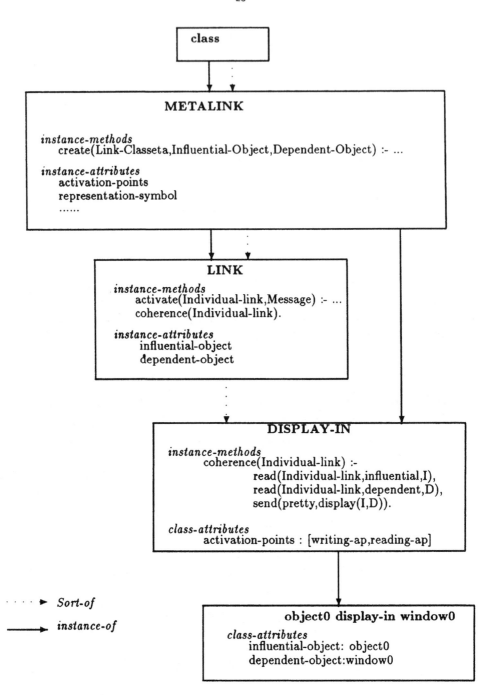

Figure 2: **Our Link Model**

CONCEPTUAL REPRESENTATION TECHNIQUES IN THE FRAMEWORK OF LARGE KNOWLEDGE BASED SYSTEMS

Gian Piero ZARRI
Centre National de la Recherche Scientifique
CERTAL - INALCO, 2 rue de Lille
75007 PARIS, France

Abstract : The "conceptual" Knowledge Representation Language (KRL) proper to a general environment for the construction of Large Knowledge Based Systems (LKBSs) involves **two different aspects**. The coding of the elementary events occurring in the real world (**descriptive data** = "Snoopy is Charlie Brown's beagle") is organized around a **"semantic predicate"**; the conceptual units constructed in this way take the name of **"predicative occurrences"**. On the other hand, the **"classes"** representing the "general categories" to which can be reduced the basic **entities** of the application domain that appear in the predicative occurrences are defined in terms of a **specialization hierarchy** ("**lexicon**" = "A beagle is a sort of hound / a hound is a dog ..."); analogously, the generic **"templates"** describing the **occurrences** are classified according to their own specialized hierarchy ("**grammar**"). The "lexicon" and the "grammar, together, set up the **definitional** component of the language.

1. Introduction

This paper describes the **"conceptual"** Knowledge Representation Language (KRL) which is at the core of a **complete environment** for the development and use of **Large Knowledge Based Systems** (LKBSs, characterized by the coexistence, in the **secondary memory**, of several thousands of "rules" and several millions of "facts"), e.g. **Large Knowledge Bases** (LKBs) or **Intelligent Information Retrieval Systems** (IIRSs). The main characteristic of the LKBSs to be produced using this environment is that (almost) all the knowledge to be inserted into these systems, concerning the **proper data** ("fact database") and the **inference procedures** ("rule base"), is coded making use of this conceptual language, a high-level representation language in the Artificial Intelligence (AI) style. Some benefits of this approach concern, for example, the reduction of the **loss of information** caused by the artificial restrictions which affect the coding and formatting operations in conventional databases, the representation of factual data under a form very suitable to the use of **complex inference procedures**, the solution of those consistency problems ("**granularity mismatch**") between "data" and "rules" which so much worry the scholars working on the integration of expert systems and classical databases. Other aspects of the environment, concerning for example the inference techniques or the knowledge acquistion tools, have been mentioned in Zarri (1988a ; 1988b).

2. Main assumptions underlying the KRL's design

The knowledge taken into account by the KRL can be classified into two categories, see other "hybrid representation systems" like KL-TWO (Vilain 1985) and KRYPTON (Brachman *et al.* 1985) :

◊ We shall refer to the **"descriptive component"** of the KRL (**factual, episodic** data) as that part of knowledge which concerns the representation of detailed, **particular** facts about individual things, characters and events. It includes such facts as : "On the 21st and 22nd October, 1988, the Bluefields town on the Atlantic coast of Nicaragua has been ravaged by the cyclone Joan" or "Snoopy is Charlie Brown's beagle".

◊ The **"definitional component"** of the KRL (**semantic, terminological** data), on the contrary, concerns **general** principles. It includes such information as : "ravage is to lay waste by plundering or destroying" ; "a cyclone is a storm or a system of winds that rotates about a center of low atmospheric pressure ..." ; "a beagle is a sort of hound / a hound is a dog of any of various hunting breeds / all dogs are animals".

The choice of this particular terminology ("descriptive component" / "definitional component") asks for some comments. In introducing KRYPTON, Brachman and his colleagues have used the term **"assertional"** to designate the component (**ABox**) that, in KRYPTON, " ... allows ... to build descriptive theories of domains of interest and to answer questions about those domains" ; the other component is the **"terminological"** one (**TBox**), allowing " ... to establish taxonomies of structured terms and answer questions about analytical relationships among these terms" (Brachman *et al.* 1985 : 418). Taking aside Brachman's insistence on the use of "structured" terms in the terminological hierarchies, the knowledge he wants to represent using the TBox tools coincides significantly with the knowledge which concerns our "definitional" component. On the contrary, it is not certain that the "assertional component" of KRYPTON really concerns the knowledge we should aim to insert in our "descriptive component" : see the example "every person with at least three children owns a car" which, in Brachman *et al.* (1985 : 418), is considered part of the "ABox" and which, according to the characteristics of **universality** of the definitional component, could be handled by introducing a hypothetical "definitional component" entity "person_with_at_least_three_children". This is why, eventually, we use the (very anodyne) terms "descriptive component" and "definitional component" in order to prevent any confusion.

This is not to say that the distribution of knowledge between our descriptive and definitional components constitutes an easy problem ; for the time being, we make use of two empiric criteria :

◊ A first criterion consists in verifying that the knowledge associated with the definitional component only refers to the **permanent** (at least in the context of a given application) **properties** (attributes) of the **single** entities (concepts) we are describing using this component, and never refers to the **particular relationships** which can associate several of these entities. If we refer again to two examples of Brachman *et al.* (1985 : 414-415), a statement such as "either Elsie or Bessie is the cow standing in Farmer Jones' field" pertain to the descriptive component ; "a family with no children" represents a constitutive property of the (possible) entity "childless_family" and must be associated with the definitional component. In some respects, this criterion is not so foreign to the Brachman's differentiation (Brachman *et al.* 1985 : 418) between **noun phrases**, to be represented using the TBox tools (here, the definitional component tools) and **sentences**, to be represented using the ABox tools (here, the descriptive component tools) ; it is also related to more "pragmatic" considerations, as the impraticability of dealing with higly structured networks of interconnected data using only the rigid mechanisms proper to the hierarchical relationships of the definitional component.

◊ A second criterion, strictly related to the first, amounts to verify if the information to be coded can be associated, implicitly or explicitly, to a well determined **point** or **interval** on the **time axis**. In this case, according to the "evolving", "dynamical" characteristics of the descriptive (episodic) knowledge in opposition to the "perennial", "universal" properties of the definitional data, we are authorized to insert this information into the **descriptive component** structures of the LKBS. For example, we shall not hesitate to consider the information : "Snoopy is Charlie Brown's beagle" as pertaining to the descriptive component because it seems reasonable to think about this information under a form like : "During a well determined **time period**, Snoopy has been the Charlie Brown's beagle", or like : "We remark **today** that Snoopy is still the Charlie Brown's beagle". Coming back to the example "a person with at least ...", it becomes now obvious that, if the information to be represented was : "In this room, now, every person with at least three childrens owns a car", we should use the **descriptive** tools in order to represent the fact that **all the particular instances** of the **definitional** entity "person_with_at_least_three_childrens" **who are now present in the room** are (may be provisionally) in possession of a car.

3.   Descriptive   component

Brachman and his collegues propose, for the ABox of KRYPTON, a language structured compositionally like a **first order predicate calculus language**. Apart from the more "theoretical" considerations expressed in previous section, we think that this pure "**logical level**" approach is not enough in order to efficiently represent intricate, real situations proper to real-life LKBSs ; for example, on a very practical ground, it may be difficult to use this "uniform" type of representation in order to **structure efficiently** the knowledge base, i.e. in order to construct powerful **"conceptual indexing"** schemata. Conceptual indexing is normally realized by conveniently choosing some "significant", "expressive" characteristics of the knowledge representation, some **"key slots"** for example (Zarri 1983).

One of the main assumptions made in the context of the **descriptive component** of the KRL is that the **informative structure** of the elementary events we take into account is **relatively stable**, so that it is possible to describe those events by making use of some sort of a "canonical" representation, see Wilensky (1987) : for example, the **"roles"** played by the entities involved in the episodes are coded by using a (*a priori* fixed) number of **"primitives"**, such as "SUBJ(ect)", "OBJ(ect)", "SOURCE", "DEST(ination)", "MODAL(ity)", etc. Accordingly, the representation of an **elementary event** pertaining to the **descriptive component** (factual data) is organized around a **"semantic predicate"** identifying the "basic" type of action, state, situation etc. described in the event. The **"entities"** (normally some **"instances"**, but see below the comment on the example of Fig. 2) which are mentioned in the event and which are, at least partly, proper to a particular application domain (corporations, financial transactions, amounts of money, stock certificates, etc. in the case of a financial applications) fill the particular **"roles"** associated with the semantic predicate. In conformity with a "case grammar" view (Sowa 1984 ; etc.) the entities are, therefore, the **"arguments"** of the semantic predicate. The semantic predicate, the arguments and the conceptual unit as a whole may be characterized by **"determiners"** (attributes) which give details about their significant aspects. For example, the predicate may be accompanied by **"modulators"**, that are there to refine or modify the original semantic meaning of the predicate ; an obvious example is the "negation" modulator which allows the happening of an elementary event to be denied ("Mary did not get the book from John"). Determiners which are associated with the arguments are the **"location attributes"** ("Mary, in Pensacola, got a book from John, in Kansas City"). Structured arguments (**"expansions"**) can be created in many ways, for example by associating to the entities (the instances) some **"quantifying"** ("all", "329" ..., see below the example of Fig. 2) or **"qualifying"** ("red", "powerful" ...) **attributes**. Determiners which refer to the global representation of the elementary event are the **"temporal attributes"**, which quantify time duration or frequency of the elementary event, or the **"identification attributes"** giving the origin of the piece of information relating this event, etc. This type of coding, a particular realization of a "predicative conceptual unit", takes the name of **"predicative occurrence"**. The general appearance of a predicative occurrence is shown in Fig. 1 ; for more details, see Zarri (1988a).

Being able to represent the elementary events in predicative occurrences is not enough to translate the original information completely. It is, in fact, necessary to represent also the **logico-semantic links** which exist between elementary events, for example between the two

---

```
{ PREDICATE :      [ modulators ]
                   ROLE - 1    { < argument > : [ location ] }
                   ROLE - 2    { < argument > : [ location ] }
                   .
                   :

                   ROLE - n    { < argument > : [ location ] } }
                   .
                   :

                   [ temporal attributes ]
                   [ identification attributes ]
                   .
                   :
```

Figure 1

---

halves of the information : "John went to the post office **in order to** send a book to Mary". In our KRL, one way to solve this problem is to use **"binding occurrences"**, i.e. **lists** - characterized by particular **binding** (ALTERN(ative), COORD(ination), ENUM(eration) and SPECIF(ication)) and **causal** roles (CAUSE, CONFER, GOAL and MOTIV(ation)) - whose elements are "labels" (addresses) of predicative occurences, see Zarri (1988a : 58-61).

We must emphasize that using a canonical representation does not entail a **systematic** decomposition into primitive : in fact, according to the views expressed by qualified researchers in the field, see for example Sowa (1984) and Wilensky (1987), the descriptive component of the KRL is represented by using a well-balanced mix of **"primitive"** and **"higher-level"** conceptual objects. As already said, roles are **primitive**. The entities of the domain, i.e. the arguments of the semantic predicate are, on the contrary, **high-level conceptual objects** which are freely chosen according to the necessities of the particular application at hand and which are **not** decomposed into primitives ; their definitions are given in the "definitional" component of the language. The semantic predicate can be chosen according to to any **"deep"** or **"surface"** option, where the choice is a completely pragmatic one, depending on architectural considerations aimed to optimize the application (very often, in order to facilitate a particular set of useful inferences) ; see Zarri (1988a : 555-556) for a discussion in this context.

We temporarily use in the project, for experiment's sake, the particular realization of a "descriptive component" language that is represented by the "metalanguage" of RESEDA, a powerful IIRS, see Zarri (1984) ; RESEDA has been utilized for several advanced applications, mainly in the historical and socio-political fields. An exhaustive description of the formal structures of the RESEDA's metalanguage and of their modalities of use can be found in Stouder (1988) ; Zarri (1988a) gives some information about the modifications already introduced into the metalanguage in order to generalize its logical design. Fig. 2 gives the (simplified) translation, in Resedian terms, of a natural language information to be coded using the descriptive component tools : "On

September 3rd, 1967, 329 Czechoslovakian intellectuals send to the Sunday Times a new declaration of protest in order to invoke the support of the western public opinion" (the original formulation has been dramatically simplified in order to keep the corresponding code within reasonable space limits).

```
a)    MOVE        SUBJ      czech_intellectual (SPECIF 329)
                  OBJ       protest_manifesto_3
                  DEST      Sunday_Times : [ London ]
                  MODAL     dispatch_12
                  [ date-1 :    3_september_1967 ]
                  [ date-2 :    ]

b)    [*] BEHAVE:  [ in_favor_of ]
                  SUBJ      western_public_opinion
                  OBJ       czech_intellectual (SPECIF all)
                  MODAL     moral_support
                  [ date-1 :    after_3_september_1967 ]
                  [ date-2 :    ]

c)    a (GOAL b)
```

Figure 2

In Fig. 2, "a" and "b" are "predicative occurrences" ; "c" is a "binding occurrence". In "a" and "b", "MOVE" and "BEHAVE" are the (deep) semantic predicates ; SUBJ(ect), OBJ(ect), DEST(ination), MODAL(ity) are roles. The arguments of the predicates (the entities of the domain), introduced by the roles, pertain to several categories : "czech-intellectual", "protest_manifest_3", "Sunday_Times", "dispatch_12", "western_public_opinion" are **"instances"** ; "moral_support" is a **"class"** which stay for all sorts of possible **concrete manifestations** of support (instances), like an "official_declaration_of_sympathy_1". In this context "moral_support" acts, therefore, as an **"implicit variable"** ; the recourse to variables is often necessary when the descriptive information represents **hypothetical events,** i.e. the **hopes, beliefs** or **intentions** of the "actors" of the chosen domain. The differentiation between "classes" and "instances" is accomplished, as usual, by verifying that a particular **proper name** can be used to identify each particular instance (see "czech_intellectual", a specific **instance** of the generic "intellectual" **class**). "Classes" are defined by using the tools proper to the **definitional component** of the KRL, see 4.2 ; when a **complex description** is associated to an "instance", this is nothing else but the **actualization** of the definition given to the class to which the instance pertains. The arguments introduced by SUBJ in a and by OBJ in b are **structured** ones (**"expansions"**), realized by using the **quantifying attributes** "all" and "329" inside a "SPECIF(ication)" list. In general, expansions are constructed by using **well-formed** combinations of lists of undefined depth, where the lists are labelled using the four "**binding roles**" already introduced, ALTERN(ative), the "disjunctive relation", COORD(ination), the "collective relation", ENUM(eration), the "distributive relation", SPECIF(ication), the "attributive relation". For uniformity's sake, the treatment of the ALTERN etc. lists is the same in the **expansions** and in the **binding occurrences** ; moreover, there is a strict symmetry between the treatment of the SPECIF lists and that of the lists appearing inside the binding occurrences and labelled by using the "causal" roles, see the occurrence "c" in Fig. 2. "London", "in_favor_of", "3_september_1967", "after_3_september_1967", "*", are all "**determiners**" : the first is a "location attribute", the second a "modulator", the third and fourth "temporal attributes", see Zarri (1983) for details about the representation of temporal data in RESEDA. The last determiner is a "conjectural validity attribute", used to make manifest that occurrence "b" is an "hypothetical" one, i.e. it represents only a desire of the SUBJ(ect) declared in occurrence "a".

4. Definitional component

On the **definitional component** side, the knowledge to be represented concerns that sort of general information which can be associated as a **definition** to :

◊   the **patterns** ("templates") which **subsume and generalize** the specific "**occurrences**" translating the elementary events of the descriptive component and their links ;

◊   the "**classes**" representing the "**general categories**" to which can be reduced all the "entities" of the application domain to be considered.

These elements are all defined by making reference to "**specialization hierarchies**", ("**is_a**" hierarchies), which (in general) are represented by an oriented graph characterized by the inheritance of properties and behaviors. The specialization hierarchy concerning **occurrences** and **templates** takes the name of **H_OCR** hierarchy, or "**grammar**" ; the hierarchy concerning the **domain entities** is the **H_ENT** hierarchy, or "**lexicon**".

4.1 Grammar

The specialization hierarchy concerning the **predicative and binding occurrences** and the corresponding **templates** (H_OCR, or "**grammar**") is not specific to a particular LKBS, to the extent that this hierarchy defines the general properties of the syntactic structures of the descriptive component and is, therefore, **domain-independent**. H_OCR (at least for the time being) is simply a "tree", i.e. multiple inheritance is not admitted here.

A common characteristic of the H_OCR and H_ENT hierarchies is that one of the **main aspects** of the "defining information" associated with the nodes of the hierarchies is given by the **"constraints"** specifying the legal set of **concrete values** (and their syntax) which can be used to construct the occurrences and to describe the status of the specific instances. Given that the formal expressions implementing these constraints can be really complex, very often constraints are only **indirectly** inserted into the definitions under the form of an association with some **"explicit variables"** x, $\dot{y}$, v, etc. In opposition to the **"implicit variables"** already introduced in 3. (and which can be considered as "pure constraints"), explicit variables are individualized by using a specific **"name"**.

For example if, in representing the predicative occurrences of the descriptive component, we make use of a "deep" semantic predicate of the type "BEHAVE" in order to identify, in the RESEDA's style, the general class of the "comportment" occurrences, a template like that of Fig. 3 (a specialization of the more general "concrete_behaviour" template) will give the general framework of the occurrence "b" in Fig. 2. Optional elements are in parentheses ; for simplicity's sake, the variables referring to the "descriptors", see 3., have been indicated only in an implicit form, and the full details of their constraints have been omitted. The restriction on the variable m indicates that the modulators "against = unfavorable behavior" and "mental = mental attitude without concrete realization" are here explicitly forbidden. Constraints delimit the **validity domain** of the template. Of course, they may also be used to express complex relationships among variables (**"semantic integrity management"**) : we have developed, for the KRL, a powerful constraint

----

```
{ concrete_favorable_behaviour_template :

    IS_A:   concrete_behaviour_template
    BEHAVE:              [ in_favor_of , m ]
           SUBJ    x :    [ < location > ]
           OBJ     y :    [ < location > ]
          ( SOURCE  z :    [ < location > ] )
          ( MODAL   u )
          ( EVENT   v )
           [ date-1 :  < behaviour_date > | < start_of_behaviour_date > ]
           [ date-2 :  < end_of_behaviour_date > ]

  m  ≠  against, mental
  x  =  < human_being > | < group_of_people > | < social_body >
  y  =  < human_being > | < group_of_people > | < social_body >
  z  =  < human_being > | < group_of_people > | < social_body >
  u  =  < concrete_behaviour_modality >
  v  =  < situation_framework  > }
```

Figure 3

----

satisfaction system which can compute all the **globally consistent assignments** for a set of variables by using local propagation, tentative assumptions and backtracking.

Besides the creation of the occurrences of the descriptive component, the templates can be used in the definition of a powerful class of inference procedures ("**conceptual rules**") to be inserted in the rule base parts of our LKBSs. They may also be used in the definition of the elements pertaining to the H_ENT (lexicon) hierarchy, see 4.2., in the construction of complex conceptual structures "à la Schank", etc.

4.2 Lexicon

The specialization hierarchy concerning the **domain entities** (H_ENT, or "lexicon") is, in contrast to what we have seen for the H_OCR hierarchy, particular to a specific LKBS, to the extent that its elements (and their definitions) give the general background of a particular application field and are subjected to change when another field must be taken into account.

The elements of the lexicon can be defined according to several strategies. For example, it is possible to derive a definition of these elements simply by determining their **positions** inside the graph, i.e. by determining, following the "is_a" links, **the ordered set of their "generic" terms**. In this way, "beagle" is defined only by the fact of being a "**specific**" term of "hound" ("beagle" pertains to the type "hound") ; "hound" is specific of "hunting_dog", etc. ; all these terms pertain to the sub-graph which has "animal" as the top-level node. The nodes are **labelled** by using only the "coded name" of the corresponding element. Several applications of the RESEDA system have been realized using, for the definition of the classes, only this type of "naive" semantic definition.

On the other hand, the definition of entities which are of particular importance from the point of view of a given application cannot be given satisfactorily by this type of representation only, and must be **augmented** by a **formal description** of the **outstanding characteristics** of the entities ; this formal description can be read as a **universally quantified sentence**. The simplest way to furnish these characteristics is to use some sort of "**attributes**", i.e. to associate a "**frame**" (a complex label) to the nodes of the oriented graph. Frames are **well-known** semantic structures used in the knowledge representation domain, see Bobrow and Winograd (1977), Stefik (1979), Fikes and Kehler (1985), etc. : therefore, I will limit myself to mention here some of the main decisions taken for our KRL in a frame context.

◊ In the definitional component of the KRL, a frame is composed of a **name** (the label of the class to be defined) and a **set of slots** (attributes). In contrast with the decision taken for the roles of the occurrences in the descriptive component, and in accordance with the general philosophy of the frame languages, **no set of primitive attributes has been selected as**

standard slots (remember that the definitions of the H_ENT hierarchy change according to the application domains). To stick to a well-known example, the class "employee" could be defined in term of the non-standard slots "name", "age", "sex", and "hobbies" (inherited for example from the parent-node, the class "person"), in addition to more specific attributes which we can define for this specific entity, as "job_title", "division" and "employee_number".

◊ In order to understand correctly the philosophy that inspires the construction of a H_ENT hierarchy, we must emphasize that the basic building block of this hierarchy is **still** the "is_a" relation, to be interpreted as an operator giving rise to **universally quantified sentences** ("if someone is an employee, **then** he **necessarily** is a person"). The respect of this interpretation could suffice to rule out a lot of very speculative problems such as those discussed in Brachman (1983 ; 1985), and originated by the use of inconsistent examples in the style of "bird is_a flying_thing" or "grey_elephant is_a yellow_elephant", where these examples, of course, **cannot** be read as universally quantified sentences. This postulate about universal statements, which is valid in what concerns the relationships between the **nodes** of the hierarchy, **does not apply**, on the contrary, to the **sets of slots and fillers** to be associated with these nodes, and translating our knowledge about some interesting properties of the entities of the domain. The values assumed by these properties can, therefore, **be overridden**. The value "can_fly", which would normally be inherited by "ostrich", is **explicitly cancelled** for this particular class ; this has no consequence on the relationships between "ostrich" and his parent-node "bird", because "ostrich" is still necessarily a "bird".

◊ An exception to the rule stating that slots are not primitive conceptual objects is given by a series of slots which have been **specialized** in order to add to the standard "is_a" the possiblity of using other forms of relations among entities. For the time being, we admit the "member_of" ("has_member") and "part_of" ("has_part") slots, corresponding to the well-known **abstraction hierarchies**, "grouping" (= "member_of") and "aggregation" (= part_of") used in the semantic models of the database domain ; see for example Schiel (1989) for a formal definition. We can note that the relationships "member_of" and "part_of" can only be used to link **classes with classes** ("cardinals" **member_of** "college_of_cardinals") or **instances with instances** ("cardinal_Glemp" **member_of** "college_of_cardinals_27", where this last instance represents the actual composition of the college), but not classes with instances. The relation "is_a" ("has_specializations") is reserved to the links **between classes ; classes and instances** are linked by the relation "instance_of" ("has_instances").

◊ Another form of specialization consists in using the names of **procedures** in order to fill some particular slots ; in particular, a **complete characterization** of an entity can be obtained if the **formal description** of its **typical behaviour** ("behavioural rules") is added to the normal, "static" attributes. For the "employee" class, typical behavioural rules can be "hiring_procedures", "firing_procedures", "social_insurance_calculation", etc. In conformity with the general characteristics of the KRL, see also 4.1, these behavioral rules are implemented in a "declarative" style using the "templates" of the H_OCR hierarchy.

◊   In the definitions of the entities of the H_ENT hierarchy, the **normal** slots can be simply filled using the names of other **classes** (implicit variables) already defined inside the H_ENT hierarchy. Slots are **multivalued** : in order to facilitate the establishment of **complex associations of fillers**, the "binding roles" introduced in 3. can be used. However, when the expression of the filler becomes too complex, **explicit variables** accompanied, as usual, by **constraints** are normally used ; variables and constraints can be **inherited**. For the "person" and "employee" classes, the constraint on the variable inserted in the "age" slot will specify that, in the concrete **instances** ("employee_132"), this slot should contain a number between 0 and 120. **A last, very important, possibility concerns the use of the H_OCR elements** (with variables and constraints) **as fillers**.

◊   The H_ENT hierarchy is, **in general**, an oriented graph admitting multiple inheritance with exceptions. The problem linked with the presence of "exceptions" should be dealt with by using, as usual, an algorithmic expression of the intuitive **"specialization principle"** stating that subclasses should override superclasses. We are taking into consideration, for the time being, an adaptation of the solution proposed by Brewka (1987), consisting in the use of a three-place "predicate" to express the information that an entity x is **"exceptional"** with respect to a property of a (very general) parent entity z if x is a specific term of a more specialized entity y for which different information regarding this property is available

5. Conclusion

In this paper, I have described the "conceptual" Knowledge Representation Language (KRL) proper to a general environment for the construction of Large Knowledge Based Systems (LKBSs). This language involves **two different aspects**. The coding of the elementary events occurring in the real world (**descriptive data** = "Snoopy is Charlie Brown's beagle") is organized around a **"semantic predicate"**; the conceptual predicative units constructed in this way take the name of **"predicative occurrences"**. On the other hand, the **"classes"** representing the general categories to which can be reduced all the basic **entities** in the application domain that appear in the predicative occurrences are defined in terms of a **specialization hierarchy** ("lexicon" = "A beagle is a sort of hound / a hound is a dog ...) ; analogously, the generic **"templates"** describing the **occurrences** are classified according to their own specialized hierarchy (**"grammar"**). The "lexicon" and the "grammar, together, set up the **definitional** component of the language.

References

BOBROW, D.G., and WINOGRAD, T. (19977) "An Overview of KRL, a Knowledge Representation Language", Cognitive Science, 1, 3-46.

BRACHMAN, R.J. (1983) "What IS-A Is and Isn't : An Analysis of Taxonomic Links in Semantic Networks", IEEE Computer, 16, n° 10, 30-36.

BRACHMAN, R.J. (1985) " 'I Lied about the Trees' Or, Defaults and Definitions in Knowledge Representation", AI Magazine, 6, n° 3, 80-93.

BRACHMAN, R.J., FIKES, R.E., and LEVESQUE, H.J. (1985a) "KRYPTON : A Functional Approach to Knowledge Representation", in Readings in Knowledge Representation, Brachman, R.J., and Levesque, H.J., eds. Los Altos: Morgan Kaufmann.

BREWKA, G. (1987) "The Logic of Inheritance in Frame Systems", in Proceedings of the Tenth International Joint Conference on Artificial Intelligence - IJCAI/87. Los Altos: Morgan Kaufmann.

FIKES, R., and KEHLER, T. (1985) "The Role of Frame-Based Representation in Reasoning", Communications of the ACM, 28, 904-920.

SCHIEL, U. (1989) "Abstractions in Semantic Networks : Axiom Schemata for Generalization, Aggregation and Grouping", ACM Sigart Newsletter, n° 107, 25-26.

SOWA, J.F. (1984) Conceptual Structures : Information Processing in Mind and Machine. Reading (Mass.): Addison-Wesley.

STEFIK, M. (1979) "An Examination of a Frame-Structured Representation System", in Proceedings of the Sixth International Joint Conference on Artificial Intelligence - IJCAI/79. Los Altos: Morgan Kaufmann.

STOUDER, L. (1988) RESEDA, le métalangage (Conv. INALCO/CIMSA SINTRA n° 0223A). Vélizy: Division CIMSA SINTRA de Thomson-CSF.

VILAIN, M. (1985) "The Restricted Language Architecture of a Hybrid Representation System", in Proceedings of the Ninth International Joint Conference on Artificial Intelligence - IJCAI/85. Los Altos: Morgan Kaufmann.

WILENSKY, R. (1987) Some Problems and Proposals for Knowledge Representation (UCB/CSD Report n° 87/351). Berkeley: University of California Computer Science Division.

ZARRI, G.P. (1983) "An Outline of the Representation and Use of Temporal Data in the RESEDA System", Information Technology : Research and Development, 2, 89-108.

ZARRI, G.P. (1984) "Expert Systems and Information Retrieval : An Experiment in the Domain of Biographical Data Management", in Developments in Expert Systems, Coombs, M.J., ed. London: Academic Press.

ZARRI, G.P. (1988a) "Conceptual Representation for Knowledge Bases and 'Intelligent' Information Retrieval Systems", in Proceedings of the Eleventh International ACM Conference on Research and Development in Information Retrieval, Chiaramella, Y., ed. Grenoble: Presses Universitaires (PUG).

ZARRI, G.P. (1988b) "Knowledge Acquisition for Large Knowledge Bases Using Natural Language Analysis Techniques", Expert Systems for Information Management, 1, 85-109.

Efficient Frame Systems

Dario Giuse
The Robotics Institute, Carnegie Mellon University
Pittsburgh, PA 15213 - U.S.A.

Abstract: Frame systems occupy an important place among formalisms for computer-based knowledge representation. A common concern about frame systems is that they are not efficient enough. We argue that this is not necessarily true of all possible systems, and that the trade-off between representational power and efficiency has not been fully explored. It is possible, in particular, to design frame systems that retain much of the flexibility while providing excellent performance. Such systems are well suited for applications that need flexible knowledge representation but cannot afford the high performance price.

Introduction

Ever since the introduction of the programmed digital computer, the need for computers to manipulate information from the real world has been apparent. A distinction has emerged between programs that manipulate regular, simple-structured data and programs that manipulate less structured information, normally referred to as *knowledge*. The problem of representing this information in a way that is best suited for use by a computer program is known as *knowledge representation*.

Different mechanisms have been proposed to represent knowledge for use by a computer program, and *frame systems* are among the most successful. The frame model provides a great deal of flexibility and great representational power. In spite of the wealth of work, however, the space of possibilities for frame-based representation has not been explored in its entirety. The lower end of the spectrum, in particular, has only been covered lightly. This region offers several advantages of its own: Frame systems at the low end of the spectrum combine great simplicity with good performance, and are well suited for applications that do not fit the systems at the opposite end.

The next section presents a brief overview of some influential frame systems. We then introduce the distinction between low-end frame systems and the more usual high-end systems, and justify the need for low-end frame systems. The remaining portion of the document describes a specific example of a low-level knowledge representation system and shows how its features form a natural complement to those of the more complex systems.

1. Frame Systems

The origins of frame systems can be found in ideas first expressed by Minsky [15], but actually originated much further back in the history of philosophy. For example, Anderson et al. [1] trace some of the ideas all the way back to Aristotle's associationism. Mac Randal [13] provides a good historical introduction to the field of semantic networks and frame systems, and an in-depth discussion of the semantics of various frame systems.

The first computer implementation of Minsky's ideas came with Quillian's PhD thesis in 1966, which was aimed at the problem of natural language understanding. Quillian [20] [19] used the term *semantic memory* to describe his formalism. Each node in the system corresponded to a linguistic concept (a *word concept*) and represented the "meaning" of a word. Other work soon followed, such as that by Shapiro [21] who gave a model of semantic network, and by Woods [25] who emphasized the precise description of the semantics of nodes and links in semantic networks.

Probably the best-known example of frame system is KL-ONE, developed by Brachman [2] [4], which embodies many of the notions found in modern semantic networks. One of its primary goals was to investigate the so-called *epistemological adequacy* of frame systems, i.e., what could and could not be represented by frame systems and what type of semantics should be built into them. The system includes a powerful set of features such as multiple inference strategies and the so-called *classifier*, which automates the placement of frames within a taxonomy. Brachman [4] gives a comprehensive description of the system and the underlying philosophy.

Another paper by Brachman [3] had a fundamental influence on the development of modern frame systems. In that paper Brachman posed basic questions about the semantics of frame systems and clarified important issues which had often been muddled in previous systems. The paper also made a clear distinction among the different levels in frame systems: the *implementation level*, the *logical level*, the *conceptual level*, and the *linguistic level*. Each level builds on the previous ones and provides a foundation for the next level up.

Other frame systems developed more recently were greatly influenced by KL-ONE and its derived systems. An example of the current generation of tools is SRL, developed by Fox et al. [6], which includes user-definable customizations such as user-defined inheritance paths, relations, contexts, and support for object programming in the form of procedural attachments. As with many AI tools designed within the last decade, SRL was later developed commercially to become CRL [12].

1.1 High-end Systems

Most frame systems described in the literature have emphasized powerful knowledge representation and inferencing, possibly at the expense of performance. The reasons for this bias toward the high end are several, and high-end systems of this kind have made significant contributions to the field of computer-based knowledge representation. The high end of the spectrum has been, and will continue to be, the place where most advances in frame-based knowledge representation take place.

The reverse side of the coin is that high-end systems tend to be complex, and their performance is not always adequate. One should draw a clear distinction between problems that are inherently hard, and therefore require complex solutions, and problems that are inherently simple. It is acceptable for solutions to complex problems to be expensive, but unfortunately high-end systems often exhibit poor performance on simple problems as well.

Many systems which provide fully general support for features such as meta-knowledge and alternative world reasoning fail to optimize the simple cases which occur so often in real applications. Simple problems are treated just like complex problems and suffer from an undue performance penalty. High-end systems, moreover, are large and complex software artifacts, and thus they quickly become difficult to maintain as they grow. Most chances for performance improvements in such large systems are effectively lost.

A final, well-known problem with most high-end systems is that they are monolithic environments which make it virtually impossible to scale down application programs for smaller hardware platforms. Moving an application program originally developed in a high-end system to the delivery environment sometimes requires rewriting the entire application.

1.2 Low-end Systems

The low end of the spectrum of frame systems has not been explored nearly as much as the high end. Many important practical applications of frame systems have been precluded by this relative lack of interest in efficient knowledge representation. Low-end systems cannot compete with high-end ones on the basis of features and representational power. They can, however, provide three advantages over the more conventional high end of the spectrum. These advantages justify the need for more research in the low-end area.

The first, and more obvious, advantage is *efficiency*. If properly designed, a low-end knowledge representation system can offer superior performance, often approaching that of conventional data structures. The later sections of this paper present an actual example of a knowledge representation system, named KR, which substantiates this claim.

The second advantage is *simplicity*. A low-end frame system typically offers only a fraction of the functionality found near the high end of the spectrum, and therefore it is much easier to understand and use. Equally important, it is easier to debug and maintain, which generally means that it also more robust.

The third advantage is *flexibility*. The kernel of a low-end knowledge representation system is very small and thus very flexible. A low-end system may be the ideal environment for studying the relative impact of different knowledge representation features, since its flexibility enables each feature to be implemented and evaluated separately.

The following sections describe in detail a low-end frame-based knowledge representation system named KR. We present an overview of KR and position it within the spectrum of frame systems. We then present some data which describe the performance of the system, and examples of applications which use it as their sole form of knowledge representation.

2. The KR System

KR is a knowledge representation system implemented in Common Lisp [22]. It follows in the tradition of frame systems, but it has a distinct position within the low end of the spectrum. KR shares this area with few other frame systems; the most noteworthy of these is FrameKit, described by Nyberg [18], which also provides a simplified knowledge representation framework.

2.1 General Features

The central concept in KR is the *schema*, which may contain as many slots as needed. A schema consists of a name, a set of slots, and a set of values for each slot. A *slot* behaves as an attribute/value pair: the slot name indicates the attribute name, and the slot values (if any) indicate its values. *Values* are the actual data items stored in the schema.

Inheritance is used extensively in KR to allow a schema to inherit slots and values from other schemata. Inheritance achieves three purposes: It reduces network size; it helps maintain consistency; and it allows local knowledge to override global knowledge. Inheritance reduces network size because whenever a piece of information for a schema is the same as in a more general one, the information need only appear once. Inheritance helps maintain consistency because it enables a local change to be immediately visible everywhere in the network. Finally, inheritance allows local redefinition of global knowledge, since a local value simply overrides any value which might otherwise be inherited. These features are illustrated in Fig. 2-1, which shows their effect on a very simple network.

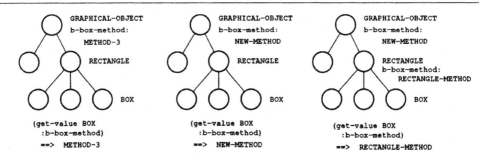

Figure 2-1: Three effects of inheritance

Inheritance in KR is user-defined. In addition to a handful of predefined relations that perform inheritance (of which IS-A is the most typical example), application programs are free to define new inheritance relations. New relations may be defined in any order and at any time during execution.

A *relation* is a slot which acts as a link between schemata. Any relation may be defined to have inverse relations, and thus to have an inverse link be created automatically when needed.

Relations and their inverses are maintained transparently by KR. All side effects of any modification to the values in a slot which is a relation are immediately computed and installed in the network of schemata. For example, consider the situation where the following schemata are defined:

```
BLOCK-1       is-a : rectangle
              part-of : aggregate-12 aggregate-10
AGGREGATE-12  is-a : aggregate
              components : base-3 block-1 block-8
```

Eliminating the value AGGREGATE-12 from the slot PART-OF in BLOCK-1 also eliminates the inverse pointer from AGGREGATE-12. This keeps the network in a consistent state.

2.2 The Functional Interface

The interface from the application program to KR is implemented as a LISP package which exports a handful of functions. Earlier reports [7] [10] give a complete description of the functional interface and the suggested programming style for KR users. The number of functions is extremely small as compared to that of typical high-end knowledge representation systems.

NAME	DESCRIPTION	COMMENTS
Predicates and Query Functions		
SCHEMA-P	is object a schema?	
RELATION-P	is object a relation?	
HAS-SLOT-P	does object have this slot?	*possibly with inheritance*
Schema Manipulation Functions		
PS	print current status of a schema	
CREATE-SCHEMA	create a new schema	
DELETE-SCHEMA	delete a schema	*deals with relations*
CREATE-RELATION	create a new relation	*possibly with inheritance*
DELETE-SLOT	delete a slot from a schema	*deals with relations*
DOSLOTS	iterate a function over all slots in a schema	
Value Manipulation Functions		
GET-VALUE	retrieve slot value	*has SETF form*
GET-VALUES	retrieve all slot values	*has SETF form*
GET-LOCAL-VALUES	retrieve slot values	*no inheritance*
DOVALUES	iterate a function over all values in a slot	
SET-VALUE	set slot value	*SETF for get-value*
SET-VALUES	set all slot values	*SETF for get-values*

Table 2-1: The functional interface of KR: main functions

Table 2-1 shows the main functions in the interface, broken down into major categories. The table contains the function names and a brief description of the function; additional comments are in the right-hand column.

2.3 Some Applications

Several application programs have been developed which use KR for knowledge representation. Some of them use a mixture of KR and conventional data structures, while others rely entirely on KR.

The first application we developed using KR was the Chinese Tutor [8] [9], an intelligent tutoring system designed to teach Chinese to English speakers. The Chinese Tutor uses KR as its sole form of knowledge representation. KR is used, among other things, to store the online dictionary of Chinese characters and words, complete with English translations and various structural hierarchies. The evaluation of the student's familiarity with the language and a simple system of rules is also stored in a network of schemata.

The second major application of KR is the Garnet User Interface Development Environment [16], an advanced user interface development environment currently under development at the Computer Science Department of Carnegie Mellon University. We are using KR extensively to implement a graphical object system [24], a constraint satisfaction system [11], and a graphical object editor [17] for the interactive creation of user interfaces.

Other applications are also being developed at Carnegie Mellon, especially in the area of speech understanding research [26]. Most users have mentioned simplicity and excellent performance as the deciding factors which motivate them to use KR.

2.4 The Advantages of Simplicity

Simple frame systems like KR enable experimentation of a type that would be difficult with high-end frame systems. An intriguing line of research is the evaluation of the *relative cost of each knowledge representation feature*. Since so few complex features are hard-wired in KR, each feature can be evaluated independently.

The best example to date of this line of research was the implementation of a one-way constraint satisfaction system on top of KR. The main features of this system, which is closely modeled after Coral [23], are its transparency (access to slots with constraints is indistinguishable from access to regular slots) and its automatic maintenance of constraints among values.

The system is implemented as a separate layer built on top of KR. Constraints are implemented as *formulas*, which specify how the value in a slot depends on values in other slots. Any change to those other values causes the formula to be re-evaluated; in practice, lazy evaluation causes formulas to be only recomputed when needed. The experiment yielded a system which is now being used in several application programs, most notably a constraint-based graphical system [17] for designing user interfaces. Performance is very good, due to the use of lazy evaluation. The system is quite general and can be used to implement a broad class of constraint-based applications.

A second advantage of simplicity is that low-end systems such as KR are suitable for non-LISP environments. We are currently in the process of implementing an experimental

version of KR in the C programming language. Preliminary results suggest that this system
may provide a viable alternative to more static knowledge representation for languages such
as C.

3. Evaluation

We now present an evaluation of KR along three different lines: performance, simplicity, and
support for applications. We will attempt to characterize KR by comparing it to other frame
systems and to other programming paradigms, such as conventional data structures and
objected-oriented programming systems.

3.1 Performance

We begin this section by showing a short table with performance figures for KR in Common
Lisp (see Table 3-1). These figures were collected on an IBM RT workstation running CMU
Common Lisp [14] under the Mach operating system. All figures refer to compiled code and
are expressed in microseconds per call.

GET-VALUE (1st slot):	14.4 μsec
GET-VALUE (2nd slot):	20.6 μsec
GET-VALUE (for each extra slot):	6.2 μsec
GET-VALUE (1 level of inheritance):	52.2 μsec
GET-VALUE (2 levels of inheritance):	84.0 μsec
SET-VALUE:	59.3 μsec

Table 3-1: Performance of the basic KR access functions (for IBM RT)

The table indicates that KR performs quite well. To put those figures in perspective, consider
that an empty function call and return in the same environment takes about 10 microseconds.
The time to execute the simplest and most commonly used accessor macros, GET-VALUE and
GET-VALUES, is of the order of less than 2 function calls. Similar results were obtained on a
Symbolics 3640 Lisp Machine.

Table 3-2 gives a simple measure of the complexity of KR versus two other frame systems:
the number of functions and special variables in the program interface. KR and FrameKit
belong to the low end of the spectrum; CRL is a commercial, high-end system.

As the table shows, the difference between low-end and high-end systems is quite marked.
The CRL interface contains a total of 139 exported symbols (103 functions plus 36 special
variables), whereas KR only has 28. Most CRL functions, moreover, have a fairly complex
structure and take optional arguments and keyword arguments. FrameKit, a low-end frame
system, is much closer to KR in pursuing a streamlined interface.

Finally, Table 3-3 compares the execution times for some of the most common functions in
different representation systems. Each entry in the table indicates the actual execution time in
microseconds. When the operation generates temporary storage (garbage), this is indicated by

FUNCTION GROUP:	KR	FRAMEKIT	CRL
create	4	11	16
access	6	12	33
update	7	17	30
information	7	8	8
debugging	2	3	2
o-o, demons	2	1	14
miscellaneous	0	4	0
TOTAL:	28	43	103
special variables	0	13	36
TOTAL SYMBOLS:	28	56	139

Table 3-2: Complexity of the functional interface for different frame systems

a second number in parentheses which shows the number of bytes allocated per operation.

	LISP	KR	FRAMEKIT	CRL
get-value (1 0)	5.7	14.4	493.0 *(80 bytes)*	118.0
get-value (4 0)	5.7	33.0	518.7 *(80 bytes)*	142.6
get-value (1 1)	-	52.2	2090.0 *(240 bytes)*	417.3
get-value (1 4)	-	145.3	3962.5 *(576 bytes)*	1191.0
set-value (1 0)	10.0	59.3	4921.8 *(576 bytes)*	465.3

Table 3-3: Execution times for various representation systems (IBM RT)

Each row is labeled with the name of the operation and two numbers. The first number indicates the position of the slot (in most frame systems, the access time is position-dependent). The second number determines the levels of inheritance; 0 means that the slot is local and no inheritance is used. The second row, for example, shows the execution time for retrieving the fourth local slot (i.e., with 0 levels of inheritance); the fourth row shows the time to retrieve the first slot from a schema 4 levels up in the hierarchy.

The column labeled "LISP" shows figures for a straightforward implementation where a LISP structure was used to simulate conventional data structure access. These figures give the lower bound for the access time. Times in the "LISP" column show the slot access time (which is position-independent) and the slot update time. Inheritance is, of course, not applicable to this simple data structure.

Table 3-3 clearly expresses the large difference in performance among different systems. Whereas the cost of a GET-VALUE operation in KR is only 2.5 times that of the fastest possible LISP access, the cost becomes 20.7 times in CRL. The performance ratio between KR and CRL (a reasonably optimized high-end system) is around 5.2 for the simplest operations and 7.3 for operations with inheritance.

The figures for FrameKit deserve a little explanation. While FrameKit is a low-end system, as shown by its reduced functional interface (see Table 3-2), its performance is actually significantly worse than that of CRL. This is because FrameKit has not undergone any optimization, and thus it suffers from all the usual overhead for the simple cases. Careful optimization should bring the performance to more acceptable levels.

3.2 Comparison with Object-Oriented Systems

Low-end frame systems provide much greater flexibility than most object-oriented programming languages. This, together with good performance, makes them suitable for a large class of object-oriented applications. Consider, for example, KR versus CLOS, the Common Lisp Object System [5].

CLOS offers the familiar notions of instance, class, and meta-class. All CLOS classes are instances of some other class, and the details of the inheritance path are specified at class-creation time. Slots within an instance may be specified as local (each instance contains storage for the slot) or shared. This decision must be made at class-creation time, and is not meant to be altered dynamically.

KR, on the other hand, has no notion of predefined classes or metaclasses. Inheritance of values is determined dynamically, rather than at compile time; any object may inherit values or slots from any other object. Inheritance may be overridden locally as needed; values are inherited on demand, rather than being copied into each object.

Instance slots in CLOS are normally of the *local* type. In this case, storage for a slot is allocated at instance creation time, and the class cannot influence the value of the slot afterwards. In KR, by contrast, storage is never allocated by default. Values are inherited from parent objects, and the inheritance path is evaluated each time the value is needed. An inherited value may be overridden simply by specifying a local value. In CLOS terms, this would be equivalent to an automatic conversion from a shared slot to a local slot, except of course that this is on a per-instance, rather than per-class, basis. Deleting a local slot in KR automatically reverts to the default, inherited situation.

In spite of its greater flexibility, however, KR is actually *more efficient* than CLOS. Moreover, developing object-oriented applications in KR requires less effort than in CLOS. Both claims are substantiated in [11], which discusses the relative performance of the two systems and compares two different implementations of the constraint system described previously. That paper shows that KR clearly outperforms CLOS on a variety of low-level benchmarks and on more complex application programs. KR is very efficient in performing inheritance, and therefore it can yield extremely compact systems.

4. Future Work

Important research topics remain to be addressed in the area of frame systems. Some of them can best be addressed within the framework of low-end frame systems such as KR. One such topic is the evaluation of the impact of different features on performance and complexity.

While high-end frame systems offer an all-or-nothing choice, systems at the low end of the spectrum show the potential for a careful, independent evaluation of each feature, thus providing designers and users with realistic data about expected costs and benefits.

We have performed one such experiment, by adding constraint satisfaction to the system and evaluating its effect on implementation and performance. Similar questions that will have to be addressed in future research concern the impact of:

- Alternative world reasoning (*contexts*) capabilities.
- User-defined inheritance paths and search strategies (such as breadth-first versus depth-first).
- Used-defined slot and value restrictions and, more generally, *meta-knowledge*.
- Separate inference mechanisms, such as those available in KL-ONE.

Based on the results of these evaluations, it may become possible to build "knowledge representation toolkits" from which users could select only the features they need. This approach should produce systems that are easier to customize as needed. This would open new possibilities for the problem of converting existing AI systems and applications to smaller software environments and hardware platforms.

A second area of research that becomes possible with low-end knowledge representation systems is that of aggressive storage reduction. For applications that need extremely large knowledge bases, this may well be the dominant factor. Low-end systems are ideal candidates for research on aggressive storage reduction techniques, possibly by trading flexibility for data compactness. This type of research would be prohibitively expensive in the domain of high-end frame systems.

Finally, low-end frame systems are ideal candidates for research into non-LISP implementations. Simplicity becomes a fundamental benefit when working with languages such as C which do not provide the rich data manipulation capabilities of LISP. The potential for excellent performance makes this a promising direction for future research. While we have begun a limited research in this direction, much work remains to be done before the possibilities of this approach are exhausted.

5. Conclusions

Research on frame-based knowledge representation has been mostly concentrated on the high end of the spectrum and has emphasized representational power and flexibility over performance. While this direction of research has yielded important theoretical and practical progress, it is unfortunate that the reduced emphasis on performance has originated the myth that semantic networks are only appropriate for large, complex AI applications.

It is time to correct this problem by placing equal significance on simplicity and efficiency. The domain where such issues can best be addressed is that of low-end frame systems, which emphasize economy while still retaining most of the flexibility of frame-based knowledge representation. This line of research will yield a better understanding of the relative costs of different knowledge representation features which are currently lumped together in high-end frame systems.

This paper has used KR, a low-end frame-based knowledge representation system, to show the main differences among the two types of frame systems. KR is a simple, very efficient knowledge representation system which implements the basic paradigm of semantic networks and offers such features as multiple values, fully dynamic inheritance, multiple inheritance, and user-defined relations.

Low-end frame systems such as KR provide a natural complement to the more traditional, high-end ones. This region of the power/performance spectrum shows an amount of flexibility and efficiency that is not usually found elsewhere. Besides being useful systems in their own right, low-end frame systems should also act as an incentive for implementors of any knowledge representation mechanism to regard simplicity and performance as essential features that cannot be sacrificed.

Acknowledgments

This research was sponsored by the Defense Advanced Research Projects Agency (DOD), DARPA Order No. 4976, under contract number F33615-87-C-1499, monitored by the Avionics Laboratory, Air Force Wright Aeronautical Laboratories, Aeronautical Systems Division (AFSC), Wright Patterson AFB, Ohio 45433-6543. The views and conclusions are those of the author and should not be interpreted as representing the official policies, either expressed or implied, of the Defense Advanced Research Projects Agency or the US Government.

References

1. Anderson, J.R. and Bower, G.H.. *Human Associative Memory.* Holt, New York, 1973.

2. Brachman, R.J. *A structural paradigm for representing knowledge.* Ph.D. Th., Harvard University, Cambridge, MA, May 1977.

3. Brachman, R.J. On the epistemological status of semantic networks. In *Associative Networks: Representation and Use of Knowledge by Computers*, Academic Press, New York, 1979, pp. 3-50.

4. Brachman, R.J. and Schmolze, J.G. "An overview of the KL-ONE knowledge representation system". *Cognitive Science 9*, 2 (April-June 1983), 170-216.

5. Linda G. DeMichiel. "Overview: The Common Lisp Object System". *LISP ard Symbolic Computation 1*, 3/4 (January 1989), 227-244.

6. Fox, M.S., Wright, J.M., and Adam, D. Experiences with SRL: an analysis of a frame-based knowledge representation. First International Workshop on Expert Database Systems, 1984.

7. Dario Giuse. KR: an efficient knowledge representation system. Tech. Rept. CMU-RI-TR-87-23, The Robotics Institute, Carnegie-Mellon University, October, 1987.

8. Dario Giuse. "LISP as a rapid prototyping environment: the Chinese Tutor". *LISP and Symbolic Computation 1*, 2 (September 1988), 165-184.

9. Dario Giuse. Intelligent Tutoring Systems for Foreign Language Acquisition. proceedings of the Asia-Pacific Conference on Computer Education (APCCE 88), Shanghai, China, 1988, pp. 33-58.

10. Dario Giuse. KR: Constraint-Based Knowledge Representation. Tech. Rept. CMU-CS-89-142, Computer Science Department, Carnegie-Mellon University, April, 1989.

11. Dario Giuse. Frame Systems as Object-Oriented Systems. Submitted for publication.

12. *Knowledge Craft Reference Manual.* Carnegie Group, Inc., Pittsburgh, PA, 1986.

13. Mac Randal, D. Semantic Networks. In *Approaches to knowledge representation: an introduction*, Research Studies Press, Inc., Forest Grove, OR, 1988, pp. 45-79.

14. David B. McDonald. CMU Common Lisp User's Manual - Mach/IBM RT PC Edition. Tech. Rept. CMU-CS-87-156, Computer Science Department, Carnegie-Mellon University, September, 1987.

15. Minsky, M.. *Computers and thought.* McGraw Hill, New York, 1963.

16. Brad A. Myers. The Garnet User Interface Development Environment: A Proposal. Tech. Rept. CMU-CS-88-153, Carnegie-Mellon University, September, 1988.

17. Brad A. Myers, Brad Vander Zanden, and Roger B. Dannenberg. Creating Graphical Objects by Demonstration. Submitted for Publication.

18. Nyberg, E.H. The FrameKit user's guide. Center for Machine Translation, Carnegie Mellon University, March, 1988.

19. Quillian, M.R. "Word concepts: a theory and simulation of some basic semantic capabilities". *Behavioral Science 12* (1967).

20. Quillian, M.R. Semantic Memory. In *Semantic Information Processing*, The MIT Press, Cambridge, MA, 1968, pp. 227-270.

21. Shapiro, S.C. "Representing and locating deduction rules in a semantic network". *SIGART Newsletter 63* (June 1977), 14-18.

22. Steele, G.L.. *Common LISP - The Language.* Digital Press, Burlington, MA, 1984.

23. Pedro A. Szekely and Brad A. Myers. "A User Interface Toolkit Based on Graphical Objects and Constraints". *Sigplan Notices 23*, 11 (Nov. 1988), 36-45.

24. Brad Vander Zanden, Brad A. Myers, Dario Giuse, and John Kolojejchick. An Incremental Automatic Redisplay Algorithm for Graphic Object Systems. Submitted for Publication.

25. Woods, W.A. What's in a link: foundations for semantic networks. In *Representation and Understanding: Studies in Cognitive Science*, Academic Press, New York, 1975, pp. 35-82.

26. Sheryl R. Young, Alexander G. Hauptmann, Wayne H. Ward, Edward T. Smith, and Philip Werner. "High-level Knowledge Sources in Usable Speech Recognition Systems". *Communications of the ACM 32*, 2 (February 1989), 183-194.

First Order Theories of Quantification

Arkady Rabinov

Computer Science Department
Stanford University
Stanford, California 94305

Abstract

Many applications of logic to AI require that propositions be reified, i.e., made elements of the domain of discourse. This is needed, in particular, in formalizing reasoning about knowledge and about preconditions of actions. Difficulties arise when the quantificational structure of propositions is essential. We show how ideas from combinatory logic can be used to deal with this problem. This approach allows us to construct first order theories in which lambda-abstraction and quantification can be easily expressed as terms of the language.

1 Introduction

McCarthy [1] suggested First Order Theories of Propositions, in which propositions formally are the objects of theories and therefore it is possible to express various relationships between propositions. He showed how the relationship between a complex proposition and the propositions representing its parts can be described axiomatically. This approach works very well for quantification free propositions. For example, if the term $at(b, l)$ represent the fact that block b is at the location l, and the fact that block b is red is represented by the term $color(b, Red)$, where at and $color$ are the functions in our first order logic, then the function and can be used to form the term $and(at(b, l), color(b, Red))$ to represent a conjunction of these two propositions. He described the basic property of function and by the axiom

$$true(and(f1, f2)) \equiv true(f1) \wedge true(f2), \tag{1}$$

where $true$ is a unary predicate, expressing the truth value of a proposition. Similarly, for the functions or and not we have axioms

$$true(or(f1, f2)) \equiv true(f1) \vee true(f2), \tag{2}$$

$$true(not(f)) \equiv \neg true(f). \tag{3}$$

Things turned out to be not so smooth when McCarthy included propositions expressing quantification. In the corresponding section McCarthy wrote that he is not so confident in the approach presented there. The problems become clear when we try to express quantification by the straightforward use of function *exists* as we did with propositional connectives. If we write something like

$$exists(x, f(x)), \tag{4}$$

then, since formally speaking the variable x is free in this term, we have contrary to our expectations and intuition:

$$a = x \land true(exists(x, f(x))) \supset true(exists(x, f(a))).$$

To avoid this problem, the bound variable x in (4) is considered to be a constant in the underlying first order theory, but as the result of this the axiomatic description of the function *exists* becomes complicated, if possible at all. The problem lies in the fact that function *forall* should be applied to lambda expressions, and we are not able to construct them.

We are going to show how further reification, combined with ideas from combinatory logic, can be used to form the theories of propositions in which quantifications can be easily expressed. Section 2 contains an example from the formal theories of action which shows potential application of theories of quantification. This example sheds also some light on the way of solving the problem. Section 3 contains the technical details of a proposed solution. Section 4 shows how the proposed solution can be used. In Section 5 we prove some theorems about the proposed solution.

2   Blocks world example

In 1986 Lifschitz [2] proposed an axiomatic description of causal connection between actions and changes. In his approach, fluents are not functions but the objects in the universe, and each fluent describes a particular aspect of the world. Formally, the truth value of a particular fluent (and therefore of a particular aspect of the world) in a particular situation can be retrieved using the predicate *holds*, so formula $holds(at(B1, L), S0)$ would tell us whether block $B1$ is at location L in the situation $S0$. His method is in the framework of the situation calculus and based on circumscription of two predicates *causes* and *precond*. The formula $precond(f, a)$ expresses the notion that fluent f must hold in a particular situation for the action a to be successful in that situation. He illustrated his method with a simple example from the blocks world. He considered some blocks; each of them can be located on the table or on the top of some other block. Given a block b the function *top* can be used to obtain a location $top(b)$ on the top of the block b. (Following McCarthy, we will omit the parentheses for unary functions and will write *top b*.) Blocks can be moved, and the term $move(b, l)$ denotes the action of moving the block b to the location l, where *move* is a binary function. Block b cannot be moved if its top is not clear. To express this formally, we would like to write something like:

$$precond(clear\ top\ b, move(b, l)).$$

The next question is how to express the notion *clear*? If there is only a finite number of blocks (for example 2 blocks) and we have names (constants) in our language for all of them, then we can view *clear top b* as an abbreviation for:

$$and(not\ at(B1, top\ b), not\ at(B2, top\ b)).$$

On the other hand if we do not have enough constants or if we want to allow an arbitrary number of blocks, we will need terms representing quantified proposition to express the notion that the top of a block is clear. Lifschitz solved this problem by introducing additional fluent *clear(l)* which represents the fact that there are no blocks at the location *l*; he considered it "non-primitive" and described its behavior by the following axiom [1] :

$$holds\ (clear(l), s) \equiv \forall b \neg holds\ (at(b, l), s). \tag{5}$$

But it would be more convenient if, whenever we need a new term expressing a quantified proposition, we were able to form it without the necessity to extend the language by a new fluent constant. This would also make it unnecessary to add new axioms like (5), each time we introduce terms expressing new quantified propositions.

As we noted earlier, our main problem is the impossibility to form the terms representing lambda expressions. The Formal Theories of Action can give us the idea how to solve this problem. In McCarthy's original formalization fluents were the functions in the first order theories, which were defined on situations. In order to avoid unintended models Lifschitz needed to axiomatize relationship between actions and fluents per se, i.e. between actions and lambda expressions of a very special form. To achieve this goal, he made them into objects of the universe [2] so *at(b, l)* now represents the property of block *b* being at location *l*. The truth value which was represented earlier by the term *at(b, l, s)* now can be represented by the term *value(at(b, l), s)* or by the formula *holds (at(b, l), s)*. In order to be able to construct various lambda expressions we need to proceed with reifying the terms of our language. For example instead of function *at* we should have the constant *at*. The only function we should have which deals with fluents or building blocks for fluents should be the function *apply*. Then *at(b, l)* should be written as *apply(apply(at, b), l)* and the lambda expression $\lambda l.at(b, l)$ can be easily constructed as *apply(at, b)*.

But what about the term $\lambda b.at(b, l)$? In order to be able to construct arbitrary lambda expressions from the elementary blocks we need to introduce combinators as objects of our first order logic.

3   Combinators and Theories of Quantification

Combinators were invented by Schönfinkel. We assume that the reader has some familiarity with the topic; see [5].

---

[1]Perlis[3] went to ultimate end in this direction by adding an infinite number of terms (one for each wff in the language). As the result, an appropriate axiom or axioms had to be added for each of these terms.

[2]Actually Kowalski [4] earlier and for a different purpose used fluents as objects of the universe.

Our goal is to be able to construct terms representing quantified propositions. We use a multi-sorted logic, and we assume that we have a sort h which represents truth-valued terms. We also have some other domain specific sorts, which, together with h, are called atomic sorts. The first step in the direction of our goal is an introduction of additional sorts. Namely for each two sorts α and β we also require to have a sort $\alpha \to \beta$. Such sorts are called compound sorts. Intuitively, the sort $\alpha \to \beta$ represents functions from objects of sort α into objects of sort β, but formally they are just objects of our universe.

The only function dealing with the terms representing propositions is the function *apply*. Actually for any two sorts α and β we have a function $apply_{\alpha\beta}$, such that its first argument has the sort $\alpha \to \beta$, its second argument has the sort α and the result has the sort β. All other domain specific functions, which we would like to have, should be made into the constants of appropriate sorts. For example, the above mentioned function *at* will become a constant of the sort $b \to l \to h$ (we assume that $\to$ is right associative). To make our formulas more readable, we introduce "syntactic sugar". The term $T_1(T_2)$ is an abbreviation for the term $apply(T_1, T_2)$; here sort of T_1 must be of the form $\alpha \to \beta$, where α is a sort of T_2. The sorts of T_1 and T_2 uniquely define which of the *apply* functions used, and consequently define the sort of the result to be β. We also abbreviate the term $apply(apply(T_1, T_2), T_3)$ as $T_1(T_2, T_3)$, etc.

Our next step is the introduction of combinators. We introduce combinators as constants of our language. For each two sorts α and β there must exist a constant $K_{\alpha,\beta}$ of sort $\alpha \to (\beta \to \alpha)$. For each three sorts α, β and γ there must exist a constant $S_{\alpha,\beta,\gamma}$ of sort $(\alpha \to \beta \to \gamma) \to (\alpha \to \beta) \to \alpha \to \gamma$.

We have the following two axiom schemas:

$$K(x1, x2) = x1 \tag{6}$$

and

$$S(x1, x2, x3) = x1(x3)(x2(x3)). \tag{7}$$

These schemas are instantiated for particular sorts.

We have the following fact, well known in combinatory logic:

Theorem 1 *For each term T_1 and variable x there exists a term T_2, such that for each term T_3 of the same sort as x*

$$T_2(T_3) = [T_3/x]T_1,$$

where $[T_3/x]T_1$ defined to be the result of substituting T_3 for every occurrence of x in T_1.

Given T_1, such term T_2 can easily be constructed by a standard algorithm (compare [5]), and we denote this term by $\lambda^* x.T_1$.

Having now lambda expressions at our disposal, we are ready to construct the terms representing quantified propositions. For each atomic sort α (except h) we have a constant $forall_\alpha$ of the sort $(\alpha \to h) \to h$ and we have the following axiom:

$$true(forall_\alpha(y)) \equiv \forall x\, true(y(x)). \tag{8}$$

Here y is a variable of the type $\alpha \to h$, and x is a variable of the type α. We define $exists_\alpha(y)$ to be an abbreviation for $not(forall_\alpha(not(y)))$. From axioms (3) and (8) it follows that

$$true(exists_\alpha(y)) \equiv \exists x \; true(y(x)).$$

We add some syntactic sugar by writing $Forall(x, T)$ instead of $(forall_\alpha \; \lambda^* x.T)$ and $Exists(x, T)$ instead of $(exists_\alpha \; \lambda^* x.T)$; the sort of x uniquely defines the sort α.

If we also add axioms (1), (2) and (3) to the axioms (6) – (8), considering them to be sugared version of appropriate axioms for *apply* then we will have the following

Theorem 2 *Let A be a formula such that all its atomic parts have the form $true(T_i)$. Let $T0$ be a term constructed from A by replacing all occurrences of subformulas of the form $true(T_i)$ by the term T_i, subformulas of the form $A1 \wedge A2$, $A1 \vee A2$, $\neg A1$, $\forall x(A1)$ or $\exists x(A1)$ by the terms $and(A1, A2)$, $or(A1, A2)$, $\neg(A1)$, $forall(x, A1)$ or $exists(x, A1)$, respectively. Then*

$$true(T0) \equiv A.$$

4 Examples

We illustrate these ideas by some examples.

In the area of reasoning about knowledge, we can be interested in expressing the fact that a particular robot $R1$ knows that all robots are in the office. This can be written as

$$knows(R1, forall \; \lambda^* r. \; in(Office, r)),$$

which is a sugared version of the formula:

$$knows(R1, apply(forall_r, apply(in, Office))).$$

We can also have an axiom:

$$knows(r, forall_r(x)) \supset \forall r1 \; knows(r, x(r1)).$$

In our last example we return to the blocks world as described in [2] and Section 2. In formalizing this example we will use the ideas described in previous section. We will slightly simplify this example by omitting the insignificant for us possibility of painting blocks.

Since we are interested in the situation calculus and formalizing actions, our basic atomic type will be the fluent sort f instead of the sort h, and instead of predicate *true* we will use predicate *holds* with two arguments, a fluent and a situation. Our additional atomic domain specific sorts are locations l and blocks b. These three atomic sorts are augmented with the compound sorts. As described above, we have constants K and S and the function *apply*. We have domain specific constants $B_0, \ldots, B_N$ of the sort blocks, $Table$ of the sort locations, top of the sort $b \to l$. We consider the sort of primitive fluents p to be a subsort of the sort f, and we have the constant at of the sort $b \to l \to p$. As usual, we have the constants $forall_l$ and $forall_b$. This describes the part of our language which deals with propositions related to fluents. We also have some additional sorts which do not participate in combinatory logic: actions a and situations s. The constant $S0$ is of the sort s. The function $result(a, s)$ produces a situation, and the function $move(b, l)$ produces an action. Besides the predicate $holds$ we also have the predicates $cause(a, p, f)$, $precond(f, a)$. Our axiom set follows the axioms of [2], but notice that the term $at(b, l)$ is a new syntactic sugar for the term $apply(apply(at, b), l)$; the term $clear(l)$ is just an abbreviation for the term

$$forall(\lambda^* b.\ not(at(b, l)))$$

or for a less sugared version

$$forall_b(S(K\ not, S(at, K\ l)));$$

$true$ is an abbreviation for $or(at(B_0, Table), not(at(B_0, Table)))$, and $false$ is an abbreviation for $and(at(B_0, Table), not(at(B_0, Table)))$.

The axioms are

$$b = B_0 \vee \ldots \vee b = B_N \tag{9}$$

$$holds(at(b, Table), S0), \tag{10}$$

$$holds\ (at(b, l1), s) \wedge holds\ (at(b, l2), s) \supset l1 = l2, \tag{11}$$

$$causes(move(b, l), at(b, l), true), \tag{12}$$

$$l \neq l1 \supset causes(move(b, l), at(b, l1), false), \tag{13}$$

$$l \neq Table \supset precond(clear(l), move(b, l)), \tag{14}$$

$$precond(clear(top\ b), move(b, l)), \tag{15}$$

$$precond(false, move(b, top(b))). \tag{16}$$

We have also the Law of Change:

$$success(a, s) \wedge causes(a, p, f) \supset (holds(p, result(a, s)) \equiv holds(f, s)), \tag{17}$$

and the Law of Inertia:

$$\neg affects(a, p, s) \supset (holds(p, result(a, s)) \equiv holds(p, s)), \tag{18}$$

where

$$affects(a, p, s) \equiv success(a, s) \wedge \forall f\ causes(a, p, f)$$

and

$$success(a, s) \equiv \forall f(precond(f, a) \supset holds(f, s)).$$

We also include axioms (1)-(3), (6), (7) and (8), with the subformulas of the form $true(f)$ replaced by the subformulas $holds(f, s)$; for example, axiom (1) becomes

$$holds(and(f1, f2), s) \equiv holds(f1, s) \wedge holds(f2, s).$$

By B we denote the conjunction of all these axioms. As in [2], we circumscribe the predicates $cause$ and $precond$, while the predicate $holds$ is allowed to vary.

By axioms (1)-(3), (6), (7) and (8) we postulated some properties of our theory, but are these postulates consistent. The following theorem gives the answer.

Theorem 3 *B has a minimal model.*

In the next section we construct a minimal model of B in which fluents have the intuitively expected values.

If we follow [2] or [6], our example can be easily generalized to the models with arbitrary universes. We should notice that in the general case there will be many non-isomorphic minimal models, but for any ground atom its truth value would be the same in all these models. Consequently, our axioms are sufficiently strong.

One of the deficiencies of the Formal Theories of Action was somehow artificial and unintuitive division of fluents into primitive and non-primitive classes. It was not clear to which class a particular fluent should belong. We should also notice that our approach helps to clarify this. In our theories, all domain specific fluents are primitive, while the fluents built using constants representing sentential connectives, quantification and combinators are non-primitive.

5 Model of B

We start with the description of the universe. For the situations and actions we use the sets of ground terms of our language as the domains.

We have the following atomic sorts: locations l, blocks b, fluents f and its subsort – primitive fluents p. In order to build a model we consider three additional languages. The first one is a two-sorted first order language L': sort b has constants $B_0, \ldots, B_N$ and sort l has a constant $Table$; this language has one function $top(b) \to l$ and one predicate $at(b, l)$. The second – L'' is a system of typed combinatory logic with three atomic types: blocks – b, with the constants $B_0, \ldots, B_N$; locations – l, with the constant $Table$; there is no constants of the fluent type – f or of its subtype – primitive fluents p. We have one constant top of the type $b \to l$ and one constant at of the type $b \to l \to p$. We also have constants and, or, not, $forall_l$ and $forall_b$ of appropriate types. It is obvious that we have the same set of types in L'' as the set of sorts in our language. The closed normal terms of the language L'' of a particular type will be the domain for the corresponding sort of our language.

Our third language – L'''. It is very close to L''. The difference is that it does not have the constants $forall$, but have the following constants $F_1^l, \ldots, F_i^l, \ldots$ and $F_1^b, \ldots, F_i^b, \ldots$ of the type $f \to f$.

The same symbols can stand for or be parts of the terms of L, L', L'' or L''', it will be always clear from the context to which language a particular instance of a symbol belongs. Since we are going to introduce some functions which map terms between languages, we need to distinguish between the use of parentheses as metasymbols and the use of them as parts of terms of L'' and L'''. Therefore we are going to use brackets [and] in forming terms of L'' and L'''.

For any term T of L'' or L''' we denote by $\overline{T}$ the result of normalization of T. It is always exists for typed combinatoric logic and by Church-Rosser theorem it is uniquely defined.

Our next step is an interpretation of the constants and an interpretation of the functions. We interpret each constant of L as the same constant term of L for $S0$ and as the constant term of L'' for all others.

For any two term $T1$ of sort block and $T2$ of sort location, we interpret $move(T1, T2)$ as a term $move(T1, T2)$ in L and similarly for the function $result$. For any two terms $T1 \in L''$ and $T2 \in L''$ of appropriate types we define

$$apply(T1, T2) = \overline{[T1 \ T2]}.$$

We interpret predicates $cause$ and $precond$ as the strongest predicates satisfying axioms (12)-(16).

To interpret predicate $holds$ we need to define some additional functions. The function FE maps L'' into L''' as follows: it replaces i-th occurrence of the symbol $forall$ (either $forall_b$ or $forall_l$) by the term $\lambda^* y. \ [F_i^l[y \ l_i]]$ (for $forall_l$) or by the term $\lambda^* y. \ [F_i^b[y \ b_i]]$ (for $forall_b$).

We also need functions FE_n which are different from FE in one respect: they start enumeration from number n.

Lemma 1 *If $T \in L'''$ of an atomic type is normal then T contains neither K nor S.*

Proof. By induction on the length of T. Consider the first symbol of T. If it is K or S then it is clear from consideration of the types of K and S that T cannot be both normal and of atomic type. Therefore the first symbol of T must be one of the following:

- *and* - then it follows from type considerations that T has a form $[[and \ T1]T2]$ where $T1$ and $T2$ also are of type f;

- similarly for *or* and *not*;

- if the first symbol is F then T must have the form $[F \ T1]$ where $T1$ is of type f;

- *at* – then it follows from type consideration follows that T must be of the form $[[at \ T1]T2]$ where $T1$ and $T2$ are both of atomic types;

- similarly for the symbol *top*;

- if the first symbol of T is $Table$ or B_i or a variable then T must coincide with this symbol.□

In the following definition and the Lemma 2 the letter x in the variable symbols or in the superscripts of F_i^x stands for l or b.

Definition: variable x_i which occurs in a term T is bound in the terms

1. $[F_i^x \ T]$;

2. $[[[K F_i^x]T_1]T]$, where T_1 is some term;

3. $[[S[KF_i^x]][[S[[SK]K]][Kx_i]]]$;

4. in any term $T1$ of which T is subterm if x_i is bound in T.

Definition: the term $T0 \in L'''$ is sentence if every variable occuring in $T0$ is bound in $T0$.

Lemma 2 *If $T0$ is sentence then $\overline{T}0$ is also a sentence.*

It is enough to prove that one contracting preserves the property of being a sentence. In the proof of the Lemma the word 'bound' always means 'bound in $T0$' and the word 'subterm' means 'subterm of $T0$'.

Notice that if $T1$ and $T2$ are both subterms of $T0$ then one must occur: they are disjoint or they coincide or one is proper subterm of another. Since contraction does not generate new variables we only have to prove that the variable which was bound before contraction is also bound after contraction.

Consider a variable x_i and let T_b be a subterm of the forms 1., 2. or 3., so that T_b provides binding for x_i. Let T_r be a redex we are going to contract. If T_r and T_b are disjoint then obviously the binding is preserved across the contraction.

In none of the cases of T_b is redex and therefore can not coincide with T_r.

Consider the case when T_r is a proper subterm of T_b. If it is subterm of T in case 1. or it is subterm of T or $T1$ in case 2. then binding is preserved across contraction. If T_r coincide with $[[KF_i^x]T1]$ in case 2. then x_i, being a subterm of T, is also bound after contraction according to the case 1. No redex term can be a proper subterm of T_b in case 3.

Now consider the case when T_b is a proper subterm of T_r. Consider two subcases:
a) $T_r = [[KV]U]$, in this case T_b must be a subterm of V or U which means that either binding is preserved across contraction or occurrence of x disappeared after contraction. In any case property of being sentence is preserved.
b) $T_r = [[[ST1]T2]T3]$, in this case T_b can be either:
subterm of $T1$, $T2$ or $T3$ in which case binding is preserved across contraction or T_b can be of the form 3. and coincides with $[[ST1]T2]$, in this case T_r has a form

$$[[[[S[KF_i^x]][[S[[SK]K]][Kx_i]]]T3]$$

and after contraction it will have the form

$$[[[KF_i^x]T3][[[S[[SK]K]][Kx_i]]T3]]$$

and x_i is still bound according to the case 2.$\square$

We define the function $Pred$ which maps the normal terms of atomic types of L''' into formulas and terms of L' by induction as follows:

$$Pred([[and\ T1]\ T2]) = Pred(T1) \wedge Pred(T2),$$

$$Pred([[or\ T1]\ T2]) = Pred(T1) \vee Pred(T2),$$

$$Pred([not\ T]) = \neg Pred(T),$$

$$Pred([F_i^x\ T]) = \forall x_i Pred(T),$$

$$Pred([[at\ T1]\ T2]) = at(Pred(T1), Pred(T2)),$$

$$Pred([top\ T1]) = top(Pred(T1)),$$

constants and variables of atomic types are mapped into the same constants and variables of L'.

By Lemma 1 the normal terms of atomic types of L''' do not contain constants K and S and therefore our definition is sufficient.

Our next step is interpretation of the predicate *holds*. We are going to do it by induction on the length of the terms for situations. This induction is correct since all situation in our universe are ground terms. Consider fixed situation s in the situation domain of our universe. For the primitive fluents, we define the truth value of $holds([[at\ B_i]Table], s)$ and $holds([[at\ B_i][top\ B_j]], s)$ by initial conditions or by the Laws of Change and Inertia.

For this particular situation, consider auxiliary boolean function hld_s defined on the the sentences of L'. For any closed term $T \in L''$ of the type f we define $Pred1(T) = Pred(\overline{FE(T)})$. The restriction of this function on primitive fluents is obviously injection and its range is all ground atoms of L'. We are using this function to define hld_s for the ground atoms as follows:

$$hld_s(Pred(\overline{FE(T)})) = holds(T, s), \tag{19}$$

where T is a primitive fluent. Having defined hld_s for the ground atoms we are now can define hld_s for all sentences by induction on the height of the formulas in a usual way:

$$hld_s(A1 \wedge A2) = hld_s(A1) \wedge hld_s(A2), \tag{20}$$

$$hld_s(A1 \vee A2) = hld_s(A1) \vee hld_s(A2), \tag{21}$$

$$hld_s(\neg A1) = \neg hld_s(A1), \tag{22}$$

$$hld_s(\forall b\ (A)) = \forall_{b=B_0,...,B_N} hld_s(A), \tag{23}$$

$$hld_s(\forall l\ (A)) = \forall_{l=Table,[top\ B_0],...,[top\ B_N]} hld_s(A), \tag{24}$$

$$hld_s(\exists b\ (A)) = \exists_{b=B_0,...,B_N} hld_s(A), \tag{25}$$

$$hld_s(\exists l\ (A)) = \exists_{l=Table,[top\ B_0],...,[top\ B_N]} hld_s(A). \tag{26}$$

We now can use the function $Pred1$ to define $holds(T, s)$ for all closed terms of L'' of the type f as follows:

$$holds(T, s) = hld_s(Pred1(T)), \tag{27}$$

here we used the fact that for each closed term T of the type f in L'' the function $Pred1$ is defined and $Pred1(T)$ by Lemma 2 is a sentence of L'. We now have to prove that axioms B hold in a just built structure.

Axioms (9), (10), (12), (13), (14), (15), (16), (17) and (18) follow from our definition of domain for blocks, definition of *precond* and *cause* and definition of *holds* for primitive fluents. The axiom (11) can be easily proven by induction on the length of the situation terms.

We are going now to prove (1). Let $T1$ and $T2$ be two elements of the domain of the sort f. Consider the term $T0 = apply(apply(and, T1), T2)$. According to our definition of the function apply

$$T0 = \overline{((and\ T1)T2)}$$

and therefore

$$T0 = ((and\ \overline{T1})\overline{T2}).$$

Consider some fixed situation s. By our definition

$$
\begin{aligned}
holds(T0, s) &= hld_s(Pred1(T0))\\
&= hld_s(Pred(\overline{FE(T0)}))\\
&= hld_s(Pred(\overline{FE([[and\ T1]T2])}))\\
&= hld_s(Pred(\overline{[[and\ FE(T1)]FE_n(T2)]}))\\
&= hld_s(Pred([[and\ \overline{FE(T1)}]\overline{FE_n(T2)}]))\\
&= hld_s(Pred(\overline{FE(T1)}) \wedge Pred(\overline{FE_n(T2)}))\\
&= hld_s(Pred(\overline{FE(T1)})) \wedge hld_s(Pred(\overline{FE_n(T2)}))\\
&= hold(T1, s) \wedge hold(T2, s),
\end{aligned}
$$

here n is the number of F_i^x symbols in $T1$. We used here also the following obvious fact: for any term $T \in L''$ the corresponding formula $Pred(FE_n(\overline{T}))$ can be derived from $Pred(FE(\overline{T}))$ by reversible renaming of variables, and therefore for any closed term T by our definition of hld_s

$$hld_s(Pred(FE_n(\overline{T}))) = hld_s(Pred(FE(\overline{T}))).$$

Proofs for axioms (2) and (3) are similar.

We are now going to prove that axiom (8) holds in our structure. Consider arbitrary element of domain for the sort $l \rightarrow h$, i.e. arbitrary term T of the type $l \rightarrow h$. Let $T0 = apply(forall_b, T)$. For the fixed situation s, we have

$$
\begin{aligned}
holds(T0, s) &= hld_s(Pred1(T0))\\
&= hld_s(Pred(\overline{FE(T0)}))\\
&= hld_s(Pred(\overline{FE([forall_b\ T])}))\\
&= hld_s(Pred(\overline{[(\lambda y.[F_1^b[y\ b_1]])FE_2(T)]}))\\
&= hld_s(Pred(\overline{[F_1^b[FE_2(T)\ b_1]]}))\\
&= hld_s(Pred(\overline{[F_1^b FE_2([T\ b_1])]}))\\
&= hld_s(Pred([F_1^b \overline{FE_2([T\ b_1])}]))\\
&= hld_s(\forall b_1(Pred(\overline{FE_2([T\ b_1])})))\\
&= \forall_{b=B_0,\dots,B_N} hld_s(Pred(\overline{FE_2([T\ b])}))\\
&= \forall_{b=B_0,\dots,B_N} hld_s(Pred(\overline{FE([T\ b])}))\\
&= \forall_{b=B_0,\dots,B_N} holds([T\ b])\\
&= \forall_{b=B_0,\dots,B_N} holds(apply(T, b), s)\\
&= \forall b\ holds(apply(T, b), s).
\end{aligned}
$$
(28)

The proof of axiom (8) for locations is similar. The proofs for axioms (6) and (7) follow immediately from Church-Rosser theorem.

It is obvious that the model just constructed is minimal.

6 Acknowledgements

The ideas presented in this paper have evolved over discussions with Vladimir Lifschitz, to whom I am indebted for his time and patience. I would also like to thank John McCarthy and Michael Gelfond for useful discussions related to the subject of this paper.

References

[1] McCarthy, J., "First Order Theories of Individual Concepts and Propositions", in Hayes, J., Michie, D., and Mikulich, L. (eds.), *Machine Intelligence* **9**. Chichester, UK: Ellis Horwood, 1979, pp. 129-147

[2] Lifschitz, V., Formal theories of action, *The Frame Problem, Proc. of the 1987 Workshop* (1987) 35-57.

[3] Perlis, D., Languages with Self-Reference I: Foundations, *Artificial Intelligence* **25** (1985) 301-322.

[4] Kovalski, R., *Logic for Problem Solving*, New York, NY, North Holland, 1979, p. 136.

[5] Hindley, J. and Seldin, J., *Introduction to Combinators and λ-Calculus*, Cambridge, Great Britain, University Press, 1986.

[6] Lifschitz, V. and Rabinov, A., Miracles in Formal Theories of Action *Artificial Intelligence* **38** 225-237.

A Horn Clause Theory of Inheritance and Temporal Reasoning

Stephen G. Pimentel and John L. Cuadrado
Computer and Software Engineering Division
Institute for Defense Analyses
1801 N. Beauregard Street
Alexandria, VA 22311

Abstract

In this paper, we present a logic-based theory for the performance of two types of common-sense reasoning: *inheritance* and *temporal reasoning*. The inheritance part of the theory is modeled on frame-based systems, while the temporal reasoning component is based on the event calculus of [Kowalski and Sergot 86]. The entire theory is axiomatized using Horn clauses augmented with negation as failure. A knowledge representation facility incorporating this work, called the *Temporal Frame System,* has been implemented in Prolog and is being used in the development of a natural language processing system.

Area: Knowledge Representation

1. Introduction

In this paper, we present a logic-based formalization of two types of commonsense reasoning: *inheritance* and *temporal reasoning*. The inheritance part of the theory is a formalization of frame-based systems allowing multiple inheritance with exceptions. Such systems have been studied extensively in AI [Touretzky 86; Etherington 88] and form the backbone of many knowledge representation systems.

The temporal reasoning component is intended to handle the problem of "temporal projection," which can be characterized as follows: given a set of facts describing the state of the world and general rules of causality within a domain, how can one infer the consequences of specific events? In particular, we wish to discover what facts are true over particular intervals of time. The technique we adopt for this problem is based on the event calculus of [Kowalski and Sergot 86].

Both the inheritance and temporal parts of the theory are axiomatized using Horn clauses augmented with negation as failure. Furthermore, the axioms of the theory, viewed as a logic program, have the important property of *stratification* [Przymusinski 88]. A logic program is stratified when it is free of "recursion through negation." Intuitively, this means that negation can be used only with predicates that have already been fully defined (without the use of negation). Stratification is an important property because, within stratified logic programs, negation as failure can be used for general-purpose nonmonotonic reasoning in a well-defined fashion. In addition, negation as failure within this setting has been shown to be equivalent to other major nonmonotonic formalisms, such circumscription, default logic, and autoepistemic logic [Przymusinski 88]. The precise role played by stratification in our approach to temporal reasoning is discussed in [Pimentel and Cuadrado 89].

The work presented in this paper has been incorporated into a knowledge representation facility called the *Temporal Frame System* (TFS), which has been implemented in Quintus Prolog. TFS allows a knowledge engineer to describe a domain by entering a frame hierarchy into the system using a high-level frame language, which is compiled into Prolog. At present, we have assembled a large knowledge base categorizing everyday concepts, such as vehicles, buildings, common physical objects, spatial concepts, human characteristics, mental states, etc. We have also constructed a detailed categorization of the various classes of events important in our domain. Classes of events are represented using case frames similar to those of [Charniak 81].

TFS is currently being used as the knowledge representation component of a natural language processing system. The input to the system consists of English descriptions of events in which temporal ordering plays an important role. Both the parsing and the semantic analysis of the system are performed using the Definite Clause Translation Grammar formalism of [Abramson 84]. The semantic translation rules are very similar to those of a case grammar [Bruce 75], and their output consists of instances of case frames. In the final stage of processing, temporal reasoning is performed over these instances of case frames, and the results are displayed in a graphical interface implemented in X-windows. The implementation of TFS now stands at about 5000 lines of code, including the frames comprising the knowledge base. Nevertheless, the core axioms dealing with inheritance and temporal reasoning are remarkably simple. In the remainder of the paper, we will ignore issues concerning natural language processing as well as the details of our specific knowledge base and focus on the inheritance and temporal reasoning axioms.

2. Inheritance System

One of the chief forms of commonsense reasoning is the ability to reason with general information which is subject to exceptions in more specific cases. This type of reasoning can be nicely captured by *inheritance systems*, in which a class of objects inherits properties from its subsuming classes, unless the properties are overridden by explicitly recorded exceptions. It is the possible presence of exceptions which makes inheritance reasoning nonmonotonic. An inheritance system is said to allow *multiple* inheritance if a class can have more than one superclass; otherwise, it allows only *single* inheritance. It has been the goal of much recent work in this area to formalize multiple inheritance with exceptions. Our particular interest is focused on *class/property* inheritance systems, in the terminology of [Touretzky 86], of which frame-based systems are representative. In such systems, the set of concepts is partitioned into classes and properties, and the subsumption relations among the former are held to be strict (exception-free). Exceptions are allowed only in the association of properties with classes.

Logic-based formalizations of inheritance systems have tended to divide into two types, depending on the manner in which classes and properties are represented. The most obvious representation follows the natural ontology of first-order logic by assigning a predicate to each class and each property. For example, we might have

    four_wheels(X) ← auto(X).
    auto(X) ← jeep(X).
    jeep(jeep23).

and so on. This style of encoding inheritance systems in first-order logic originated with [Hayes 79], although that work handled only exception-free systems. [McCarthy 86, section 12] shows how this representation can be extended to handle properties with exceptions using prioritized circumscription. [Etherington 88] describes a similar extension, only using default logic instead of circumscription. Finally, [Gelfond and Lifschitz 88] give a method for compiling McCarthy's prioritized circumscription encoding into Horn clauses with negation as failure; unfortunately, their technique works only for single inheritance.

The second logic-based representation of inheritance systems reifies classes and properties by assigning them variables and constants. For example, we might have

    no_of_wheels(auto,4).
    specializes(jeep,auto).
    instantiates(jeep23,jeep).

and so forth. Note that the binary predicate 'no_of_wheels' serves in effect as a *slot* of the class 'auto'. [McCarthy 86, section 8] sketches a method for encoding multiple inheritance with exceptions in this representation using formula circumscription. [Brewka 87] fleshes out McCarthy's method to show how a full-fledged frame system can be handled. Among other things, Brewka's system involves reifying slots as well as classes and properties, so that instead of no_of_wheels(auto,4), we would have something like has_slot(auto,no_of_wheels,4).

Below, we develop a frame system which is rather close to Brewka's, except that we use Horn clauses with negation as failure instead of circumscription. As in most frame systems, we distinguish between *frames*, which denote classes of individuals, and *instances* of frames, which denote single individuals. A frame is permitted to inherit from any number of other frames. Instances, on the other hand, are restricted to inherit from a single frame. (This restriction is not important, since the parent frame of an instance can itself participate in multiple inheritance.)

The basic predicates required by the system are as follows. We use instantiates(I,F) to indicate that I is an instance of the frame F, while specializes(F1,F2) indicates that the frame F1 represents a subclass of the frame F2. The predicate has_slot(F,S,V) indicates that each instance of the frame F has value V for slot S unless the instance is *exceptional*. (Our notion of exceptionality is precisely defined below.) Finally, holds(I,S,V) indicates that the instance I has value V for slot S. The value of a slot for an instance may either be explicitly recorded for that instance or inherited from above.

The following four axioms govern the behavior of the frame system. First, we define the relation 'ako' as the transitive closure of 'specializes':

```
ako(F1,F2) ←
    specializes(F1,F2).
ako(F1,F3) ←
    specializes(F1,F2),
    ako(F1,F3).
```

Second, we define the relation 'isa' as the extension of 'instantiates' to superclasses:

```
isa(I,F) ←
    instantiates(I,F).
isa(I,F2) ←
    instantiates(I,F1),
    ako(F1,F2).
```

Third, we stipulate that slot values are inherited from frames to their instances, unless the instance is exceptional:

```
holds(I,S,V) ←
    isa(I,F),
    has_slot(F,S,V),
    ¬ exceptional(I,S,F).
```

The negation of 'exceptional' in the above axiom is the crucial place at which negation as failure comes into play. Fourth, we specify that an instance is exceptional with respect to a slot of some frame if there is a *more specific* frame from which it could inherit a different value for that slot.

```
exceptional(I,S,F2) ←
    isa(I,F1),
    has_slot(F1,S,V1),
    has_slot(F2,S,V2),
    ¬ V1 = V2,
    ako(F1,F2).
```

Given these axioms, it is straightforward to record any set of frames and instances. A frame 'frame1' is encoded simply by asserting any number of clauses of the form specializes(frame1,F) and has_slot(frame1,S,V). (Recall that a frame may have any number of superclasses.) The representation of an instance is only slightly more complex. Each instance 'instance1' will have exactly one clause of the form instantiates(instance1,F). For each value 'value1' of a slot 'slot1', we will assert

```
holds(instance1,slot1,value1).

exceptional(instance1,slot1,F) ←
    has_slot(F,slot1,V),
    ¬ V = value1,
    isa(instance1,F).
```

The latter clause insures that values different from 'value1' will not be inherited by the instance.

The frame system as defined correctly implements the intuition that slot values from more specific frames should override values from less specific frames. However, one should note that in cases where two or more frames are of *incomparable specificity,* it is possible for an instance to inherit *multiple* values for a slot. (The alternate strategy of returning *no* values in these cases does not have as elegant a Horn clause implementation.)

Although we have only defined "default" values for frames (i.e. values which can be over-ridden by exceptions), most frame systems also allow the use of "necessary" values which hold for all instances of a frame without exception. It is straightforward to add this feature to our theory. (Essentially, we must extend 'has_slot' with an additional *facet* argument and write an additional axiom for 'holds' governing inheritance of necessary values.) Our implementation of TFS includes this feature, although we have no need to discuss it in this paper.

3. Temporal Reasoning

The second form of commonsense reasoning which has been incorporated into our system is *temporal reasoning*. We have adopted the event calculus of [Kowalski and Sergot 86] for this purpose, modifying it for integration with the inheritance system of the previous section. The event calculus is a formalism for reasoning about time and change which takes the *event* as its basic object. Since it is axiomatized using Horn clauses with negation as failure, it is well-suited to our purpose.

An event is a distinguished point in time at which one or more facts concerning the domain changes in truth value. In the event calculus, events are reified and then described using "semantic cases," as in a case grammar [Bruce 75]. For example, the sentence "Frank Burns enters the restaurant and gives his coat to the doorman," would generate two events, represented by

```
instantiates(e1,enter).
holds(e1,agent,burns1).
holds(e1,destination,restaurant1).
```

```
instantiates(e2,give).
holds(e2,agent,burns1).
holds(e2,patient,coat1).
holds(e2,recipient,doorman1).
```

(We have omitted the 'exceptional' clauses for brevity.) Each of the above sets of clauses for 'e1' and 'e2' constitute an instance of a *case frame* [Charniak 81]. The case frames themselves are associated with event classes, such as 'enter', 'give', etc., and are arranged in an inheritance hierarchy.

What domain facts can be inferred from, say, the clauses for 'e2'? Prior to the event 'e2', Burns is in possession of the coat, while afterwards, it is in the doorman's possession. As of yet, we have no way of representing temporally scoped facts of this sort. We have seen that the predicate holds(I,S,V) is used to indicate timeless and unchanging facts; a similar four-place predicate will give us the desired representation for facts which are temporally scoped.

Specifically, we will use holds(I,S,V,after(E)) to indicate that the instance I has value V for slot S *for a period of time beginning with event E.* Likewise, holds(I,S,V,before(E)) will indicate that the instance I has value V for slot S for a period of time *ending* with event E. Therefore, in the previous example we would infer something like

```
holds(burns1,possess,coat1,before(e2)).
holds(doorman1,possess,coat1,after(e2)).
```

In our system, temporally scoped facts of this sort are derived from instances of case frames using domain-dependent rules, such as

```
holds(A,possess,P,before(E)) ←
    holds(E,agent,A),
    holds(E,patient,P).
holds(R,possess,P,after(E)) ←
    holds(E,recipient,R),
    holds(E,patient,P).
```

As a result, there is no need for additional inheritance axioms governing the four-place version of 'holds'.

Note that a temporally scoped fact makes explicit reference to only a single event, giving us only a single end-point of its temporal extent. What we would really like to know, if possible, is the entire extent of time over which the fact persists. This extent can be determined by the axioms of the event calculus. We assume that we are given at least a partial order over events, represented by the predicate precedes(E1,E2). Then, the persistence of a fact between two events is expressed by

```
persists(I,S,V,E1,E2) ←
    holds(I,S,V,after(E1)),
    holds(I,S,V,before(E2)),
    precedes(E1,E2),
    ¬ broken(I,S,V,E1,E2).
```

Negation as failure plays a critical role in the definition of persistence: we can have persists(I,S,V,E1,E2) only if ¬broken(I,S,V,E1,E2). This makes the predicate 'persists' nonmonotonic. The predicate 'broken' is true when a fact is known not to hold continuously between two events. It is defined by

```
broken(I,S,V1,E1,E2) ←
    holds(I,S,V2,after(E)),
    related(V1,V2),
```

```
        precedes(E1,E),
        precedes(E,E2).
broken(I,S,V1,E1,E2) ←
        holds(I,S,V2,before(E)),
        related(V1,V2),
        precedes(E1,E), .
        precedes(E,E2).
```

Two values (for a given slot in a given instance) are 'related' if they are either identical or incompatible.

```
related(V,V).
related(V1,V2) ←
        incompatible(V1,V2).
```

The predicate 'incompatible' is domain-dependent and indicates that a slot cannot take on the two given values simultaneously. Finally, to test the truth value of a fact at the time of an arbitrary event, we can use the predicate 'holds_at', defined by

```
holds_at(I,S,V,E) ←
        persists(I,S,V,E1,E2),
        precedes(E1,E),
        precedes(E,E2).
```

The above axioms yield a simple and effective means of querying the frame system for temporally scoped facts. However, in the application for which we are using TFS, we do not simply want to test whether some fact holds at a given time, but rather to construct a complete *history* of certain slots in our frame instances. Consider, for example, a slot 'location' in an instance 'person1'. We would want to compute all possible solutions of

$$persists(person1,location,L,E1,E2).$$

Such a set of solutions represents the "history" of the location of 'person1'. In our application, histories are computed and recorded for each slot value and then displayed on a graphical user-interface.

For such an application, the normal Prolog computation strategy has a major flaw. The use of negation as failure presupposes that we will evaluate the 'persists' predicate by backward chaining each time we wish to examine its solution. However, if *records* of these solutions have been made, negation as failure gives us no mechanism for retracting invalidated records when the slot values of frame instances change.

This difficulty is remedied in our system by the use of a *truth maintenance system* (TMS) [Doyle 79]. After a solution has been found for an event calculus predicate, it is cached in the TMS with a justification. When some event is added or deleted from the frame system, the truth maintenance algorithm automatically withdraws solutions to

$$persists(I,S,V,E1,E2)$$

which are no longer valid. Hence, while negation as failure is used for computing periods, the TMS handles the retraction of already-computed periods after alteration of frame instances. The use of truth maintenance with the event calculus is discussed in detail in [Pimentel and Cuadrado 89].

4. Conclusions and Further Research

In this paper, we have shown how two important forms of commonsense reasoning (inheritance and temporal reasoning) can be integrated into a single theory via a Horn clause axiomatization. While this result is quite useful, there are still many areas of commonsense reasoning that have not been addressed. One central area is that of *reasoning about knowledge.* Such a capability is crucial in order for our system to model the behavior of inteligent agents within its domain.

A promising approach to reasoning about knowledge is the technique adopted in [Moore 80]. Moore takes the possible-world semantics of a modal logic of knowledge and directly axiomatizes those semantics in first-order logic. This allows one to efficiently reason about knowledge using purely first-order proof techniques. Furthermore, Moore's axioms can be represented as Horn clauses, making it straightforward to integrate his technique into our system. [Appelt 85] has applied Moore's representation to planning in the context of natural language generation.

References

Abramson, H., "Definite Clause Translation Grammars," *Proceedings of the IEEE Logic Programing Symposium,* 1984.

Appelt, D., *Planning English Sentences,* Cambridge University Press, 1985.

Brewka, G., "The Logic of Inheritance in Frame Systems," *Proceedings IJCAI-87,* 1987.

Bruce, B., "Case Systems for Natural Language," *Artificial Intelligence* 6, 1975.

Charniak, E., "The Case-Slot Identity Theory," *Cognitive Science* 5, 1981.

Doyle, J., "A Truth Maintenance System," *Artificial Intelligence,* 12, 1979.

Etherington, D., *Reasoning with Incomplete Information,* Chapter 4, Morgan Kaufmann, 1988.

Gelfond, M., and Lifschitz, V., "Compiling Circumscriptive Theories into Logic Programs: Preliminary Report," *Proceedings AAAI-88,* 1988.

Hayes, P., "The Logic of Frames," *Frame Conceptions and Text Understanding,* D. Metzing (ed.), Walter de Gruyter and Co., 1979.

Kowalski, R., and M. Sergot, "A Logic Based Calculus of Events," *New Generation Computing,* 4, 1986.

McCarthy, J., "Applications of Circumscription to Formalizing Common-Sense Knowledge," *Artificial Intelligence,* 28, 1986.

Moore, R., *Reasoning About Knowledge and Action,* Technical Report No. 191, SRI International Artificial Intelligence Center, 1980.

Pimentel, S., and J. Cuadrado, "The Event Calculus and Consistency Maintenance," to appear, 1989.

Przymusinski, T., "On the Relationship Between Logic Programming and Non-monotonic Reasoning," *Proceedings AAAI-88,* 1988.

Touretzky, D., *The Mathematics of Inheritance Systems,* section 2.19, Morgan Kaufmann, 1986.

EXPLICIT CONTEXT-BASED BLACKBOARDS
ENHANCING BLACKBOARD SYSTEMS PERFORMANCE

Cheng-Seen Ho
Department of Electronic Engineering
National Taiwan Institute of Technology
43 Keelung Road, Section 4
Taipei, Taiwan 10772

Abstract

Inference engine in blackboard systems is better viewed as a process of matching potential knowledge sources with promising solution areas. To manifest this feature, a context-based blackboard is proposed as an explicit component to summarize, in terms of contexts, meta-level information about ordinary blackboards. It is so organized that a list of promising solution areas, a list of potential knowledge sources, and their best match can be proposed effectively and efficiently. The concept of context is properly elaborated and comprehensively used in the design of the blackboard. This approach improves the system performance by providing a balanced status feedback between potential knowledge sources and promising solution areas for system control and replanning. It also enhances the system performance by supporting viewpoint reasoning to allow reasoning on a single solution space from different aspects and various meta-level applications, e.g., viewpoint explanation, knowledge acquisition, etc.

I. Introduction

Traditional blackboard systems contain only one domain blackboard. Control information is stored in a separate, global database, while scheduling criteria are incorporated in a sophisticated scheduler [4,7,10,11]. The scheduler is responsible for selecting a knowledge source (KS) for execution at each cycle. It is more or less a conventional viewpoint of solution space search. It blurs an important difference between blackboard systems and other paradigms of problem solving, i.e., opportunistic scheduling. This unique feature can be described as follows. The inference engine is working both on the search of prominently promising solution areas and on potentially invocable KSs. A matched pair between KSs and solution areas is then selected for further processing. The match promises the selection has the best opportunity to achieve a better solution. Based on this match viewpoint the solution space should be able to suggest something so that we can identify those areas, which if explored will lead to a better solution.

To endow solution space this capability, a separate blackboard, called context-based blackboard (CNTXTBBD), is proposed. It is organized as an explicit common data pool so that *system status* can be effectively and efficiently summarized and presented for the inference engine. By system status we mean information for various control requirements, e.g., scheduling, execution monitoring, performance fine tuning, or subsequent replanning. The concept of context is so elaborated and employed in the design of the blackboard that it may reflect system status in suitable contexts and propose both promising solution areas and invocable KSs. Since the blackboard is treated as a separate, meta-level blackboard we can employ the same blackboard techniques to fulfill this requirement.

The idea of employing CNTXTBBDs is not only helpful in capturing the essential feature of the inference engine in blackboard systems, but also helpful in examining and refining many previously developed ideas in blackboard systems. For instance, problems caused by the "rigid" structure of hypothesis network, i.e., inflexibility of combining hypotheses into a network and incapability of reflecting the significance of supporting hypothesis networks to a supported node [10], can be solved. Moreover, this separate blackboard allows us to develop new concepts and applications to enhance the system performance.

The idea is more useful if applied in generalized blackboard systems, e.g., Hearsay-III [5], and BB1 [6]. The distinction of the BB1 architecture is the flexibility and adaptability in system control, since criteria can be explicitly put on the control blackboard for flexible scheduling, and planning decisions on the control blackboard can be modified for adaptive planning. Several issues, however, are not well addressed. One is that criteria are guidelines for planning and scheduling, information to apply these guidelines on has to be gathered from the domain blackboard, which in general is not well organized for quick status reference. Difference between ratings of plan decisions and domain hypotheses is not properly identified. Their use in selecting *mixed* KS activation records for scheduling does not make strong sense. Finally, local competition is not explored in control blackboard. These issues can be solved without sacrificing the flexibility and adaptability for system control if the architecture is enhanced with explicit CNTXTBBDs.

Next section will discuss a traditional blackboard architecture with a CNTXTBBD incorporated. Section III then details the design of CNTXTBBDs. Section IV will discuss how to incorporate CNTXTBBDs into generalized blackboard systems and summarize the benifit of this configuration. Issues related to the implementation and application of the system can be referenced from [8].

II. An Architecture For Traditional Blackboard Systems with Context-Based Blackboards

Fig. 1 (next page) gives an overall architecture of a traditional blackboard system with a CNTXTBBD. Basically, it includes two blackboards and two types of KSs. *Domain blackboard* contains the actual (partial or complete) loci of domain activities representing the function subsystem of the problem solving. *CNTXTBBD* summarizes the information on domain blackboard and provides various aspects of meta-level information for control and other applications. KSs which are associated with specific blackboards are called *blackboard KSs*. They monitor the state of the predefined blackboard, execute whenever the monitoring conditions become true, and produce on the same blackboard whatever results are appropriate. *System KSs* are KSs which integratively propose a best matched pair of KS and solution area for processing. They are executed in a simple control loop and serve as the inference engine of the blackboard system.

Domain blackboard may contain as many levels as appropriate for the target domain. Each level may have his own data structure so that domain *islands* (hypotheses) on the level can be represented in a way most suitable for the domain. KSs associated with each level represent different categories of object level knowledge for the problem.

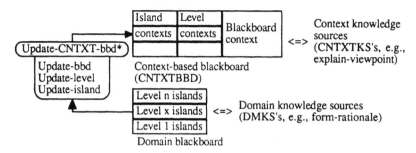

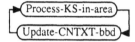

Fig. 1 An architecture for traditional blackboard systems with a context-based blackboard

CNTXTBBD contains three regions: island contexts, level contexts, and blackboard contexts to store *contexts* for domain islands, levels, and blackboards, respectively. *Contexts may be thought as meta-level manifestation of domain objects* (islands, levels, or blackboards). They contain all meta-level information about the corresponding objects and inter-relationships among them. KSs associated with the blackboard may work for viewpoint explanation or help the domain knowledge acquisition process.

The ultimate goal of the inference engine is the decision of a matched pair between KSs and solution areas at each specific time. System KS "update-CNTXT-bbd" contains a group of system KSs, which monitor changes on domain blackboard and reflect these changes on CNTXTBBD by making and propagating changed meta-information about domain objects, including inter-relationships among updated objects. A list of workable pairs of KSs (in terms of "surrogates") and solution areas (in terms of islands) will finally appear in the "blackboard context" on the CNTXTBBD. At this point, the inference engine may apply current control constraints and select the best matched pair for processing by "process-KS-in-area." Note that the processing modifies the domain blackboard and recycles the loop.

III. Detailed Design of Context-Based Blackboards

One effective way to reflect the domain blackboard for the use of control is to represent it in multiple, different perspectives on CNTXTBBD so that the inference engine may take advantage of different aspects of the same domain status. Context mechanisms, long time used in AI circles as hypothetical reasoning and partitioning mechanisms [1,3], can be elaborated for this representation.

In general, contexts can be used as a partitioning tool to partition the domain blackboard and represent partitioned solution spaces in the CNTXTBBD. If the partitioning is based on the islands on the domain blackboard, we may define an island on each level of the blackboard as an *island context* and associate with it relevant information about the island, e.g., island justification, annotation, competition weight, etc. A bucket-based merge mechanism can be applied to merge these island contexts within an entire level into a *level context*, which allows us to focus on areas needing to work. Finally, a *blackboard context* representing the whole blackboard can be thought as a merged context of all level contexts in the blackboard. Since level and blackboard contexts store much more abstract information, part of re-computing process in the scheduling mechanism of [7] can be sped up.

If instead, the partition is based on the inference relationship among islands, we can represent the networks of nodes (islands) which are related to an island during the inference process as its contexts. We will call subnetworks which support the reasoning of a higher level node its *precontexts*. The supernetwork which is supported by a lower level node will be termed its *postcontext*. Since KSs may take proper forms of precontexts for an island, *precontexts represent different viewpoints of different KSs on the same island*. Thus, we can measure and evaluate the significance of an island in different aspects (viewpoints) and provide cooperative reasoning among multiple (possibly conflicting) viewpoints. Postcontexts of two islands will intersect at a higher level island if they are inside the precontexts of the latter island. They hence provide a way for the recognition and evaluation of potential competition or cooperation between two KSs working on different islands inside precontexts (probably different) of the same higher level island. Since precontexts provide a way to dynamically select proper nodes from a supporting network as a viewpoint and postcontexts allow the recognition of two interacting precontexts, problems with rigid network structure of blackboard hypotheses no longer exist.

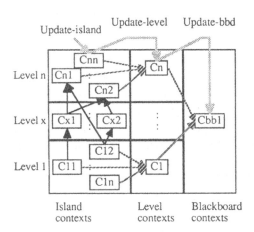

Fig. 2 The context-based blackboard

Fig. 2 shows the configuration of the CNTXTBBD, which integrates these two elaborations of the context concept. Regions of island contexts and level contexts contain as many levels as domain blackboards, while blackboard contexts contain only one level. Since we are talking about traditional blackboard systems, criteria for rating the weights of domain objects in following explanation are treated as being hardwired inside KSs. They, however, can be put on proper blackboards in generalized blackboard systems to get flexible control (see Section IV and [9] for detail).

A. Island contexts - Each island on the domain blackboard has a corresponding island context on CNTXTBBD. For instance, island context C11 on level 1 may contain context information for island H11 on the same level of the domain blackboard. A frame-based data structure for island contexts (for implementation see [8]) is shown in Fig. 3.

```
NAME: identity of the island context
MERGER: level context which the island context is part of
ISLAND-ID: identity of corresponding island
RATIONALE: reasons of creating the island
ANNOTATION: description of the island
LOCATION: location of the island
BIRTH:
        CREATOR: KS which creates the island
        CREATED-TIME: time the island is created
STATISTICS:
        ESTIMATED-WEIGHT: estimated weight before the island is created
        ISLAND-WEIGHT: weight of the island after its birth
        ISLAND-WEIGHT-VARIANCE: distribution of weight deviation inside the island
        TYPE-OF-CREATION: {planning, expectation-driven, event-driven}
        TYPE-OF-USAGE: {planning, expectation-driven, event-driven}
        STATUS: {dead, alive, verifying, etc.}
        CORRECTNESS OF ESTIMATION: a ratio of ESTIMATED-WEIGHT to modified
            ISLAND-WEIGHT
PRECONTEXTS: subnetworks supporting the island
        PRECONTEXT-1: relevant subnet interested by following viewers
            VIEWERS: KSs that take this viewpoint
            VIEWPOINT-STATUS: {dead, alive, verifying, etc.}
            VIEWPOINT-WEIGHT: computed weight of the subnet
            RATIONALE: reasons of taking this viewpoint
            ANNOTATION: description of the viewpoint
        PRECONTEXT-2: ...
POSTCONTEXT: super-network supported by the island
```

Fig. 3 The data structure of island contexts

Slot LOCATION specifies where the corresponding island is located. Its format depends on the structure of the domain blackboard. It is one of the several island retrieval mechanisms used in the system (ref. [8] for more). ESTIMATED-WEIGHT in slot STATISTICS is the weight estimation of the island before it is actually produced. Its value may be computed from various knowledge, e.g., the LOCATION of the to-be-produced island, its relationships with neighboring islands, etc. (See subsection "B. Level contexts" for detail.) This estimation serves as a credibility measure of the island compared with many other to-be-produced islands.

ISLAND-WEIGHT, on the contrary, is the actual weight determined by the system after it is produced. Its value may be exclusively decided by the CREATOR. Or, it may be modified by surrounding islands or supporting islands. The effect from surrounding islands is reflected in ISLAND-WEIGHT-VARIANCE of the *next higher level island* supported by the island. In other words, the ISLAND-WEIGHT-VARIANCE of an island describes the similarity of the next lower level islands which construct the island. Thus, with the same ISLAND-WEIGHT, a small value of ISLAND-WEIGHT-VARIANCE seems to suggest that this island be constructed from lower level islands of the same "feathers." The effect from supporting islands is reflected in the VIEWPOINT-WEIGHT of a specific PRECONTEXT, to be explained in slot VIEWPOINT-WEIGHT.

TYPE-OF-CREATION specifies how an island is created and TYPE-OF-USAGE pecifies how it can be used in reasoning. These slots allow us to intermingle different types of inference processes in the same framework. Thus, an island may be created from and used by data-driven, plan-oriented (goal-directed), or model-based (expectation-driven) process.

STATUS of an island context indicates the processing state of the island, i.e., how much work has been done and how much left to be done. Its values are strongly dependent upon domains. In general, it may take on at least one of two values: dead or alive. An island context will be marked temporarily dead if the corresponding island contradicts with current active constraints or is not promising enough to continue work. The concept can be elaborated further. Imagine that the contexts on CNTXTBBD are windows and the STATUS of each context works as a switch to control the transparence of the context. If the STATUS is marked dead, the context is closed, that is, the window is painted dark and the corresponding island is invisible. Its effect is that the corresponding island is "removed" from the domain blackboard. The overall result is that we can only see those portions of domain blackboard that are visible through lightened (not dead) contexts defined on CNTXTBBD. We will use the term "shadow blackboard" to denote visible portions of the blackboard.Thus, contexts with STATUS turn the CNTXTBBD into a mask. Lightened windows on the mask create a shadow blackboard out of the domain blackboard. (To get more detailed distinction between states, a shadow blackboard can be *colored* to denote islands contained are of a specific state.)

As noted before, we allow KSs to work on different aspects of subnetworks which support the same island. They indicate their viewpoints (aspects) by creating different precontexts for the island. This concept complicates the concept of shadow blackboards by introducing different masks on the same CNTXTBBD via different viewpoints and projecting different shadow blackboards out of the same domain blackboard. Shadow blackboards thus represent different interpretations (or viewpoints) of a single blackboard via precontexts. If we define "viewpoints reasoning" as the capability of reasoning on the same solution space from different aspects, shadow blackboards represent different solution spaces under different viewpoints. The importance of the concept of shadow blackboards is that it allows us to fast recognize an isolated solution space under a specific viewpoint. It also allows us to evaluate the compound influence of different viewpoints by overlapping relevant shadow blackboards together, a key activity in viewpoint reasoning.

VIEWPOINT-STATUS of a specific precontext, indicates the processing states of the specific network, e.g., how much work has to be done from the network. It can be marked dead by the VIEWERS and works as a global switch to control the transparence of the whole precontext, which in turns controls the interaction of shadow blackboards and facilitates various viewpoints reasoning. VIEWPOINT-WEIGHT of a specific precontext denotes the supporting weight of the subnetwork. Its value is computed from the ISLAND-WEIGHTs of islands inside the precontext. Currently, a bayesian inference-like propagation rule is being investigated for the computation and propagation of ISLAND-WEIGHTs inside the network. This value is used to modify the local measure ISLAND-WEIGHT of the supported island to reflect "global" significance of the island, in the sense of its relation to previously processing history, from the viewpoint. Thus, each viewpoint may has his own weight value for the island by modifying the value ISLAND-WEIGHT. While more than one viewpoint is working toward the same island, VIEWPOINT-WEIGHT and VIEWPOINT-STATUS serve as important measures for competition or cooperation.

Each island eatails a default precontext. It includes all lower levels of islands which support the island. (Thus, all other precontexts are selective subsets of this precontext.) The VIEWPOINT-WEIGHT of this precontext (coupled with ISLAND-WEIGHT-VARIANCE) will translate the ISLAND-WEIGHT into a modified island-weight. With this modified island-weight, we may talk about correctness of estimation by dividing ESTIMATED-WEIGHT by modified island-weight. This ratio, put in CORRECTNESS-OF-ESTIMATION, may serve as a successful measure of estimation. It works as a learning index for us to ree-valuate the knowledge used in estimation and improve subsequent estimation.

Precontexts and postcontexts are depicted in Fig. 2 by solid arrows. Suppose that KSs, say, KS1 and KS2, are only interested in the inference relationship between level 1 and level n, i.e., it does not need to look at the detailed, intermediate inference levels. Then, Cn1 may contain a precontext ((Cn1 C11 C12)) for (KS1 KS2) to denote that Cn1 is "inferred" from C11 and C12. Some other KSs may be interested in the relationship between Cx1 on level x and Cn1 on level n instead, then Cn1 will contain another precon-text ((Cn1 Cx1)). The default precontext for Cn1 is ((Cn1 Cx1 C12) (Cx1 C11)).

The postcontext of C12 is represented as a list of higher level nodes, e.g., (Cn1 Cx2 Cn2). Since the only purpose of postcontexts is to quickly determine whether or not two islands are supporting the same higher level island, mark-and-test mechanism is employed to perform the interaction of two postcontexts. From the intersected island, if any, we may evaluate the influence of this two islands on the higher level one and notice and resolve any competition or cooperation. Dotted arrows in Fig. 2 denote the MERGER rela-tionship among contexts to be described below.

B. Level contexts - Each level of the domain blackboard is represented as a level context. For instance, level context C1 merges island contexts on level 1, i.e., C11, C12, and C13. Fig. 4 shows the data structure of a level context.

    NAME: identity of the level context
    LEVEL-ID: identity of corresponding level
    ANNOTATION: description of the level
    MERGER: blackboard context which the level context is part of
    BUCKETS-LIST: a list of buckets according to the level structure
    TRIGGERED-KSS-LIST: a list of triggered KS surrogates
    INVOCABLE-KSS-LIST: a rated list of invocable KS surrogates
    PROMISING-AREA-LIST: a rated list of promising solution areas
    STATISTICS:
        DEGREE-OF-COMPLETION: percentage of nonempty buckets
        LEVEL-WEIGHT-MEAN: average weight of the whole level
        LEVEL-WEIGHT-VARIANCE: deviation of weight on the level
    BUCKET1:
        ISLAND-CONTEXTS-LIST: island contexts in this bucket
        BUCKET-BEST: the best status of the bucket
        AGE-OF-BUCKET-BEST: for how long the best has elapsed
        BUCKET-WEIGHT-MEAN: average weight of the bucket
        BUCKET-WEIGHT-VARIANCE: deviation of weight of the bucket
    BUCKET2: ...

Fig. 4 The data structure of level contexts

The concept of *buckets* is employed as a merging mechanism. For simplicity, we only consider levels with two dimensions as in Hearsay-II. (For levels with complicated structure as in [2], extensions along new dimensions are straightforward.) All lightened island contexts describing islands of the same location are merged into a bucket. Buckets are then concatenated according to the level structure of the domain blackboard. If a gap exists between two near-adjacent buckets, a gap bucket containing an empty island context is created for the gap. If islands are not located exactly at the same area, e.g., one may totally subsume another, or they may partially overlap, a bucket is created whose size covers all of the overlapped islands. For those islands whose size is smaller than the bucket, they are elongated along shorter dimensions with empty island contexts inserted.

Against those existing island contexts inside the list of buckets in each level, KSs whose "triggering patterns" are satisfied will be identified and noted in terms of surrogates in TRIGGERED-KSS-LIST. A triggered KS surrogate will be rated and put into the INVOCABLE-KSS-LIST if its "triggering context" is also satisfied. (See subsection "D. Knowledge sources" for the description of triggering patterns, triggering contexts, and surrogates.) Criteria for the weight rating of KS surrogates may consider characteristics of triggering islands and triggered KSs, e.g., the weight of triggering islands, the credit of KSs, etc. Each bucket hence works as a local competition arena since islands inside the same bucket compete for the determination of the invocation of better KSs. A threshold can be set so that more than one KS surrogate may be selected from the same triggering islands. The final determination of selecting which KS depends on how well its action matches the potential solution areas. Note that the processing of these lists can be done in parallel, since it is localized in each level.

Now, we have to derive the PROMISING-AREA-LIST from the same list of buckets. Several attributes are important in identifying and rating potential areas. BUCKET-WEIGHT-MEAN and BUCKET-WEIGHT-VARIANCE define the static behavior of a bucket. They will be used in the computation of LEVEL-WEIGHT-MEAN and LEVEL-WEIGHT-VARIANCE as the statistics of the whole level. BUCKET-BEST is defined as a characteristic value of a bucket. It can be computed simply by taking on the weight of the highest-rated island inside the bucket. A more general way may consider the STATUS, ISLAND-WEIGHT with modification from ISLAND-WEIGHT-VARIANCE and/or VIEWPOINT-WEIGHT from a specific viewpoint of the highest-rated island, etc. For gap buckets, it is set to zero so that any areas inside the bucket deserving exploration can be singled out as soon as possible by the following method.

Potential areas should lie inside the buckets which if explored lead to a better partial solution. First step is to locally evaluate each island context: all island contexts (empty or not) inside a same bucket are estimated and compared to see how much they may improve the characteristic value of the bucket. Factors affecting the estimation are characteristics of each island context (area) and the bucket. For instance, the location of the area, island STATUS, ISLAND-WEIGHT-VARIANCE, and BUCKET-BEST. A heuristic threshold can be set to select all areas with high potential. Now comes the global evaluation: all selected areas from all buckets will be compared according to their relative degrees of improvement over their specific buckets. Factors to consider during this step include relative attribute values of buckets, such as BUCKET-BEST, LEVEL-WEIGHT-MEAN, BUCKET-WEIGHT-MEAN, BUCKET-WEIGHT-VARIANCE, AGE-OF-BUCKET-BEST, which may serve as an indication of whether or not it is worth exploring the same bucket any more, and so on. Example uses of these parameters would be if one of the location weights of two islands improves its BUCKET-BEST much more than the other, then it is rated higher. If all other conditions of two buckets are evaluated equal, areas with the one of higher BUCKET-WEIGHT-VARIANCE may suggest higher weight. The estimated value will be used as the importance measure of each area and put inside the island context as its ESTIMATED-WEIGHT. A heuristic threshold can be set to select all islands with higher ESTIMATED-WEIGHT and rate them into a weight descending PROMIS-ING-AREA-LIST.

Level statistics also contain DEGREE-OF-COMPLETION, which measures the percentage of non-empty buckets on the level, i.e., buckets having been processed so far. Level statistics makes it viable and meaningful for the comparison among all levels to choose the best level and the best island to work on in blackboard context described below.

C. Blackboard contexts - The whole domain blackboard is represented as a blackboard context on the CNTXTBBD. For instance, domain blackboard, say BB1, is summarized in the blackboard context Cbb1. Fig. 5 gives the data structure of a blackboard context.

NAME: identity of the blackboard context
BBD-ID: identity of corresponding blackboard
ANNOTATION: description of the blackboard
SORTED-LEVEL-CONTEXTS-LIST: a descending list of level contexts according to LEVEL-
      WEIGHT, LEVEL-WEIGHT-DEVIATION, and DEGREE-OF-COMPLETION
WORKABLE-KSS-AREA-LIST: a list of paired KS surrogates and workable solution areas
UNMATCHED-KSS-LIST: a list of KS surrogates which are not matched
UNMATCHED-AREA-LIST: a list of solution areas which are not matched
FOCUS: focus of attention of the blackboard system
      LEVEL: level id to be processed
      ISLAND: island id to be processed
      KS: knowledge source id to be executed
STATISTICS:
      BBD-WEIGHT-MEAN: averaged weight over LEVEL-WEIGHTs of all the level contexts
      BBD-WEIGHT-VARIANCE: deviation of weight of the blackboard
SHADOW1: shadow blackboard
      ANNOTATION: description of this shadow
      RATIONALE: reasons of creating this shadow
      PRODUCERS: KSs responsible for creating the shadow
      ENLIGHTENED-CONTEXTS-LIST: list of contexts producing this shadow
      STATUS: {dead, alive, current}
SHADOW-2: ...

Fig. 5 The data structure of blackboard contexts

A blackboard context contains two important attributes for focus control: WORKABLE-KSS-AREA-LIST and FOCUS. WORKABLE-KSS-AREA-LIST contains workable pairs of KS surrogates and solution areas. In general, a KS surrogate is *paired* twith a solution area if the action of the KS will be in the area and the area is contained in the PROMISING-AREA-LIST of any level. In planning-oriented problem solving, however, planner normally enforces specific constraints on areas (e.g., work on which level), or on KSs (e.g., select which category of KSs). These constraints may work as filters to speed up the pairing process. For instance, constraints on areas may work as a pre-filter to exclude irrelevant levels before pairing. Other constraints can also be applied during the pairing. For instance, we may merge all level contexts into a sorted list by evaluating DEGREE-OF-COMPLETION, LEVEL-WEIGHT, and LEVEL-WEIGHT-VARIANCE of each level. The list may work as a filter to exclude some unimportant levels.

There are solution areas and KSs which are not matched during the pairing process. UNMATCHED-AREA-LIST contains those promising but unmatched areas. If some of them are highly weighted, they may be set as goals on the domain blackboard for search of KSs which might eventually make the area workable, a process quite like GPS [1]. Similarly, UNMATCHED-KSS-LIST might be used to derive areas that must be first explored if to make the execution of the KS feasible.

A *matching process* is then applied to each pair of the WORKABLE-KSS-AREA-LIST and select a best matched pair as FOCUS, under control constraints currently operative. FOCUS normally contains KS id, level id, and island id to be processed. If the pairing is impossible (e.g., a null WORKABLE-KSS-AREA-LIST), or any unmatched object (area or KS) is weighed much higher than the best matched pair, the FOCUS will be set to the unmatched object to solicit further processing.

BLACKBOARD-WEIGHT-MEAN and BLACKBOARD-WEIGHT-VARIANCE describe the static behavior of the blackboard. They may be used as a competition measure if more than one blackboard is competing with one another (cf. two CNTXTBBDs used in Section IV). Shadow blackboards are represented in the blackboard context as SHADOWs. A shadow may be made unseen to the system by setting the STATUS to be "dead." STATUS of current-focused shadow is marked "current", which is alive, of course. Conceptually, system may simultaneously handle all live shadows in order to make reasoning on relevant shadows.

D. Knowledge sources - KSs responsible for updating of CNTXTBBD are marked on Fig. 2. "Update-island" updates an island context according to the change of the corresponding island. It includes the updates of its precontexts and/or postcontext. It also propagates this change to related island contexts. "Update-level" propagates the change of an island context to related level context. It includes updates of proper lists of the level context, especially PROMISING-AREA-LIST and INVOCABLE-KSS-LIST. "Update-bbd" propagates the change of the level context to relevant blackboard context. It includes the pairing process to propose WORKABLE-KSS-AREA-LIST and matching process to select the FOCUS. Each KS is of a stereotyped structure of Fig. 6.

```
NAME: name of the KS
ANNOTATION: behavior description of the KS
CATEGORY: {system, CNTXT, domain, etc.}
CONTROL-ATTRIBUTES:
     PREMISE-CONTEXT:
          PATTERN: definition of variables and values for triggering islands
          CONTEXT: definition of variables and values for execution
     CONCLUSION-CONTEXT:
          PATTERN: definition of variables and values for triggering islands
          CONTEXT: definition of variables and values to be satisfied
     TRIGGERING-CONTEXT: {premise-context, conclusion-context}
     WEIGHT: importance of the KS
     RELIABILITY: correctness percentage of the KS outcome
     EFFICIENCY: how fast (in percentage) this KS is to produce the outcome
ACTION: the way to make the change as specified in CONCLUSION-CONTEXT
```

Fig. 6 The stereotyped structure of knowledge sources

The CATEGORY of a KS declares how it will be used. System KSs, e.g., update-island, update-level, update-bbd, and process-KS-in-area (ref. Fig. 1) are categorized as "system." Blackboard KSs are categorized according to the blackboard with which the KSs are associated. For instance, "explain-viewpoint" with CNTXTBBD is of "CNTXT" type, while "form-rationale" with domain blackboard is of "domain" type. Recall that the category can be used as a filtering parameter in the pairing process of WORKABLE-KSS-AREA-LIST.

All KSs contain three major parts. A PREMISE-CONTEXT declares the condition that must be satisfied if to execute the KS. A CONCLUSION-CONTEXT expects what the result would be once the KS is executed. Both are refined into two parts: PATTERN, on when to trigger the KS, and CONTEXT, for the environment under which the KS will be executed if in PREMISE-CONTEXT or for the possible outcome of the KS if in CONCLUSION-CONTEXT. Triggering a KS does not guarantee the execution of the KS unless the variables specified in CONTEXT are satisfied. The TRIGGERING-CONTEXT determines how the KSs will be triggered and used. It will be triggered and used in forward-chaining if taking on the value of premise-context. And PATTERN of PREMISE-CONTEXT will be used as its triggering pattern. By taking on the value of conclusion-context it will be used in backward-chaining with PATTERN of CONCLU-SION-CONTEXT as its triggering pattern. Finally, ACTION specifies how (via procedure, rules, or expectation models) to make the CONCLUSION-CONTEXT true.

WEIGHT specifies the importance of the KS compared with others. RELIABILITY and EFFICIEN-CY record the credit of the KS. These parameters determine static competition priority of a KS. By referencing the CNTXTBBD and performing proper statistics, the system operation history may suggest new values for these parameters.

Blackboard KSs are of the same data structure as system KSs. Whenever a blackboard KS is ready for triggering, the system will create a *surrogate* representing this specific instance of triggered KS. The surrogate should entail information about this instance, i.e., instance environment. It will be put on the relevant level in the level contexts region of the CNTXTBBD and processed until it is selected as the FOCUS, when the corresponding blackboard KS will be executed. [8] gives detailed structure of KS surrogates.

Meta-level applications can be developed by attaching suitable blackboard KSs to CNTXTBBD. For instance, "explain-viewpoint" may be established as a blackboard KS with CNTXTBBD to explain a designated viewpoint. Execution of this KS may go like this. First, we expand domain blackboard with an extra level called "interface level" for users to post questions and read answers. The CNTXTBBD will have a corresponding level, which is specially designed to contain only two portions, one for question contexts and the other for answer contexts. Posted questions are then reflected on the question contexts area. "Explain-viewpoint" is set to monitor question contexts area and act on answer contexts area. Thus, it may be triggered by posted question contexts. The same pairing and matching process in other levels will be applied to select a match. If "explain-viewpoint" is finally selected to work on the answer area, it will be executed, e.g., it will retrieve the annotation of the precontext defined by the designated viewpoint. Since this level will compete with other levels in the blackboard context, the importance of user interface against the system activities can be adjusted per domain required.

IV. Context-Based Blackboards in Generalized Blackboard Systems

In addition to domain blackboard, a generalized blackboard sytem contains *planning* and *constraint* blackboards. Planning blackboard contains partial states of planning-oriented activities, i.e., partial plans, such as overall goals and refined subgoals. Constraint blackboard contains all constraints regulating both planning and domain blackboards, i.e., relevant to system problem solving, e.g., plan generation strategies, plan coordination strategies, long-term or short-term policies, scheduling criteria, monitoring and control criteria, etc. Each blackboard entails suitable KSs. For instance, "planner" with planning blackboard may be invoked under suitable strategy on the constraint blackboard and generate more detailed subplans. A conflict-set queue can be set up to store all KS surrogates which are ready to execute. These surrogates compete with each other for the best selection.

Here is how we incorporate CNTXTBBDs into this generalized architecture. First, a CNTXTBBD is established to reflect domain status. By looking at planning blackboard as just another domain blackboard (domain of developing plans) we may establish another CNTXTBBD to reflect planning blackboard. WORKABLE-KSS-AREA-LISTs of these two CNTXTBBDs have to compete (probably via a special criterion) for the final best. Various criteria we talked about in the design of CNTXTBBDs now can be brought to the surface, i.e., on constraint blackboard. One implication of this architecture is that two CNTXTBBDs will feed information back for the updates of constraints on constraint blackboard. This updating on constraint blackboard retain the flexibility and adaptability described in BB1. Moreover, problem of inefficient feedback in generalized blackboard systems (cf. BB1) can be overcome by the quick reference of system status on CNTXTBBD. Local competition that is not well explored is manifested in buckets of context-blackboards. Mixing different interpretations of certainty factors in planning and domain blackboards can be alleviated since different criteria are applied to separate CNTXTBBDs. The final competition among different blackboard contexts using specialized criteria will minimize the interaction.

References

[1] A. Barr and E. A. Feigenbaum, Eds., *The Handbook of Artificial Intelligence*, Vol. I & II, W. Kaufman, Los Altos, CA, 1981.

[2] D. D. Corkill, K. Q. Gallagher and K. E. Murray, "GBB: A Generic Blackboard Development System," In *Proc. Fifth National Conference on Artificial Intelligence (AAAI-86)*, 1008-1014, 1986.

[3] N. M. Delisle and M. D. Schwarts, "Contexts - A Partitioning Concept for Hypertext," *ACM Transactions on Office Information Systems 5* (2), 168-186, April 1987.

[4] L. D. Erman, F. Hayes-Roth, V. R. Lesser and D. R. Reddy, "The Hearsay-II Speech Understanding System: Integrating Knowledge to Resolve Uncertainty," *ACM Comput.Surveys 12* (2), 213-253, 1980.

[5] L. D. Erman, P. E. London, and S. F. Fickas, "The Design and an Example Use of Hearsay-III," In *Proc. Seventh International Joint Conference on Artificial Intelligence (IJCAI-81)*, 409-415, August 1981.

[6] B. Hayes-Roth., "A Blackboard Architecture for Control," *Artificial Intelligence 26*, 251-321, 1985.

[7] F. Hayes-Roth and V. R. Lesser, "Focus of Attention in the Hearsay-II Speech Understanding System," In *Proc. Fifth International Joint Conference on Artificial Intelligence (IJCAI-77)*, 27-35, Aug. 1977.

[8] C. S. Ho, "Enhancing Blackboard Systems Performance with Explicit Context-Based Blackboards," Technical Report, National Taiwan Institute of Technology, 1989.

[9] C. S. Ho, "Making Blackboard Shell More General," Technical Report, National Taiwan Institute of Technology, 1989.

[10] V. R. Lesser and L. D. Erman, "A Retrospective View of the Hearsay-II Architecture," In *Proc. Fifth International Joint Conference on Artificial Intelligence (IJCAI-77)*, 790-800, August 1977.

[11] H. P. Nii, "Blackboard Systems: The Blackboard Model of Problem Solving and the Evolution of Blackboard Architectures - Part one," *The AI Magazine*, 38-53, Summer 1986.

Reasoning with the Unknown[*]

Nuno J. Mamede,[†] Carlos Pinto-Ferreira, João P. Martins

Instituto Superior Técnico
Technical University of Lisbon
Av. Rovisco Pais
1000 Lisboa, Portugal

Abstract

We define a logical system with four values, the traditional truth values T and F and two "Unknown" values. An inference system based on this logic has the capability to remember all the paths followed during an attempt to answer a question. For each path it records the used hypotheses (the hypotheses that constitute the path), the missing hypothesis (when the path did not lead to an answer), and why it was assumed as missing. The inference system takes special care with missing hypotheses that are contradictory with any hypothesis that is being considered. An inference system with these capabilities can report the answers found and the reasons that prevented the inference of other potential answers. This capability can be used to plan reasoning, to perform default reasoning, and to reason about its own knowledge.

1 Introduction

Although computers are faster than they were some years ago, the computational work required by an inference system to answer a question is sometimes so extensive that some applications remain useless. McKay proposed associating resources with each question [McKay 81]. This permits controlling the maximum computational effort that can be used to answer each question. If wanted, it is possible to resume a computation giving it more resources. But the decision to give more resources is based on the user's intuition, since the inference system does not report the paths it was following and where the computation was suspended.

[*]This work was partially supported by Fundação Luso Americana para o Desenvolvimento (FLAD), by Instituto de Engenharia de Sistemas e Computadores (INESC), and by Grant 87-107 of Junta Nacional de Investigação Científica e Tecnológica (JNICT).

[†]This paper describes research done during the months of March, April and May 1989 at the Department of Computer Science, State University of New York at Buffalo.

It is also well known that for most question-answering systems, when they do not produce a result they do not give the user the reasons why they could not find an answer to a question. We think this is something that must change: inference systems must justify why they could not answer a question.

Our proposal consists of combining the resources approach with the capability to inform the user about paths that have been followed and the impediments, if any, that have already been found for each of them. The possible impediments are of two kinds: either some knowledge is absent from the knowledge base or the resources were insufficient. These two situations are differentiated whenever reporting to the user. We also propose to inform the user whenever the absent knowledge if introduced in the knowledge base would contradict an existing proposition.

The inference system we propose is based on a logic with four values, which is introduced in the next section. Sections 3 and 4 introduce the connectives. Sections 5 and 6 discuss "supported wffs". Section 7 presents a logic that relies on the notion of relevancy.

2 The four values

If someone is asked if the color of Napoleon's horse was pink, four possible answers can be expected: (i) I know it is pink (since I was told so or it can be inferred given the knowledge I have available); (ii) I know it is not pink (mutatis mutandis); (iii) I know that I don't know whether it is pink or not (since either I don't have such information or I can't infer it from what I know); (iv) I do not know if it is pink or not (but, perhaps I could find an answer if I think a little more about it).

As far as the last answer is concerned, what we would like to hear from an intelligent reasoner with common sense would be something like: "Do you want me to spend more resources elaborating on this particular subject?"

We have talked about resources, but we have not referred what they mean to us: something that is consumed by the inference system (computer) when it is trying to answer a question. For instance, McKay proposed using as resource unit the operation of matching a proposition (or a pattern) with the knowledge base [McKay 82].

The values of our logic are based on the above expected states of knowledge, which are epistemological states. The values of our many-valued logic are intended as epistemic, rather than ontic, in character. Let us give them names:

KT (Known True): know it has been told so, (with the available knowledge and the available resources);

KF (Known False): know that it has been denied, (with the available knowledge and the available resources);

KN (Known Neither): know that it has been told nothing. It has not been told it and neither it has been denied (with the available knowledge and the available resources);

U (Unknown): don't know if it has either been told, or has been denied because we did not look for (there were no resources available).

The values KN and U represent to different states of knowledge, the first one is a "state of knowledge" and the second one is a "state of ignorance". The KN value means that it is *known that it is unknown*, and the U value means that it is *not known if it is either known or not known.*

There are many 3-valued systems which add a third value to the two standard values, True and False [Lukasiewicz 20] [Bochvar 39] [Kleene 52]. The motivation for the third value in these logics were different: Lukasiewicz deals with future contingent statements; Bochvar intends to supply a solution to the semantic paradoxes; Kleene's intends to accommodate undecided mathematical statements. In all these tree-valued logics the third value has the intention to fill a gap between the two standard values. A detailed description of these logics can be found in [Rescher 69] and [Turner 84].

Belnap's four valued logic had the intention to disable that minor inconsistencies in the data lead (as in classical logic) to irrelevant conclusions [Belnap 77]. The two values added by Belnap are "none" (told neither True neither False), and "both" (told both True and False).

Ackermann argues that the main motivation for considering many-valued logics is to sanction fewer arguments as valid than do standard logics [Ackermann 67, p. 43]. However this is not our intention, we do not want to sanction fewer arguments as valid than do SWM logic[1] [Martins 83]. On the contrary, *our motivation is to determine the conditions that must be satisfied in order to sanction failed arguments.*

We would like to notice that our logic only enables to express explicitly that a proposition is either Known True or Known False, and implicitly that a proposition is Known Neither, not telling the computer that it is either Known True or Known False. The available resources will determine which propositions will be Unknown. The vocabulary available is the same as in the classical logic.

3   The connectives NOT, AND, and OR

We stipulate that the negation of a KT proposition is a KF proposition; the denial of a KF is KT; the denial of a KN is still KN; and the denial of U is still U. This definition is classical on true and false; see Table 1a.

A	¬A
KT	KF
KF	KT
KN	KN
U	U

a) NOT

∧	KT	KF	KN	U
KT	KT	KF	KN	U
KF	KF	KF	KF	KF
KN	KN	KF	KN	U
U	U	KF	U	U

b) AND

∨	KT	KF	KN	U
KT	KT	KT	KT	KT
KF	KT	KF	KN	U
KN	KT	KN	KN	U
U	KT	U	U	U

c) OR

Table 1: Truth table for the NOT, AND and OR connectives

If either component in a conjunction is KF, the conjunction is KF; if both components are KT, the conjunction is KT; if either component is U and the other one is not KF, the disjunction is U; and in all other cases the conjunction is KN (see Table 1b).

The above definition says that if one of the conjuncts is KN and the other is U then the conjunction is U, which means that it is not known if the conjunction is either

---

[1] We took SWM logic as the starting point for developing our logic.

KT, KF or KN. This state of uncertainty is due to the value of the conjunct that has value U (it is not known if it is either KT, KF or KN). If, for instance, this conjunct becomes KF then the conjunction becomes F too, the state of uncertainty is removed.

If either component in a disjunction is KT, the disjunction is KT; if both components are KF, the disjunction is KF; if either component is U and the other one is not KT, the disjunction is U; and in all other cases the disjunction is KN (see Table 1c). The reasoning used to justify the fact that the conjunction has value U, when one conjunct is KN and the other is U can be used for the disjunction too.

These connectives are consistent with all usual connectives with respect to the values KT and KF. Note that all the three tables preserve many properties of the classical two-valued connectives.

We introduce a semantics for the logic involving the three defined connectives, in the usual way. Given an arbitrary set-up s, which is a mapping of atomic formulas into the set {KT, KF, KN, U}, we can extend a mapping of all formulas into the set {KT, KF, KN, U} in the standard inductive way:

$$s(A \wedge B) = s(A) \wedge s(B)$$
$$s(A \vee B) = s(A) \vee s(B)$$
$$s(\neg B) = \neg s(B)$$

This tells what the value of a formula A is: the value of the formula A in s, i.e., s(A). The following propositions are logical equivalences:[2]

$$A \vee B \equiv B \vee A \qquad\qquad A \wedge B \equiv B \wedge A$$
$$A \vee (B \vee C) \equiv (A \vee B) \vee C \qquad A \wedge (B \wedge C) \equiv (A \wedge B) \wedge C$$
$$\neg(A \wedge B) \equiv \neg A \vee \neg B \qquad \neg(A \vee B) \equiv \neg A \wedge \neg B$$
$$\neg\neg A \equiv A$$

For our purposes, the following propositions can be taken as being almost logically equivalent in spite of the fact that they are not truly logically equivalent:

$$(A \wedge (B \vee C)) \equiv^* (A \wedge B) \vee (A \wedge C)$$
$$(A \vee (B \wedge C)) \equiv^* (A \vee B) \wedge (A \vee C)$$

We will explain this for the first proposition. There are two (out of 64) possible combinations of truth values (of A, B, and C) that raised this problem: either A is KN, B is KT, and C is U; or A is KN, B is U, and C is KT. Since we know that both conjunction and disjunction are commutative, we can reduce both assignments to one, for example, the first one. So the value of (A ∧ (B ∨ C)) is KN and the value of ((A ∧ B) ∨ (A ∧ C)) is U. In first place, the difference is not "serious", since both values correspond to an indeterminate state of knowledge, it would be catastrophic if we had obtained contradictory values (KT and KF). If the U value (of C) is considered as temporary, then independently of the next value of C the value of ((A ∧ B) ∨ (A ∧ C)) is KN. A similar justification can be given for (A ∨ (B ∧ C)) ≡* (A ∨ B) ∧ (A ∨ C).

Golshani [Golshani 85] describes a four-valued logic with truth tables for the OR and the AND connectives similar to the ones presented here. The purpose of both logics is similar. The aim of Golshani's work is to give answers as precise as possible to any query to a data-base in the presence of incomplete information; his interpretation for the "new" values is: "the type of the argument is correct but the function cannot have

---

[2]We say that two propositions are logically equivalent when for any combination of truth values of their atomic constituents, both propositions will have the same value.

a value for it" (our KN value) and "The argument given to the function is of the correct type, but the corresponding result is not available at the present time" (our U value).

We argued that "A∨B" should be KT if "A" is KN and "B" is KT, (Table 1c), because the truth of one disjunct is sufficient to determine the truth of the whole disjunction, regardless of the value of the other disjunct. However, we assign KN to "A∨B" when "A" and "B" are KN; and so, in particular, we assign KN to "A∨ ¬A" when "A" and "¬A" are KN. But, "A∨ ¬A" should be KT independently of the value of "A". This suggests that we must have a different assignment to "A∨ ¬A" than to "A∨B", when both disjuncts are KN. The same thing can be said when both disjuncts are U. The conjunction (Table 1b) suffers from a similar problem.

This same problem has been pointed out by other many-valued logics: Haack discusses this referring the 3-valued logic of Kleene [Haack 78, pp. 215–216]; Rescher uses the Lukasiewicz 3-valued logic [Rescher 69, pp. 171–173].

The solution to this problem requires the use of *non-truth-functional-logics* defined by Rescher: "I propose to characterize as *quasi-truth-functional* systems of propositional logic defined by truth-tables ...., in which some connectives are governed by *many-valued* functions of the truth-values of their variables." [Rescher 62, p. 2].

We adopt a similar approach and our system is not truth-functional, but quasi-truth-functional, see Table 2. For instance, in the previous example (when both disjuncts are KN), two values can be assigned to the disjunction: KT and KN, which is represented in Table 2 by the pair "(KT,KN)".

	A∧B				A∨B			
	KT	KF	KN	U	KT	KF	KN	U
KT	KT	KF	KN	U	KT	KT	KT	KT
KF	KF	KF	KF	KF	KT	KF	KN	U
KN	KN	KF	(KF,KN)	U	KT	KN	(KT,KN)	U
U	U	KF	U	(KF,U)	KT	U	U	(KT,U)

Table 2: Quasi-truth-functional table for the AND and OR connectives

4 Entailment

Entailment has generated lots of controversy between logicians, philosophers and AI researchers. We do not want to aggravate this quarrel, but we have to position ourselves in this dispute. We think that for *our* proposes,[3] the best interpretation of "A entails B" or "B follows logically from A" is that A is relevant to B.[4]

We are not going to present a full semantics for entailment, but rather discuss it informally. When "A→B" is KT but we know either that we don't know nothing about "A" or it is KF, then the traditional two valued logic cannot conclude anything about "B". In our four-valued logic this corresponds to saying that "B" is known to be not known[5] (value KN). But if "A" is not known because resources were not enough (value

---

[3] We are thinking in a Question-Answering system able to perform Common Sense Reasoning.

[4] With "relevant" we mean that A can be used to derive B.

[5] If "A→B" is the only knowledge about "B".

U) then we can say that "B" is also not known because resources were not enough, with more resources perhaps we could know something about "A" and consequently about "B". Of course if "A" is KT then we can conclude that "B" is also KT.

This behavior can lead to a proposition having different values. Suppose the following propositions are KT: "A→C", "B→C", and "A". Since "A→C" and "A" are KT, we can conclude that "C" is also KT. On the other hand, since we know "B→C" is KT, and we do not know anything about "B" we can conclude that "C" is KN. We have said that "C" has simultaneously the value KT and the value KN.

This is a new way to look at the values, they are related with the propositions that were used to determine them. They are "special" values, and should be interpreted as possible values, or the value of the proposition if a different value is not "proposed" too. For example, "C" is KT, if we consider the propositions "A→C" and "A", and is KN, if we consider only propositions "B→C" and "B" (which is KN).

We can think of a function Υ that decides which is the value of a proposition when *different* values have been "proposed":

$$\Upsilon(v_1 \ldots v_n) = \left\{ \begin{array}{ll} KT, & \text{if } \exists(i)\colon 1\leq i\leq n\colon v_i = KT, \\ KF, & \text{if } \exists(i)\colon 1\leq i\leq n\colon v_i = KF, \\ KN, & \text{if } \forall(i)\colon 1\leq i\leq n\colon v_i \neq KF \text{ and } v_i \neq KF, \end{array} \right.$$

This function enables a proposition being simultaneously KT and KF, which should be interpreted, as usual, as a contradiction. A formal description of the entailment rules can be found in Section 4.

5   An example

Let's suppose that our knowledge base has the following propositions:

    A) "It is summer" → "I go to the beach"
    B) ("It is warm" ∧ "It is sunny") → "I go to the beach"
    C) "It is clear" → "It is sunny"
    D) "It is warm"
    E) "It is not clear"

Suppose we want to know the truth value of the proposition "I go to the beach", and that the available resources are not enough to know propositions D, and E. So propositions A, B, and C are KT, propositions D and E are U. In this environment, there are two possible paths that can be used to find the truth value of "I go to the beach". Each path can be thought as a sub-context of the context in which we are reasoning, and "I go to the beach" can have different values in each sub-context.

In the example, we are considering, the two paths that can be used to find the value of "I go to the beach" are:

    sub-context-1: A (and "It is summer" is KN)
    sub-context-2: B and C (D and E are U)

In sub-context-1 "I go to the beach" has the value KN,[6] and in sub-context-2 has the

---

[6] When the antecedent of an entailment is KN and the entailment is KT, then the consequent is KN.

value U.[7] But to know that "I go to the beach" has two different possibilities to be derived (and in this case two different values) is not enough. We would like to receive ·the following answer: *"I go to the beach" has the value KN and can be deduced in two ways: 1) Using proposition A; but since I do not know anything about "It is summer", the value of "I go to the beach" is KN; 2) Using propositions B, and C; but since resources were not enough, and consequently the value of propositions E and B is U, the value of "I go to the beach" is U.*

If we give more resources to the system, enough to find propositions D and E, then we would like to receive the following message: *"I go to the beach" has the value KN and can be deduced in two ways: 1) Using proposition A; but since I do not know anything about "It is summer", the value of "I go to the beach" is KN; 2) Using propositions B, C and D; the value of "I go to the beach" is KN (This path cannot be used to derive proposition "I go to the beach" since one of the requirements "It is clear" is contradictory with the asserted proposition E).*

If we now introduce the proposition:

F) "It is summer"

and, if we ask again the system about "I go to the beach", we would like to receive the following message: *"I go to the beach" has the value KT and can be deduced in two ways: 1) Using proposition A and F the value of "I go to the beach" is KT; 2) Using propositions B, C and D; the value of "I go to the beach" is KN (This path cannot be used to deduce proposition "I go to the beach" since one of the requirements "It is clear" is contradictory with the asserted proposition E).*

The information necessary to produce the above (hypothetical) reports is computed by the inference rules, described in Section 7, and stored in a structure described in the next section.

6 Supported wffs

We took as the starting point for developing our logic the SWM system [Martins 83] [Martins and Shapiro 88], and the next sub-section describes the objects, which the SWM system deals with: *supported wffs*. The objects of our logic, the *conditional supported wffs* are described in Sub-section 6.2. Sub-section 6.3 shows how to interpret conditional supports in terms of the values of the logic described in the previous sections.

6.1 The SWM system

The SWM system associates each wff[8] with an *origin set*, which references every hypothesis used in its derivation [Martins and Shapiro 88]. In order to record contradictions, each wff and its corresponding origin set are associated with a set, called the *restriction set*, that contains information about which sets unioned with the wff's origin set produce an inconsistent set. To know whether a given wff was introduced as a hypothesis or was derived from other wffs each wff is associated with an identifier, called *origin tag*. The origin tags take one value from the set {*hyp, der, ext*}: *hyp* identifies

---

[7] When the antecedent of an entailment is U and the entailment is KT, then the consequent is U; so "It is sunny" is U. When both conjuncts are U the conjunction is also U, so the antecedent of B is U. Since the antecedent of B is U and B is KT then the consequent of B is U.

[8] The standard formation rules for wffs were assumed.

hypotheses, *der* identifies normally derived wffs, and *ext* identifies special wffs whose OS was extended and has to be treated specially in order to avoid the introduction of irrelevancies.[9]

The SWM system deals with objects called *supported wffs*. A supported wff consists of a wff and an associated triple, its *support*, containing an *origin tag* (OT), an *origin set* (OS), and a *restriction set* (RS). The support is not part of the wff itself but rather associated with a particular occurrence of the wff.

The OS and the OT of a supported wff are related with a *particular derivation*. Once a supported wff is generated, its OT and OS remain constant.

6.2 The conditional support

The SWM's support is used to record the hypotheses used in the derivation of a wff. Since we want to register the absent hypotheses that if present enable the derivation of a wff, we have to extend the SWM's support. An extended support is used to record the hypotheses needed to derive a wff where some of them may not be available at the moment. This new support is called *conditional support* to the, and the new supported wffs *conditional supported wffs*. As in the SWM system, multiple derivations are memorized in different conditional supported wffs.

In a system with limited resources there are two possible reasons to justify the absence of a wff: (i) it cannot be derived; (ii) there are not enough resources. We also want to know whenever an absent premise is contradictory with any other wff that is being considered. We store all this information in the conditional support.

A conditional supported wff consists of a wff and an associated quintuplet containing an *origin tag* (OT), an *origin set* (OS), a *neither set* (NS), an *unknown set* (US) and a *contradictory set* (CS).

The SWM's restriction sets were very important to the theoretical development of the SWM system [Martins 83, p. 3.58], but the computation of the RSs is very expensive and they are only used to check if a new context is known to be inconsistent. Since it is possible to achieve the same functionality with a less expensive procedure [Shapiro 89], we removed them from the conditional support.

The OT has exactly the same interpretation as in the SWM logic. The OS, NS, US and CS are sets of hypotheses. The union of the four sets, of a conditional supported wff, determines exactly which hypotheses were used to derive the wff: the OS contains the hypotheses that already exist; the NS contains the hypotheses that do not exist and the equivalent propositions could not be derived; the US contains the hypotheses that are not possible to know if they exist, or if they can be derived since the available resources are insufficient; the CS contains the hypotheses that are contradictory with another wff.[10]

A conditional supported wff with empty NS, US, and CS must be interpreted in the same way as SWM's supported wffs: the wff is a hypothesis or has been successfully deduced. If at least one of these sets is not empty then the conditional supported wff can be interpreted two fold:

1. the derivation of the wff was blocked. The OS contains the hypotheses that were used so far in the attempt to derive the wff. The NS, US and CS contain exactly

---

[9]A detailed discussion of this issue can be found in [Martins and Shapiro 88, p. 37].

[10]It is not necessary that the contradictory wff be a hypothesis.

the premisses that are necessary to derive the wff, but were not available. The NS contains the premisses that are not hypotheses and their derivation was unsuccessful. The US contains the premisses that the available resources did not allow to look for. The CS contains the premisses that are contradictory with another conditional supported wff.

2. the derivation of the wff is conditional. If all the hypotheses of NS, US and CS would be present then the wff would be derived and the hypotheses used to derive it would be given by the union of OS, NS, US and CS. If the CS is not empty then a contradiction may be derived.[11]

We have some preference for the second interpretation since it is a positive (optimist) reading of a failure and simultaneously all sets that constitute a conditional support share the same kind of information: the hypotheses necessary to derive a wff.

6.3 The semantics of the conditional support

The conditional support is a "mirror" of the truth-value of a conditional supported wff $\langle A, t, o, n, u, c \rangle$:

- if the n, u and c are empty sets then A has the truth value KT;
- if either n or c are not empty sets but u is then A has the truth value KN;
- If u is not an empty set then A has the truth value U.

We say that a wff A has the value KF when the wff $\langle \neg A, t, o, \{\}, \{\}, \{\} \rangle$ is present in the knowledge base.

7 The Inference Rules

Most of the inference rules presented herein are generalizations of the SWM's inference rules. The word "generalization" means that the requirements that were imposed on the OSs, are now imposed to the NSs, USs, and CSs too.

To compute the OT of a conditional supported wff resulting from the application of the rules of inference, we use SWM's function Λ defined as follows:

$$\Lambda(\alpha, \beta) = \begin{cases} ext, & \text{if } \alpha = ext \text{ or } \beta = ext, \\ der, & \text{otherwise}; \end{cases}$$

$$\Lambda(\alpha, \beta, \ldots, \gamma) = \Lambda(\alpha, \Lambda(\beta, \ldots, \gamma)).$$

Hypothesis (Hyp) The rule of hypothesis allows us to add new information to the knowledge base: for any wff A we may add the supported wff $\langle A, hyp, \{A\}, \{\}, \{\}, \{\} \rangle$ to the knowledge base, provided that A has not already been introduced as a hypothesis.

Neither (Neither) The rule of Neither allows the introduction of knowledge that is both absent and not derivable: for any wff A we may add the supported wff $\langle A, hyp, \{\}, \{A\}, \{\}, \{\} \rangle$ to the knowledge base, provided that neither A nor $\neg A$ have already

---

[11]In the set of hypotheses under consideration unioned with the hypotheses of the CS.

been introduced as hypotheses, they have not been derived, and they cannot be derived using the inference rules here presented.

Unknown (Unkn) This rule enables the introduction of wffs when there are no available resources to know if they either have been introduced as hypotheses, or can be derived: for any wff A we may add the supported wff $\langle A, hyp, \{\}, \{\}, \{A\}, \{\}\rangle$ to the knowledge base, provided the resources available do not permit to know if neither A nor $\neg A$ have already been introduced as hypotheses or been derived.

Implication Introduction ($\rightarrow$I) This rule is a generalization of the traditional relevant rule to introduce entailments: from $\langle B, der, o, n, u, c \rangle$ and any hypothesis $H \in o$, or $H \in n$, or $H \in u$, or $H \in c$, infer $\langle H \rightarrow B, der, o - \{H\}, n - \{H\}, u - \{H\}, c - \{H\}\rangle$.

Notice that any hypothesis in the OS, NS, US or CS of B *is necessary* in its derivation, and thus it implies B under the assumption of the remaining hypotheses. The hypothesis H is subtracted to all hypotheses sets, but it is present in only one of the sets.

Modus Ponens—Implication Elimination (MP) Next rule is a generalization of the SWM's rule of Modus Ponens:

MP$_1$ From $\langle A, t_1, o_1, n_1, u_1, c_1 \rangle$, $\langle A \rightarrow B, t_2, o_2, n_2, u_2, c_2 \rangle$, infer $\langle B, \Lambda(t_1, t_2), o_1 \cup o_2, n_1 \cup n_2, u_1 \cup u_2, c_1 \cup c_2 \rangle$.[12]

Next rule enables the introduction of the antecedent of the entailment as a hypothesis, when it is contradictory with another wff present in the knowledge base:

MP$_2$ From $\langle \neg A, t_1, o_1, \{\}, \{\}, \{\}\rangle$, $\langle A \rightarrow B, t_2, o_2, n_2, u_2, c_2 \rangle$, infer $\langle B, \Lambda(t_1, t_2), o_2, n_2, u_2, c_2 \cup \{A\}\rangle$.[12]

Modus Tollens—Implication Elimination (MT) Next rule is a generalization of the SWM's rule of Modus Tollens:

MT$_1$ From $\langle A \rightarrow B, t_1, o_1, n_1, u_1, c_1 \rangle$, $\langle \neg B, t_2, o_2, n_2, u_2, c_2 \rangle$, infer $\langle \neg A, \Lambda(t_1, t_2), o_1 \cup o_2, n_1 \cup n_2, u_1 \cup u_2, c_1 \cup c_2 \rangle$.[12]

Next rule enables the introduction of the negation of the consequent of the entailment as a hypothesis, when it is contradictory with another wff present in the knowledge base:

MT$_2$ From $\langle A \rightarrow B, t_1, o_1, n_1, u_1, c_1 \rangle$, $\langle B, t_1, o_1, \{\}, \{\}, \{\}\rangle$, infer $\langle \neg A, tags, o_1, n_1, u_1, c_1 \cup \{\neg B\}\rangle$.[12]

Negation Elimination ($\neg$E) From $\langle \neg\neg A, t, o, n, u, c \rangle$ infer $\langle A, \Lambda(t.t), o, n, u, c \rangle$.

And-Introduction ($\wedge$I)

$\wedge$**I$_1$** From $\langle A, t_1, o, n, u, c \rangle$ and $\langle B, t_2, o, n, u, c \rangle$, infer $\langle A \wedge B, \Lambda(t_1, t_2), o, n, u, c \rangle$.

$\wedge$**I$_2$** From $\langle A, t_1, o_1, n_1, u_1, c_1 \rangle$, $\langle B, t_2, o_2, n_2, u_2, c_2 \rangle$, and either $o_1 \neq o_2$, or $n_1 \neq n_2$, or $u_1 \neq u_2$, or $c_1 \neq c_2$, infer $\langle A \wedge B, ext, o_1 \cup o_2, n_1 \cup n_2, u_1 \cup u_2, c_1 \cup c_2 \rangle$.

And-Elimination ($\wedge$E) From $\langle A \wedge B, t, o, n, u, c \rangle$ and $t \neq ext$, infer either $\langle A, der, o, n, u, c \rangle$ or $\langle B, der, o, n, u, c \rangle$ or both.

---

[12]There is the possibility that the computed OT be *der*. For a complete discussion on this subject see [Mamede and Martins 89].

Or-Introduction $(\vee I)$[13] From $\langle \neg A \rightarrow B, t_1, o, n, u, c \rangle$ and $\langle \neg B \rightarrow A, t_2, o, n, u, c \rangle$ infer $\langle A \vee B, \Lambda(t_1, t_2), o, n, u, c \rangle$.

Or-Elimination $(\vee E)$

$\vee E_1$ From $\langle A \vee B, t_1, o_1, n_1, u_1, c_1 \rangle$, $\langle \neg A, t_2, o_2, n_2, u_2, c_2 \rangle$, infer, $\langle B, \Lambda(t_1, t_2), o_1 \cup o_2, n_1 \cup n_2, u_1 \cup u_2, c_1 \cup c_2 \rangle$

$\vee E_2$ From $\langle A \vee B, t_1, o_1, n_1, u_1, c_1 \rangle$, $\langle \neg B, t_2, o_2, n_2, u_2, c_2 \rangle$, infer, $\langle A, \Lambda(t_1, t_2), o_1 \cup o_2, n_1 \cup n_2, u_1 \cup u_2, c_1 \cup c_2 \rangle$.

$\vee E_3$ From $\langle A \vee B, t_1, o_1, n_1, u_1, c_1 \rangle$, $\langle A \rightarrow C, t_2, o_2, n_2, u_2, c_2 \rangle$, and $\langle B \rightarrow C, t_3, o_2, n_2, u_2, c_2 \rangle$, infer $\langle C, \Lambda(t_1, t_2, t_3), o_1 \cup o_2, n_1 \cup n_2, u_1 \cup u_2, c_1 \cup c_2 \rangle$.

Universal Introduction $(\forall I)$ From $\langle B(t), der, o \cup \{A(t)\}, n, u, c \rangle$, in which $A(t)$ is a hypothesis which uses a term (t) never used in the system prior to A's introduction, infer $\langle \forall(x)[A(x) \rightarrow B(x)], der, o, n, u, c \rangle$.[14]

Universal Elimination $(\forall E)$ From the supported wffs $\langle \forall(x)[A(x) \rightarrow B(x)], t_1, o_1, n_1, u_1, c_1 \rangle$, and $\langle A(d), t_2, o_2, n_2, u_2, c_2 \rangle$, in which "d" is any individual symbol, infer $\langle A(d) \rightarrow B(d), \Lambda(t_1, t_2), o_1 \cup o_2, n_1 \cup n_2, u_1 \cup u_2, c_1 \cup c_2 \rangle$

Existential Introduction $(\exists I)$ From $\langle A(d), t, o, n, u, c \rangle$ in which "d" is an individual constant, infer $\langle \exists(x)[A(x)], \Lambda(t, t), o, n, u, c \rangle$.

Existential Elimination $(\exists E)$ From $\langle \exists(x)[A(x)], t, o, n, u, c \rangle$ and any individual constant "d" that was never used before, infer $\langle A(c), \Lambda(t, t), o, n, u, c \rangle$.

8 Conclusion

The main objective of this work is to provide a mechanism that will properly explore the introduction of resources in inferences systems. It is our opinion that an inference system based on our concepts will provide the information necessary to perform a wide sort of tasks, such as planning, to carry out default reasoning and hypothetical reasoning, and reasoning about its own knowledge.

We have presented a logic with four-values the Known True, Known False, Known Neither and Unknown. The basic justification for the introduction of the two "new" values was the necessity to distinguish between "not finding an answer but resources were not a problem", from "not finding an answer but with more resources perhaps an answer could be found". The semantics of NOT, AND, and OR was presented, and entailment was treated informally.

We also discussed a natural deduction system based on this logic. This system has the capability to remember the hypotheses used to derive a given wff, where some of them may not be available. Our system has not been implemented yet.

---

[13] We are considering only the *intentional sense* of the or. For a discussion between the *intentional sense* and the *functional sense* refer to [Martins 83] [Martins and Shapiro 84].

[14] According to this rule of inference, the universal quantifier can only be introduced in the context of an implication. This is not a drawback, as may seem at first, since the role of the antecedent of the implication (A(x)) is to define the type of objects that are being quantified. This is sometimes called relativized quantification.

The rules of inference presented do not reflect the quasi-truth-functional tables given at the end of Section 3. The detection and handling of contradictions, the existence of rules of inference capable to updating the conditional supports when new hypotheses are introduced, and enabling the derivation of negation, constitute work in progress.

Acknowledgement

Many thanks to Bill Rapaport, Stuart Shapiro, and John Kearns for their comments on earlier versions of this paper and for their general discussions while the research was in progress.

References

Ackermann R., *An Introduction to Many-valued Logics*, New York: Dover Publications Inc., 1967.

Belnap N., "A Useful Four-valued Logic", in *Modern Uses of Multi-valued Logic*, G. Epstein and M. Dunn (ed.), Dordrecht: Reidel, 1977.

Bochvar D., "On Three-valued Logical Calculus and its Application to the Analysis of Contradictions", *Matematiceskij Sbornik* **4**, pp. 353–369, 1939.

Golshani F., "Growing Certainty with Null Values", *Information Systems* **10**, No. 3, pp. 289–297, 1985.

Haack S., *Philosophy of Logics*, Cambridge, UK: Cambridge University Press, 1978.

Kleene S., *Introduction to Metamathematics*, New York: Van Nostrand, 1952.

Lukasiewicz J., "Many-Valued Systems of Propositional Logic", in McCall (ed.), *Polish Logic: 1920-1939*, Oxford, pp. 16–18, 1930.

Mamede N. and Martins J., "Reasoning with the Unknown", GIA Technical Report 89/3, Instituto Superior Técnico, Technical University of Lisbon, 1989.

Martins J., Reasoning in Multiple Belief Spaces, Ph.D. Dissertation, Technical Report 203, Department of Computer Science, SUNY at Buffalo, 1983.

Martins J. and Shapiro S., "A Model for Belief Revision", *Proceedings Non-Monotonic Reasoning Workshop*, Menlo Park, CA: AAAI, pp. 241–294, 1984.

Martins J. and Shapiro S., "A Model for Belief Revision", *Artificial Intelligence* **35**, No. 1, pp. 25–79, 1988.

McKay D., "Monitors: Structuring Control Information", Thesis proposal, Department of Computer Science, SUNY at Buffalo, 1981.

Rescher N., "Quasi-Truth-Functional Systems of Propositional Logic", *The Journal of Symbolic Logic*, **27**, No. 1, pp. 1–10, 1962.

Rescher N., *Many-valued Logic*, McGraw-Hill, 1969.

Shapiro S., personal communication, 1989

Turner R., *Logics for Artificial Intelligence*, Chichester, UK: John Wiley & Sons, 1984.

PATH - BASED INFERENCE IN SNeBR [1]

Maria R. Cravo and *João P. Martins*
Instituto Superior Técnico
Technical University of Lisbon
Av. Rovisco Pais, 1000 Lisboa,   Portugal

Abstract

Path-based inference allows the inference of the existence of an arc between two nodes based on the existence of a path of arcs between those nodes. Path-based inference has been used in the SNePS Semantic Network Processing System for several years. When SNePS was extended to include belief revision (giving rise to SNeBR) the path-based inference capability was lost, because no study had been done to decide how to compute the dependency (on other nodes) of the node generated by path-based inference.

In this paper we discuss how to incorporate path-based inference in a semantic network used for belief revision (SNeBR) and show how to compute the dependency of the nodes generated by path-based inference. The techniques that we develop can be used to incorporate belief revision techniques in networks based in hierarchies.

1. INTRODUCTION

SNeBR (SNePS with Belief Revision) [Martins 83], [Martins and Shapiro 88] is a belief revision system based on the logic SWM. SNeBR is implemented in SNePS [Shapiro 79], [Shapiro and Rapaport 87]. In SNeBR we can introduce hypotheses, reason from them, and, whenever a contradiction is derived the system identifies those (and only those) hypotheses that underly the contradiction. This is possible because each proposition in SNeBR is associated with all the hypotheses that were *really* used in its derivation. Up to now the only inference allowed in SNeBR is node-based, i.e., the inference proceeds according to patterns of nodes.

In this paper we discuss how to introduce path-based inference in SNeBR (inference that relies on the existence of a path between nodes). Path-based inference, although less general than node-based inference, is much more efficient. The main issue in the integration of path-based inference in SNeBR concerns the computation of the hypotheses that underly a newly generated node.

---

[1]   This work was partly supported by Junta Nacional de Investigação Científica under grant 87-107.

The paper is divided into five main sections. In the first one we present some fundamental concepts of the SWM logic; in the second, we introduce SNeBR and discuss node-based inference; then we discuss path-based inference, presenting a syntax for specifying paths and a description of some of the paths that we allow; we then discuss the process of computation of the hypotheses associated with a newly derived node, using path-based inference; and, finally, we present an example of path-based inference.

2. SWM

SWM is a logic that has been developed to support belief revision systems [Martins 83], [Martins and Shapiro 88]. One of the main issues in these systems is the possibility of identifying dependencies among propositions; this is important because once a contradiction is detected we want to find out *exactly* which hypotheses underly the contradictory propositions.

SWM is loosely based on the relevance logic of [Anderson and Belnap 75] and associates each derivation of a proposition with three items:

1. An *origin tag* that tells how the proposition was derived. An origin tag can either be "hyp" if the proposition was introduced as an hypothesis; "der" if it was derived according to the rules of relevance logic; or "ext" if it was derived in a special way (for a detailed description of these values refer to [Martins 83]);

2. An *origin set* that contains *exactly* those hypotheses that underly the derivation of the proposition. The origin set is computed whenever a proposition is derived;

3. A *restriction set* that contains those sets of hypotheses that are known to be incompatible with the proposition's origin set. These sets are propagated through the application of rules of inference and are updated whenever contradictions are detected.

SWM deals with *supported propositions* which are of the form $< A, \tau, \alpha, \rho>$, where A is a proposition, τ its origin tag, α its origin set, and ρ its restriction set. The triple (τ, α, ρ) is called the *support* of the proposition A. If the same proposition is derived in several different ways there will be several supported propositions with the same proposition and we say that the proposition has different supports.

The rules of inference of SWM make use of several functions that compute the origin tag, origin set, and restriction set of the derived propositions. For the purpose of this paper we will mention two of them, $\wedge$ and μ, without a detailed explanation about how they work; this can be found in [Martins 83] and [Martins and Shapiro 88]. The function $\wedge$ takes as arguments the origin tags of two propositions to be combined by a rule of inference and produces the origin tag of the resulting proposition; the function μ takes as arguments a set of restriction sets and a set of origin sets and μ $(\{r_1, ..., r_m\}, \{o_1, ..., o_n\})$ produces the restriction set of a proposition resulting from the application of a rule of inference, where r_1, ..., r_m are the restriction sets of the propositions to be combined and $o_1, ..., o_n$ are their origin sets.

3. SNeBR

SNeBR is an assumption-based belief revision system [Martins 83], [Martins and Shapiro 88] based on SWM and implemented in SNePS [Shapiro 79], [Shapiro and Rapaport 87]. SNeBR is a propositional semantic network, i.e. propositions are represented by nodes.

In SNeBR there are nodes and arcs. Nodes represent concepts and arcs represent non-conceptual relations *between* concepts. The arcs are defined by the user. For each arc defined by the user (descending arc) SNeBR creates an ascending arc (representing the converse relation). Besides nodes and arcs there is another kind of objects in SNeBR, the supports, which are associated with every node that represents a proposition and which correspond to the proposition's support(s) in SWM's sense.

In Figure 1 we show SNeBR's representation of the propositions "Rover is a dog" and "dogs are a subclass of mammals". In this figure, m1 represents the proposition that "Rover is a dog". This proposition is associated with a support which is not shown in the figure. The arcs member and class are descending arcs defined by the user. Besides these arcs there exist arcs labeled member− from Rover to m1 and class− from dogs to m1. Something similar holds for node m2 that represents the proposition that "dogs are mammals".

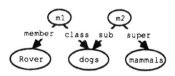

Figure 1: Representation of "Rover is a dog" and "dogs are a subclass of mammals"

In Figure 2 we show the representation of the proposition that says that "if someone is a member of a class and that class is contained in a superclass then that someone is also a member of the superclass". This figure uses a non-standard connective, "and-entailment" whose description can be found in [Shapiro 79] and [Martins and Shapiro 88].

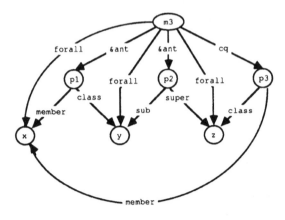

Figure 2: Representation of the proposition ∀x,y,z [(member (x,y) & subclass (y,z) → member (x,z)]

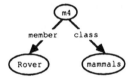

Figure 3: Representation of "Rover is a mammal"

From the propositions of Figures 1 and 2, SNeBR is able to deduce (using node-based inference) that "Rover is a mammal" (Figure 3) and associates this new proposition with the corresponding support. For example, if both m1, m2, and m3 were introduced as hypotheses, the support of m4 would be (der, {m1, m2, m3}, { }). The inference is node--based because it proceeds according to the existence of instances of patterns of nodes: p1 which is in antecedent position of a rule matches m1 with the substitution {x / Rover, y / dogs}, p2, which is also in antecedent position of the rule, matches m2 with the substitution {y / dogs, z / mammals} and thus we may infer an instance of the pattern p3 with the substitution {x / Rover, y / dogs, z / mammals} (m4).

4. Path - Based Inference

The result obtained at the end of the previous section could have been obtained in a rather different way: suppose that we have the network shown in Figure 1 and that we tell the system that whenever the sequence of arcs member- / class / sub- / super is found from a node x to a node y then it can infer the existence of the sequence of arcs member- / class from node x to node y; under these circumstances the system could be able to infer the node m4 of Figure 3.

However, the way m4 is derived is very different from the previous derivation: rather than relying on the existence of instances of patterns of nodes in the network we rely on the existence of a sequence of arcs *(path)* from a node to another, this is *path-based inference* [Shapiro 78], [Srihari 81].

We now concentrate on how to define path-based inference in SNeBR and how to propagate dependencies of propositions. We will only show some of the path-based inference rules we can use in SNeBR. For a full description of these rules as well as a discussion of the differences we introduced to the SNePS path-based inference refer to [Cravo and Martins 89].

4.1. Defining Path-Based Inference Rules

A path-based inference rule is of the form

$$(<R1> , <R2>) \leftarrow <path>$$

where <R1> and <R2> are arcs and <path> is a path as described below. From this rule, and the existence of the path <path> from node x to node y we can infer a new node with arc <R1> to x and arc <R2> to y. In an informal way, the path described at the outset of Section 4 could be specified as:

$$(member, class) \leftarrow member-/class/sub-/super$$

where, as will be described, "/" represents composition of arcs.

Formally, a <path> is either the sequence of an ascending arc followed by a descending arc (elementary path) or is composed in the following ways[2]:

1. *Composition*: If *P* is a <path> from x to y and Q is a <path> from y to z then P/Q is a <path> from x to z;

2. *Composition-* *: If P composed with itself zero or more times is a path from x to y then P* is a <path> from x to y;

3. *Union*: If either P or Q are a <path> from x to y then P ∪ Q is a <path> from x to y;

4. *Intersection*: If P is a <path> from x to y and Q is a <path> from x to y then P & Q is a <path> from x to y.

---

[2] There are other ways to form paths which are described in [Cravo and Martins 89].

As an example, the following rule generalizes the path-based inference rule given earlier in this section:

$$(\text{member}, \text{class}) \leftarrow \text{member-} / \text{class} / (\text{sub-} / \text{super}) *$$

4.2. Inference Rules for Path-Based Inference

We will now describe rules of inference that allow the computation of the support of propositions generated during path-based inference. In these rules, the letters x, y, and z represent nodes; the letters Q, R, and S represent paths; and the letters a and b represent arcs.

The rules of inference are divided into three groups:

1. *CONVERSION RULES*:

   These are rewrite rules that allow the transformation of a node in the network in an expression containing relations and vice versa.

   1.1. *Node-to-Expression Rule*: From the node represented in Figure 4 with support (t, o, r) we can write $<(x \ a\text{-}/b \ y), t, o, r>$;

   1.2. *Expression-to-Node Rule*: From $<(x \ a\text{-}/b \ y), t, o, r>$ we can write the node of Figure 4 with support (t, o, r).

Figure 4: Node is the network

---

2. *PATH RULES*

   There is one of these rules for each of the possible ways of defining <path> and they define the support of the node resulting from the inference.

   2.1. *Composition Rule*: From $< x \ Q \ y, t_1, o_1, r_1 >$ and $< y \ R \ z, t_2, o_2, r_2 >$ we can deduce $<x \ Q/R \ z, \wedge (t_1, t_2), o_1 \cup o_2, \mu(\{r_1, r_2\}, \{o_1, o_2\})>$;

   2.2. *Composition- * Rule*: From $< x \ R \ y, t, o, r >$ we can deduce $< x \ R^* \ y, t, o, r >$; from $< x \ R^* \ y, t_1, o_1, r_1 >$ and $< y \ R \ z, t_2, o_2, r_2 >$ we can deduce $< x \ R^* \ z, \wedge (t_1, t_2), o_1 \cup o_2, \mu(\{r_1, r_2\}, \{o_1, o_2\}) >$;

   2.3. *Union Rule*: From $< x \ R \ y, t, o, r >$ and $R \in \{Q, S\}$ we can deduce $< x \ Q \cup S$

y, ∧ (t, t), o, r >;

2.4.   *Intersection Rule:* From < x Q y, t_1, o_1, r_1 > and < x R y, t_2, o_2, r_2 > we can

deduce <x Q&R y, ∧ (t_1, t_2), o_1 ∪ o_2, μ({r_1, r_2}, {o_1, o_2})>.

3. ← *ELIMINATION RULE*:

This rule allows the application of a path-based inference rule by removing the symbol
"←" (Note the similarity with modus ponens):   From < x R y, t_1, o_1, r_1 > and < (a, b)
← R, t_2, o_2, r_2 > we can deduce < (x a-/b y), ∧ (t_1, t_2), o_1 ∪ o_2, μ ({r_1, r_2}, {o_1,
o_2}) >.

A deduction involving path-based inference will involve the application of the node-to-
-expression rule to one or more nodes of the network, followed by the necessary path rules,
followed by the ← elimination rule, followed by the application of the expression-to-node
rule.

The inference rules were written so that a node corresponding to a proposition generated
during path-based inference would have the same support as if it were produced using node-
-based inference.

5. Example

We will now present an example of a deduction using path-based inference. It involves
inheritance of properties, a case where path-based inference is well applicable. Suppose that
our network contains the nodes represented in Figure 5, corresponding to the propositions

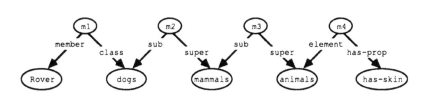

Figure 5:   Representation of the propositions
"Rover is a dog", "dogs are mammals","mammals are animals", and "animals have skin".

"Rover is a dog" (m1), "dogs are mammals" (m2), "mammals are animals" (m3), and
"animals have skin" (m4). We will assume that all these nodes were introduced as
hypotheses. Suppose, furthermore, that we introduce the following path-based inference
rule:

<(element, has-prop) ← member- / class / (sub- / super)* / element-

/ has-prop, hyp, {m5}, { }> [3]   (1)

Informally, this rule states that an object has a given property if its class or one of its superclasses has that property.

Using these propositions, we could derive that "Rover has skin" in the following way:

1. We apply the node-to-expression rule to nodes m1, m2, m3, and m4 obtaining the following supported wffs:

    <Rover member- / class dogs, hyp, {m1}, { }>   (2)

    <dogs sub- / super mammals, hyp, {m2}, { }>   (3)

    <mammals sub- / super animals, hyp, {m3}, { }>   (4)

    <animals element- / has-prop has-skin, hyp, {m4}, { }>   (5)

2. We apply the composition-* rule to (3) and (4) to obtain:

    <dogs (sub- / super)* animals, der, {m2, m3}, { }>   (6)

3. We apply the composition rule to (2) and (6) to obtain:

    <Rover member- / class / (sub- / super)* animals, der, {m1, m2, m3},

    { }>   (7)

4. We apply the composition rule to (7) and (5) to obtain:

    <Rover member- / class / (sub- / super)* / element- / has-prop

    has-skin, der, {m1, m2, m3, m4}, { }>   (8)

5. We apply the ← elimination rule to (1) and (8) to obtain:

    <Rover element- / has-prop has-skin, der, {m1, m2, m3, m4, m5},

    { }>   (9)

6. We apply the expression-to-node rule to (9) to obtain the node of Figure 6 with support

    (der, {m1, m2, m3, m4, m5}, { })

---

[3] This proposition is represented in the network by node m5, whose representation we do not show.

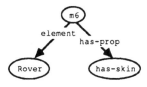

Figure 6: Representation of the proposition "Rover has skin"

6. Conclusion

We discussed how to introduce path-based inference in SNeBR, an assumption- -based belief revision system. The bulk of the work corresponded to the definition of a syntax to define paths and the study of how to propagate dependencies among the propositions involved in the deduction so that the resulting propositions have adequate support.

The importance of the work reported concerns, not only SNeBR, but mainly corresponds to a study of how to incorporate techniques of belief revision (the computation of dependencies) to networks based on hierarchies.

7. References

Anderson A.R. and Belnap N.D., *Entailment, The Logic of Relevance and Necessity*, Vol. 1, Princeton, N.J.: Princeton University Press, 1975.

Cravo M.R. and Martins J.P., "Integração da Inferência Baseada em Caminhos em SNeBR", GIA Relatório Técnico 89/1, Lisboa, Portugal: Instituto Superior Técnico, 1989.

Martins J.P., "Reasoning in Multiple Belief Spaces", Technical Report 203, Buffalo, N.Y.: Department of Computer Science, State University of New York at Buffalo, 1983.

Martins J.P. and Shapiro S.C., "Reasoning in Multiple Belief Spaces", *Proc. IJCAI-83*, pp. 370-373, 1983.

Martins J.P. and Shapiro S.C., "A Model for Belief Revision", *Journal of Artificial Intelligence*, Vol. 35, N. 1, pp. 25-79, May 1988.

Shapiro S.C., Path-Based and Node-Based Inference in Semantic Networks", *Theoretical Issues in Natural Language Processing 2*, pp. 219-225, 1978.

Shapiro S.C., "The SNePS Semantic Network Processing System", in *Associative Networks: Representation and Use of Knowledge by Computers*, Findler (ed.), New York, N.Y.: Academic Press, pp. 179-203, 1979.

Shapiro S.C. and Rapaport W.J., "SNePS Considered as a Fully Intensional Propositional Semantic Network", in *The Knowledge Frontier: Essays in the Representation of Knowledge*, Cercone and McCalle (eds.), New York, N.Y." Springer-Verlag, pp. 262-315, 1987.

Srihari R., "Combining Path-Based and Node-Based Inference in SNePS", Technical Report 183, Buffalo, N.Y.: Department of Computer Science, State University of New York at Buffalo, 1981.

RELEVANT COUNTERFACTUALS

Luís Moniz Pereira and **Joaquim Nunes Aparício**

Artificial Intelligence and Logic Programming Group
Universidade Nova de Lisboa
2825 Monte da Caparica, Portugal

Abstract

Our aim is to present here a proposal of counterfactual truth value evaluation, based on a notion of relevance, which we compare to classical counterfactual evaluation. Informally we demand that the truth value of the counterfactual (or conditional) implication p > q should depend on the existence of a deduction of q that requires the truth of p, in some appropriate nearest world. We believe that relevance of counterfactuals is important in A.I. and illustrate that with examples.

1. Introduction

The ultimate motivation for this work is to explore, in the context of other types (c.f. section future explorations) of non-monotonic reasoning, and later within the logic programming paradigm, a suitable proposal for counterfactual reasoning.

Lewis [1] is an excellent classic essay on counterfactuals. Ginsberg [2] provides a good introduction to counterfactuals and their need in AI, and shows that his definition of counterfactual truth, based on a proposed maximum similarity, satisfies Lewis' axioms. Nute [4] gives a comprehensive recent overview on Conditional Logic. Our concern is with the notion of relevant worlds among alternative ones, not with the particular logic used in each world. In fact, our approach seeks to characterize worlds used for the evaluation of a counterfactual, where the truth of the premises is essential (i.e. relevant) for a classical deduction of the conclusion. This method is distinct from the use of some relevance logic [6,7,8,9] within each world.

In the second section Lewis' classic proposal for counterfactuals is introduced, as well as some examples. In the third and fifth sections we present our proposal. In the fourth section a definition for similarity (from [2]) is introduced. In the sixth some examples are examined and we contrast both approaches and argue in favour of ours. In the seventh we define relevant counterfactuals in terms of classical ones. In the remainder we refer to open problems and future explorations.

2. Lewis' counterfactuals

Counterfactuals are usually defined based on the notion of possible (or alternative) worlds, and the definition of the truth value of the counterfactual p > q[1] considers the possible worlds "maximally similar" to the world where the counterfactual is to be evaluated. We don't need to quantify how similar two worlds S_1 and S_2 are, but only to define a partial order between worlds (set of formulas) enabling to find whether S_1 is more similar than S_2 with respect to S.

Given a definition of similarity relation $\geq_F$ that nests layers of similar worlds relative to F, obeying some reasonable precepts[2], Lewis [1] defines p > q to be true in some world F only in either of two cases:

(A) if there exists some world U such that:
(A1) p is true in U and
(A2) p → q is true in any world V with $V \geq_F U$ (i.e. if V is any world at least as similar to F as U is, q will hold in V if p does[3]);
(B) if there is no possible world U in which p holds (p > q is vacuously true).

Lewis uses □→ in place of >. Let p-world mean a world where p holds. He also provides a "might" counterfactual defined as p ◇→ q $=_{def}$ ~(p □→ ~q), meaning "there is a nearest p-world where p → q".

The counterfactual implication is also equivalently defined by Lewis [1] in a different way, directly based on a notion of maximally similar worlds. Let $f(p,w)$ stand for the set of nearest p-worlds from w.

$$p >_w q =_{def} f(p,w) \subset [\![q]\!] \tag{1}$$

where f is a selection function (page 57 in [1]), where $[\![q]\!]$ represents the set of worlds in which q is true, and meaning: "the counterfactual implication p > q is true in the world w iff in all the nearest p-worlds from w, q is also true", or in other words if the set of the nearest p-worlds is a subset of the q-worlds.

Lewis derives a similar equivalent definition for the "might" counterfactual implication:

---

[1] We represent the counterfactual "if it would be the case that a then b" by a > b.
[2] (i) The relation is transitive. (ii) For any worlds J and K, either $J \geq_F K$ or $K \geq_F J$. (iii) F $\geq_F$ F. (iv) For any world $J \neq F$, $J >_F F$.
[3] Note that it is not required that the U in (A) be the most similar world to F that enjoys (A1) and (A2) above. Thus, choosing as U a similar world obeying (A1), makes (A2) easier to evaluate.

$$p \leftrightarrow_w q \equiv f(p,w) \cap [\![q]\!] \neq \{ \} \qquad\qquad (1')$$

meaning "there is a nearest p-world from w such that q is true"

Example

Let $S_1 = \{p, q\}$ and $S_2 = \{p, p \rightarrow q\}$, and the counterfactual $p > q$. S_1 and S_2 are two cases where the antecedent of the counterfactual is already true. For both S_1 (and also S_2) the set of its most similar worlds is the set containing just itself, and for these worlds whenever p is true q is true and so $p \rightarrow q$ is true. Later we shall argue that in the first case (set S_1), this result is not very interesting since q is already true anyway.

Note that no full definition of similarity was required in this example. It is not our aim to discuss preferable or possible defining forms of similarity between worlds. In fact, we will use later a notion of maximum similarity taken from [2], since we can elect to choose, in (A) above, always the most similar world U to F just like in Lewis' above definition (1).

3. Relevance in counterfactual reasoning

Our aim is to capture a notion of relevance between the antecedent and consequent of a counterfactual implication. In world S_1 the truth value of **q** does not depend on the truth value of **p**, while in S_2 there is a connection between the truth values of **p** and **q**. In other words, in S_1 the counterfactual implications $p > q$ or $\sim p > q$ are true whatever the truth value of the antecedent may be: it's truth is independent from it. In other words, the antecedent is irrelevant for the consequent.

This happens because whenever q is true, any counterfactual $X > q$, is true because of (A2); or because of (B) if X is false everywhere. The same isn't true for S_2.

To try to capture the notion of counterfactual relevance first we need to define a generalization of the selection function f of (1), where now the second argument may be a set of worlds instead of being a single world. If S is a set of worlds we redefine f, in terms of its previous definition, as:

$$f(p,S) =_{def} \bigcup_{i \in S} f(p,i) \qquad\qquad (2)$$

We can define the relevant counterfactual implication "if it would be the case that p then it would relevantly be the case that q" as follows:

$$p >_R q =_{def} (f(p,\{w\}) \subset [\![q]\!]) \wedge (f(p, f(\sim q, f(p,\{w\}))) \cap [\![q]\!] \neq \{ \}) \quad (3)$$

where f is our generalization of the selection function; thus the previous $f(p,w)$ becomes now $f(p,\{w\})$.

Recall that the first part of the definition is the same as the classical one in (1), and we add the extra condition

$$f(p, f(\sim q, f(p,\{w\}))) \cap [\![q]\!] \neq \{\} \tag{4}$$

so (3) could also be written as

$$p >_R q \equiv p > q \wedge (f(p, f(\sim q, f(p,\{w\}))) \cap [\![q]\!] \neq \{\}) \tag{3'}$$

The extra condition (4) says that "for some element of $f(p,\{w\})$ there must exist a nearest ~q-world, in relation to which there must exist some nearest p-world where q holds".

Some remarks are in order:

i) The motivation for (4) is to test implicational relevance in each $f(p,\{w\})$: first alternative nearest worlds are found where any proofs of q in $f(p,\{w\})$ are inhibited; next, in some such world, q must be reobtained when p is introduced.

ii) By (3) the set of worlds where $p >_R q$ is true is a subset of the worlds where $p > q$ is true; in other words:

$$p >_R q \rightarrow p > q.$$

iii) (4) also shows that $p >_R q$ is true just in those cases where a p-world exists because otherwise the first set of the intersection in the left-hand side of (4) is $\{\}$.

iv) By (4) $p >_R q$ only if there exists a p-world such that q holds; so if $p \equiv F$ then $p >_R q$ is false, though $p > q$ is vacuously true.

We similarly define a relevant might counterfactual:

$$p \diamondsuit\!\!\rightarrow_R q =_{def} p \diamondsuit\!\!\rightarrow q \wedge (f(p, f(\sim q, f(p,\{w\}))) \cap [\![q]\!] \neq \{\})$$

4. Maximum similarity between worlds according to Ginsberg

For convenience we recall some definitions and results from [2][4]:

Consider a consistent world S and the counterfactual $p > q$:

(i) if $S \models p$ the closest world in which p holds is S itself

(ii) if $S \not\models p$ and $S \not\models \sim p$ the closest world is $S \cup \{p\}$

(iii) if $S \models \sim p$ one just needs to identify the worlds obtained by minimally removing formulas from S until ~p cannot be deduced anymore

Let the collection of maximally close possible worlds for p in S be:

$$W(p,S) =_{def} \{T \subseteq S \mid T \not\models \sim p \text{ and } T \subset U \subseteq S \Rightarrow U \models \sim p\} \tag{5}$$

Now, for all cases, the counterfactual $p > q$ is defined to be true in a world S iff for every $T \in W(p,S)$, $T \cup \{p\} \models q$. He shows that the definition of possible worlds obeys the

---

[4] See [2] for some remarks on other accounts of similarity.

Gärdenfors axioms [5] (cf. section 8), which characterize Lewis' system, and so complies with Lewis' semantics. Ginsberg's p > q corresponds to defining, in **(1)**:

$$f(p,S) =_{def} \{T \cup \{p\} \mid T \in W(p,S)\}$$

In the sequel, whenever necessary, we will use Ginsberg's maximum similarity relation, though other definitions could, of course, be retained.

5. Relevant closest worlds

One outstanding issue regarding $p >_R q$ is to define "q-relevant p-world nearest to w". Till now we have only provided a necessary criterium for the truth of $p >_R q$ in the present world, additionally to the classic requirement for the $p > q$. The criterium requires the existance of some world $U \in f(p, f(\sim q, f(p,\{w\}))) \cap [\![q]\!]$. A p-world belonging to $f(p,\{w\})$ is a q-relevant p-world nearest to w iff it originates, by the previous formula, some such world U. As a result of the way f was defined in the previous section, the formulas of U are contained in the corresponding $f(p,\{w\})$ worlds; thus all the proofs of q relying on p in U exist also in the latter.

Let V be a q-relevant p-world nearest to w. We define $W_R(p,q,w)$, the set of "q-relevant maximally close possible worlds for p in w", as follows:

$$W_R(p,q,w) =_{def} \{ T \mid \text{for each } V, T = V - \{p\} \text{ if } p \notin w \text{ else } T = V\}$$

Equivalently it can be defined as:

$$W_R(p,q,w) =_{def} \{ T \in W(p,w) \mid T \cup \{p\} \text{ is q-relevant p-world nearest to w } \}$$

6. Examples of application

Example 1
Consider the following interpretation:

$p \equiv$ tweety is a bird, and $q \equiv$ tweety flies

Consider again the world $S_1 = \{p, q\}$ and the counterfactual $p >_R q$; then:

$$f(p,S_1) = S_1$$

$$f(\sim q,S_1) = \{ \{p, \sim q\} \}$$

$$f(p,f(\sim q,f(p,S_1))) = \{ \{p, \sim q\} \}$$

and so

$$f(p,f(\sim q,f(p,S_1))) \cap [\![\,q\,]\!] = \{\}$$

and thus $p >_R q$ is false: there is no relevance, in world S_1, between flying and being a bird.

Consider the set $S_2 = \{p, p \to q\}$ and again the counterfactual implication $p >_R q$; then:

$$f(p,S_2) = S_2$$

$$f(\sim q,S_2) = \{\{p,\sim q\}, \{p \to q,\sim q\}\}$$

$$f(p,f(\sim q,S_2)) = \{\{p,\sim q\}, \{p,p \to q\}\}$$

and so

$$f(p,f(\sim q,f(p,S_2))) \cap [\![\,q\,]\!] = \{\{p,p \to q\}\} \neq \{\}$$

and thus $p >_R q$ is true since $p > q$ is also true. In S_2 there is a clear expression of the relevance of being a bird to flying. Note also that $W_R(p,q,S_2) = S_2$.

Example 2
Consider again the set $S_1 = \{p,q\}$ and the counterfactual $\sim p >_R q$:

$$f(\sim p,S_1) = \{\{\sim p,q\}\}$$

$$f(\sim q,\{\sim p,q\}) = \{\{\sim p,\sim q\}\}$$

$$f(\sim p,\{\}) = \{\{\sim p,\sim q\}\}$$

and so

$$f(\sim p,f(\sim q,f(\sim p,S_1))) \cap [\![\,q\,]\!] = \{\}$$

thus the counterfactual $\sim p >_R q$ is false, though $p > q$ is true.

Example 3
Consider the set $S_3 = \{p \to q, \sim p \to q\}$ and the counterfactual $p >_R q$:
Let S' be $f(p,S_3) = \{\{p, p \to q, \sim p \to q\}\}$
Let S" be $f(\sim q,S') = \{\{\sim q, p, \sim p \to q\}\}$
$$f(p,S") = \{\{p, \sim q, \sim p \to q\}\}$$
and so
$$f(p,f(\sim q,f(p,S_3))) \cap [\![\,q\,]\!] = \{\}$$

and thus the counterfactual $p >_R q$ is false, though $p > q$ is true. Symmetrically, $\sim p >_R q$ will also be false. In fact, q is true independently of the value of p; hence the irrelevancy result.

Example 4
Consider the counterfactual implication $\sim q >_R \sim p$ (if tweety would not fly it would not be a bird). We argue that the implication must be false in the world $S_1 = \{p,q\}$ since in it it is not relevant to being a bird to be able to fly. We have in this case:

Let S' be $f(\sim q,S_1) = \{\{p, \sim q\}\}$

Since $f(\sim\sim p,S') = S'$

$f(\sim q, f(\sim\sim p, f(\sim q, S_1))) = \{\{p, \sim q\}\}$

so, and as $\sim q \to \sim p$ is false in this world (equivalently, $\{\{p, \sim q\}\} \cap [\![\sim p]\!] = \{\}$), we have $\sim q >_R \sim p$ is false.

On the other hand, if we consider again the world $S_2 = \{p, p \to q\}$, one might expect $\sim q >_R \sim p$ to be true since there is now some relevance for being a bird regarding the ability to fly (syntactically expressed by the material implication $p \to q$).

For this case we have:

Let S' be $f(\sim q, S_2) = \{\{p, \sim q\}, \{p \to q, \sim q\}\}$

Let S" be $f(\sim\sim p, S') = \{\{p \to q, p\}, \{\sim q, p\}\}$

$f(\sim q, S") = \{\{p, \sim q\}, \{p \to q, \sim q\}\}$

and so there is a world where $\sim q \to \sim p$ (equivalently: $\{\{\sim q, p \to q\}\} \cap [\![\sim p]\!] \neq \{\}$), but $\sim q >_R \sim p$ is false, since $\sim q > \sim p$ is false (there is a nearest $\sim q$-world, $\{p, \sim q\}$ where $\sim q \to \sim p$ is false).

Important remark

Note also that although from a model-theoretical standpoint S_1 and S_2 are equivalent, in that $S_1 \models p$ iff $S_2 \models p$, we draw from them quite different relevant counterfactual conclusions. This holds also for the classical counterfactual, but only our approach justifies the rôle played by the difference in representation.

Thus, though $p >_R q$ is true, its contrapositive $\sim q >_R \sim p$ is false. In general, as for regular counterfactuals, the rules of contraposition, transitivity, and strengthening of the antecedent, are not valid for relevant counterfactuals. The results depend of course on the similarity measure used. For instance, in example 3, if implications such as $p \to q$ are only removed after facts, because they are considered laws, then we would indeed have $\sim q > \sim p$. Alternatively, one might consider the facts hard. and the theory (in the form of implications) as flimsy.

Example 5

Let $S_4 = \{a \to p, b \to p, a \vee b\}$ and consider the counterfactual implication $\sim a >_R p$. Note that $S_4 \cup \{\sim a\} \models p$, so $\sim a > p$ is true; here we have:

$S' = f(\sim a, S_3) = \{\{\sim a, a \to p, b \to p, a \vee b\}\}$

$S" = f(\sim p, S') = \{\{\sim p, \sim a, a \to p, b \to p\}, \{\sim p, a \to p, a \vee b, \sim a\}\}$

$f(\sim a, f(\sim p, f(\sim a, S_3))) = S" = \{\{\sim p, \sim a, a \to p, b \to p\}, \{\sim p, a \to p, a \vee b, \sim a\}\}$

and

$f(\sim a, f(\sim p, f(\sim a, S_3))) \cap [\![p]\!] = \{\}$

so $\sim a >_R p$ is false.

Example 6

Consider the following domain (borrowed from [3]):

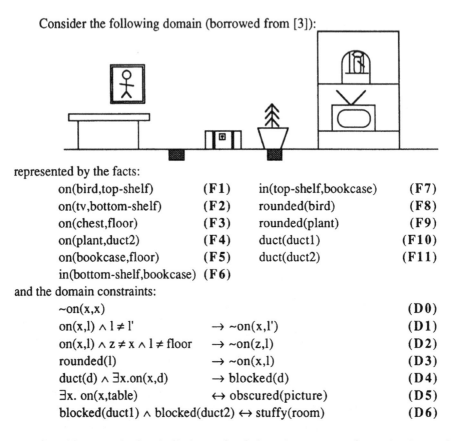

represented by the facts:

on(bird,top-shelf)	**(F1)**	in(top-shelf,bookcase)	**(F7)**
on(tv,bottom-shelf)	**(F2)**	rounded(bird)	**(F8)**
on(chest,floor)	**(F3)**	rounded(plant)	**(F9)**
on(plant,duct2)	**(F4)**	duct(duct1)	**(F10)**
on(bookcase,floor)	**(F5)**	duct(duct2)	**(F11)**
in(bottom-shelf,bookcase)	**(F6)**		

and the domain constraints:

$\sim$on(x,x)		**(D0)**
on(x,l) $\wedge$ l $\neq$ l'	$\rightarrow$ $\sim$on(x,l')	**(D1)**
on(x,l) $\wedge$ z $\neq$ x $\wedge$ l $\neq$ floor	$\rightarrow$ $\sim$on(z,l)	**(D2)**
rounded(l)	$\rightarrow$ $\sim$on(x,l)	**(D3)**
duct(d) $\wedge$ $\exists$x.on(x,d)	$\rightarrow$ blocked(d)	**(D4)**
$\exists$x. on(x,table)	$\leftrightarrow$ obscured(picture)	**(D5)**
blocked(duct1) $\wedge$ blocked(duct2) $\leftrightarrow$ stuffy(room)		**(D6)**

For this example the similarity notion is based upon removing only clauses from the facts (and none from the domain constraints), for which we will give the steps for evaluating relevant counterfactuals according to expression **(4)**, in the world S defined by the set of all clauses above.

Consider the counterfactual, "**if the tv would be on the bottom-shelf then the bird would be on the top-shelf**": on(tv,bottom-shelf) $>_R$ on(bird,top-shelf).

S'= f(on(tv,bottom-shelf),S) = S

Let S" be f($\sim$on(bird,top-shelf),S) = S – {on(bird,top-shelf)} $\cup$ {$\sim$on(bird,top-shelf)}

then f(on(tv,bottom-shelf),S_1) = S' since on(tv,bottom-shelf) is already true.

Since f(on(tv,bottom-shelf),f($\sim$on(bird,top-shelf),S')) $\cap$ $[\![$on(bird,top-shelf)$]\!]$ = { }, we have that on(tv,bottom-shelf) $>_R$ on(bird,top-shelf) is false. However, the classical version of this counterfactual is true, which seems pointless.

This happens in general when we are trying to evaluate the counterfactual p > q in a world S which already has the formulas p and q (i.e. S = S'$\cup$ {p,q}).

Consider the counterfactual "**if the tv would be on the table then the picture would be obscured**": on(tv,table) $>_R$ obscured(picture).

Let S' be f(on(tv,table),S) = S - {on(tv,bottom-shelf)} $\cup$ {on(tv,table)}

Let S" be f(~obscured(picture),S') = S' - {on(tv,table)} $\cup$ {~obscured(picture)}

f(on(tv,table),S") = S" $\cup$ {on(tv,table)}

Thus as S' $\models$ obscured(picture) by **(D5)** and {on(tv,table)}, the counterfactual is true.

In this case classical counterfactual implication gives the same result.

One interesting case to analyze is the counterfactual "**if the tv were not on the bottom-shelf then the room could be stuffy**": ~on(tv,bottom-shelf) $>_R$ $\not\models$ ~stuffy(room).

Let S' be f(~on(tv,bottom-shelf),S) = S - {on(tv,bottom-shelf)} $\cup$ {~on(tv,bottom-shelf)}

Let S" be f(~stuffy(room),S') = S' $\cup$ {~stuffy(room)}

f(~on(tv,bottom-shelf),S") = S" and S" $\cap [\![\not\models$ ~stuffy(room) $]\!]$ = { }

and in this case the counterfactual is false.

On the other hand, if we want to assume the tv not being on bottom-shelf means it being at some place else in S, we can do it by stating that everything except the floor is on something:

$$\exists y \ on(x,y) \leftarrow x \neq floor \qquad\qquad \text{(D7)}$$

which we add as another domain constraint.

In this case we will have instead

$$f(\text{~on(tv,bottom-shelf)},S") \cap [\![\not\models \text{~stuffy(room)}]\!] \neq \{ \}$$

since, given **(D7)**, it is not possible to disallow ~on(tv,duct1) and hence $\not\models$ ~stuffy(room) in S". Now the counterfactual becomes true.

Other examples of the application of counterfactual reasoning in domains such as planning and diagnosis can be found in [2].

7. Definition of relevant counterfactuals in terms of classical ones

An equivalent definition to **(4)** is

$$p >_R q \equiv (p \: \square\!\!\rightarrow q) \wedge (p \leftrightarrow (\text{~}q \diamond\!\!\rightarrow (p \diamond\!\!\rightarrow q))) \qquad\qquad \text{(6)}$$

where the extra condition can be rephrased as:

"there exists one most similar p-world such that there exists one most similar ~q-world such that, relative to it, there exists a p-world such that p → q". In fact, looking at the extra condition in (4) it can be read, as another way of expressing the above rephrasing of the extra condition in (6) when (1') is taken into account, so they ought to be equivalent.

Note that in (1) the counterfactual implication is indexed by the world where it is evaluated. In the case of (6) the inner counterfactual connective $\leftrightarrow$ is implicitly indexed by the set of worlds where it must be evaluated:

$$p >_R q \equiv (p \,\square\!\!\rightarrow_w q) \wedge (p \leftrightarrow_w (\sim q \leftrightarrow_{f(p,w)} (p \leftrightarrow_{f(\sim q,f(p,w))} q))) \qquad (6')$$

and using (1') with the generalization of f, the embedded connectives rewrite to $f(p,f(\sim q,f(p,\{w\}))) \cap [\![q]\!] \neq \{\}$, which is the extra condition in (4).

Now let's show how the connective $>_R$ can be expressed solely in terms of the $>$ connective. This might be of interest in order to verify whether Gärdenfors' axioms for Lewis' system hold (cf. open problems) when we replace the classic connective of counterfactual implication by the relevant counterfactual connective. Furthermore it also shows another rephrasing of relevancy by interpreting that equivalent formulation.

Recall that $p \leftrightarrow q =_{def} \sim(p \,\square\!\!\rightarrow \sim q)$ so (4) becomes successively:

$$p >_R q \equiv (p \,\square\!\!\rightarrow q) \wedge (p \leftrightarrow (\sim q \leftrightarrow (p \leftrightarrow q)))$$

$$p >_R q \equiv (p \,\square\!\!\rightarrow q) \wedge \sim(p \,\square\!\!\rightarrow \sim(\sim q \leftrightarrow (p \leftrightarrow q)))$$

$$p >_R q \equiv (p \,\square\!\!\rightarrow q) \wedge \sim(p \,\square\!\!\rightarrow \sim\sim(\sim q \,\square\!\!\rightarrow \sim(p \leftrightarrow q)))$$

$$p >_R q \equiv (p \,\square\!\!\rightarrow q) \wedge \sim(p \,\square\!\!\rightarrow \sim\sim(\sim q \,\square\!\!\rightarrow \sim\sim(p \leftrightarrow q)))$$

and finally

$$p >_R q \equiv (p \,\square\!\!\rightarrow q) \wedge \sim(p \,\square\!\!\rightarrow (\sim q \,\square\!\!\rightarrow (p \,\square\!\!\rightarrow \sim q))) \qquad (7)$$

or, changing notation

$$p >_R q \equiv (p > q) \wedge \sim(p > (\sim q > (p > \sim q))) \qquad (7')$$

We can read (7') as stating that, besides the classical condition $p > q$, for $p >_R q$ to be true, $p > (\sim q > (p > \sim q))$ must be false, i. e., there must exist a world w where p is true and $p \rightarrow (\sim q > (p > \sim q)) \equiv F$; since p is true $(\sim q > (p > \sim q)) \equiv F$ in w, i.e. there must exist a world v where ~q is true and $\sim q \rightarrow (p > \sim q) \equiv F$; since ~q is true, $p > \sim q \equiv F$ in v. So there exists a world such that p is true and $p \rightarrow \sim q \equiv F$, which means that $\sim q \equiv F$ and so $q \equiv T$. (Compare this reading with that of (6).)

Special cases of $p >_R q$ which differ from $p > q$:
- if p is false in every world (this is the case defined as **vacuously true** in [1]), $p >_R q$ becomes false.
- if ~q is true in every world: $p \,\square\!\!\rightarrow \sim q$, is always true, and so are $\sim q \,\square\!\!\rightarrow (p \,\square\!\!\rightarrow \sim q)$ and $(p \,\square\!\!\rightarrow (\sim q \,\square\!\!\rightarrow (p \,\square\!\!\rightarrow \sim q)))$; thus $p >_R q$ is false.

These cases are coherent with the intended meaning of $p >_R q$, which requires relevancy.

8. Open problems

The counterfactual truth-value is dependant on the knowledge representation clause set used; i.e., given two sets S_1 and S_2 which are equivalent from the model-theoretical point of view, the same counterfactual implication may give different results, a point already made by Ginsberg [2]. It seems an expected result when the definition of similarity is based only on a syntactic notion, since the same models may be obtained from several syntactically different clause sets. Further exploration of this representation issue is needed.

On the other hand, different proposals for counterfactual evaluation capture different epistemological interpretations. Our proposal seems to give more intuitive results than Ginsberg's, since it requires a notion of relevance between the antecedent and the consequent of the implication. This seems evident by comparing results on the two sets of clauses $S_1=\{p, q\}$ and $S_2=\{p, p \rightarrow q\}$, as in examples 1 and 2.

Another topic of interest is to verify whether Gärdenfors' axioms (cf. [5,2]) for Lewis' system hold when we replace the classic connective of counterfactual implication by the relevant counterfactual one, and to compare both systems on an axiomatic basis.

9. Future explorations

Counterfactual reasoning involves the ability to answer "what-if" questions: e.g. "would C be true if H were true ?". It also involves the ability to deal with "what-if" of hypothetical statements: e.g. "C would be true if only H were made to be true". In both cases, H may be inconsistent with the present theory T, which has to be minimally revised to accommodate the set of hypothesis H. Concepts which are of the essence here include:

• the idea of minimality, according to preferred criteria;

• H must be relevant to C; even if C is already true, because H may lend extra support to C. This is crucial if other supports of C may be withdrawn.

We want to explore, in some more general framework for non-monotonic knowledge, hypothetical reasoning, counterfactual reasoning, default and abductive reasoning. There seems to exist some relations between these reasoning schemes; given a theory:

i) in **abductive reasoning** one <u>finds</u> additional consistent assumptions that condition an answer;

ii) in **default reasoning** one <u>makes</u> consistent retractable additional assumptions to derive an answer;

iii) in **counterfactual reasoning** one <u>imposes</u> assumptions, that in general require modifying the theory so as to restore consistency before obtaining an answer.

One interesting general point is that counterfactual reasoning can show how something can be made true even if it isn't, which is a form of abductive reasoning. One interesting problem is the definition of these reasoning schemes in a framework where the frame problem and the qualification problem are "already" solved.

We assumed here a simple definition of similarity between worlds. In a more general framework, alternative definitions for similarity may be used (e.g. default knowledge may be questionable whereas domain constraints may never be retracted, and assumed true for all worlds), thus directing the searching for possible worlds. Anyway, from the implementation point of view this approach still leads to an explosion of the possible worlds, since it seems that in the most realistic models of the real world most of the rules are "default" ones.

Acknowledgements

ESPRIT BRA on Computational Logic (COMPULOG), Instituto Nacional de Investigação Científica, Gabinete de Filosofia do Conhecimento, Junta Nacional de Investigação Científica e Tecnológica.

References

1. Lewis, D., Counterfactuals, Harvard University Press, Cambridge, MA. Revised edition, 1986.
2. Ginsberg, Matthew L., *Counterfactuals*, Artificial Intelligence **30** (1986), pp. 35-79.
3. Ginsberg, Matthew L., Smith, David E., *Reasoning about Action I:A Possible Worlds Approach* Artificial Intelligence **35**, pp. 165-195, 1988.
4. Nute, Donald, *Conditional Logic*, in Handbook of Philosophical Logic Vol .2, pp. 387-439, (eds. D. Guenthner and D. Gabbay), D. Reidel, 1986.
5. Gärdenfors, P., *Conditionals and changes of belief*, Acta Philos. Fennica **30** (1978), pp. 381-404.
6. Anderson and Belnap, Entailment: The Logic of Relevance and Necessity, Princeton University Press, 1975.
7. Read, S., Relevant Logic, Basil Blackwell, 1988.
8. Routley, F.R. et al. Relevant Logics and their rivals, Atascadero, California, 1982.
9. Dunn, J.M., *Relevant Logic and Entailment*, in Handbook of Philosophical Logic, Vol 3, pp. 177-224, (eds. D. Guenthner and D. Gabbay), D. Reidel, 1986.

Non-monotonic Reasoning with the ATMS

F. Zetzsche
Battelle-Institut e.V.
Am Römerhof 35
6 Frankfurt a.M. 90
West Germany

Abstract

By viewing a default rule $t_1 \ldots t_n; U s_1 \ldots U s_m / t$ as a monotonic ATMS justification with assumptions $U s_i$, we are able to prove a 1-1 correspondence between the admissible extensions (well-founded labellings) of a Doyle-like TMS and certain extensions of the associated ATMS.

To obtain this result, we modelled the TMS as a non-monotonic reasoning system according to Reiter and the ATMS as a (classical) monotonic reasoning system. The result is therefore interesting in the more general context of non-monotonic reasoning as well.

1   Introduction

To solve problems it is usually necessary to state assumptions and to retract them in case of a conflict. Reason Maintenance Systems, formerly called Truth Maintenance Systems, are designed to support a problem solver in this respect.

In this paper we are concerned with two of the most popular systems of this kind, namely the TMS of Doyle [4] and the ATMS (assumption based truth maintenance system) of de Kleer [1]. The two systems mainly differ in the following point. Whereas the TMS allows non-monotonic justifications but restricts the problem solver to one context, the ATMS supports monotonic justifications only but enables reasoning in multiple contexts.

The computation of certain "extensions" may be seen as a central task of both systems. In this paper we will show that for every Doyle-like TMS specification there is an associated ATMS specification, such that the extensions of the one system correspond 1-1 to the extensions of the other. In order to do this, we view a default rule $t_1 \ldots t_n; U s_1 \ldots U s_m / t$ as a monotonic ATMS justification with assumptions $U s_i$. The admissible extensions (well founded labellings) of the TMS will then correspond bijectivly to those ATMS extensions C with the property $t \in C \Leftrightarrow U t \notin C$.

Our result contributes to a better understanding of the relationship between assumption and justification based reason maintenance systems. Especially, it provides the foundation for an integrated non-monotonic ATMS.

To prove our result, we have modelled the TMS as a non-monotonic reasoning system according to Reiter [8] and the ATMS as a (classical) monotonic reasoning system. Hence, the result is interesting in the general context of non-monotonic reasoning, too.

Non-monotonic reasoning with the ATMS has also investigated by de Kleer [2] and Dressler [5], but in both approaches a rigorous formal treatment is lacking. Furthermore, both suggested modellings seem to be incorrect. In section seven we give an example which indicates some shortcomings in the case of Dressler's approach, as a more detailed discussion is not possible within the scope of this paper.

The paper is organised in the following way: First, we give the relevant definitions of a monotonic and non-monotonic reasoning system respectively. We then formulate the concepts of the TMS and the ATMS in terms of the associated reasoning systems. With these preliminaries we are able to state and prove our claim. We conclude the paper with a detailed discussion of the example mentioned above.

2 Monotonic Reasoning Systems

Both, the TMS of Doyle and the ATMS of de Kleer are defined by an operational semantic, i.e. the system behavior is defined by procedures that perform some kind of computations. Therfore, one way to compare the two systems would be to show that they perform similar computations. However, we prefer a comparison on a more abstract level.

For this we need the notion of derivability. In the monotonic case the definitions are standard, so we treat this point in some brevity.

Definition 2.1 A monotonic reasoning system is a triple (M, R, A), consisting of

- a non-empty set M,

- a non-empty set R of (formal) expressions

$$\frac{t_1 \ldots t_n}{t}$$

with $t_1 \ldots t_n, t \in M$, $n \geq 0$,

- a (possibly empty) set A, with $A \subseteq M$.

The elements of R are called rules and the elements of A are called axioms. In case $A = \emptyset$ we simply denote the system by (M, R). Often the involved sets are required to fulfil certain additional requirements like, for example, the recursivity of R. For our purpose, however, the above definition is sufficient.

Definition 2.2 Let (M, R, A) be a monotonic reasoning system. We define the associated funktor $\Gamma \in 2^M \to 2^M$ by

$$\Gamma = \lambda X. X \cup \{t \mid \exists \frac{t_1 \dots t_n}{t} \in R \wedge t_1 \dots t_n \in X\}.$$

The following theorem is an immediate consequence of the definition of Γ.

Theorem 2.3 Γ is monotonic and continuous w.r.t to the (natural) cpo-structure on 2^M.

We are now able to formalize the concept of derivability.

Definition 2.4 Let $X \subseteq M$. We define the set $C(X)$ of all elements that are derivable from X by $C(X) = \bigcup \Gamma_i(X)$, where

$$\Gamma_0(X) = X \cup A; \quad \Gamma_{i+1}(X) = \Gamma(\Gamma_i(X))$$

For $t \in M$ we also denote $t \in C(X)$ by $X \vdash t$ and call t derivable from X.

Finally we give the usual fixpoint characterization of $C(X)$.

Theorem 2.5 $C(X)$ is the least fixpoint Y of Γ fulfilling $X \cup A \subseteq Y$.

3 The ATMS

An ATMS maintains the derivations of a problem solver in form of a labeled dependency network. The nodes of the network represent propositions in which the problem solver is interested. Some nodes may be labeled as assumptions, all other nodes are required to have at least one justification in form of a list of nodes. The ATMS uses these justifications to compute all minimal sets of assumption for every node that justify that node. Given this labelling, it is straightforward to determine the context of a consistent set of assumptions, i.e. the set of all nodes that are justified by these assumptions. Actually, the determination of contexts and extensions (maximal contexts) may be considered to be the central task of an ATMS.

We now formalize the ATMS specification given in [1]. We will consider the ATMS as a monotonic reasoning system as described in the preceding section. It can be shown, that our formalization is correct w.r.t. the computing of labellings as given in [1], see [10].

Definition 3.1 An ATMS specification (N, A, J, Nog) is given by the following data:

- a non-empty set N, whose elements are called nodes.

- a set A, disjoint with N, whose elements are called assumptions

- a non-empty set of justifications J, i.e. expressions of the form

$$n_1 \dots n_k; a_1 \dots a_m \Rightarrow n$$

where $n_1 \dots n_k, n \in N$ and $a_1 \dots a_m \in A$. Here, the list n_i and the list a_j may be empty.

- a set $Nog \subseteq 2^A$, whose elements are called nogoods.

A set of assumptions is called an environment.

Definition 3.2

- $Env = 2^A$. The elements of Env are called environments.

Every ATMS can be associated with a monotonic reasoning system in a natural way, with the set of axioms taken to be empty.

Definition 3.3 Let (N, A, J, Nog) denote an ATMS specification. We then define the associated monotonic reasoning system $(N \cup A, R)$ by the set of rules R given by

$$R = \{\frac{n_1 \dots n_k, a_1 \dots a_m}{n} \mid [n_1 \dots n_k; a_1 \dots a_m \Rightarrow n] \in J\}.$$

Definition 3.4 Let $E \in Env$.

- E is called consistent (inconsistent), in case $E \notin Nog$ ($E \in Nog$).

- If $C(E')$ is maximal in $\{C(E) \mid E \text{ consistent}\}$, then $C(E')$ is called an extension and E' is called an interpretation of $C(E')$.

We will show later (Lemma 6.5) that for every extension there is exactly one interpretation.

Our definition of inconsistency (nogoods) is less specific then that given in [1], where

$$E \in Nog \Leftrightarrow E \vdash \perp,$$

with a special node $\perp \in N$. In the case that this definition is used, the ATMS will be called a Basic-ATMS.

Definition 3.5 A Basic-ATMS is a 4-tuple $(N, A, J, Nog, \perp)$, consisting of an ATMS specifikation (N, A, J, Nog) where $\perp \in N$ and $E \in Nog \Leftrightarrow E \vdash \perp$.

However, we will show that this simple notion of inconsistency will not be sufficient for modelling non-monotonic justifications.

4 Non-monotonic Reasoning Systems

In this section we state some important formal definitions of a Reiter-like non-monotonic reasoning system. Thereto we closely refer to the definitions given in Reiter [8]. We conclude this section with a straightforward alternative characterization of the so called (admissible) extensions. In spite of the simplicity of the characterization it seems to be new, and, especially, it differs from the one given in [8]. We will use this characterization in the next section to justify our modelling of a TMS as a non-monotonic reasoning system.

In the framework of this paper we can hardly give an introduction to the subject of non-monotonic reasoning. We therefore assume that the reader is familiar with default rules like "if $t_1 \ldots t_n$, then t, unless there is evidence for one of $s_1 \ldots s_m$".

Definition 4.1 A non-monotonic reasoning system is a triple (M, R, A), consisting of

- a non-empty set M,

- a non-empty set R of expressions

$$\frac{t_1 \ldots t_n; U s_1 \ldots U s_m}{t}$$

  where $t_1 \ldots t_n, s_1 \ldots s_m, t \in M$, $n, m \geq 0$,

- a (possibly empty) set A, where $A \subseteq M$.

The elements of R are called rules and the elements of A are called axioms. The above U-symbol is short for the unless-quantor and will be interpreted as a bijection of M into a set disjoint to M. Of course, any other syntactic representation of the rules that seperates the list t_i from the list s_j, would also be appropriate. As in the monotonic case we denote the system simply by the pair (M, R) if the set of axioms is empty.

We can also identify an associated functor for non-monotonic reasoning systems, as given in the following definition.

Definition 4.2 Let (M, R, A) be a non-monotonic reasoning system and $X \subseteq M$. We then define the funktor $\Gamma^X \in 2^M \to 2^M$ by

$$\Gamma^X = \lambda Y. Y \cup \{t \mid \exists \frac{t_1 \ldots t_n; U s_1 \ldots U s_m}{t} \in R, \ t_i \in Y, \ s_j \notin X\}.$$

Again, the following theorem is trivial.

Therorem 4.3 Γ^X is monotonic and continuous w.r.t. the cpo-structur on 2^M.

Note that Γ^X is not monotonic in X, i.e. $X \subseteq X'$ does not necessarily imply $\forall Y (\Gamma^X(Y) \subseteq \Gamma^{X'}(Y))$.

The next definition and theorem are analogous to 2.4 and 2.5 respectively.

Definition 4.4 Let $X, Y \subseteq M$. We define $C^X(Y)$ by $C^X(Y) = \bigcup \Gamma_i^X(Y)$, where

$$\Gamma_0^X(Y) = Y \cup A, \ \Gamma_{i+1}^X(Y) = \Gamma^X(\Gamma_i^X(Y))$$

Theorem 4.5 $C^X(Y)$ is the least fixpoint Z of Γ^X, where $Y \cup A \subseteq Z$.

As shown in Reiter [8], theorem 2.1, his notion of extension may be characterized by the following definition.

Definition 4.6 Let $X, Y \subseteq M$ and $A \cup Y \subseteq X$. X is called an admissible extension of Y iff $X = C^X(Y)$.

To establish the connection to the TMS we need the following definitions.

Definition 4.7 Let (M, R, A) be a non-monotonic reasoning system and $X, Y \subseteq M$.

- Y is called closed w.r.t. X, if for all $\frac{t_1 \ldots t_n ; U_{s_1} \ldots U_{s_m}}{t} \in R$ we have:

$$(t_1 \ldots t_n \in Y) \wedge (s_1 \ldots s_m \notin X) \Rightarrow (t \in Y)$$

We are calling X closed, if X is closed w.r.t. X.

- X is called grounded in Y, if $X \subseteq C^X(Y)$.

Our definition of groundedness differs a little bit from the one given in [7] but can be easily shown to be equivalent.

The following theorem characterizes the admissible extensions as the closed and grounded subsets of M.

Theorem 4.8 Let $X, Y \subseteq M$ and $A \cup Y \subseteq X$. Then we have: X is an admissible extension of Y iff X is closed and grounded in Y.

Proof Obviously, for all $Z \subseteq M$ we have $\Gamma^X(Z) = Z$ iff Z is closed w.r.t. X. Therfore $X = \Gamma^X(X)$ iff X is closed. The rest follows from the fact that for every fixpoint Z of Γ^X where $A \cup Y \subseteq Z$ and $Z \subseteq C^X(Y)$ we have $Z = C^X(Y)$, for $C^X(Y)$ is the least fixpoint Z of Γ^X where $Y \cup A \subseteq Z$. Δ

5 The TMS

Like the ATMS the TMS maintains the derivations of the problem solver in a labeled dependency network, however, the TMS allows non-monotonic justifications which consist of an inlist and an outlist. According to these justifications the TMS marks a node in or out. A node is marked in iff there is at least one justification for that node that is marked in. A justification is marked in iff all nodes in the inlist are marked in and all nodes of the outlist are marked out.

If the non-monotonic justifications are interpreted as the rules of a non-monotonic reasoning system with an empty set of axioms, it is straightforward to see that there is a 1-1 correspondence between the set of all nodes that are marked in and the closed subsets of the reasoning system.

To avoid circular justifications the labellings are required to fulfil an additional property, which is called well-foundedness. As noticed by Reinfrank [7] this property is equivalent to the property of groundedness of the reasoning system.

Accepting these equivalences, a TMS may be formalized as a non-monotonic reasoning system (note theorem 4.8). In this sense the computation of some of the admissible extensions may be considered to be the central task of the TMS. In the next section we will show that the ATMS is able to compute them as well.

6 TMS-ATMS

In this section we show that for every non-monotonic reasoning system there is an associated ATMS specification, such that the admissible extensions of the non-monotonic reasoning system correspond bijectivly to the extensions of the ATMS.

By modelling axioms as rules, we may assume in the following that the set of axioms of the non-monotonic reasoning system is empty.

Definition 6.1 Let (M, R) be a non-monotonic reasoning system. We then define the associated ATMS (M, A, J, Nog) by

$$A = \{Us \mid s \in M\}$$
$$J = \{[t_1 \ldots t_n; Us_1 \ldots Us_m \Rightarrow t] \mid \frac{t_1 \ldots t_n; Us_1 \ldots Us_m}{t} \in R\}$$
$$Nog = \{E \mid \neg(\forall s(s \in C(E) \Leftrightarrow Us \notin E))\}$$

Note that according to this definition the non-monotonic rules in R are interpreted as monotonic justifications with assumptions Us, which may be read as "it is consistent to assume $\neg s$" or "s can not be derived".

Theorem 6.2 Let (M, R) be a non-monotonic reasoning system and (M, A, J, Nog) the associated ATMS. Let adE the set of all admissible extensions (of the empty set) and Ext the set of all ATMS extensions. For $X \subseteq M$ let $E(X) = \{Ut \mid t \notin X\}$. Then the mapping

$$\lambda X.C(E(X))$$

defines a bijection $adE \rightarrow Ext$.

Proof We prove the theorem in four steps:

Lemma 6.3 $X \in adE \Leftrightarrow X = C(E(X)) \setminus E(X)$.

Proof We refer to the notation from the section on monotonic and non-monotonic reasoning systems. Let $X, Y \subseteq M$. From the definition of Γ and Γ^X we immediately have (note $M \cap A = \emptyset$)

$$\Gamma^X(Y) = \Gamma(Y \cup E(X)) \setminus E(X).$$

In the same manner we derive

$$\forall i : \Gamma_i^X(Y) = \Gamma_i(Y \cup E(X)) \setminus E(X).$$

Taking the union over all $\Gamma_i^X(Y)$, we finally have

$$C^X(Y) = C(Y \cup E(X)) \setminus E(X),$$

which was to be proved (for $Y = \emptyset$).

Lemma 6.4 Let $X \in adE$, then $C(E(X)) \in Ext$.

Proof We first show $E(X) \notin Nog$, i.e.

$$\forall s(s \in C(E(X)) \Leftrightarrow Us \notin E(X)).$$

Because of $s \notin E(X)$ the claim follows from the following equivalences

$$s \in C(E(X)) \Leftrightarrow s \in X \Leftrightarrow Us \notin E(X)$$

using the result of lemma 6.3.

Let $E = E(X)$. It remains to show, that $C(E)$ is maximal. Assume the contrary. Then there exists a $F \in Env$ where

$$C(E) \subseteq C(F), \; C(E) \neq C(F)$$

and $F \notin Nog$. But then there is a $Ut \in F$ where $Ut \notin E$, because otherwise we would have $F \subseteq E$ and thereby $C(F) \subseteq C(E)$, i.e. a contradiction.

From $Ut \in F$ and $F \notin Nog$ we may deduce $t \notin C(F)$. Because of $X \cup E = C(E) \subseteq C(F)$ we also have $t \notin X$, i.e $Ut \in E$, a contradiction!

The next lemma proves the injectivity of our mapping.

Lemma 6.5 Let $E, F \in Env$ and $C(E) = C(F)$. Then $E = F$.

Proof From $E \subseteq C(E)$ it follows $E \subseteq C(F)$. Since assumptions can not be derived we must have $E \subseteq F$. Similar arguments show $F \subseteq E$.

It remains to show the surjectivity of our mapping.

Lemma 6.6 Let $Y = C(E)$ where $E \notin Nog$. Let $X = C(E) \setminus E$. Then $X \in adE$ and $E = E(X)$.

Proof First note that due to lemma 6.5 X is well defined. Because of $E \notin Nog$ and $Y = C(E)$ we have

$$Ut \in E \Leftrightarrow t \notin Y \Leftrightarrow t \notin X$$

and thereby $E = E(X)$. From the definition of X and lemma 6.3 we deduce $X \in adE$. This concludes the proof of our lemma and also the proof of the theorem. $\triangle$

Note that in lemma 6.6 we did not explicitly require $Y \in Ext$. Together with the other lemmas we therefore have

Corollary 6.7 Let $Y = C(E)$ and $E \notin Nog$. Then $Y \in Ext$, i.e. all contexts are maximal.

Remark 6.8 Looking again to the above nogood specification

$$Nog = \{E \mid \neg(\forall s(s \in C(E) \Leftrightarrow Us \notin E))\}$$

it can be seen that we require for every context $C(E)$ and every $s \in M$ either $s \in C(E)$ or $Us \in C(E)$), but not both. It is now natural to ask, whether the condition

$$\neg((s \in C(E)) \wedge (Us \in C(E)))$$

(i.e. $s, Us \vdash \perp$ in the basic ATMS) would also be sufficient. That this is not the case is shown by an example due to Junker [6]. We will discuss this example in detail in the next section.

7 Example

Regard the following rules of a non-monotonic reasoning system:

$$\frac{}{a}, \quad \frac{a; Ub}{c}, \quad \frac{a; Uc}{d}.$$

It is easy to see that there is exactly one admissible extension, namely $\{a, c\}$. On the other hand the justifications

$$\Rightarrow a, \ a; Ub \Rightarrow c, \ a; Uc \Rightarrow d, \ s; Us \Rightarrow \perp, (s = a, b, c, d)$$

generate two Basic-ATMS extensions: $\{Ub, Ud, a, c\}$ and $\{Uc, a, d\}$.

This example points out that in general it isn't possible to do without the requirement $s \in C$ or $Us \in C$ for a context C. Note, that in the above example, the second extension contains neither b nor Ub.

Furthermore the example points out that the requirement $s \vee Us$ may not be viewed as an input to an extended ATMS or other similar systems. This is because we do not want to construct extensions that fulfil the constaint, but to rule out all those extensions that don't. For example, regard the following hypothetical inferences of a corresponding system: "It has to be $b \vee Ub$. Ub causes a contradiction. Thererfore it has to be b." So such a system would incorrectly construct the extension $\{Uc, a, b, d\}$.

As a matter of fact, exactly those inferences are made by Oskar Dressler's non-monotonic ATMS, [5]. Therefore, we think that Dressler's ATMS does not implement non-monotonic reasoning in the sense of Reiter's default logic. Instead, we think that Dressler has implemented some kind of negation, where it is possible to handle assumptions of the form $\neg s$.

Finally, for the sake of clarity, we would like to state the correct procedure for computing the admissible extensions again. First, compute all extensions C of the associated Basic-ATMS as indicated above. Then disregard all those that fail the test $\forall s (s \in C \vee Us \in C)$. From those extensions left remove all elements of the form Us, i.e. all assumptions. In this way all the admissible extensions of the non-monotonic system are obtained (refer lemma 6.6 und theorem 6.2).

8 Outlook

Currently we are working towards an integrated non-monotonic ATMS. That is, we want to handle non-monotonic justifications in the sense of this paper that support ordinary ATMS assumptions. The problem hereby is the correct computation of the admissible extensions of a given consistent environment of ordinary assumptions. Although it is not immediately appearant, this problem is much harder than the computation of the admissible extensions as indicated by the above example, but has hopefully been solved by now.

9 Conclusion

We have shown that a Doyle-like TMS can be modelled as a non-monotonic reasoning system according to Reiter. Furthermore, we have shown that the admissible extensions of such a non-monotonic reasoning system correspond bijectivly to certain extensions of the ATMS. For this purpose we have modelled the ATMS as a (classical) monotonic reasoning system. Our result therefore contributes to the area of truth maintenance and non-monotonic logics as well.

10   Acknowledgements

I would like to thank Oskar Dressler, Ulrich Junker, Michael Reinfrank, and Georg Zinser for valuable discussions. It seems, that Junker has independently derived a similar result.

This work has been supported by the "Bundesministerium für Forschung und Technik", West Germany, under the TEX-B project.

References

[1] Johan de Kleer. An Assumption Based TMS. *Artifical Intelligence, 28:127-162, 1986*

[2] Johan de Kleer. Extending the ATMS. *Artifical Intelligence, 28:163-196, 1986*

[3] Johan de Kleer. Problem solving with the ATMS. *Artifical Intelligence, 28:197-224, 1986*

[4] Jon Doyle. A Truth Maintenance System. *Artificial Intelligence,12:231-272, 1979*

[5] Oskar Dressler. Extending the Basic ATMS. *ECAI'88*

[6] Ulrich Junker. Einige Bemerkungen zu O.Dressler, Non-Monotonic Justifications for the Basic ATMS. *GMD, F3-HIS*

[7] Michael Reinfrank. An Introduction to Non-Monotonic Reasoning. *Technical Report MEMO-SEKI-85-02, Universität Kaiserslautern, June 1985*

[8] R. Reiter. A Logic for Default Reasoning. *ARTIFICIAL INTELLIGENCE 13*

[9] R. Reiter and J de Kleer. Foundations of Assumption-Based Truth Maintenance. *Proceedings AAAI-87, pp. 183-188*

[10] Frank Zetzsche. Einige Ergebnisse zur formalen Begründung des ATMS. *TEX-B Memo 43-88*

On the classification and existence of structures in default logic

Aidong Zhang [*]   Wiktor Marek[*]

Department of Computer Science
University of Kentucky
Lexington, KY 40506-0027

Abstract

We investigate possible belief sets of an agent reasoning with defaults. Besides of Reiter's extensions which are based on a proof-theoretic paradigm (similar to Logic Programming), other structures for default theories, based on weaker or different methods of constructing belief sets are considered, in particular, weak extensions and minimal sets. The first of these concepts is known to be closely connected to autoepistemic expansions of Moore, the other to minimal stable autoepistemic theories containing the initial assumptions. We introduce the concept of ranking collection of defaults and investigate the properties of largest ranking subset of the family D, determined by W. We find a necessary and sufficient condition for a weak extension to be an extension in terms of ranking. We prove that for theories (D, W) *without* extension, the least fixed point of the associated operator (with weak extension or minimal set as a context) is an extension of suitably chosen (D', W) with $D' \subseteq D$. We investigate conditions for existence of extensions and introduce the notion of perfectly-ranked set of defaults and its variant of maximally perfectly-ranked set. Existence of such set of defaults turns out to be equivalent to existence of extension. Finally, we investigate convergence of algorithm for computing extension.

1   Introduction

Default logic deals with default theories - pairs (D, W), where W is a collection of formulas and D is a collection of defaults that are used as non-monotonic inference rules to generate possible sets of consequences for W. In default logic, although it is widely agreed that an extension of $\Delta = (D, W)$ is precisely a set of reasonable beliefs of Δ, various default theories happen to have no extensions. In general default logic, so far, there is no simple syntactic characterization of default theories which have or do not have extensions. Some

---

[*] Work partially supported by National Science Foundation grant RII 8610671 and the Commonwealth of Kentucky EPSCoR program.

particular classes of default theories which guarantee existence of extensions have been introduced, such as Reiter's normal default theories and Etherington's semi-normal and ordered default theories([9,2,1]). But there is only a restricted progress in general case, because default rules' context-sensitive characteristics make the situation complicated.

Konolige([3]) investigates correspondence of default logic to autoepistemic logic. He indicates that an extension in default logic corresponds exactly to a strongly-grounded expansion in autoepistemic logic. It turns out that the definition of strongly-grounded expansion needs to be further strengthened ([4]) in order to reconstruct the extensions in the autoepistemic environment. Furthermore, Marek and Truszczyński([7]) have complemented Konolige's work by indicating the role of generating defaults in this context. In [7] the authors introduce the class of weak extensions of a default theory. These structures happen to correspond to expansions in autoepistemic logic. This indicates why weak extensions should be studied on their own. Moreover, the definition of extension in default logic is very strong, perhaps even too strong to penetrate and capture the properties of general default theories, and so we may weaken the conditions to present more significant results in general default logic. This is, in particular, the purpose of this paper and also of [7].

In this paper, we focus on several types of structures for default logic. Two weaker types of structures – weak extensions and minimal sets are defined and compared with Reiter's extensions. A default theory may have a weak extension or minimal set but no extension. However, a default theory always has some minimal sets. Weaker types of extensions or structures are meaningful in that they provide us with efficient ways to delineate default theories and means to discuss them when the theories under consideration have no extension. We also get additional information about extensions for subtheories of default theories. One important application for the theories of other types of structures in default logic is the development of a theory for defaults revision systems. Based on the relations among different kinds of structures, we show how we can revise a default theory to guarantee existence of extensions (possibly for subtheories, though). By introducing a definition of ranking on default rules, we get a method of checking which default theories have extensions. This gives rise to an alternative method of constructing an extension. It turns out that an extension can be constructed by finding a maximally perfectly-ranked set. An algorithm to construct extensions based on this existence principle is proposed. The algorithm can not only converge dynamically on every extension of given default theory but also detect abnormal defaults. Detection in our algorithm is particularly useful since a default theory with abnormal defaults seems unreasonable even if it has an extension. This problem is specially critical in practical applications.

Due to the space constraints we omit proofs. A detailed account is provided in [12].

2 Definitions

In this paper, we consider the language **L** of propositional logic.

As introduced by Reiter in ([9]), a default is an expression of the form:

$$d = \frac{\alpha : \beta_1, \ldots, \beta_n}{\omega}$$

where $\alpha, \beta_1, \ldots, \beta_n, \omega \in \mathbf{L}$. α is called the *prerequisite* of the default, $\beta_1, \ldots, \beta_n$ are called *justifications*, and ω is called *conclusion*. For convenience, we denote the prerequisite of the default d by $p(d)$, its set of justifications by $j(d)$ and its conclusion by $c(d)$. Considering its intuitive meaning, a default d is an inference rule which says: for some set of beliefs, if $p(d)$ is believed, and all justifications in $j(d)$ are "possible"(i.e. their negations are not in the belief set), then we accept the conclusion $c(d)$.

A *default theory* is a pair (D, W) where D is a collection of defaults and $W \subseteq \mathbf{L}$. By using a fixed-point of an operator, *Reiter*([9]) proposed a precise definition of an *extension* for a default theory. In this paper, we use a more intuitive and equivalent definition given by theorem 2.1 in ([9]). We say that a theory T is an extension if it is Reiter's extension. For completeness sake, we give the definition of the extension below.

Definition 1 *Let $\Delta = (D, W)$ be a default theory and $E \subseteq \mathbf{L}$. Define an operator $R^{D,E}(\cdot)$ as follows:*

$$R^{D,E}(S) = Cn(S \cup \{c(d) : d \in D \text{ where } p(d) \in S \text{ and } \forall_{\beta \in j(d)} \neg\beta \notin E\})$$

Then we iterate operator $R^{D,E}$ on W:

$$R_0^{D,E}(W) = Cn(W),$$

for $n \geq 0$,

$$R_{n+1}^{D,E}(W) = R^{D,E}(R_n^{D,E}(W)),$$

thus,

$$R_{n+1}^{D,E}(W) = Cn(R_n^{D,E}(W) \cup \{c(d) : d \in D \text{ where } p(d) \in R_n^{D,E} \text{ and } \forall_{\beta \in j(d)} \neg\beta \notin E\}),$$

where Cn is the consequence operation of the propositional logic.
Finally, we define:

$$R_\infty^{D,E}(W) = \bigcup_{n=0}^{\infty} R_n^{D,E}(W)$$

E is an extension of (D, W) iff E is equal to $R_\infty^{D,E}$, the least fixed-point of the operator $R^{D,E}$ over W.

From **definition 1**, we see that E is an extension of (D, W) if and only if the formulas of E are precisely those formulas that can be derived from W by means of propositional consequences and defaults treated as context-sensitive inference rules with the context E itself. In default logic it is widely agreed that any reasonable conclusions should reside in an extension of the default theory under consideration([1]).

But some default theories suffer from incoherence problem, which means they have no extensions. To deal with this issue, we introduce two other structures. One structure called *weak* extension is defined as follows:

Definition 2 *Let $\Delta = (D, W)$ be a default theory and $E^w \subseteq \mathbf{L}$, E^w is a weak extension of Δ iff*

$$E^w = Cn(W \cup \{c(d) : d \in D \text{ where } p(d) \in E^w \text{ and } \forall_{\beta \in j(d)} \neg\beta \notin E^w\}).$$

The concept of weak extension is weaker than that of extension because when we reconstruct E^w and try to use a default rule, we take arbitrary prerequisites from E^w and not only those that has been proved. Hence the structure of weak extension allows for founding the belief on unproven statements, it is just enough that the reasons for accepting them are on the list (and not necessarily are already proven!).

In [7] it is shown that the concept of weak extension is equivalent to that of expansion in autoepistemic logic under Konolige's translation. This indicates that weak extensions are associated with the mode of reasoning used in autoepistemic logic and that default logic provides a vehicle for a faithful simulation of autoepistemic reasonings assuming we use a different type of structure (weak extension).

Another structure considered here is *minimal set*.

Definition 3 *Let $\Delta = (D, W)$ be a default theory and $E^m \subseteq \mathbf{L}$. E^m is a minimal set of Δ iff E^m is a minimal collection satisfying following:*
(1) $W \subseteq E^m$.
(2) $Cn(E^m) = E^m$
(3) For each $d \in D$, if $p(d) \in E^m$ and $\forall_{\beta \in j(d)} \neg\beta \notin E^m$, then $c(d) \in E^m$.

Thus the idea behind the minimal set is this: We require that the belief set of the agent be closed under Cn, defaults from D and contain W. The principle of parsimony tells us that these should be the only reasons to accept the sentence in belief set - hence the minimality. Obviously, we can see that minimal sets of a default theory are all candidates that have to be checked for extensions. There is a closed connection between minimal sets and minimal Herbrand models for general logic programs, but we shall not pursue this line of analogy here.

Every default theory $\Delta = (D, W)$ possesses at least one minimal set. The intuitive explanation for this is that a candidate for minimal set can be built by adding the negation of a justification of $d \in D$ to block it whenever d may give rise to incoherence of the theory under consideration. Hence, as in [7], all candidates for minimal sets have following "normal form":

$$S = Cn(W \cup U_1 \cup U_2),$$

where $U_1 \subseteq \{\neg\beta : \beta \in \cup_{d \in D} j(d)\}$, $U_2 \subseteq \{c(d) : d \in D\}$, and $U_1 \cap U_2 = \emptyset$.

One particular type of minimal sets, which satisfies $|U_1| = 1$, is called *linear minimal set*. Linear minimal sets have some special property. We discuss it in following section.

3 Relations among various types of structures for default theories

First of all, we give some additional definitions. Generally, our notation follows that of Reiter.

Definition 4 *Let $\Delta = (D, W)$ be a default theory and $E \subseteq \mathbf{L}$. The set of generating defaults for E with respect to Δ is defined to be*

$$GD(E, \Delta) = \{d : d \in D \text{ where } p(d) \in E \text{ and } \forall_{\beta \in j(d)} \neg\beta \notin E\}.$$

and for a set of defaults D, the consequents of D is defined to be

$$Cs(D) = \{c(d) : d \in D\}.$$

Similar definition can be found in Reiter([9]). Here, however, E is an *arbitrary* set of formulas, not necessarily an extension.

Theorem 1 *Every extension of* (D, W) *is both a weak extension and a minimal set of* (D, W).

The proof of **theorem 1** is a slight variation of the one in [9] for the **theorem 2.5**.

The converse of **theorem 1** does not hold. In general, as shown in the following examples, weak extensions or minimal sets do not need to be extensions.

Example 1

$$W = \emptyset$$

$$D = \{\frac{A : B}{B}, \frac{B :}{A}\}$$

$\Delta = (D, W)$ has an unique extension $Cn(\emptyset)$ but two weak extensions $Cn(\emptyset)$, $Cn(\{A, B\})$. $Cn(\emptyset)$ is also a minimal set.

It is routine to give an example of a default theory with no extensions at all. But such a default theory may still have weak extensions or minimal sets. It is natural then to ask whether a structure that is both weak extension and minimal set of (D, W) must be an extension. The following example shows that it is not so.

Example 2

$$W = \{A \Rightarrow B\}$$

$$D = \{\frac{B :}{A}, \frac{: \neg A}{A}\}$$

$\Delta = (D, W)$ has no extensions, but it has an unique weak extension and minimal set $Cn(\{A, B\})$. This indicates the possibility of yet other class of structures for default theories. We will not pursue this avenue here.

Notice that minimal sets do not coincide with weak extensions, that is, a minimal set does not have to be a weak extension (nor conversely).

Example 3

$$W = \emptyset$$

$$D = \{\frac{: \neg A}{A}\}$$

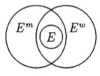

Fig. 1

$\Delta = (D, W)$ has no extensions or weak extensions. Yet, $Cn(\{A\})$ is a minimal set.

The relations among three kinds of extensions can be depicted as in **Fig.1**, in which each circle is supposed to represent the space of a type of extensions.

Weak extensions and extensions seem to share much similarity. In [7], it is shown that for prerequisites-free default theories, classes of weak extensions and extensions coincide. Here we consider analogous problem for general default theories. First of all, we need a definition:

Definition 5 *Let $\Delta = (D, W)$ be a default theory and $D^* \subseteq D$, D^* is* **ranked** *iff it can be classified into following:*

$D_0^* = \{d : d \in D^* \text{ where } p(d) \in Cn(W)\}$

and, for $n > 0$,

$D_n^* = \{d : d \in D^* - \bigcup_{i=0}^{n-1} D_i^*, \ p(d) \in Cn(W \cup Cs(\bigcup_{i=0}^{n-1} D_i^*))\}$

$D^* = \bigcup_{i=0}^{\infty} D_i^*$

Intuitively, ranking serves to classify defaults into levels such that the prerequisites of defaults in each level are consequents of combining W with conclusions of defaults in lower levels. Ranking has an effect similar to that of stratification for general logic programs.

Proposition 1 *Given a default theory $\Delta = (D, W)$ and a ranked set $D^* \subseteq D$, if D_0^* is empty then D^* is empty.*

Proposition 2 *Every default theory (D, W) possesses the largest ranked set of defaults $D^* \subseteq D$. This set contains all defaults that may be applied in process of constructing extensions.*

With the definition of ranked sets, the relation between weak extension and extension becomes clear in view of the following theorem.

Theorem 2 *Given a default theory $\Delta = (D, W)$ and its weak extension E^w, E^w is an extension of Δ if and only if $GD(E^w, \Delta)$ is ranked.*

This theorem shows that the only difference between extension and weak extension is the ways of treatment of prerequisites of defaults in their construction. Hence when we try to determine whether $E \subseteq \mathbf{L}$ is an extension of $\Delta = (D, W)$, as long as E is a weak extension, we can totally omit justifications of d for d belongs to $GD(E, \Delta)$. In a sense, the defaults from $GD(E, \Delta)$ become context-independent, and we reason as within the classical logic with additional rules.

In **example 1**, $GD(Cn(\{A, B\}), \Delta) = D$ is not ranked, hence $Cn(\{A, B\})$ is not an extension.

We turn out to the issue of defaults revision problem. If a default theory $\Delta = (D, W)$ has no extension, it is of interest to find a subset $D^* \subseteq D$ such that (D^*, W) possesses an extension. One particularly interesting question is the problem of finding maximal subset $D^* \subseteq D$ to generate extensions.

Theorem 3 Let a default theory $\Delta = (D, W)$ have no extension. If E^w is a weak extension of Δ, then there exists a $D^* \subseteq D$, such that $R_\infty^{D, E^w}(W)$ is an unique extension of (D^*, W).

This theorem is proved by constructing D^* as $GD(E^w, \Delta)$. Similarly, a property for minimal sets holds as well.

Theorem 4 Let a default theory $\Delta = (D, W)$ have no extension. If E^m is a minimal set of Δ, then there is a $D^* \subseteq D$, such that $R_\infty^{D, E^m}(W)$ is an unique extension of (D^*, W).

The **theorem 4** is an important tool for defaults revision. The reason for this is the following. On one hand the belief set of the agent should be an extension of the default theory (D, W). On the other hand initial theory (D, W) may have no extension. However as pointed before (D, W) definitely possesses a minimal set. The **theorem 4** tells us that at a price of discarding some defaults from D we can find a $D^* \subseteq D$ such that the iterated computation $R_\infty^{D, E}(W)$ corresponding to a minimal set E is an extension of (D^*, W). This indicates that a theory (D, W) that has no extension is "too big", there are too many defaults to provide with the data W an extension. If we accept the proof concept as adopted in default logic (that is "prove the prerequisite, see that justifications consistent") then the collection of formulas provable in this way(with a minimal set servicing as context) is an extension. This phenomenon occurs, however, only when (D, W) has no extension.

D^*, in above, may not be the maximal subset of D to guarantee extensions. But if a default theory has a linear minimal set, as mentioned in section 2, then the following theorem holds.

Theorem 5 Let a default theory $\Delta = (D, W)$ have no extension. If Δ possesses a linear minimal set E^m, then $D - \{d : d \text{ is blocked by } U_1 \text{ in } E^m\}$, denoted as D^*, is a maximal subset of D to generate extensions and $R_\infty^{D, E^m}(W)$ is an extension of (D^*, W).

4   Existence of various of structures

As mentioned in Etherington([1]), an extension is a set of beliefs which are in some sense "justified" or "reasonable" in light of what is known about a world. Hence every reasonable conclusion should reside in an extension of the default theory under consideration. Since some default theory may have no extension, the most significant work is to find a existence principle deciding which theories have or do not have extensions and how to revise the given default theory to possess extensions. In this section we focus on existence issue. Reiter([9]) has proved that every normal default theory must have at least one extension. Etherington proposed some sufficient conditions for semi-normal default theories which guarantee existence of extensions. Now we discuss general default theories.

Since extensions form an antichain under inclusion, hence, if $\Delta = (D, W)$ has an extension $E = Cn(W)$ then E is the unique extension of Δ. Reiter([9]) has pointed out that a closed default theory (D, W) has an inconsistent extension if and only if W is inconsistent. Hence without lose of generality, we assume W is consistent in the rest of the paper.

For a default theory $\Delta = (D, W)$ and $d \in D$, if $c(d) \in Cn(W)$, then we consider d to be **useless**. In the rest of the paper, we assume that there is no useless d in D.

The following definitions are steps in an alternative characterization of default theories that possess extensions.

Definition 6 *Given a default theory $\Delta = (D, W), D^* \subseteq D$ is perfectly-ranked iff D^* is ranked such that for each $d \in D^*$,*

$$\forall_{\beta \in j(d)} \neg \beta \notin Cn(W \cup Cs(D^*)).$$

Notice that when D^* is perfectly-ranked, $Cn(W \cup Cs(D^*))$ is consistent. The point is that, since an inconsistent extension contains all formulas of **L**, if $Cn(W \cup Cs(D^*))$ is inconsistent, then every justification of $d \in D^*$ can be refuted. Thus, D^* cannot be perfect.

Definition 7 *Given a default theory $\Delta = (D, W)$, $D^* \subseteq D$ is maximally perfectly-ranked iff D^* is perfectly-ranked, and for each $d \in D$, if $p(d) \in Cn(W \cup Cs(D^*)), \forall_{\beta \in j(d)} \neg \beta \notin Cn(W \cup Cs(D^*))$, then $d \in D^*$.*

A perfectly-ranked collection of defaults may not be maximally perfectly-ranked. That is why some default theories have no extensions.

Lemma 1 *Let $\Delta = (D, W)$ be a default theory, and assume that W is consistent. Then: Δ has an unique extension $E = Cn(W)$ iff for every ranked $D^* \subseteq D$, $\forall d \in D_0^*, \exists_{\beta \in j(d)} \neg \beta \in Cn(W)$. (That is, empty collection of defaults is a maximally perfectly-ranked set of defaults for (D, W)).*

Theorem 6 *Let $\Delta = (D, W)$ be a default theory, and assume W is consistent. Δ has an extension iff there exists a $D^* \subseteq D, D^*$ is maximally perfectly-ranked.*

The proof of above theorem tells us, in fact, more, namely that if $D^* \subseteq D$ is a maximally perfectly-ranked set of (D, W), then $Cn(W \cup Cs(D^*))$ is an extension.

There is a simple construction of maximally perfectly-ranked set of defaults for normal default theories, which coincides with the construction of extensions. Hence we have following corollary.

Corollary 1 *Every normal default theory of (D,W) possesses at least one $D^* \subseteq D$ such that D^* is maximally perfectly-ranked.*

The **theorem 5** provides a necessary and sufficient condition for existence of extensions in general default theories. It is based on an approach different both from the original construction of Reiter[9](fixed point of the operator Γ) and "strong context dependent proofs" of Marek and Truszczyński[7]. We use here ranked subsets of D as a primary vehicle of investigation and show that existence of a maximally perfectly-ranked subset is equivalent to existence of extension.

The actual process of computing an extension can be reconstructed from this principle. We discuss it in next section.

We address now the problem of existence for other types of structures. As concerns the existence of minimal set, it always exists. However, it should be mentioned that some default theories may hold inconsistent minimal sets. For a given default theory (D,W) and a collection of formulas S, let property $\Psi(S)$ include:
(a) $W \subseteq S$.
(b) $Cn(S) = S$.
(c) For each $d \in D$, if $p(d) \in S$ and $\forall_{\beta \in j(d)} \neg\beta \notin S$, then $c(d) \in S$.

Let Φ be the set of all collections that satisfy the property Ψ. Φ is nonempty since **L** itself is a member of Φ. The classification of Φ under inclusion constructs families(Different families may not be disjoint, e.g., **L** belongs to every family of classification under consideration). There exists a minimal collection with property Ψ in each family. A theorem is followed from this fundamental principle and the detail of the proof is in [7].

Theorem 7 *For every (D,W) there exists a minimal set.*

Turning to the existence of weak extensions, let us note that a closed under consequence theory S is a weak extension of (D,W) if and only if $E(S)$ is an expansion of $tr(D,W)$ (where $tr(\cdot)$ is Konolige's translation of (D,W) into autoepistemic logic, cf [3,6,7,5]).

5 Constructing extensions

Using Reiter's approach, Etherington([1]) presents a procedure in which extensions are constructed by a series of successive approximations. In this section we propose an alternative algorithm which attempts to converge on a maximally perfectly-ranked set of defaults for (D,W). Then following **lemma 1** and **theorem 5**, extensions are constructed simply as consequences of combining W with conclusions of all defaults in the maximally perfectly-ranked set.

Algorithm 1
$i \leftarrow 0; T \leftarrow false;$
$D_0 \leftarrow$ *find largest ranked set of D ;*
repeat

if *for each $d \in D_i$ and $\forall_{\beta \in j(d)} \neg \beta \notin Cn(W \cup Cs(D_i))$*
then
    D_i *is a maximally perfectly-ranked set;*
    $T \leftarrow true$
else
    $D_{i+1} \leftarrow D_i;$
    while *for $d \in D_{i+1}$ and $\exists_{\beta \in j(d)} \neg \beta \in Cn(W \cup Cs(D_{i+1}))$* **do**
        $D_{i+1} \leftarrow D_{i+1} - \{d\};$
        $D_{i+1} \leftarrow$ *find largest ranked set of D_{i+1}*
    endwhile;
    while *for $d \in D - D_{i+1}$ and $\{d\} \cup D_{i+1}$ is ranked*
            and $\forall_{\beta \in j(d)} \neg \beta \notin Cn(W \cup Cs(D_{i+1}))$ **do**
        $D_{i+1} \leftarrow D_{i+1} \cup \{d\}$
    endwhile;
    if $D_{i+1} = D_j (0 \leq j \leq i)$
    then
        $\bigcup_{n=j}^{i+1} D_n$ *contains abnormal defaults;*
        $T \leftarrow true$
    else $i \leftarrow i + 1;$
until $T = true;$

According to proposition 2, those defaults in D which cannot be ranked at all do not have any influence on extensions, thus we simply omit them at the beginning of the **algorithm 1**.

In **algorithm 1**, D_0 is the largest ranked subset of D. For $i \geq 0$, whenever D_i is not perfect, D_{i+1} is constructed using two loops. The first loop, starting at D_i, produces D_{i+1} converging on a perfectly-ranked subset, by deletion of some defaults whose justifications are refuted. To make sure it is maximal, in the second loop, any default $d \in D$ such that $\{d\} \cup D_{i+1}$ is ranked and $j(d)$ can not be denied is added to D_{i+1}. Thus each $D_i (i \geq 0)$ is large enough to be a candidate for maximally perfectly-ranked set. Then the perfectness is checked.

According to Etherington([1]), an incoherent default theory is a theory which has no extension. Intuitively, such default theory has the property that "any set of formulas small enough to be an extension is too small and any set large enough is too large". There are two kinds of defaults to make this situation possible. We call these defaults "abnormal". One kind is defined as "self-abnormal", that is, the conclusions of defaults refute the justifications of themselves. Another kind of abnormal defaults is "circular-abnormal" defaults, which means there is a circular dependency among a group of defaults such that the justifications of some defaults in the group are refuted by conclusions of other defaults residing in the same group but after their deletion we may be forced (by maximality) to include them again. Both kinds of abnormal defaults have this property that "not applying them force their application and converse". Hence abnormal defaults may give rise to incoherence of default theories, as shown in following example.

Example 4

$$W = \emptyset$$

$$D_n = \{\frac{: \neg p_1}{p_2}, \frac{: \neg p_2}{p_3}, \ldots, \frac{: \neg p_n}{p_1}\}$$

(D_n, W) has no extension whenever n is odd. For n=1, $\frac{: \neg p_1}{p_1}$ happens to be a "self-abnormal" default; for $n > 1$ and n to be odd, all defaults of D_n consist of a set of "circular-abnormal" defaults.

Note, however, that there exist examples of default theories which possess extensions because their abnormal defaults are blocked by conclusions of other defaults.

Lemma 2 *If $\Delta = (D, W)$ is a finite default theory, then* **algorithm 1** *fails to converge on a maximally perfectly-ranked set only if for some $i > 0$, $D_i = D_j (0 \le j \le i - 1)$.*

Lemma 3 *Given a finite default theory $\Delta = (D, W)$, if in* **algorithm 1**, *for some $i > 0, D_i = D_j (0 \le j \le i - 1)$, then $\bigcup_{n=j}^{i} D_n$ contains abnormal defaults.*

Theorem 8 *Every default theory $\Delta = (D, W)$ without abnormal defaults has at least one extension.*

Since Etherington's ordered, semi-normal default theories do not exhibit cyclic behavior, hence his default theories have no abnormal defaults and **algorithm 1** converges on a maximally perfectly-ranked set of defaults. It is of interest if there exists a syntactic characterization of general default theories which do not have abnormal defaults. This algorithm solves this problem dynamically.

The **algorithm 1** suffers the same problem as Etherington's, that is, nonconverging computations. However, our algorithm always stops. It either finds an extension or else detects abnormal defaults. We consider it the most important feature of the algorithm. A default theory with abnormal defaults seems unreasonable even if it has extensions. This problem is specially critical when we deal with practical applications since the existence of abnormal defaults always holds a danger to make the default theory incoherent.

There is another similarity between our algorithm and Etherington's, that is, the nondeterminism concerning the selection of defaults to be processed. The nondeterminism is necessary since the relative coherence among defaults may depend upon the order in which they are chosen, giving rise to multiple extensions. In particular, for every extension there exists a selection strategy which makes the algorithm to produce that extension and for every abnormal set of defaults there is a strategy which makes the algorithm to detect it. Consequently, a theorem similar to Etherington's follows:

Theorem 9 *There exists a converging computation such that the* **algorithm 1** *converge on a maximally perfectly-ranked set $D^* \subseteq D$ if and only if (D, W) has an extension of $Cn(W \cup Cs(D^*))$.*

6 Conclusions

Using concepts weaker than that of *extension* (weak extension, minimal set), we have shown how to assign possible sets of consequences (belief sets of an agent) to default theories that have no extension. This allows us to introduce a default revision method for theories without extensions.

In addition, we found that minimal sets, which are defined by a different paradigm than extensions (minimalistic rather than proof-theoretical) are closely related to extensions. This seems to confirm extensions as a focal point of default theory.

Finally, a novel characterization of extensions gives rise to a new algorithm for computing extensions and detects abnormality in the initial set of defaults.

7 Acknowledgments

We are grateful to Mirek Truszczynski for suggestions which helped to clarify many of the ideas presented in the paper.

References

[1] D.W. Etherington. (1987) *Formalizing Nonmonotonic Reasoning System*, Artificial Intelligence Journal 37, pp.41-85.

[2] W. Lukaszewicz. (1987) *Two Results on Default Logic*, Computers and Artificial Intelligence, vol.6, pp. 329-343.

[3] K. Konolige. (1988) *On the Relation between Default and Autoepistemic Logic*, Artificial Intelligence Journal 35, pp.343-382.

[4] K. Konolige. Electronic private communication.

[5] W. Marek. (1986) *Stable Theories in Autoepistemic Logic*, to appear in Fundamenta Informaticae.

[6] W. Marek, M. Truszczyński. (1988) *Autoepistemic Logic*, submitted.

[7] W. Marek, M. Truszczyński. (1988) *Relating Autoepistemic and Default Logics*, Technical Report, Department of Computer Science, University of Kentucky.

[8] R.C. Moore. (1985) *Semantical Considerations on Non-Monotonic Logic*, Artificial Intelligence Journal 25, pp. 75-94.

[9] R. Reiter. (1980) *A Logic for Default Reasoning*, Artificial Intelligence Journal 13, pp. 81-132.

[10] R. Reiter. (1987) *Nonmonotonic Reasoning*, Ann. Rev. Comput. Sci 2, pp.147-186.

[11] R.C. Stalnaker. (1980) *A note on nonmonotonic modal logic*, unpublished manuscript.

[12] A. Zhang, W. Marek. (1989) *On the classification and existence of extensionss in default logic*, Technical Report 137-89, Department of Computer Science, University of Kentucky.

Inscription — A Rule of Conjecture

Carlos Pinto-Ferreira
João Pavão Martins

Instituto Superior Técnico
Technical University of Lisbon
Av. Rovisco Pais
1000 Lisboa, Portugal

Abstract

Conjectural reasoning, introduced by McCarthy's circumscription is one of the most important non standard methods of inference. It allows the generation of plausible conclusions, plausibility being defined on the basis of a minimization criterion.

Inscription — a dual of circumscription — is another method for "jumping to conclusions" based on a maximization criterion suitable for inductive reasoning.

Examples of circumscription and inscription and an application of inscription to inductive reasoning are presented.

1   Introduction

Since perfect and exhaustive knowledge about the *real* world is unattainable, intelligent agents, when interacting with the environment, have to be capable of inferring conclusions and taking decisions under partial knowledge. In these circumstances, pure deductive reasoning provides only incomplete results — the set of conclusions logically implied by the available knowledge — which is likely to be insufficient in most practical applications. Therefore, except for reasoning about toy worlds, where deduction can be useful, other mechanisms of inference have to be provided to an agent for generating not only logical but plausible conclusions as well. Generalizing from examples — induction — and reasoning by analogy are examples of such methods.

Conjectural reasoning, introduced by McCarthy with circumscription [1] [2], is another non deductive inference based method, providing ways to "jump to conclusions". It is worthwhile to note that conclusions obtained from deductive reasoning are indefeasible since, as mentioned, they are *logically* implied by the available knowledge. Further aggregation of knowledge doesn't invalidate the conclusions already derived, its number growing monotonically. Such methods of inference are called *monotonic*. On the other hand, what underlies inference in conjectural reasoning is not only logical implication but some criterion of plausibility, allowing the choice of a class of conclusions among the possible ones. Some of those conclusions may have to be abandoned in face of contrary evidence; further acquisition of knowledge will eventually reduce the number of already inferred conclusions. These are *non-monotonic* reasoning mechanisms. Non standard methods of inference rely on the concept of "plausible reasoning" which has the following characteristics:

- *Consistency*: The inferred conclusions have to be consistent with the available knowledge.

- *Preference*: Among several possible conclusions, an ordering criterion allows for the choice of a preferred one.

The purpose of this paper is to present another rule of conjecture — inscription — which is based on an ordering criterion, dual of McCarthy's circumscription. Examples of circumscription and inscription and an application of inscription to inductive reasoning are also presented.

2 Inscription — a model theoretic approach

Inscription will be presented using the preferential-models approach developed independently by Shoham [5], and Besnard and Siegel [6]. In particular, Besnard an Siegel theoretical framework is suitable for defining different plausible inference methods like Closed World Assumption (CWA) [7], subimplication [8], and circumscription [1] [2].

As mentioned, the central issue in strictly deductive reasoning is the concept of logical consequence: given a belief set[1] Γ and a sentence ϕ, ϕ is said to be a logical consequence of Γ iff *all* models[2] of Γ are also models of ϕ.

Suppose, on the other hand, that only *some* models of Γ are also models of ϕ. If there is a criterion for preferring these models, ϕ is a plausible consequence of Γ under the given criterion.

---

[1] A belief set is a finite set of first order wffs (well formed formulae).

[2] A model of a sentence ϕ is an interpretation satisfying ϕ; a model of a belief set Γ is an interpretation satisfying every sentence of Γ.

As an example [3], consider the following belief set Γ_1:

$$\forall x.\ Quaker(x) \Rightarrow Pacifist(x) \tag{1}$$

$$\forall x.\ Pacifist(x) \Rightarrow \neg Republican(x) \tag{2}$$

$$Quaker(Dupont) \tag{3}$$

$$\neg Republican(Dupond) \tag{4}$$

The domain consists of two objects, denoted by two constants, $D = \{Dupont, Dupond\}$. Notice that neither $Pacifist(Dupond)$ nor $\neg Pacifist(Dupond)$ are logical consequences of Γ_1. Thus, these two wffs don't belong to the logical closure of Γ_1, i.e., to the theory[3] T generated by Γ_1.

However, given the fact that most individuals are pacifists, $Pacifist(Dupond)$ can be considered an acceptable *conjecture*. Informally, a conjecture is a piece of knowledge which does not follow logically from the available evidence not being, however, against it. It will be said that $Pacifist(Dupond)$ is a plausible consequence of Γ_1.

Or conversely, knowing that most individuals are non-pacifists it will be plausible to accept $\neg Pacifist(Dupond)$.

The following intends to introduce this plausibility approach. Let M_1 and M_2 be two different models, generating respectively two theories T_1 and T_2 which are extensions of theory T. Recall that an extension of a theory T is the set of all logical consequences of Γ (the belief set generating T) together with other wffs representing assumed beliefs.

Let T_1 include

$$Quaker(Dupont) \tag{5}$$

$$Pacifist(Dupont) \tag{6}$$

$$\neg Pacifist(Dupond) \tag{7}$$

$$\neg Republican(Dupont) \tag{8}$$

$$\neg Republican(Dupond) \tag{9}$$

Let T_2 include

$$Quaker(Dupont) \tag{10}$$

$$Pacifist(Dupont) \tag{11}$$

$$Pacifist(Dupond) \tag{12}$$

$$\neg Republican(Dupont) \tag{13}$$

$$\neg Republican(Dupond) \tag{14}$$

Notice that T_1 and T_2 are consistent theories whereas $T_1 \cup T_2$ is not.

---

[3] A theory is a set of wffs closed under logical implication.

Now, suppose that there are sufficient reasons to accept the conjecture that *the only pacifists are those individuals that must be pacifists*, given the available knowledge. This corresponds to minimize the extension[4] of predicate *Pacifist* in Γ_1, i.e., to *circumscribe* the predicate *Pacifist* in the belief set Γ_1. Therefore, the underlying criterion for choosing a theory is, in this case, the one which minimizes the number of objects having a certain predication P. In the given example, it corresponds to choosing model M_1.

On the other hand, the *inscription* of a predicate P in a belief set Γ corresponds to prefer the model(s) maximizing the number of objects with predication P in Γ. In the example given, to inscribe the predicate *Pacifist* in Γ_1 corresponds to choosing the extension T_2.

Notice that what underlies this preference approach is a different interpretation of certain constant relation symbols corresponding to the predicates in Γ_1. For instance, in the example given, between models M_1 and M_2 there are constant relation symbols with the same interpretation (e.g., *Quaker*) and others having different interpretations (e.g., *Pacifist*).

Besnard and Siegel preferential-models approach establishes the preference between two models N and M considering a partition Π of the set of all constant relation symbols R, $\Pi = < R_=, R_+, R_-, R. >$.

Model N is preferred to model M relatively to the partition Π iff the following conditions are met:

- $R_=$ is the subset of R corresponding to those predicates having the same interpretation in M and N.

- R_+ is the subset of R such that the extension of every corresponding predicate in N is a superset of the same predicate in M.

- R_- is the subset of R such that the extension of every corresponding predicate in N is a subset of the same predicate in M.

- $R.$ is the subset of R corresponding to those predicates allowed to vary in M and N.

Besides that, M and N share the same domain of objects and the constant function symbols have the same interpretation in both models. Of course,

$$R = R_= \cup R_+ \cup R_- \cup R. \tag{15}$$

Therefore, a particular partition defines a method for plausible inference. For example, Circumscription of a predicate R_0 in a belief set Γ including predicates

---

[4]The extension of a predicate P is the set of all objects having the predication P.

$R_0, R_1, ..., R_i, R_j, ...R_n$ with predicates $R_1, ..., R_i$ allowed to vary, corresponds to the partition:

$$\Pi_c = < R_=, \{\}, \{R_0\}, \{R_1, ..., R_i\} > \qquad (16)$$

In the given example, the circumscription of predicate $Pacifist$ in Γ_1, corresponds to:

$$\Pi_1 = < \{Quaker, Republican\}, \{\}, \{Pacifist\}, \{\} > \qquad (17)$$

Allowing a predicate to vary means to allow for different interpretations to it between the compared models.

The following definition formally introduces the concept of inscription.

Definition: A formula ϕ follows from a belief set Γ by inscription of a predicate R_0 with varying relations $R_1, ..., R_i$ iff ϕ belongs to a theory extension corresponding to a preferred model defined on the basis of the partition

$$\Pi_i = < R_=, \{R_0\}, \{\}, \{R_1, ..., R_i\} > \qquad (18)$$

So, ϕ is a plausible R_0-inscriptive conclusion of Γ, denoted by:

$$\Gamma \models_{INSCR(R_0)} \phi \qquad (19)$$

In the given example, the inscription of predicate $Pacifist$ in belief set Γ_1 corresponds to the following partition:

$$\Pi_2 = < \{Quaker, Republican\}, \{Pacifist\}, \{\}, \{\} > \qquad (20)$$

Thus, $Pacifist(Dupont)$ and $Pacifist(Dupond)$ follow from inscription of predicate $Pacifist$ in Γ_1.

However, the given definition doesn't provide a constructive way to compute inscription. To do this, a similar approach to the one taken by Genesereth and Nilsson in circumscription [4] (pp. 132-137) will follow.

The central idea is to transform a problem of plausible reasoning into a problem of deductive inference through the determination of an adequate formula to be conjoined with the initial belief set. Let Γ be a belief set, P a predicate and ϕ a plausible P-inscriptive conclusion of Γ:

$$\Gamma \models_{INSCR(P)} \phi \qquad (21)$$

To compute inscription of P in Γ, a formula ψ_P (ψ_P containing the predicate P) will be sought, such that:

$$\Gamma \wedge \psi_P \models \phi \qquad (22)$$

In other words, the central idea is to find a formula ψ_P to conjoin with the belief set Γ such that the plausible P-inscriptive conclusions of Γ are logical consequences of $\Gamma \wedge \psi_P$.

Thus, ϕ being satisfied in maximal models of Γ will be also satisfied in all models of $\Gamma \wedge \psi_P$.

To determine ψ_P, consider a predicate Φ with the same arity[5] of P and let $\Gamma(\Phi)$ be the belief set Γ in which all occurrences of P are substituted by Φ.

Observe that any model of

$$(\forall x\ P(x) \Rightarrow \Phi(x)) \wedge \neg(\forall x\ \Phi(x) \Rightarrow P(x)) \wedge \Gamma(\Phi) \qquad (23)$$

is not a maximal model of Γ in predicate P[6], since Φ satisfies Γ and Φ is a proper superset of P. In other words, from the first two conjuncts of (23) it is observed that there are elements having the predication Φ which have not the predication P, the extension of Φ being a proper superset of the extension of P. The third conjunct allows the conclusion that Φ satisfies the belief set Γ.

Notice that the formula

$$\forall\Phi\ \neg((\forall x\ P(x) \Rightarrow \Phi(x)) \wedge \neg(\forall x\ \Phi(x) \Rightarrow P(x)) \wedge \Gamma(\Phi)) \qquad (24)$$

is a P-maximal model of Γ, this being so because it corresponding to the negation of (23) for all Φ.

So, (24) is a way for obtaining the desired formula ψ_P, the inscription of P in Γ being the conjunction of Γ with (24):

$$INSCR[\Gamma; P] \equiv \Gamma \wedge \forall\Phi\ \neg((\forall x\ P(x) \Rightarrow \Phi(x)) \wedge \neg(\forall x\ \Phi(x) \Rightarrow P(x)) \wedge \Gamma(\Phi)) \qquad (25)$$

or,

$$INSCR[\Gamma; P] \equiv \Gamma \wedge (\forall\Phi\ (\Gamma(\Phi) \wedge (\forall x\ P(x) \Rightarrow \Phi(x))) \Rightarrow (\forall x\ \Phi(x) \Rightarrow P(x))) \qquad (26)$$

Introducing the abbreviations:

$P \leq \Phi$ for $\forall x\ P(x) \Rightarrow \Phi(x)$,

$P < \Phi$ for $(P \leq \Phi) \wedge \neg(\Phi \leq P)$, and

$P = \Phi$ for $(P \leq \Phi) \wedge (\Phi \leq P)$, (24) can be rewritten as:

$$INSCR[\Gamma; P] \equiv \Gamma \wedge \forall\Phi\ (\Gamma(\Phi) \wedge P \leq \Phi)) \Rightarrow (\Phi \leq P) \qquad (27)$$

Notice that the provided formula for computing inscription is a second order formula (it is quantified universally over a predicate); however, there are cases in which easier ways to compute inscription are available. Consider the following theorems:

---

[5] The arity of a predicate is the number of arguments of the predicate.
[6] Notice that x can be a tuple of variables.

THEOREM 1: Let $\Gamma(P)$ be a belief set containing a predicate P. Let P' be a predicate with the same arity of P, not defined in terms of P.

If $\Gamma(P) \models \Gamma(P') \wedge (P \leq P')$, then $INSCR[\Gamma; P] \equiv \Gamma(P) \wedge (P' = P)$.

Proof: Assume the conditions of the theorem, i.e.,

$$\Gamma(P) \models \Gamma(P') \wedge (P \leq P') \tag{28}$$

Left to right: Using the definition of inscription and specializing for predicate P', results after the application of *modus ponens*,

$$\Gamma(P) \wedge (P' = P) \tag{29}$$

Right to left: Using the condition $\Gamma(P) \wedge (P' = P)$ a contradiction is found negating the intended result, $INSCR[\Gamma; P]$.

Q.E.D.

THEOREM 2: Let $\Gamma(P)$ be a belief set which can be written in the form:

$$(E_2 \leq P) \wedge (P \leq E_1) \wedge E_3 \tag{30}$$

where E_1, E_2, and E_3 are formulae that contain no occurrences of P. Then,

$$INSCR[\Gamma; P] \equiv (E_2 \leq P) \wedge E_3 \wedge (P = E_1) \tag{31}$$

Proof: Since $(E_2 \leq P) \wedge (P \leq E_1) \wedge E_3$ logically implies $(E_2 \leq E_1) \wedge E_3$, the conditions for Theorem 1 are met.

Q.E.D.

As an example of application of these theorems to compute inscription consider the belief set Γ_2:

$$\forall x.\, Quaker(x) \Rightarrow Pacifist(x) \tag{32}$$

$$\forall x.\, Pacifist(x) \Rightarrow \neg Republican(x) \tag{33}$$

The inscription of predicate $Pacifist$ in Γ_2, yields:

$$INSCR[\Gamma; pacifist] \equiv \forall x\, [pacifist(x) \Leftrightarrow \neg republican(x)] \wedge$$
$$[quaker(x) \Rightarrow \neg republican(x)] \tag{34}$$

Whereas the circumscription of predicate $Pacifist$ yielding:

$$CIRC[\Gamma; pacifist] \equiv \forall x\, [pacifist(x) \Leftrightarrow quaker(x)] \wedge$$
$$[republican(x) \Rightarrow \neg quaker(x)] \tag{35}$$

3 Using Inscription for Induction

Consider the following example of induction [4] (pp.162-164):

> "We are asked to select a card of our choice from a deck of cards. If we select a "good card", we are given a reward; otherwise, we get nothing. We know that in the past people have been given rewards for the four of clubs, for the seven of clubs, and for the two of spades, but not for the five of hearts or for the jack of spades. Assuming that we are not allowed to repeat a card that already has been selected, which card should we choose?"

Summarizing, the known "good cards" are the 4♣, the 7♣ and the 2♠. On the other hand the known "bad" cards are the 5♡ and the J♠.

Noticing that spades and clubs are black cards and 2, 4, and 5 are numbered ones, consider the belief set Γ_3 (consistent with the previous knowledge):

$$\forall x\,(Num(x) \wedge Black(x)) \Rightarrow Reward(x) \tag{36}$$

$$\forall x\,((\neg Num(x) \wedge Black(x)) \vee (Num(x) \wedge \neg Black(x))) \Rightarrow \neg Reward(x) \tag{37}$$

Now, suppose that it is adopted the point of view that the only rewarded cards are those that must be rewarded given the available knowledge.

This corresponds to circumscribe the predicate $Reward$ in Γ_3, yielding:

$$
\begin{aligned}
&\forall x\,(Reward(x) \Leftrightarrow (Num(x) \wedge Black(x)))\wedge \\
&\quad ((Num(x) \wedge Black(x)) \Rightarrow \\
&\qquad \neg((\neg Num(x) \wedge Black(x)) \vee (Num(x) \wedge \neg Black(x))))
\end{aligned}
\tag{38}
$$

Using the above conjecture, it can be concluded that *the only rewarded cards are numbered and black ones*, a somewhat pessimistic conclusion.

Now, what to do when there are no numbered and black cards left in the deck? In this case, it is wise to use a more optimistic criterion which correspond to the inscription of the predicate $Reward$ in Γ_3, using Theorem 2:

$$
\begin{aligned}
&\forall x\, Reward(x) \Leftrightarrow \\
&\quad \neg((\neg Num(x) \wedge Black(x)) \vee (Num(x) \wedge \neg Black(x))) \wedge \\
&\quad ((Num(x) \wedge Black(x)) \Rightarrow \\
&\qquad \neg((\neg Num(x) \wedge Black(x)) \vee (Num(x) \wedge \neg Black(x))))
\end{aligned}
\tag{39}
$$

This formula being equivalent to:

$$\forall x\, Reward(x) \Leftrightarrow ((Num(x) \wedge Black(x)) \vee (\neg Black(x) \wedge \neg Num(x))) \tag{40}$$

So, from now on, it will be acceptable to choose not black and not numbered cards, say a queen of diamonds, $Q\diamond$.

4 Conclusions

Informally speaking, inscription is a method for setting an "upper bound" on the extension of a predicate (the one being inscribed) in a belief set. This can be helpful, as in the previous example, where it has provided a way of making decisions under incomplete knowledge.

Since inscription is a perfect dual of circumscription, the inscription of a predicate P in a belief set Γ corresponds to the circumscription of a predicate Q in Γ, being

$$\forall x\, Q(x) \Leftrightarrow \neg P(x) \tag{41}$$

This can be easily demonstrated using the Besnard and Siegel preferential-models approach.

Therefore, performing circumscription and inscription of the same predicate P on a belief set allows the assessment of opposite criteria (e.g., pessimistic and optimistic, rare and frequent) shedding light on the constraints imposed by the belief set relatively to the extension of the predicate.

McCarthy's circumscription states "these are the *only* objects that *must* have the predication P" whereas inscription establishes "these are *all* the objects that *can* have the predication P".

5 Acknowledgment

Many thanks to Nuno J. Mamede and Maria R. Cravo for their useful comments and suggestions on an early versions of this paper.

This research was supported in part by the "Junta Nacional de Investigação Científica e Tecnológica" (Portugal) under grant 87-107.

References

[1] McCarthy J., "Circumscription — A form of non-monotonic reasoning", *Artificial Intelligence 13*, pp. 27-39, 1980.

[2] McCarthy J., "Applications of Circumscription to Formalizing Common-sense knowledge", *Artificial Intelligence 28*, pp. 89-116, 1986.

[3] Hanks S. e McDermott D., "Default reasoning, nonmonotonic logics, and the frame problem", *Proceedings of the Fifth National Conference on Artificial Intelligence*, pp. 328-333, 1986.

[4] Genesereth M.J. and Nilsson N.J., *Logical Foundations of Artificial Intelligence*, Los Altos, CA: Morgan Kaufmann, 1987.

[5] Shoham Y., "Nonmonotonic Logics: Meaning and Utility", *Proceedings of the Tenth International Joint Conference on Artificial Intelligence*, pp. 388-392, Milan, Italy, 1987.

[6] Besnard P. and Siegel P., "The Preferential-Models Approach to Non-Monotonic Logics", *Non-Standard Logics for Automated Reasoning*, Ed. Smets, Mamdani, Dubois, and Prad. New York. Academic Press, pp. 137-161, 1988.

[7] Reiter R., "On Closed World Databases", *Logic and Databases*. Ed H. Gallaire and J. Minker, pp 55-76. New York: Plenum Press, 1978.

[8] Bossu G., and Siegel P., "Saturation, Non Monotonic Reasoning, and The Closed World Assumption", *Artificial Intelligence 25*, pp. 13-63, 1985.

Algorithmic Debugging of Prolog Side-Effects

Luís Moniz Pereira and Miguel Calejo[1]
Logic Programming and Artificial Intelligence Group
Universidade Nova de Lisboa (UNL)
2825 Monte da Caparica
Portugal

Abstract

Prolog side-effects are typical necessary evil. Convenient logic program properties no longer hold, and upsetting practical problems sprout, namely the debugging of programs with side-effects is harder. This paper attempts to reduce the magnitude of such problems, by formulating a framework for the algorithmic debugging of logic programs with side-effects, encompassing both input/output (I/O) and internal database (DB) ones. Our debugging framework [Pereira Calejo 88] is reviewed and extended for that purpose. The new methods extend the scope and differ, significantly, from those developed in the context of [Pereira 84 86].

In what refers DB side-effects, we extend our suspect sets to include additional suspects: those contained in the partial derivations leading to 'assert' and 'retract' calls. For I/O we define an additional type of bug related to the I/O side-effect notion of *segment* (or trace) of a goal, and introduce a corresponding additional type of suspect set. This approach allows us to apply the same diagnosis algorithms already developed for programs without side-effects. We make some reasonable assumptions in either case, so as to render the implementation amenable and to avoid extorting excessive information from the user.

These extensions are being implemented in our HyperTracer debugger [Pereira Calejo 89a, 89b], incurring in tolerable overhead, mostly confined to actual use of the extensions.

1. Introduction

We address here the following problem: given a buggy Prolog program with I/O or DB side-effects, how can one debug it systematically ?

A partial answer is given to this problem, by extending our previous debugging framework [Pereira Calejo 88] to deal with such side-effects. This follows in the vein of work on algorithmic debugging by [Shapiro 82] and by one of the authors [Pereira 86]. References to other authors will be found herein.

---

[1] Phone: (+351) (1) 295 4464 (ext.1360)   Telex: 14542 FCTUNL P
FAX:(+351)(1)295 4461
ARPA:mc%host.fctunl.rccn.pt@mitvma.mit.edu
UUCP...{mcvax,inria}!inesc!unl!mc
Bix: mcalejo   Applelink:IT0083

Shapiro defined one basic scheme we still adopt: an oracle (i.e., the programmer) answers queries posed by the debugger regarding the intended semantics of the (buggy) program; given enough queries, the debugger eventually localizes a source of the bug to an incorrect clause or an uncovered goal.

Our previous work follows and extends this basic approach. To do so it:

- defines a single diagnosis algorithm, "Select&Query", which is a uniform "Divide and Query "-like algorithm [Shapiro82] for all terminating bug types, taking into account both unsuccessful and successful derivations, and adding heuristics which order suspect sets

- covers larger Prolog subsets then previous approaches, namely all uses of the cut

- relies on an oracle acceding correct type information about the program and correctness declarations (whenever available)

- allows mixed initiative browsing [Pereira Calejo 87, Eisenstadt Brayshaw 88] of executions: either directed by the user or else by the diagnosis algorithm. The result of the latter is advice on which node to inspect next; such advice can be envisaged as an indirect browsing user command, a consequence of the declarative information proffered in answer to debugger queries.

Arithmetic and other builtins with localized semantics were already dealt with in this framework. Thus we're not considering such builtins as "side-effects" in the context of this paper.

The Rational Debugger [Pereira 84 86], by one of the authors, already allowed programs to contain side-effects. Essentially it logs I/O and DB side-effects to consume them during recomputations, and warns the user whenever a detected buggy clause exists because previously asserted. However it doesn't include methods to specifically deal with side-effect induced bugs.

To the best of our knowledge, there hasn't been yet any work till now on specific methods for Prolog side-effects.

In this paper such methods are introduced, integrated with the debugging framework referred above into our HyperTracer implementation (cf.below). We start by reviewing the framework, and then go on to present its extensions for DB and I/O side-effects. Next we exhibit a small HyperTracer session and draw some conclusions.

2 Our debugging framework revisited

For convenience, we provide below an abridged description of our debugging framework. The reader should refer to [Pereira Calejo 88,89a] for more details.

2.1. Goal behavior, bug manifestation, bug instance, bug

A goal's *behavior* is the triple <goal call, its solution sequence, failure information>. Each of these we call a *goal behavior aspect*. Failure information can be simply the solution sequence itself. The *oracle* is a subsystem which includes the user knowledge, and whatever type information is available about the program, regarding the correctness of particular goal behaviors. If the goal behavior displeases the oracle, then it's a *bug manifestation* - either a *missing solution*, a *wrong solution*, or an *inadmissible goal call*. Otherwise it's a *correct* goal. When not inadmissible then it is *admissible*.

Whether it is legitimate to call such oracle knowledge "declarative" or "operational" is perhaps a polemic issue. We certainly argue that it is *not* operational: such statements characterize the intended semantics by referring to a sequence of goal (atom) behaviors instead of to a set of true ground atoms as usual, but they manage to abstract entirely from the *context* of the goal.

For example, saying that "a goal G is inadmissible" means "no matter what the behavior aspects, there's no behavior with G as goal call in the intended semantics"; it does *not* assume awareness of whatever execution strategy caused G to be an activated goal. In the extensions for side-effects below we strived to retain this non-operational flavor.

One or more *bug instances* may be responsible for a bug manifestation, and they may be of the following types:

wrong clause instance - a clause instance whose head is incorrect but whose body goals are all correct

incomplete predicate definition - a predicate definition which produces less solutions for a particular goal then it should, but each of whose children produce all solutions expected

inadmissible call - a goal G which the oracle deems to violate some expected type, but whose father doesn't (i.e. is an admissible goal) and, furthermore, whose other children called before G are all correct.

Each of these bug instances is an instance of a bug in the program text (e.g. wrong clause, incomplete predicate definition or inadmissible atomic goal) - a *bug*. A bug may deliver several bug instances.

Nontermination of programs is not treated specifically. We simply allow the user to interrupt an execution, and let him browse it afterwards, hoping he finds one of the bug manifestations above, that then allows the standard method to be used.

2.2.   Suspect sets[2]

Consider the traditional 4-port execution box for Prolog procedures/predicates (call, exit, redo, fail), as described by [Byrd 80]. A goal G is *under* another goal A if G is called inside A's execution box. G is a *child* of A if it is under A and it is an instance of a goal in the body of a clause matching A. Notice that these are *dynamic* relations, based on some concrete execution.

---

[2]Detailed definitions in [Pereira Calejo 88]

The "**wrong solution suspects**" set for goal G and solution S, WSS(G,S), contains the AND-tree nodes supporting the wrong solution. It also contains[3] the negations of goals under G (via their MSS sets defined below) that have failed before brother cuts: because had they succeeded, the cut would have avoided that particular wrong solution.

The "**missing solution suspects**" set for a goal G, MSS(G), contains all goals under G that have failed completely[4], after producing their solution sequences. Any of them may be responsible for the missing solution. MSS also contains the nodes of AND-subtrees (via its WSS sets) that lead to cuts: because had such an AND-subtree failed the cut wouldn't be reached and other alternatives might have been be tried.

The "**inadmissible goal suspects**" set for a goal G under an admissible goal T, IGS(G,T), contains the AND-tree nodes leading to the G call. It also contains the negations of goals (via its MSS sets) that have failed before cuts and could have prevented the path to G, had they succeeded.

We say that a suspect *supports* some buggy goal behavior aspect if it is contained in the suspect set for that aspect. Notice that all suspects in MSS and WSS of a goal are under it, and all those in IGS are not.

PROPOSITION 1 Given a bug manifestation, there is a bug instance in the suspect set supporting it [Pereira Calejo 88].

Example Consider the following program:

```
(1)  a(Y):-b(Y),!,c(Y).
(2)  a(Y):-d(Y),h(Y).
(3)  a(Y):-e(Y),!,f(Y),g(Y).

(4)  e(_).     (5)  f(1).    (7)  g(1).    (8)  h(3).
               (6)  f(2).
```

The suspect sets for top goal a(X) are:
```
MSS(a(X)) = {<a(X),[clauses (1), (2), and (3)]>, <b(X),[]>, <d(X),[]>, e(X),
             <f(X),[clauses (5) and (6)]>, <g(1),[clause (7)]>, <g(2),[clause (7)]> }
WSS(a(X),a(1)) = { <b(X),[]>, e(X),  f(1),  g(1),  (a(1):-e(1),!,f(1),g(1)) }
```
For the inadmissible call d(X) they are:
```
IGS(d(X),a(X)) = {<b(X),[]>, (a(X):-d(X), h(X))}
```

Notice that the suspect sets for a goal behaviour are unique for a given execution, and are independent of the diagnosis process. Oracle information will be used only to prune these sets during diagnosis[5]. Whether the program is actually buggy depends only on the detection of a bug manifestation. Suspect sets are the same, irrespective of whether a bug manifestation actually occurs.

---

3 This is one feature on which our work significantly departs from previous ones.

4 And hence "used up" the complete definitions of the matching predicates, namely the last part which implicitly states "there are no more solutions". A more formal presentation of this can be found in [Bruffaerts and Henin 88], whose meta interpreter provides explanations for failures in pure Prolog.

5 Other suspect set refinements can be done without oracle knowledge. Cf. [Pereira Calejo 88].

2.3. Diagnosing

To detect a bug we search for a bug instance in the execution tree producing some bug manifestation, more specifically in the supporting suspect set for thet manifestation.

Built-in predicates are always omitted from suspect sets, as their behavior is (or should!) be always correct[6]. The same holds for predicates declared correct; such declarations (e.g., [Pereira 86, Pereira Calejo 88]) can be regarded as extended oracle knowledge, as explored in [Drabent et al. 88].

Consider a top goal's bug manifestation and some goal G in its supporting suspect set. Clearly, if we're looking for some bug instance, and if G's behavior is correct, we can at least for the moment[7], discard all suspects supporting it: because no matter what bug instances might incorrectly support G, at least another bug instance exists elsewhere. If G's behavior is incorrect however, we can proceed with G as the new top goal bug manifestation.

Given a bug manifestation and its corresponding suspect set S, we show the user the behavior for some goal G supporting it, and ask whether it is correct or exhibits a bug manifestation. Whatever the answer, we pursue a single bug instance: if G is correct, we remove its supporting suspect set from S and continue with the smaller set; else we switch to the suspect set supporting the new bug manifestation.

To select some such goal G we use a divide and conquer algorithm which ensures a minimum[8] next suspect set, whatever the oracle's answer might be. The algorithm admits a list of assumptions about the location of bug instances, which it may withdraw later if needed. It also allows restrictions on possible suspects, depending on possible heuristics in force. Both assumptions and heuristics are used to attempt making the next suspect set smaller *and* more likely to contain a bug instance, by using extra information.

This uniform diagnosing framework, as well as the underlying divide and conquer algorithm, was inspired in Shapiro's [Shapiro 82] treatment of the simpler problem for pure Prolog and wrong solutions only.

Next we introduce extensions to accommodate side-effects.

3. Internal (DB) side-effects

We assume that buggy *internal* side-effects (assert, retract, and the like) have manifested themselves as some buggy top goal behavior. (Assuming otherwise would force us to extend our defined notion of "goal behavior" to include any goal execution's associated database state changes.)

---

[6]There's a single exception for type violations in calls to built-ins, which constitute inadmissible goals. Our implementation allows no more than one such goal to exist in a computation, by aborting immediately.

[7]i.e., at least until the next program change

[8]Not really, but close [Pereira Calejo 88].

Our basic idea is to extend the suspect sets, for those goal executions relying on predicate definitions modified by side-effects[9], with the suspects for changes. Accordingly, we *extend* the previous definitions for suspect sets as follows.

The **Extended wrong solution suspects set** for a solution S to goal G, $WSS_E(G,S)$, is defined similarly as before, but now extended by using MSS_E (defined below) instead of MSS, and extended also with:

a) The inadmissible goal suspects sets, IGS_E defined below, of the *assert* type calls that created clauses in WSS(G,S).

b) The IGS_E sets of *assert* type calls creating previous clauses for the predicate definitions matching goals in G's AND-tree: because such clauses may have incorrect restrictive conditions before a cut, or some cut missing, which if correct would prevent use of the matched clause .

c) The IGS_E sets of *retract* type calls affecting predicate definitions matching goals in G's AND-tree: because such calls could either retract the clause matched or prevent it to be used (if they retracted a previous clause with cuts).

EXAMPLE   Consider the program

```
(1)    a :- b, asserta(h:-c,!,d).
(2)    h :- e.
(3)    e.
(4)    b.
```

Consider that goal a has been executed and succeeded, and that afterwards top goal h produces a wrong solution using clause (2). Then $WSS_E(h)$ = { h:-e, e, <c,[]>, asserta(h:-c,!,d), b, (a :- b, asserta(h:-c,!,d)) }.

Similarly, the **Extended inadmissible goal suspects set** for a call G under a top goal T, $IGS_E(G,T)$, is defined similarly as before, but extended by using MSS_E instead of MSS, and extended also with:

d) The IGS_E sets of the *assert* type calls that create clauses in IGS(G,T).

e) The IGS_E sets of *assert* type calls creating previous clauses for the predicate definitions matching goals in T's (partial) AND-tree: because such clauses may have incorrect restrictive conditions before a cut or some cut missing, which if correct would prevent the matched clause to be used.

f) The IGS_E sets of *retract* type calls affecting predicate definitions matching goals in T's (partial) AND-tree: because such calls could either retract the clause matched or prevent it to be used (if they retracted a previous clause with cuts).

The **Extended missing solution suspects** set for a goal G, $MSS_E(G)$, is defined similarly as before, but extended by using WSS_E instead of WSS, and extended also with:

---

[9]The assert and retract calls by themselves aren't problematic: their side-effects on *other* goals are.

g) The IGS_E sets of the *retract* type calls that change predicate definitions (i.e., retract their clauses) in MSS(G).

h) The IGS_E sets of *assert* type calls creating clauses in the predicate definitions in MSS(G): because those clauses may not be producing all the solutions they were intended to produce for their fathers.

We haven't studied the relative merits of the above extensions, as some are probably more relevant than others. For example, in programs without cuts only extensions a,d,g and h are necessary. In our current implementation we arbitrated extensions a,d and g to be more relevant, and so didn't implement the other ones.

The **diagnosis** algorithm is the same as before, and it is nearly indifferent whether internal side-effects occur or not. We simply feed the algorithm with the above extended suspect sets. There are two subtleties, however:

(1) A query about the admissibility of a call producing the asserting or retracting of a clause merely concerns its potential *type-violating* character. I.e. the user may notice a type violating subgoal in its body for example, but otherwise one cannot assume the clause to be "admissible" (in the sense of trusting there are no bug instances among the suspects supporting its assertion).

(2) Furthermore, this approach does *not* take into account any relative *order* of side-effects, as we don't find it reasonable to presuppose the user aware of thta order.

Consequently, it is occasionally possible to obtain a vacuous diagnosis[10]. Anyway, this approach is an improvement over conventional tracing methods.

For a goal execution which does not use predicates changed by assert/retract, the extended suspect sets simplify to the nonextended ones: the cases a-h above do not apply, and therefore $WSS_E=WSS$, $MSS_E=MSS$ and $IGS_E=IGS$.

4. External (I/O) side-effects

We start with an assumption:

Input side-effects (e.g. read) *are always initially considered correct* and, if later found incorrect, their cause is readily pinpointed, in the sense that the outside world - say, the user - provided them. That is, we're not yet supporting programs that rely on their own output side-effects, such as for example those involving manipulation of a file which they consume[11].

---

[10]As an example, consider a buggy predicate, whose implementation requires asserting terms in a particular order. When later diagnosing the troubles it caused, the query to the oracle about the admissibility of the assert calls does *not* take into account their ordering: the oracle will find the assert calls "admissible", so the debugger gets stuck with an identified wrong dynamically asserted clause.

[11]An interesting possibility would be to allow input side-effects to return suspect sets of their own, referring previous output side-effects affecting their external

Thus we concentrate solely on *output* side-effects (e.g. write), and will extend our previous definitions to cater for them. The previous suspect sets (WSS$_E$, MSS$_E$ and IGS$_E$) will remain unchanged, since wrong input side-effects have an immediate culprit.

4.1 Basic method

Define (output) **segment** of a goal to be the sequence of output side-effects (say, "writes") in the order they occurred in time, during that goal's execution and *under*[12] it. Notice that a segment of a goal may be chronologically interleaved with parts of segments of other goals.

Example
```
p :- write(1).    q :- write(3).
p :- write(2).    q :- write(4).
top :- p,q,fail.
```
The segment of top is [1,3,4,2]. The segment of p is [1,2].

The **Goal behavior** for a call G, as defined above in section 2.1, is now extended with G's segment as an *additional aspect*.

A goal is a **bug manifestation** if it has one or more of: a wrong solution, a missing solution, an inadmissible goal call or **wrong output** segment. Otherwise it is a **correct** goal.

The purpose of **diagnosis** given some top bug manifestation is now to locate either: a wrong clause instance, an incomplete predicate definition, an inadmissible call, or a **bad output predicate** - a predicate matching a goal with wrong output but whose children[13] all have correct behaviors. We now define an additional type of suspect set, supporting wrong output debugging.

The **output suspect set** for a goal G, **OSS(G)**, is the set of all goal calls under G.

PROPOSITION 2 Consider an (admissible) goal G with wrong output and its output suspect set OSS(G). Then there is a bug instance in OSS(G).

Informal proof: either G matches a bad output predicate or it has some incorrect child, and therefore there must be some bug instance further down the tree.

As before, we can still ignore suspects supporting goals with correct behavior. Notice that additional information is required from the oracle: whenever it states a goal to be correct it must be aware that its solutions *and* segment are correct.

Diagnosis is done as before, considering the additional type of bug manifestation (wrong output) and the associated suspect set (OSS) whenever the oracle requires it. It is easy to see that given a top goal bug manifestation, the diagnosis algorithm will find a bug instance, possibly of a different type, depending on oracle answers.

"object" (stream, graphical object with state, foreign computation,....). The assert/retract case might then be seen as a particular instance of this scheme.

[12]As defined in section 2.2.

[13]As defined in section 2.2.

Notice that although one may refine MSS(G) (the set above whose definition is closest to OSS(G)) without needing oracle knowledge, for example by using intelligent backtracking, typically one can *not* refine OSS(G), as the use of side-effects implies a strict adherence to Prolog's standard backtracking strategy! This illustrates how a semantically misbehaved language feature is paid with worse performance from a language environment tool - a debugger in our case, but also the case with partial evaluators for example.

We now introduce a refinement allowing diagnosis to start with a smaller suspect set, by using more detailed information from the oracle.

4.2 Refined method

Consider a wrong output segment for a goal G, S. Suppose that this "wrongness" can be pinpointed by the oracle by localizing a continuous nonempty (output) subsegment S', such that *no matter what the goal in the program for which S' is a subsegment, the goal's segment is wrong*. We say that S' is an **universally incorrect** behavior aspect.

This defines side-effects which are erroneous "by themselves", irrespective of the goal call (even if - we'll lift this restriction below). Following is a refined output suspect set definition taking advantage of such information.

The **refined output suspect set** for a goal G and universally incorrect subsegment S', **ROSS(G,S')**, is defined as follows: take the lowest goal call G' in OSS(G) such that its segment contains S'; then ROSS(G,S')=OSS(G') .

It is easy to see that in general ROSS(G,S') contains less suspects than OSS(G).

PROPOSITION 3 Consider a goal G with wrong output and that ROSS(G,S') can be defined for some subsegment S'. Then there is a bug instance in ROSS(G,S').

Proof: follows from proposition 2 and from our definition of universally incorrect behavior aspect.

Example Consider the following program, with top goal a:

```
a :- b, c, write(1), e.
b.
c :- write(2), d, write(w).    % w should probably be a number...
d.
e.
```

Suppose a's segment ([2,w,1]) is considered incorrect. Then OSS(a) = { a, b, c, d,e}. Furthermore, suppose that the subsegment [w] is universally incorrect, because the user expects only numbers to be printed by his program. Then ROSS(a,[w]) = {c,d}.

We'll now define an additional suspect set no longer assuming a behavior aspect to be "universally incorrect" for inadmissible goals. As a matter of fact, wrong output segments may typically be caused by an inadmissible goal.

Consider an "universally incorrect" goal subsegment, with the restriction that its incorrectness/correctness is not defined for inadmissible goals. We call that a **"nearly universally incorrect"** subsegment.

The **nearly refined suspect set**, NROSS(G,S'), is defined to be ROSS(G,S') U IGS(G',G), with G' as in the ROSS definition above. Notice that it will typically be a smaller set than OSS(G).

PROPOSITION 4 Consider a goal G with wrong output and that NROSS(G,S') can be defined for some subsegment S'. Then there is a bug instance in NROSS(G).

Proof: the only difference relative to proposition 3 is that now we're not sure whether S' can be considered wrong for goal G', as it may be inadmissible. Now if G' is admissible, then NROSS(G,S')=ROSS(G,S'), and the result follows from prop.3; otherwise, IGS(G',G) has a bug instance, from prop. 1.

The **diagnosis** process above is now naturally modified whenever the oracle requires it: if it states a subsegment S' to be *universally incorrect* or *nearly universally incorrect*, diagnosis proceeds with ROSS(G,S') or NROSS(G,S') instead of OSS(G), respectively. No other changes are necessary.

Even if the oracle is not able to proffer confidently such strong statements, it may nevertheless be useful to allow him (i.e., the user) to tentatively "proffer" them, just in order to inspect G'. This can be regarded as a debugger browsing command or as an heuristic, like other heuristics referred in [Pereira Calejo 88]: it forces suspects to be inspected by a different order, hoping to find bug instances sooner.

5. Implementation

Our debugging framework has a first incarnation in the HyperTracer debugger [Pereira Calejo 89a, 89b], currently running on the MacLogic environment [Alegria et al 89]. The "Hyper" name stems from the ability to debug several top goals simultaneously, even across DB state changes, and from some characteristics of its graphical interface.

The current HyperTracer is still too slow for practical use, as it is an experimental version implemented using a preprocessor plus "hook" predicates, written in Prolog, and running over an interpreted Prolog (C-Prolog [F.Pereira et al 83]), with little specific low-level support. However it already incorporates our mixed database-recomputation architecture [Pereira Calejo 89a], which we hope will pay dividends in the next versions. It includes the extensions for DB side-effects described above, and we're including the output side-effect diagnosis extensions. The price paid for side-effect support is restricted to logging them whenever they occur, to avoid eventual later recomputations.

Following is an actual example involving DB side-effects. Due to lack of space, we simply present the oracle interaction. The program is a Definite Clause Grammar (buggy) translator, which is used to load a particular grammar. Afterwards the user attempts parsing of the phrase "Miguel uses a debugger that debugs". Both executions are under the debugger.

The parsing produces several solutions, the first of which is wrong: it returns an unbound semantics argument. Using the HyperTracer we pinpoint the bug *in the preprocessor* after 8 "queries"[14], starting with the bug manifestation on the *grammar* parsing:

Visited Node	Oracle answer
a phrase(s(A),[miquel,uses,a,debugger,that,debugs],B)	wrong
np(x,[a,debugger,that,debugs],A)	wrong
assert((np(x,A,B):-det(x,A,C),n(x,C,D),optrel(x,D,B)))	inadmissible
transform((np(noun_phrase(A,B,C))-->det(A),n(B),optrel(C)), (np(x,D,E):-det(x,D,F),n(x,F,G),optrel(x,G,E)) ,D,E)	wrong
transform((n(A),optrel(B)),(n(x,C,D),optrel(x,D,E)),C,E)	wrong
transform(optrel(A),optrel(x,B,C),B,C)	wrong
append([],[A,B],[A,B])	correct
append([A],[B,C],[x,B,C])	wrong

The third answer is given because the user intended the semantic argument in the translated clause to be something different from "x". The bug is localized after the last oracle answer (a variable written in lowercase instead of uppercase).

6. Conclusion

Treating internal side-effects opens new perspectives for algorithmic debugging. It is now possible to apply automatic aids to find bugs manifesting across separate top goals. As in the example above, in principle one can find a bug in a program pre-processor by debugging bug manifestations in the transformed program[15].

Treating I/O side-effects also raises promising prospects. Ideally, all the relevant external actions originated within a logic programming environment might become systematically "debuggable"!

Acknowledgements

We thank Artur Dias for his help in customizing the MacLogic interface, and Luís Caires for implementing the extra Prolog builtins we needed. Also to Bruno Legeard for useful comments.

We acknowledge the support of project ESPRIT P-973 ("ALPES"), Gabinete de Filosofia do Conhecimento, Instituto Nacional de Investigação Científica, Junta Nacional de Investigação Científica e Tecnológica, and Apple Computer, Inc.

---

[14]The HyperTracer doesn't impose the notion of "answering about a node", but rather that of "calling attention to a node", which can be examined or not, strictly on user initiative. The user is free to browse any node in any executed top goal, and is not forced to answer a potential "query" immediately (or ever), but can instead examine other suspects at will.

[15]This raises the need of at least *pretty printing* of the transformed program goals (a sort of "abstraction", as in [Lichtenstein Shapiro 88]) .

References

[Alegria et al 89]	José Alegria, Artur Dias and Luís Caires, Towards Distributed Tools for Heterogeneous Logic Programming Environments, Proceedings of the 6th International Conference on Logic Programming, MIT Press 1989.
[Bruffaerts Henin 88]	Bruffaerts, A. and Henin, E., Proof Trees for Negation as Failure: Yet Another Prolog Meta-Interpreter, in Procs. 5th Int. Conf. on Logic Programming, MIT Press 1988.
[Drabent et al 88]	W. Drabent, S. Nadjm-Tehrani and J. Maluszynski, Algorithmic Debugging with Assertions, in META88 Proceedings, MIT Press 1988.
[Eisenstadt Brayshaw 88]	Marc Eisenstadt and Mike Brayshaw, The Transparent Prolog Machine: an execution model and graphical debugger for logic programming, in Journal of Logic Programming, 1988.
[Lichtenstein Shapiro 88]	Yossi Lichtenstein and Ehud Shapiro, Abstract Program Debugging, Procs. 5th Int. Conf. on Logic Programming, MIT Press 1988.
[F.Pereira Shieber 87]	Prolog and Natural-Language Analysis, Lecture Notes, Number 10, Center for the Study of Language and Information, 1987.
[F. Pereira et al 83]	Fernando Pereira et al, C-Prolog User's Manual, EdCAAD, Dept. of Architecture, University of Edinburgh, UK, 1983.
[Pereira 84]	Luís Moniz Pereira, Rational debugging of logic programs, in Proceedings of the 1st Portuguese AI Meeting, Associação Portuguesa Para a Inteligência Artificial 1985.
[Pereira 86]	Luís Moniz Pereira, Rational debugging in logic programming, in Procs. of the 3rd International Logic Programming Conference, E.Shapiro (ed.), Lecture Notes in Computer Science 225, Springer Verlag 1986.
[Pereira Calejo 87]	Luís Moniz Pereira and Miguel Calejo, "Debugging Errors in Logic Programs", proceedings of the 3rd Portuguese AI meeting, Associação Portuguesa Para a Inteligência Artificial 1987.
[Pereira Calejo 88]	Luís Moniz Pereira and Miguel Calejo, A framework for Prolog debugging, Procs. 5th Int. Conf. on Logic Programming, MIT Press 1988.
[Pereira Calejo 89a]	Luís Moniz Pereira and Miguel Calejo, How to access Prolog execution trees and its use in debugging, UNL/DI report, 1989.
[Pereira Calejo 89b]	Luís Moniz Pereira and Miguel Calejo, The HyperTracer Manual, UNL/DI report (forthcoming).
[Shapiro 82]	Ehud Y. Shapiro, Algorithmic Program Debugging, MIT Press 1982.

COOPERATING REWRITE PROCESSES REVISITED

Miguel Filgueiras

Centro de Informática, Universidade do Porto
R. das Taipas 135, 4000 Porto, Portugal

ABSTRACT

As a first step in the study of the properties of the parsing techniques based on cooperating rewrite processes used in the Spiral Natural Language system, this paper presents a description of these techniques from a formal point of view.

INTRODUCTION

In [Filgueiras 83, 84, 86] I presented a natural language (NL) system, called Spiral, that parses sentences using three layers (called "levels" in those publications) of rewrite processes. Two of these layers have their rewrite rules applied in an interleaved fashion and cooperate in scanning the surface representation and building a relational tree of the input sentence. The semantic analyser also uses rewrite processes, as prescribed in [Porto, Filgueiras], and has been the main focus of the research work carried on by our NL team at the Universidade do Porto. Results of this work include the use of the semantic analiser as a driver for menu-based NL interfaces [Filgueiras, Silva, et al.], [Filgueiras 88], an exploration on how sentences can be generated from semantic representations [Filgueiras 87], and an extension for the treatment of time and tense [Moreira 88, 89]. Current work along this line is the subject of [Tomás, Filgueiras].

During these developments some small, and scattered in time, enhancements were made to the Spiral parser, namely the introduction of context information in the rules so that some kinds of anaphoric references could be solved. However, for a better use of the parsing techniques of Spiral a detailed study of their characteristics together with a comparison with other methods is in order. A first step in this study is the description of these techniques from a formal point of view, which none of the above references attempted to give. In fact, while [Filgueiras 84] gives a detailed account of the implementation of the Spiral parser, the other descriptions [Filgueiras 83, 86] are made in broad terms and through examples. The present paper is a reduced version of [Filgueiras 89] which tries to fill in this gap and to serve as a basis for forthcoming publications on this matter.

In the sequel, I will start by introducing the general ideas used in the Spiral parser, as well as a first formalization of them in terms of rewrite processes on finite alphabets. Then the power of these rewrite processes is studied by relating them to automata. The next section gives an extension of the previous formalization that captures most of the characteristics of the Spiral parser.

BACKGROUND

Spiral parses sentences using three layers of rewrite processes. The first layer performs some deterministic operations in order to simplify the work of the subsequent layers. As this layer is not absolutely required it will be disregarded in the following discussion. Each rule of the second layer rewrites a *token list* (which contains lexical representations and/or phrase elements) into another such list and produces a (possibly void) phrase element:

$$L1 \;\; \text{-->-} \;\; L2 \; \text{-} \; E$$

This phrase element is passed to the third layer, which runs concurrently or in an interleaved fashion with the second layer. Each third layer rule specifies how a phrase element is added to a functional (relational) structure to produce a new such structure:

$$E \; + \; S1 \;\;\; \text{--->} \;\;\; S2$$

A *global rewrite process* that rewrites a pair of a token list and a functional structure into another such pair can be defined in Prolog by the following two clauses:

$$L0 \; + \; S0 \;\;\; \text{->+} \;\;\; Ln \; + \; Sn \;\;\; \text{:-}$$
$$L0 \;\;\; \text{-->-} \;\;\; L1 \; \text{-} \; E,$$
$$E \; + \; S0 \;\;\; \text{--->} \;\;\; S1,$$
$$L1 \; + \; S1 \;\;\; \text{->+} \;\;\; Ln \; + \; Sn.$$
$$L \; + \; S \;\;\; \text{->+} \;\;\; L \; + \; S.$$

When the global rewrite process is applied to a token list Li and a functional structure Si it will produce a list Lf to which no rule could be applied successfully and the structure Sf that corresponds to that part of Li that was consumed (ie., the difference between Li and Lf).

A possible interpretation of these clauses is that the second layer scans from left to right a near-surface representation of the sentence, and consumes part of it when it succeeds in applying one of its rules. The phrase element then produced, that can be seen as a more abstract representation of the consumed part, is taken by the third layer which may succeed in incorporating it in the functional structure. This idea of abstracting from a part of the sentence an element that is to be fitted in the functional structure played an important role in the design of the parser. Although it can perhaps be used to establish a psychological model of NL understanding this has not been pursued.

The above definition of the global rewrite process assumes that the rewrite rules for the second and third layers are expressed by the clause heads for the predicates "-->-" and "--->". The clause bodies may impose conditions on the application of the rules and even invoke recursively the global rewrite process for the analysis of embedded phrases.

The parsing method just described, which can be viewed in broad terms as a recursive bottom-up left-to-right process, has been employed to analyse fairly extensive subsets of both English and Portuguese.

The questions I shall try to answer in the sequel are:
- how can this parsing method be formalized and extended?
- which is the power of this method?

The reader is referred to [Hopcroft, Ullman, 69, 79] for introductory readings on automata and formal languages.

A FORMALIZATION

Let a *base level* be defined as a triplet formed by two alphabets Vb, Vu, the *own alphabet* and the *upper alphabet*, respectively, and a set of rewrite rules R. Each rule in R takes the form w -->- w'- a where w and w' are in $Vb*$ and a (the *upper symbol*) in Vu. Where needed I will resort to denoting each rule by an element of a relation like $r(w,w',a)$.

Let a *constructor* associated with an alphabet V be a partial function that from a symbol in V and a string in $V*$ produces a new string in $V*$. Constructors will be coupled with base levels to build a representation in $V*$ from a previous one and the upper symbol produced by the base level rule, and, in doing so, to act as filters by rejecting any upper symbol that does not fit in, or is incompatible with, the previous representation in $V*$. Constructors will also be used as interfaces between base levels when several of these are put together.

A *level* is an ordered pair of a base level with an upper alphabet V_u and a constructor associated with V_u.

A *closure rewrite process* for a level is denoted by

$$w - u \dashrightarrow + \quad w' - u'$$

and associates to given input strings w in V_b* and u in V_u* the results of applying one of the following:

• the results are those of the recursive application of the closure rewrite process to z_1 m and $\text{constr}(a_1, u)$, where constr is the constructor of the level, provided there is a base level rule of the form

$$z \dashrightarrow - z_1 - a_1$$

such that $w = z$ m and $\text{constr}(a_1, u)$ is defined;

• the results are the input strings.

The intended interpretation is that the base level rules rewrite prefixes of strings (starting with w, which is eventually rewritten into w'). The constructor is applied each time a base level rule is, taking as arguments the upper symbol produced by the rule and a string (initially u, which is eventually rewritten into u').

This can also be viewed as a mathematical model for a non-deterministic machine with a finite control and two tapes, initially containing w and u. In each step the machine either does nothing, or performs the following operations. It reads and erases a string z starting from the left end of the first tape, writing in the tape's left end another string z_1, and entering state a_1. The string in the second tape is then read and replaced by a string depending upon the state of the finite control and the string just read.

The definition of a closure rewrite process can be extended for more than one level. Let r_i $(1 \leq i \leq n)$ be a relational symbol of arity 3 standing for the rules of base level i with own alphabet V_{b_i} and upper alphabet V_{u_i}, such that for all $1 \leq j < n$, $V_{b_{j+1}} \supseteq V_{u_j}$ (this condition will be relaxed whenever we can guarantee that a base level does not receive unacceptable symbols from another one - note that constructors can act as filters). Let constr_i $(1 \leq i \leq n)$ be the constructor associated with base level i. The closure rewrite process for the n levels associates to $n+1$ given input strings w_i in $V_{b_i}*$ $(1 \leq i \leq n)$ and w_{n+1} in $V_{u_n}*$, the $n+1$ strings resulting from applying one of the following:

• the results are those of the recursive application of the closure rewrite process to z'_i m_i $(1 \leq i \leq n)$ and $\text{constr}_n(a_n, w_{n+1})$, provided the latter is defined and there are base level rules of the form

$$r_i(z_i, z'_i, a_i) \qquad 1 \leq i \leq n$$

such that

$$w_1 = z_1 \ m_1$$
$$\text{constr}_j(a_j, w_{j+1}) = z_{j+1} \ m_{j+1} \qquad 1 \leq j < n$$

• the results are the input strings.

In terms of the machine described above, this extension corresponds to coupling **n** such different machines, numbered from 1 to **n**, in such a way that for each **j**, with $1 \leq j < n$, the second tape of machine **j** is the first tape of machine **j+1**.

CLOSURE REWRITE PROCESSES AND AUTOMATA

Some properties concerning the power of closure rewrite processes can be established by relating these processes to automata. Strong restrictions must be put on what constructors can do in order not to pervert their passive role as filters and interfaces. I will not try to formalize those restrictions in here, although all the constructors used below will be very simple functions (in most cases they just add a symbol to the front of a string). Some of the proofs mentioned below may be found in [Filgueiras 89].

It is quite easy to prove that a closure rewrite process for a single level having a concatenation constructor has at least the power of a finite automaton. A proof consists in building such a process to simulate any automaton. Similar results can be drawn for Mealy machines (which are finite automata extended with an output alphabet and an output function which gives an output symbol for each transition) and for generalized sequential machines (GSMs) of Ginsburg (the difference to Mealy machines being that a GSM produces a string of symbols in the output alphabet instead of a single symbol in each transition).

A closure rewrite process with two levels can be constructed to simulate a given pushdown automaton (PDA). The first level is used to produce each symbol in the input (from left to right), introducing at any point an arbitrary number of occurrences of a special symbol (the empty symbol). The empty symbols may be needed to simulate ε-transitions of the PDA. The second level simulates the pushdown store and keeps a representation of the PDA current state.

Let the PDA be defined by $M = (S, I, P, t, q0, Z0, F)$ where S, I, P are the set of states, the input alphabet and the pushdown alphabet, t is a mapping from $S \times (I \cup \{ε\}) \times P$ into finite subsets of $S \times P^*$, $q0$ is the initial state, $Z0$, in P, the start symbol, and F the set of final states.

The closure rewrite process for this PDA will be as follows. The own alphabet for the first base level is the PDA input alphabet I, while its upper alphabet is $I \cup \{\$\}$, where $\$$, a symbol not in I, is used to denote an empty output. The rules in the first base level are

$$r_1(x, ε, x) \qquad \text{for every } x \text{ in } I$$

$$r_1(ε, ε, \$)$$

The constructor associated to the first base level is

$$constr_1(\$, s) = s$$

$$constr_1(x, s) = x s \text{ for each } x \text{ in } I$$

It adds every symbol in I to the front of the string, and filters out $\$$. In this way, the first level singles out each input symbol and may perform empty rewrite steps so that the number of rewrite steps in the second level becomes independent of the length of the input.

The own alphabet of the second base level is $I \cup S \cup P$ and its upper alphabet is S. I assume (without loss of generality) that S, I and P are disjoint. The set of rules for this base level is built as follows: for each (p,m) in $t(q,a,Z)$, with p and q in S, m in P^*, a in $I \cup \{\mathfrak{E}\}$, and Z in P, add the rule

$$r_2(a q Z, p m, p)$$

The constructor for this base level produces the string formed by its first argument (it forgets its second argument):

$$constr_2(x, s) = x \qquad \text{for every } x \text{ in } S$$

A closure rewrite process with these two levels applied to the input strings w, $q0$ $Z0$, $\mathfrak{E}$ will produce the strings $\mathfrak{E}$, m, f, with m in $(I \cup S \cup P)^*$, and f in F if and only if the PDA accepts (by final state) the input w.

We may conclude that a closure rewrite process with two levels has at least the power of a PDA.

From the results on GSMs and on PDAs in the previous sections it would seem that the result of increasing the number of levels is an increased power of the closure rewrite process. This idea is further supported by examples [Filgueiras 89] of closure rewrite processes with 3 levels that accept type 0 and type 1 languages (in the Chomsky's hierarchy).

However there is a serious limitation to closure rewrite processes which has to do with two aspects of their definition. In first place, rewrite rules in base levels are always applied to prefixes of strings, and this implies that those strings will be scanned from left to right. Secondly, the flow of information between levels is sequential between processes, with no feedback. This means that a certain level cannot scan an arbitrary number of times an arbitrarily long string w, because it cannot make a copy of it by itself and would have to be preceeded by an arbitrary number n of levels to produce w^n. Therefore the conclusion is that there is no way of simulating an arbitrary Turing machine with closure rewrite processes as defined, although they have more power than PDAs (as the examples in [Filgueiras 89] show).

One way of attaining the full power of Turing machines is by redefining the closure rewrite processes so that the last level sends information to the first level. This leads to the definition of *cyclic closure rewrite processes*. Let the base level i be (Vb_i, Vu_i, r_i) $(1 \leq i \leq n)$, such that for all $1 \leq j < n$, $Vb_{j+1} \supseteq Vu_j$ and $Vu_n \supseteq Vb_1$ (this condition can be relaxed as above). Let $\mathbf{constr_i}$ $(1 \leq i \leq n)$ be the constructor associated with base level $\mathbf{i}$. The cyclic closure rewrite process for the $\mathbf{n}$ levels associates to $\mathbf{n}$ given input strings $\mathbf{w_i}$ in $\mathbf{Vb_i}^*$ $(1 \leq i \leq n)$, the $\mathbf{n}$ strings resulting from applying one of the following:

    • the results are those of the recursive application of the process to $\mathbf{constr_n(a_n, \ z'_1 \ m_1)}$ and $\mathbf{z'_i \ m_i}$ $(1 < i \leq n)$, provided there are base level rules of the form

$$r_i(z_i, z'_i, a_i) \qquad 1 \leq i \leq n$$

such that

$$w_1 = z_1 \ m_1$$
$$constr_j(a_j, w_{j+1}) = z_{j+1} \ m_{j+1} \qquad 1 \leq j < n$$

    • the results are the input strings.

It is straightforward to build a cyclic closure rewrite process with two levels to simulate a given Turing machine. The idea is to have the first base level dealing with the symbols to the right of the head of the Turing machine, while the second base level stores the symbols to the left. A symbol is passed from the first to the second level whenever the head moves right, and from the second to the first whenever it moves left. This is similar to the way two-pushdown-store machines simulate Turing machines. The construction details may be found in [Filgueiras 89].

A problem that remains to be solved is the one of finding a finer characterization of the set of languages accepted by closure rewrite processes. As the previous discussion tried to show this set properly contains the set of context-free languages and is properly contained by the set of type 0 languages.

A MORE GENERAL FORMALIZATION

Instead of resorting to cyclic closure rewrite processes we may extend the definition of closure rewrite processes so that they have the power of Turing machines. The extension I explore in this section consists in letting rewrite rules act on complex terms instead of strings of atomic symbols in an alphabet. This is what an implementation in Prolog provides for free.

Let $\mathbf{T}$ be the set of terms of a logic calculus, such as the one defined by the Edinburgh Prolog syntax.

A base level is now defined as a triplet formed by two subsets $\mathbf{Tb}$, $\mathbf{Tu}$ of $\mathbf{T}$, the *own language* and the *upper language*, respectively, and a set of rewrite rules $\mathbf{R}$. Each rule in $\mathbf{R}$ takes the form

$$x \ \text{-->-} \ x' - t$$

with $\mathbf{x}$ and $\mathbf{x'}$ in $\mathbf{Tb}$ and $\mathbf{t}$ (the *upper term*) in $\mathbf{Tu}$.

A constructor associated with a language **Tl** contained in **T** is a partial function that from two terms in **Tl** produces a new such term.

A level is an ordered pair of a base level with an upper language **Tu**, and a constructor associated with **Tu**.

A closure rewrite process for a level is denoted by

$$x - u \quad \text{-->+} \quad x' - u'$$

and relates the terms x, x' in **Tb** and u, u' in **Tu**, yielding a substitution s_r by applying one of the following:

- s_p is the composition of s with the result of the recursive application of the closure rewrite process to $s.z_1$ and **constr**$(s.t_1, s.u)$, where **constr** is the constructor of the level, provided there is a base level rule of the form

$$z \quad \text{-->-} \quad z_1 - t_1$$

  where s is a substitution such that $s.x = s.z$ is the most general unifier of x and z, and **constr**$(s.t_1, s.u)$ is defined.

- s_p is a substitution such that $s_p.x = s_p.x'$ and $s_p.u = s_p.u'$ are the most general unifiers of, respectively, x and x', and u and u'.

As in the case of the previous formalization, this definition may be extended to deal with more than one level. However, a single level is enough to simulate a Turing machine. A way of doing so is to have a base level whose own language contains terms of the form **m(State, Left, Right)** where **State** is a representation of the machine state, and **Left** and **Right** are lists of the tape symbols to the left and to the right of the machine head. The construction then proceeds along the lines of the one given for cyclic rewrite processes.

In order to capture some important features of the Spiral parser I will consider now two other extensions to this definition. One of them has to do with the pairing of rewrite rules with conditions on their application. The other one allows the definition of special-purpose closure rewrite processes and their recursive use when a rewrite rule is applied.

With the above definition the only direct constraint on the application of a rewrite rule consists in that the input term (x) and the rule left-hand-side (z) must be unifiable (the requirement that **constr**$(s.t_1, s.u)$ must be defined being but a test on whether the result of applying the rule is adequate to the current context). It is useful, for practical purposes, to have the possibility of resorting to operations on terms other than unification to constrain the application of rules. This leads to the pairing of each rule with a condition on the input term, whose result will determine whether or not the rule is to be applied. A problem that I will not address in here is what kind of operations will be allowed, or, in other words, which is the language (its syntax and semantics) for the expression of such conditions. In Spiral, Prolog was used for expressing what can be regarded as conditions (pure Prolog would be enough). But other possibilities include the use of constraint languages similar to those used for unification grammars (cf. for instance [Damas, Varile] and references thereof).

In the following definition of a base level I take a language Lc, whose sentences may contain terms of Ta or Tb (the own and upper languages of the base level), together with an evaluation function that from a sentence in Lc produces a truth-value and a substitution. To each rewrite rule a sentence C in Lc is added:

$$z \text{ -->- } z_1 - t_1 \text{ if } C$$

The first rule of the definition of a closure rewrite process is modified to read:

• s_p is the composition $s_c.s_u$ with the result of the recursive application of the closure rewrite process to $s_c.s_u.z_1$ and $constr(s_c.s_u.t_1, s_c.s_u.u)$, where $constr$ is the constructor of the level, provided there is a base level rule of the form

$$z \text{ -->- } z_1 - t_1 \text{ if } C$$

where s_u is a substitution such that $s_u.x = s_u.z$ is the most general unifier of x and z, the evaluation of $s_u.C$ yields **true** and a substitution s_c, and $constr(s_c.s_u.t_1, s_c.s_u.u)$ is defined.

As we have seen above, closure rewrite processes on complex terms, rather than on symbols in alphabets, have the power of Turing machines. Therefore they will not have any additional power if we allow them to be recursively applied. However, it is useful to think of the parsing of embedded sentences in terms of recursive application of rewrite processes. On the other hand, the advantages of having special-purpose closure rewrite processes become obvious when one considers the situations in which a certain sequence of words introduces a sub-phrase of a known category (for instance, a noun-phrase that should follow a preposition, or a "whose"). In the overall bottom-up parsing, the use of such special-purpose processes introduces a top-down strategy, or to be more precise a kind of restricted bottom-up parsing, which proves to be highly efficient. To build these rewrite processes I will pair a closure rewrite process as previously defined with a condition on its application. Once more, I am not going to fix what is the language in which these conditions are specified.

I will now give the general definitions resulting from the above ideas. I still consider the set T of terms of a logic calculus, and a constraint language Lc. The definitions of constructor and level are the previous ones.

A base level is a triplet formed by two subsets Tb, Tu of T, the *own language* and the *upper language*, respectively, and a set of rewrite rules R. Each rule in R takes one of the following forms:

$$x \text{ -->- } x' - t \text{ if } C$$
$$x \text{ -->- } x' - t \text{ if } C \text{ with } crp_k(x'',w,x',t)$$

with x, x' and x'' in Tb, t (the *upper term*) and w in Tu, C a sentence of Lc, and where $crp_k(x'',w,x',t)$ denotes a closure rewrite process (as defined below).

A closure rewrite process for a level is denoted by

$$crp_i(x, u, x', u') \quad \textbf{under} \quad R_i$$

(where R_i is a sentence of Lc) and relates the terms x, x' in Tb and u, u' in Tu, yielding a substitution s_p, by applying one of the following:

• s_p is the composition of sf with the result of the recursive application of the closure rewrite process to $sf.z_1$ and $constr(t_f, sf.u)$, where $constr$ is the constructor of the level, provided the evaluation of R_i yields **true** and a substitution s_r, and

    a) there is a base level rule of the form

$$z \; \text{-->-} \; z_1 \cdot t_1 \quad \textbf{if} \quad C$$

such that:

1) there exists a substitution s_u such that $s_u \cdot s_r . x = s_u \cdot s_r . z$ is the most general unifier of $s_r.x$ and $s_r.z$,

2) the evaluation of $s_u \cdot s_r.C$ yields **true** and a substitution s_c,

3) sf is the composition of s_c, s_u and s_r,

4) $constr(\; sf.t_1, sf.u)$ is defined and $t_f = sf.t_1$;

o r

    b) there is a base level rule of the form

$$z \; \text{-->-} \; z_1 \cdot t_1 \quad \textbf{if} \quad C \quad \textbf{with} \quad crp_k(z',w,z_1,t_1)$$

such that

1) there exists a substitution s_u such that $s_u \cdot s_r . x = s_u \cdot s_r . z$ is the most general unifier of $s_r.x$ and $s_r.z$,

2) the evaluation of $s_u \cdot s_r.C$ yields **true** and a substitution s_c,

3) taking s_i as the composition of s_c, s_u and s_r, the application of the closure rewrite process crp_k to $s_i.z'$ and $s_i.w$ yields a substitution s_k.

4) sf is the composition of s_k and s_i,

5) $constr(sf.t_1, sf.u)$ is defined and $t_f = sf.t_1$.

• s_p is a substitution such that $s_p.x = s_p.x'$ and $s_p.u = s_p.u'$ are the most general unifiers of, respectively, x and x', and u and u'.

CONCLUSIONS

I presented a formalization of the parsing methods based on cooperating rewrite processes that I developed when building the Spiral NL system. This formalization is intended as a first step in a study of the properties of these methods.

A formal definition of rewrite processes working on symbols in finite alphabets was given as an introduction. A comparison of the power of these processes to automata has proved that they can recognize any context-free and some non-context-free languages, although they do not have the power of Turing machines. A finer characterization of the set accepted by these processes has been left as an open problem.

Using terms of a logic calculus instead of symbols in finite alphabets leads trivially to rewrite processes recognizing type 0 languages. The general definition of rewrite processes results from extending in this way the previous one, as well as `introducing recursion and conditions on the application of rewrite processes and of rewrite rules.

ACKNOWLEDGEMENTS

The comments made by Ana Paula Tomás, Armando Matos and Luís Damas on drafts of this paper were most helpful.

The work described herein was partially supported by Junta Nacional de Investigação Científica e Tecnológica, under research contract no. 87.336, and by Instituto Nacional de Investigação Científica.

REFERENCES

[Damas, Varile] L. Damas, G. Varile, CLG: A Grammar Formalism Based on Constraint Resolution, in this volume.

[Filgueiras 83] M. Filgueiras, A Kernel for a General Natural Language Interface, in L. Moniz Pereira, L. Monteiro, A. Porto, M. Filgueiras (eds.), Proceedings of the Logic Programming Workshop 83, Universidade Nova de Lisboa, 1983.

[Filgueiras 84] M. Filgueiras, Compreensão de Linguagem Natural: Uma Metodologia, doctoral dissertation, Universidade Nova de Lisboa, 1984.

[Filgueiras 86] M. Filgueiras, Cooperating Rewrite Processes for Natural Language Analysis, Journal of Logic Programming, vol. 3, no. 4, 1986.

[Filgueiras 87] M. Filgueiras, Generating Natural Language Sentences from Semantic Representations, A. Sernadas, J. Neves (eds.), Actas do Encontro Português de Inteligência Artificial 87, APPIA, 1987.

[Filgueiras 88] M. Filgueiras, A Query Method Driven by Semantics, Centro de Informática, Universidade do Porto, 1988.

[Filgueiras 89] M. Filgueiras, A Formalization of Parsing with Cooperating Rewrite Processes, Centro de Informática, Universidade do Porto, 1989.

[Filgueiras, Silva, et al.] M. Filgueiras, F. Silva, M.E. Pinto, A. Pinheiro, Menus Naturais, in P. Brazdil, M. Filgueiras, L. Damas, A. Matos (eds.) Actas do Encontro Português de Inteligência Artificial 86, APPIA, 1986.

[Hopcroft, Ullman, 69] J. Hopcroft, J. Ullman, Formal Languages and Their Relation to Automata, Addison-Wesley, 1969.

[Hopcroft, Ullman, 79] J. Hopcroft, J. Ullman, Introduction to Automata Theory, Languages, and Computation, Addison-Wesley, 1979.

[Moreira 88] N. Moreira, Representação Semântica de Referências Temporais em Linguagem Natural, essay submitted to the Universidade do Porto, 1988.

[Moreira 89] N. Moreira, Semantic Analysis of Time and Tense in Natural Language: An Implementation, in this volume.

[Porto, Filgueiras] A. Porto, M. Filgueiras, A Logic Programming Approach to Natural Language Semantics, Proceedings of the 1984 International Symposium on Logic Programming, IEEE, 1984.

[Tomás, Filgueiras] A.P. Tomás, M. Filgueiras, Some Comments on a Logic Programming Approach to Natural Language Semantics, in this volume.

CLG : A GRAMMAR FORMALISM BASED ON CONSTRAINT RESOLUTION

Luis Damas

Universidade do Porto, Rua das Taipas 135, 4000 Porto, Portugal

Giovanni B. Varile

CEC , 2920 Luxembourg, Luxembourg

Abstract

We present the design and implementation of a powerful grammar formalism based on constraint resolution. Constraints are expressed in a full first order language with equality allowing on top of the expression of equational, disjunctive, conjunctive, negative, implicative and if-then-else constraints. CLG has been implemented in Prolog and tested with relatively large grammars of Danish, English and German. We also report on the efficiency of the implementation and the expressive adequacy of the formalism.

keywords: Natural language processing, constraint logic programming

1 Background: Constraint Expression in Unification Grammar

Since their introduction in 1979 [Kay79], unification based grammar formalisms have enjoyed a remarkable success in computational linguistics and natural language processing in general.

Central to unification grammars is the notion of constraints, which describe the way information is to be combined by unification. While in the PATR-II formalism [Shie83], constraints can only be expressed as equations, in the FUG formalism [Kay79,Kay84], constraints are expressed as equations, alternations, by the special cset and pattern features as well as with the non-monotonic ANY value.

Several proposals have been put forward to augment the purely equational constraints of PATR-II, starting with the introduction of negation and disjunction of values by Karttunen [Kart84].

However, extending the expression of constraints beyond simple equations is not unproblematic, as pointed out by Pereira [Pere87a].

In order to clarify these problems, Kasper and Rounds [Kasp86,Roun86] have elaborated a logical calculus providing a formal semantics of disjunctive feature structure specification. This logic has been extended by Moshier and Rounds [Mosh87] to cover negation and implication giving an intuitionistic interpretation to negation. More recently, Kasper has described an extension to FUG that uses implication and a restricted interpretation of negation [Kasp88].

Although Kasper [Kasp87] has proposed an algorithm for handling grammars with a large number of disjunctions, the computational tractability of complex constraints in unification based formalism remains an open problem.

In a rather different perspective, Gazdar and his fellow researchers [Gazd86,Gazd87] propose a constraint language licensing the admissibility of categories defined within their formal framework for category definition [*ibid.*]. Their constraint language, a first order modal logic, is the meta language for formulating constraints on the well formedness of grammatical categories and in this sense is not directly part of the description of linguistic phenomena, but, rather, part of the definition of the constraints of the linguistic theory.

The difference between Gazdar's proposal and the previously mentioned constraint languages resides not only in the fact that Gazdar's is a meta constraint language, but also in that his concern is only to license grammatical categories, without being concerned with the properties of structural descriptions.

In this paper we present the main features of the CLG (Constraint Logic Grammar) formalism which allows the expression of disjunctive, conjunctive, implicative, negative and if-then-else constraints over the domain of descriptions. Our experience indicates that in the presence of non-recursive feature systems, it is possible to efficiently implement a logically sound system for expressing complex constraints.

The design of CLG was motivated by the practical needs of grammatical description and coding, while the delayed evaluation scheme chosen for the implementation was motivated by the desire to produce an efficient and logically sound implementation.

In Section 2 we present the CLG formalism and show examples of constraint expressions in grammar rules. In Section 3 we give the formal semantics of CLG grammars. The Prolog implementation of the formalism is described in Section 4. We conclude by indicating directions of future work.

2 Overview of the CLG Formalism

A CLG grammar consists of a specification of admissible complex categories, a set of grammar rules and a set of macro definitions.

Categories and category admissibility conditions are specified using a subset of Gazdar's formalism [Gaz86] which allows only the statement of implicative constraints. This paper being devoted to the description of the CLG formalism, we omit the details of the category definition, which is mentioned in this place for completeness only.

A CLG grammar rule is a pair consisting of a context free skeleton and constraints:

$$X_0[\#X_1, .., \#X_n].cs_1, ..., cs_k$$

We use [and] to separate the mother of a local tree from its daughters instead of the more common rewrite arrow. The X_i are labels (Prolog variables in the implemented system), the # represents an optional prefix operator indicating optionality or iteration (i.e. Kleene * or +) while $cs_1, \ldots, cs_k$ are the constraints to which we devote the bulk of the remainder of this section.

Constraints are expressed in a first order language with equality. Given sets *Attrs* of attribute names (constants, implemented as Prolog atoms), *Vals* of constant values, *Vars* of variables ranging over *Vals* and *Labs* of labels, we define the terms of this first order language in the following way:

$$Term = Vars + Vals + Labs + Labs \times Attrs^+$$

That is, a term is either a variable, a constant value, a label or a path expression consisting of a label and attribute names. The labels are used to refer to nodes in the description. Path expressions will not be limited to depth one since we are going to introduce category valued categories (without recursion).

The atomic constraints of CLG are the atomic formulae of the first order equational language and defined in the following way:

$$t = t' \text{ for } t, t' \text{ in } Term$$

There is a non-equational atomic constraint in the constraint language of the form *present(Label)*, which tests whether an optionally marked element was found in the input. The *present* predicate is part of the definition of the constraint language together with other predicates whose description is omitted for the sake of simplicity. We would only like to stress that the number and type of predicates can easily be changed as dictated by the requirements of the linguistic theory.

A very simple example of a CLG rule using only equational constraints is the following:

$$X_0[X_1, *X_2, X_3].X_0 : cat = np, \ X_1 : cat = det, \ X_2 : cat = adj, \ X_3 : cat = n$$

In order to facilitate grammar coding and increase their readability, the present implementation supports a syntactically *sugared* version of the abstract language used in the example above. The main property of the *sugared* language is to allow the specification of constraints with the context free skeleton:

$$X_0 : \{cat = np\}[X_1 : \{cat = det\}, *X_2 : \{cat = adj\}, X_3 : \{cat = n\}]$$

The star operator of the adjective is the Kleene star *. In the rest of this paper the examples will be given using this syntactic *sugared* notation. Note that in the last example, the labels X_i can be omitted if not otherwise needed.

We will now complete the definition of the first order constraint language. The well formed formulae of the constraint language are defined as follows:

- atomic constraints are well formed constraints (wfc)

- if C is a wfc, so is $\neg C$ (*not C*)

- if C, D are wfcs, so are $C \mid D$ (*C or D*), $C \wedge D$ (*C and D*), $C \rightarrow D$ (*material implication* and $C \leftrightarrow D$

- if C, D and E are wfcs, so is $C \rightarrow D; E$ (*if C then D else E*)

- if C is a wfc and X a variable in *Lab*, then $forall(X)\ C$ is a wfc

The semantics of constraints is implemented in a logically complete way, i.e., if M is the meaning function, then:

$$
\begin{aligned}
M[\![\neg C]\!] &= \neg M[\![C]\!] \\
M[\![C \mid D]\!] &= M[\![C]\!] \mid M[\![D]\!] \\
M[\![C \wedge D]\!] &= M[\![C]\!] \wedge M[\![D]\!] \\
M[\![C \rightarrow D]\!] &= M[\![C]\!] \rightarrow M[\![D]\!] \\
M[\![C \rightarrow D; E]\!] &= (M[\![C]\!] \rightarrow M[\![D]\!]) \wedge (M[\![\neg C]\!] \rightarrow M[\![E]\!]) \\
M[\![forall(X)C]\!] &= \text{for all } X\ M[\![C]\!]
\end{aligned}
$$

For a more detailed definition we refer the reader to section 3.

We will now give some examples in order to illustrate features of the CLG formalism. For space reasons, the examples are simplified versions of rules taken from our grammars. We will start by examining the following rule:

$S : \{cat = s,\ finite = nonfin,\ s\_type = subord\}$
    $[\ \ ^\wedge NP : \{cat = np\},$
        $VP : \{cat = vp,\ vform = base\}]$
where
    $S : diath = VP,$
    $present(NP) \rightarrow ($
        $(VP : diath = act \rightarrow NP : deep\_sf = subj)\ \ \wedge$
        $(VP : diath = pass \rightarrow NP : deep\_sf = obj))$

which states that a non-finite sentence is formed by an optional noun phrase followed by a verb phrase.

Constraints are separated from the augmented skeleton by the word *where*. The first constraint in the rule specifies that S and VP have the same value for the diathesis attribute.

The second constraint, which applies only if the optional NP is present, computes the deep syntactic function of the NP constituent based on the diathesis attribute. Note that if no value was assigned to the *diath* attribute of the VP or S components then this constraint would be kept unresolved until such an assignment took place.

As a second example consider:

$NP : \{cat = np\}$
    $[\quad \cdots,$

$$^{\hat{}}(DET : \{cat = det\}; NP : \{cat = np, case = gen\}),$$
$$\cdots,$$
$$N : \{cat = n\},$$
$$*(PP : \{cat = pp, pdist = univl; nonadjl\};$$
$$\{cat = ap, cattype = ppl\};$$
$$SBAR : \{cat = sbar, sbar\_context = np\})]$$

where

$$NP :< num, gen, case, n\_class > = N,$$
$$present(DET) \rightarrow ($$
$$(DET : lex = the \rightarrow NP : def = yes;$$
$$DET : lex = a \rightarrow NP : def = no) \wedge$$
$$(DET : cattype = demonstr \rightarrow NP : dem = DET : lex)),$$

$$\cdots$$

$$forall(PP)($$
$$(N : ers\_frame = none \wedge PP : pform = of \rightarrow PP : sf = poss) \wedge$$
$$(N : ers\_frame = subj \wedge PP : pform = of \rightarrow PP : sf = compl) \wedge$$
$$(N : ers\_frame = subj\_objnp \rightarrow ($$
$$(PP : pform = of \rightarrow PP : sf = compl2) \wedge$$
$$(PP : pform = by \rightarrow PP : sf = perj)))),$$

$$\cdots$$

where the semicolon in the augmented skeleton indicates alternation. The first constraint states that the noun phrase shares the number, gender, case and noun class with its head noun. The second constraint makes use of the $if-then-else$ construct : if the determiner is present then first, if it is *the* the noun phrase is marked as definite, else if the determiner is *a* it is marked as indefinite and second, if the determiner is demonstrative then the noun phrase attribute *dem* gets the lexical form of the demonstrative as value.

The remaining constraint illustrates the use of the *forall* construct to specify a constraint which should apply to all the constituents labelled PP in the rule.

Note that the usage made above of the $if-then-else$ construct is merely a form of hand optimization relying on the fact that *the* occurs more frequently than *a*, so that in a majority of cases the *else* part will not have to be evaluated. The more useful application of this construct is however in situations where we want to have exceptions override the general case to express a preferred interpretation:

$$if < exceptional\_case > then < exceptional\_action >$$
$$else < regular\_action >$$

By using the possibility of chaining the *if-then-else* constructs, we can achieve a sophisticated treatment of hierarchies of successively less exceptional situations.

In order to avoid the repetitive statement of constraints which apply to more than one rule, CLG supports a macro definition facility. A macro consists of a name followed by a list of label variables followed by a constraint. For instance, our grammar may contain several rules for noun phrases, all of which would have to state the first constraint above. If we now defined:

$$NP\_AGR(X,Y) \quad X :< num, gen, case, n\_class > = Y$$

we can avoid the statement of the constraint by simply adding to the constraints the name of the principle defined in the macro with the correct bindings for the variables in the macro definition $NP\_AGR(NP, N)$. Macro are especially useful when used to encode sophisticated linguistic priciples.

One final example is the following, where the use of negation and alternation is illustrated:

$$S : \{cat = s\}$$
$$[\hat{} \{cat = prep\},$$
$$(\quad \{cat = advp; ap; pp\};$$
$$SB1 : \{cat = sb\};$$
$$\ldots;$$
$$NP1 : \{cat = np\}),$$
$$V : \{cat = v\},$$
$$\ldots,$$
$$(\quad NP2 : \{cat = np\};$$
$$SB2 : \{cat = sb\}),$$
$$\hat{} NP : \{cat = np, np\_type = refl\_pron\},$$
$$\ldots]$$
$$where$$
$$\ldots,$$
$$present(NP2) \rightarrow S :< num, pers, case > = NP2,$$
$$present(SB1) \wedge SB1 : s\_type\neg = (subord; ats)$$
$$\rightarrow SB : s\_type = interr,$$
$$present(NP1) \wedge NP1 : dem\neg = den \rightarrow NP1 : dem = denne,$$
$$\ldots$$

where the semicolon indicates again alternation. The second constraint states that if the $SB1$ constituent is present and its sentence type is different from *subord* and *ats* then it is necessarily an interrogative.

A final remark: because of the lazy evaluation scheme adopted for the implementation, it can happen that not all constraints attached to partial descriptions will be resolved at the end of the grammar evaluation process. How we deal with this is explained in section 4.

3   Formal Semantics

We will define in this section a denotational semantics for CLG grammars. A meaning will be given to a CLG grammar by defining a recognition function from the domain of representations to the domain of truth values.

Starting from primitive sets *Attrs* and *Vals* of attribute names and of attribute values, we define the domains of feature bundles and of objects as follows

$$
\begin{aligned}
Fbs &= Attrs\mathord{-}>Vals_\perp && \text{feature bundles} \\
Objects &= Fbs \times Objects^* && \text{objects}
\end{aligned}
$$

where feature bundles are the information elements of representations (objects) and $Vals_\perp$ is *Vals* plus a bottom element.

The syntactic domains of our grammars are defined as follows: given sets *Vars* and *Labs* of variable symbols and of node labels, we define the following syntactic domains:

$$
\begin{aligned}
Exp &::= Labs \times Attrs \\
Constraint &::= Exp = Exp \\
&\quad| \quad \neg Constraint \\
&\quad| \quad Constraint \wedge Constraint \\
&\quad| \quad Constraint \mid Constraint
\end{aligned}
$$

$$
\begin{aligned}
Skel &= Labs \times Labs^* \\
Rule &= Skel \times Constraint^* \\
Generators &= Rule^*
\end{aligned}
$$

To define our semantic functions we still need two other domains :

$$
\begin{aligned}
r &\in VEnv = Vars \to Vals_\perp && \text{environments for variables} \\
s &\in SEnv = Labs \to Objects && \text{environments for labels}
\end{aligned}
$$

Let *TT* denote the domain of truth values. We define the following semantic functions for value expressions and constraints

$$
V : Exp \to VEnv \to SEnv \to Vals_\perp
$$

by

$$
\begin{aligned}
V[v]rs &= v \ (v \in Vals) \\
V[x]rs &= r[x] \\
V[l.a]rs &= s[l](a)
\end{aligned}
$$

and

$$
C : Constraint \to VEnv \to SEnv \to TT
$$

by

$$
\begin{aligned}
C[e_1 = e_2]rs &= V[e_1]rs = V[e_2]rs \\
C[\neg c_1]rs &= \neg C[c_1]rs \\
C[c_1 \wedge c_2]rs &= C[c_1]rs \wedge C[c_2]rs \\
C[c_1 \mid c_2]rs &= C[c_1]rs \mid C[c_2]rs
\end{aligned}
$$

To define our semantic function for generators we need a function for matching an object against a structure description

$$Match : Skel \times Objects \rightarrow SEnv + fail_\perp$$

defined by

$$Match(Label, Obj) = [Obj/Label]$$
$$Match(Label[Sk_1, ...Sk_n], (Fb, [Obj_1, ..., Obj_n])) =$$
$$[Fb/Label] * Match(Sk_1, Obj_1) * ... * Match(Sk_n, Obj_n)$$

where $*$ denotes the obvious composition of environments, i.e. $s_1 * s_2$ is different from $fail$ iff for every label l such that both $s_1[l]$ and $s_2[l]$ are defined, one has $s_1[l] = s_2[l]$, and in this case $(s_1 * s_2)[l]$ is defined for all l such that either $s_1[l]$ or $s_2[l]$ is defined. We can now define our semantic function for generators

$$S : Generators \rightarrow Objects \rightarrow TT$$

by

$$S[\![G]\!]Obj = \exists(Sk, Cs) \in G$$
$$\exists r \in VEnv$$
$$\exists s \in SEnv$$
$$\text{s.t. } s = Match(Sk, Obj)$$
$$\text{and } C[\![Cs]\!]rs = true$$
$$\text{and for every top label } l \in Sk$$
$$S[\![G]\!]s[\![l]\!] = true$$

where by top label l in a skeleton, we refer to a label occurring at depth 1, e.g. given the skeleton

$$l\,[\,l_1[l_{11}l_{12}]\,l_2[l_{21}[l_{211}]]\,]$$

the top labels are l_1 and l_2.

4 Implementation

The system described in the previous sections has been implemented in Prolog using the YAP compiler developed at the University of Porto. The implementation starts by converting a grammar using the construct $Label : feature\_name$ to a form, akin to the formalism described in the previous section, using only variables.

The parsing strategy used is a top-down recursive descent, similar to the one used by DCGs, modified to control left-recursion and handle constraints. This choice was mainly motivated by the fact that implementing other parsing strategies, such as tabular parsing, has proven problematic for unification grammars due to the need to copy partial parses (see [Pere87b]) and also to the amount of memory required to store those partial parses.

On the other hand a top-down parsing strategy provides a simpler framework in which to implement the constraint mechanism and makes better use of the constraints themselves to avoid superfluous parsings. Finally, we want to point out the advantage of compiling our grammars into executable Prolog which leads to a higher execution speed.

To control left-recursion we took advantage of the fact that the formalism does not allow erasure, and thus any rule application will consume some input. To see how we can take advantage of this, consider a left recursive DCG rule such as

$$np \rightarrow np\, n$$

In our system this will be compiled into something similar to

```
parse(np,Input,Output,Limit) :-
        compute_limit(Input,Limit,n,NewLimit),
        parse(np,Input,Input_remaining,NewLimit),
        parse(n,Input_remaining,Output,Limit).
```

where, when comparing with DCGs, we find a new parameter called Limit, which should be a tail segment of the input, the purpose of which is to specify a limit on the amount of terminals which can be consumed by the rule. Note also that before parsing the np in the rule body, we compute a new limit by searching the input backwards for the first symbol which is a starter of n thus making shorter the input usable by the recursive parsing of that np. Now, since our predicate parse fails when the Input parameter reaches the Limit parameter, we are able to avoid the familiar infinite loops found in DCGs when there is left recursion. In the actual implementation, limits are precomputed before parsing and added to the input parameters in order to avoid superfluous recomputations at parse time.

The handling of markers such as optionality and Kleene- stars is done by introducing, where needed, auxiliary parsing predicates.

The constraints are handled by adding two other parameters to the parse predicate. The first contains unresolved constraints at the start of the rule application and the second the constraints left unresolved at the end rule body. Each time a constraint is found that cannot be resolved, it is inserted in the list of unresolved constraints.

From time to time (at the start of rule application, in the current implementation) the list of unresolved constraints is re-examined and simplified. If a constraint resolves to false, that causes an immediate backtracking of the parsing process.

The list of constraints is reviewed by partially evaluating each constraint. The outcome of partially evaluating a constraint is either true, in which case the constraint is eliminated from the list, or false, which will cause backtracking, or a new, possibly simpler, unresolved constraint. Note also that this process may also produce variable instantiation as in the following example of an unresolved constraint

$$X \neq a \rightarrow a = b$$

which would reduce, by partial evaluation, to

$$X = a$$

which would cause X to be instantiated to a and would finally reduce to **true**.

To speed up the process, and to avoid superfluous re-evaluations, a list of variables occurring in each unresolved constraint is maintained, and re-evaluation takes place only when one of those variables becomes instantiated. Experimentation with varying the frequency of the re-evaluation process has produced only minor variations in the total parsing times. This is probably due to the fact that the gains of early failure are balanced by the costs of a more frequent re-evaluation of the constraints.

Note that in the actual implementation, and since we cannot rely on the existence of a main syntactic feature, this process is slightly more complex since we have to cater for complex categories. However, we can determine from the grammar a small number of attributes (i.e. a restrictor, see [Shie85]), typically two or three, which can be used as indices for applicable rules thus avoiding the need to try to parse according to every rule in the grammar.

Finally, since our implementation produces all the possible parsings by backtracking, it could become very expensive to do parsing when there were many different lexical entries for the same words. To avoid this, all the lexical entries for the same word are transformed into a single entry together with a constraint specifying the possible alternative values for its attributes and mirroring thus the effect of multiple lexical entries.

At the very end of parsing, a minimization procedure is applied to the constraints which remain unresolved, to check them for consistency and to present them in a simplified form. Note that this is possible due to the finiteness of the domain of attribute values and to the fact that, as part of the grammar definition, there is a specification of the allowed values for each attribute.

The performance of the current implementation on relatively large grammars for Danish, English and German and non-trivial input sentences is quite promising. As an example, in the case of the Danish grammar, which is the largest in the set containing 100 alternations, 60 implications and 51 negations, parsing times typically range between 0.5 and 1.5 seconds per word on a 3 Mips workstation. These results are achieved with the current prototype which is not yet optimized.

5 Future Work

The first extension to CLG which we will undertake is the incorporation of category valued categories using the formalism proposed by Gazdar [Gazd86] for defining the category structure and admissibility constraints for categories. We are confident that as long as we do not introduce a recursive feature, the problem of having complex constraints will remain computationally tractable.

Research is also in progress for incorporating separate linear precedence constraints, so that the skeletons of our grammar rules will only encode immediate dominance.

Another aspect we are examining is the possibility of modifying the abstract Prolog machine [Warr80] to directly support delayed resolution of complex constraints.

6 Conclusions

We have presented a unification grammar formalism with complex constraints and described its implementation in Prolog. We have shown that within simple non-recursive feature systems we can define and efficiently implement a formalism based on constraints expressed in a full first order language which is adequate to describe a relatively large subset of different languages such as Danish, English and German while maintaining a sound logical interpretation.

References

[Gazd86] Gazdar, Gerald, Geoffrey K. Pullum, Robert Carpenter, Ewan Klein, Thomas Hukari and Robert Levin. 1986. Category Structures. Cognitive Science Research Paper no. CSRP 071. University of Sussex, Brighton, England

[Gazd87] Gazdar, Gerald and Geoffrey K. Pullum. 1987. A Logic for Category Definition. Cognitive Science Research Paper no. CSRP 072, University of Sussex, Brighton, England

[Kart84] Karttunen, Lauri. 1984. Features and Values. In : COLING-84, 28–33.

[Kasp86] Kasper, Robert and William Rounds. 1986. A logical semantics for feature structure. In : ACL Proceedings, 24th Annual Meeting, 257–266

[Kasp87] Kasper, Robert. 1987. A Unification Method for Disjunctive Feature Description. In : ACL Proceedings, 25th Annual Meeting, 235–242.

[Kasp88] Kasper, Robert. 1988. Conditional Descriptions in Functional Unification Grammar. In : ACL Proceedings, 26th Annual Meeting, 233–240

[Kay79] Kay, Martin. 1979. Functional Grammar. In : Proceedings of the Fifth Annual Meeting of the Berkeley Linguistic Society, Christine Chiarrello et. al., eds., Berkeley Linguistic Society, Berkeley, California, 251–278

[Kay84] Kay, Martin. 1985. Parsing in functional unification grammar. In : Natural Language Parsing, David R. Dowty, Lauri Karttunen and Arnold M. Zwicky, eds., Cambridge University Press, Cambridge, England, 251–278

[Mosh87]   Moshier, M. Drew and William C. Rounds. 1987. A logic for partially specified data structures. In : ACM Symposium on the Principles of Programming Languages, Association for Computing Machinery

[Pere87a]   Pereira, Fernando C.N. 1987. Grammars and Logics of Partial Information. Technical Note no. 420, SRI International, Menlo Park, California

[Pere87b]   Pereira, Fernando C.N. and S.M.Shieber. 1987. Prolog and Natural-Language Analysis. CSLI Lecture Notes 10. Stanford, California

[Roun86]   Rounds, William C. and Robert Kasper. 1986. A complete logical calculus for record structures representing linguistic information. In : Symposium on Logic in Computer Science, IEEE Computer Society

[Shie83]   Shieber, S.M., H. Uszkorheit, F.C.N. Pereira, J.J. Robinson and M. Tyson. 1983. The formalism and implementation of PATR-II. In : Research on Interactive Acquisition and Use of Knowledge. SRI International, Menlo Park, California, 39–74.

[Shie85]   Shieber, S.M. 1985. Using Restriction to Extend Parsing Algorithms for Complex-Feature-Based Formalisms. In : ACL Proceedings, 23rd Annual Meeting, 145–152.

[Warr80]   Warren, D.H.D. 1980. An Abstract Prolog Instruction Set. Technical report 309, AI Center, SRI International, Menlo park, California

SOME COMMENTS ON A LOGIC PROGRAMMING
APPROACH TO NATURAL LANGUAGE SEMANTICS

Ana Paula Tomás, Miguel Filgueiras

Centro de Informática, Universidade do Porto
R. das Taipas 135, 4000 Porto, Portugal

ABSTRACT

The aim of this paper is to present a criticism of, and to
introduce some new ideas about the approach to natural language
semantics that has been put forward in [Porto, Filgueiras]. The main
points we will discuss are the distribution of properties among
entities, the distinction between modifiers and predications, the
concept of part of an object, and the way the Principle of
Compositionality is applied.

INTRODUCTION

The aim of this paper is to present a criticism of, and to
introduce some new ideas about the approach to natural language
(NL) semantics that has been put forward in [Porto, Filgueiras],
which we will refer to by the not very appropriate name of *ISR-
semantics*.
This approach has been used in the design of NL interfaces
[Walker, Porto], [Filgueiras 83, 84, 86], [Porto 86, 88a, 88b], of menu-
based NL interfaces [Filgueiras, Silva et al.], [Filgueiras 88], and in a
toy project on computer-aided translation [Filgueiras 87], in which
an extension for the treatment of time and tense has been developed
[Moreira 88, 89].
The present paper results from the difficulties we have
experienced when seeking possible extensions to ISR-semantics
with the purpose of increasing the expressiveness of the semantic
representation language, and of developing tools for porting NL
interfaces from one domain to another.
We will discuss some of those difficulties, presenting

whenever possible our ideas on how to overcome them. Before this discussion a brief description of ISR-semantics is given taking as a basis its 1984 version [Porto, Filgueiras]. Our criticism also applies to the version in [Porto 88a, 88b], as the main ideas of the previous one have been kept.

BACKGROUND

The Logic Programming approach to NL semantics put forward in [Porto, Filgueiras] must be seen as defining a language of representations for the semantics of NL sentences (the *intermediate semantic representations*, or **ISR**s for short), **and** as prescribing a certain method for building those representations. These two aspects of the approach cannot be separated. As mentioned above we adopt the (not very appropriate) name *ISR-semantics* for referring to this approach.

The method for building an ISR for a sentence is a bottom-up rewrite process using the well-know Principle of Compositionality (stating that the semantics for the whole is built from the semantics for its parts). In ISR-semantics each rewrite step of the semantic representation is (notionally) made only when the syntactic analyser establishes a syntactic function between two constituents. This restrictive view causes a good level of independence between syntax and semantics, and makes possible the indexing of semantic information by syntactic functions, which is a distinctive feature of this approach.

The ISR language is used to represent both entities (individuals or enumerations of individuals) and predications (basically extended first-order predicate logic expressions). We are not going to give a detailed description of this language. Some examples of phrases and sentences together with their ISRs will be presented instead:

```
"fungus"              fungus : F
"the fungus"          the - fungus : F

"every Portuguese fungus"
      every - fungus : F ! grows_in(F,portugal)

"every fungus has more than 2 colours"
              for( every - fungus : F,
                      for( sup(2) - colour : C,
                              colour(F,C) ))
```

"all colours of each fungus are bright"
```
for( all - colour : C !
    for( each - fungus : F,
         colour(F,C) ),
    bright(C) )
```

The bottom-up rewrite process used to produce the ISR for a sentence in a NL interface takes as base elements data from the lexicon: simple entities for nouns, and a representation of the word for the other lexical categories (for instance, the preposition "of" may be represented just by the atom **of** - in some cases a more complex term may be used). Each rewrite step applies a *semantic rule* that builds a new ISR from the previous one and from another ISR (for a sub-phrase), lexical information on a word (or a word sequence — e.g., complex determiners), or both.

Semantic rules are grouped by syntactic functions and are implemented in Prolog as predicates, like

snc(In, P, Ic, Inc)

("**snc**" stands for semantics of noun and complement) read as: the ISR **Inc** is built from the ISR **In** for the noun, from the preposition **P** and from the **Ic** for a noun-phrase. For instance,

```
snc(fungus : F,
    of,
    place : P,
    fungus : F ! grows_in(F,P) )
snc(fungus : F,
    of,
    month : M,
    fungus : F ! grows_during(F,month,M) )
```

These examples show two important characteristics of ISR-semantics. The first is that *syntactic* words like prepositions are not assigned an interpretation at the lexical level, but are interpreted when sufficient context is available. The second is the fact that in each step the previous ISR can be rewritten into a completely different structure.

ISR-semantics has been proved to be adequate as a basis for the implementation of NL interfaces, its main advantages being: the independence from the syntactic formalism employed, the easiness of translation of ISRs into expressions that can be used for accessing knowledge bases, and the possibility of splitting the set of semantic rules into general rules and domain-dependent ones, which leads to a high level of portability between applications. In the next sections we address some of its negative points and make some suggestions on how to remedy them.

DISTRIBUTIVENESS

Verbs such as "to distinguish", "to differ", "to resemble" often entail a relation between an abstract entity and several concrete entities forcing a distribution of a property among them (e.g., "size" in "the boletus badius differs from the amanita muscaria in size"). The same would happen if some conjunctions were treated (e.g., "brown" in "the boletus badius and the amanita muscaria are brown")

A suitable ISR for the sentence "The colour distinguishes the boletus badius from the boletus lanatus" is

    for(the - colour : C1 ! colour(boletus_badius, C1),
        for(the - colour : C2 ! colour(boletus_lanatus, C2),
        C2\=C1))).

In accordance with the principles of ISR-semantics, it has to be built from the ISRs for its parts:

    the - colour : C
    the - fungus : boletus_badius
    the - fungus : boletus_lanatus

in which there is only one variable for "colour". One way of getting "the colour of the boletus lanatus" and "the colour of the boletus badius" bound to different variables, is to duplicate that variable. More complex operations would have to be performed to build the ISR for "the *colour of the cap* distinguishes the boletus badius from the boletus lanatus" from the one for "the colour of the cap", which is

    the - colour : C ! for(the - cap : Cap, colour(Cap,C))

since we want to refer not only to two colours but also to two caps. In general this method would become extremely inefficient.

This might lead us to consider the rôle of predications, and even to question how compositionality is being used (we will return to this point later). For the time being, we just observe that descending arbitrarily complex terms, like the one for "the intensity of the brightness of the colour of the cap", to find the entity to be restricted may not be practical.

With a richer and more complex type hierarchy we could have solved the problem by rewriting the entity type into **cap_colour**, instead of restricting the abstract entity **the - colour:C**. But, relevant information on quantification might then be lost. It is not reasonable to assume that, for example "the colour of *a* part", "the colour of *any* part", "the colour of *two* parts", have different types.

On the other hand, we were implicitly classifying "of the cap" as a modifier of "colour" in the sense that it modifies the type of the object it is applied to. Therefore, the claim in [Porto, Filgueiras] that there is no need to distinguish between modifiers and predications would have to be discussed. Indeed, we will discuss it below but for stronger reasons.

A closer look into other ways of building an ISR for "X *differs from* Y *in* Attribute" led us to conclude that an attribute in this context should rather be something like a function.

What we then suggest is the definition of new constructs of the ISR language denoting functions. The *domain* of each function specifies the most general type of the objects that can be its argument, while its *codomain* specifies the least general type of the objects that result from its application. A function is denoted by **TCd @ TD**, where **TCd** is the codomain type and **TD** the domain type.

Depending on the database domain, the ISRs for "colour" could be **colour@object**. After applying it to a concrete object whose type conforms to the type of the function domain we would have an entity. Therefore, "the colour of the boletus badius" would be represented by the ISR

the - colour : C ! colour(C, boletus_badius)

Restrictions by predications and quantifications on functions imply restricting each set that belongs to the function codomain. As an example, "the colour" could then be denoted by **the-colour@object**.

Examples such as "the intensity of the colour", suggest that the *composition* of functions may also have to be used. In that case the ISR could be something like

the - intensity @ (the - colour @ object)

although this notation suffers from the same flaws the ISR notation had when complex terms are to be dealt with.

MODIFIERS VERSUS PREDICATIONS

When dealing with restrictions on noun-phrases, it is usual to make a distinction between modifiers and predications [Pereira] or describers and classifiers [Winograd]. As Winograd points out "there is no good formalism for establishing this distinction" [Winograd].

In ISR-semantics, and as we have already mentioned, it has been taken for granted that the notion of predication was enough to capture the meaning of NL sentences [Porto, Filgueiras]. However, the examples below seem to contradict this position.

In broad terms, we will take a *modifier* to be a restriction on an entity that constrains its type, while a *predication* specifies some additional information about it. Taking types as sets, this has similarities to "distinguishing what the sentence is predicating of each set and what the sentence is predicating of each individual set members" [Webber].

The implementation of this classification of restrictions is not straightforward, due not only to the vagueness of that classification, but also to the possible need for context information that is not available when the principles of ISR-semantics are observed.

In some cases, for some particular domains, it is possible to fix the rôles of certain restrictions exclusively as modifiers, or as predications. For instance, "front" when qualifying "legs" of animals will normally be taken as a modifier. But, the same does not apply to "black" in the sentence "the animal with strong black legs" which has the two readings (among others):

"the animal whose black legs are strong",

"the animal whose legs are black and strong"

depending on whether "black" is regarded as a modifier. ISRs for these readings would be:

the - animal : A !
    for(plural - leg:L ! (leg_of(A,L) & colour(L,black)),
               resist(L,strong)),

and

the - animal : A !
    for(plural - leg:L ! leg_of(A,L),
               colour(L,black) & resist(L,strong))

the difference lying on the relative positions of the quantifier "**plural**" and the restriction "**colour(L,black)**", implying distinct quantifier scopes.

These ISRs could not have been built in a reasonably simple way under the assumptions made in the ISR-semantics. Instead, we would get

the - animal:A !
    for(plural - leg:L ! (colour(L,black)&resist(L,strong)),
        leg_of(A,L))

which is closer to "the animal with [some of the] legs [in the set of all legs] that are black and strong". In spite of its similarity to the second ISR above, it would be quite complex to obtain the first one. Part of the reason for this is, once more, the bottom-up rewrite process and the way compositionality is implicitly used.

These examples establish the need for distinct denotations of modifiers and predications in the ISR language. A possible approach is to consider a modifier part and a predication part in the restriction of an entity. The distinction would be made during the rewrite process by domain rewrite rules that specify the rôle of the restriction to be added.

Thus, in case "black" is regarded as a modifier, the ISR for "strong black legs" would be

    plural - leg:L % colour(L,black) ! resist(L,strong)

where % is supposed to bind more tightly than !. Its intended meaning is "black legs that are strong". When "black" is classified as a predication, the ISR would be

the - cap/F ! of(each - fungus:F)

where "**of(QE)**" is a new construct in the ISR language. Its intended meaning is that the quantified entity given as argument has the part-entity that "**of**" is predicating. Therefore, the quantifier of the argument has a wider scope than that of the part-entity.

We have extended the above notions to deal with modification and quantification on part-entities when the relationship to their possessors is not one-to-one. However, a detailed discussion of these extensions is not within the scope of this paper.

COMPOSITIONALITY

In this section we address the problem of whether the Principle of Compositionality as used in ISR-semantics should be put aside.

We recall that in ISR-semantics, the ISR for a part of a sentence is built by a bottom-up recursive rewrite process on the ISRs for subparts related by a syntactic function. The base elements for this process are representations attached to words and contained in the lexicon. Then, this process is similar to the one used in Montague semantics [Dowty].

From a theoretical point of view, and as a new ISR is produced in each rewrite step, the method seems absolutely foolproof. The information carried by the ISRs for the parts, together with the syntactic function, should be enough to build the ISR for the whole. Nevertheless, the complexity of the analysis that has to be performed on the previous ISRs, often makes the rewrite step so burdensome that from a practical point of view it is better to adopt any other construction method.

Before proceeding to the presentation of an example that illustrates this point, we would like to refer to the interesting (and convincing) discussion on compositionality by Hintikka [Hintikka]. One of the flaws that is there attributed to compositionality is the so-called *inside-out principle*: the fact that the construction of a semantics representation is made (in the majority of the approaches that adopt compositionality) from the inner parts to the outer parts of the sentence. Hintikka presents several examples of sentences in which information from the outer parts is crucial to determine the meaning of the inner ones.

We arrived (independently) at the same conclusions when looking at sentences like

"the ostrich with strong long legs"
"the kangaroo with strong long legs"

plural - leg:L ! (colour(L,black) & resist(L,strong))

which denotes "legs that are strong and black". By analogy, we would represent "exquisite Asiatic countries" by either

plural - country:C % in(C,asia) ! exquisite(C)

o r

plural - country:C ! (in(C,asia) & exquisite(C)).

A striking point is that when analysing "animal with strong black legs", the distinction is of great importance, while for "animal of exquisite Asiatic countries" the entities we want to arrive at are exactly the same, that is

animal:A !

   for(plural - country:C ! (in(C,asia) & exquisite(C)),
   lives(A,C)).

This explains the already mentioned claim made in [Porto, Filgueiras]. However, this claim does not take into account the scope problems that arise when modifiers act on *parts of objects*.

PARTS OF OBJECTS

   ISR-semantics has been mostly used in NL interfaces to databases or knowledge bases. Often, we want to talk about objects that are not explicitly represented in the database. For example, let us consider a database describing the characteristics of the cap of each fungus without having a representation of fungi caps. A sentence like "the colour of the cap of the boletus lanatus" refers to "cap" which would be represented (in ISR-semantics) by the ISR, **cap:C**. One of the problems this puts is that of finding what the variable **C** stands for, as there is no representation for fungi caps in the database. Another one is that the connection between "c a p" and the fungus that possesses it would be rendered by a relation, like the one i n

the - cap : C ! cap_of(C, boletus_lanatus)

which is quite meaningless, or at least of no use in accessing data.

   A possible solution to the first problem could be the use of a tuple of the characteristics of the cap as its representation. But, in general this seems a fairly complicated and artificial approach.

   What we propose is to treat the objects of this kind as *special* functions when in isolation, called *part-functions*, and as special entities, called *part-entities*, after having related them to another entity.

   In the sentence, "the colour of the cap of each fungus" one would have for "cap"

cap @/ fungus

and for "the cap of each fungus"

in which "ostrich"/"kangaroo" in the outer noun-phrase forces different preference readings of "long" — taken as either a predication, or a modifier:

> "the ostrich whose legs are strong and long"
> "the kangaroo whose long legs are strong".

On the other hand, when analysing sentences such as

> "the colour of the strong long legs"
> "the animal of exquisite Asiatic countries"

there is even no need to distinguish between modifiers and predications.

These examples suggest that a better method for building ISRs would be to proceed from left to right in the sentence, propagating and using the information gathered from the previous parts of the sentence to understand its subsequent parts. We are not yet in a position to make a concrete proposal for this, and we hope to do so in the near future.

CONCLUSIONS

We have presented a few points of the Logic Programming approach to NL semantics of [Porto, Filgueiras] that we think must be subject to a thorough revision because of the difficulties in their use for practical purposes. For some of them we have suggested possible ways of extending or modifying that approach so as to simplify its use.

The need for distribution of a given property among entities has led us to propose introducing denotations for functions in the ISR language. The distinction between modifiers and predications was then addressed. Evidence in its support has been given, and a denotation for modifiers proposed. Having considered parts of objects and some of the quantifier scoping problems they involve, we found that special part-functions and part-entities are useful extensions to the ISR language. Finally, we briefly discussed the central problem of whether compositionality, as used in ISR-semantics, makes it difficult rather than simplifies the task of building semantic representations for certain sentences.

ACKNOWLEDGEMENTS

The work described in this paper was partially supported by

Junta Nacional de Investigação Científica e Tecnológica, under research contract no. 87.336, and by Instituto Nacional de Investigação Científica.

REFERENCES

[Dowty] D. Dowty, R.Wall, S. Peters, Introduction to Montague Semantics, Reidel, (1981) 1985

[Filgueiras 83] M. Filgueiras, A Kernel for a General Natural Language Interface, in L. Moniz Pereira, L. Monteiro, A. Porto, M. Filgueiras (eds.), Proceedings of the Logic Programming Workshop 83, Universidade Nova de Lisboa, 1983

[Filgueiras 84] M. Filgueiras, Compreensão de Linguagem Natural: Uma Metodologia, doctoral dissertation, Universidade Nova de Lisboa, 1984

[Filgueiras 86] M. Filgueiras, Cooperating Rewrite Processes for Natural Language Analysis, Journal of Logic Programming, vol. 3, no. 4, 1986

[Filgueiras 87] M. Filgueiras, Generating Natural Language Sentences from Semantic Representations, A. Sernadas, J. Neves (eds.), Actas do Encontro Português de Inteligência Artificial 87, APPIA, 1987

[Filgueiras 88] M. Filgueiras, A Query Method Driven by Semantics, Centro de Informática, Universidade do Porto, 1988

[Filgueiras, Silva, et al.] M. Filgueiras, F. Silva, M.E. Pinto, A. Pinheiro, Menus Naturais, in P. Brazdil, M. Filgueiras, L. Damas, A. Matos (eds.) Actas do Encontro Português de Inteligência Artificial 86, APPIA, 1986

[Hintikka] J. Hintikka, J. Kulas, The Game of Language, Reidel, (1983), 1985

[Moreira 88] N. Moreira, Representação Semântica de Referências Temporais em Linguagem Natural, essay submitted to the Universidade do Porto, 1988

[Moreira 89] N. Moreira, Semantic Analysis of Time and Tense: An Implementation, in this volume

[Pereira] F. Pereira, Logic for Natural Analysis, Technical note 275, SRI International, 1983

[Porto 86] A. Porto, Semantic Unification for Deduction in Knowledge Bases, Report DI/UNL-70/86, Universidade Nova de Lisboa, 1986

[Porto 88a] A. Porto, A Framework for Deducing Useful Answers to Queries, in M. Tokoro (ed.), Proceedings of the IFIP WG 10.1 Workshop on Concepts and Characteristics of Knowledge-Based Systems, North-Holland, 1988

[Porto 88b] A. Porto, Representação de Conhecimentos e

Programação em Lógica, Universidade Nova de Lisboa, 1988.

[Porto, Filgueiras] A. Porto, M. Filgueiras, A Logic Programming Approach to Natural Language Semantics, Proceedings of the 1984 International Symposium on Logic Programming, IEEE Press, 1984

[Walker, Porto] A. Walker, A. Porto, KBO1 - A Knowledge-based Garden Store Assistant, in L. Moniz Pereira, L. Monteiro, A. Porto, M. Filgueiras (eds.), Proceedings of the Logic Programming Workshop 83, Universidade Nova de Lisboa, 1983

[Webber] B.L. Webber, So what can we talk about now?, in M. Brady, R. Berwick (eds.), Computational Models of Discourse, MIT Press, 1983

[Winograd] T. Winograd, Language as a Cognitive Process, Addison-Wesley, 1983

Semantic Analysis of Time and Tense in Natural Language: an implementation

Nelma Moreira

Universidade do Porto, R. das Taipas 135, 4000 Porto, Portugal

Abstract

In this paper a model for temporal references in natural language (NL) is studied and a Prolog implementation of it is presented. This model is intended to be a common framework for semantic analysis of verb tenses and temporal adverbial phrases. The time model choosen was based on time intervals and temporal relations. The notion of "proposition type" and temporal concepts of tense, aspect, duration, location and iteration were represented as temporal relations between some special time intervals and temporal quantifiers over time intervals. The implementation consisted in extending an existing semantic analyser based on the approach to NL semantics of [Por Fil 84]. Area: Natural Language Understanding

1 Introduction

In this paper a model for temporal references in natural language (NL) is studied and a Prolog implementation of it is presented. This model is intended to be a common framework for semantic analysis of verb tenses and temporal adverbial phrases. The reason for having such a common framework is the well-know fact that the meaning of the temporal expressions in NL sentences, and mainly of verb tenses, is not a one-to-one map from the morphosyntactic forms. The meaning of verb tenses and auxiliaries is different in different NL languages, and even in a given language that meaning relies on several factors: the verb's inherent meaning, the nature of the verb's arguments (definiteness/mass nouns) and adverbials, if present.

This work is part of a research on NL understanding within the Logic Programming paradigm and in particular of a toy project on the construction of a computer-aided translation (CAT) system [Fil84,Fil86,Fil87]. The approach used in the construction of this CAT system is based on the translation of the source language into an abstract language - *interlingua* - from which the target language is subsequently generated. Corresponding to a NL sentence a syntactic analyser produces a functional (relational) structure from which the semantic analyser builds an "intermediate semantic representation" of the sentence: an element of the *interlingua*. The Logic Programming approach to NL semantics put forward in [PorFil84] — to be referred to as *ISR-semantics* — must be seen as defining that language and as prescribing a method for building those representations. [Fil86], [Por88] for some descriptions and [TomFil89] (where a brief description is also made) for some comments and extensions.

Our aim was to develop an extension to the ISR language for the treatment of time and tense, and the following steps were considered:

$$\text{Morphosyntactic forms} \rightarrow \text{Temporal Concepts} \rightarrow \text{Formal Representation} \rightarrow \text{ISR}$$

The temporal representation scheme was based on previous works on this subject. Among others [Bru72], [BenPar78], [Mou78], [Dow79], [Bac81], were valuable references. A similiar formal model was found in [Eyn87].

2 Background

We assume that a NL sentence describes some situation (or state of affairs) which is valid in some time period (for which it is said to hold or occur). This time period is normally related with other time periods (namely, the so called time of speech) and it can be explicitly or implicitly referred in the sentence. Each NL sentence can be splitted into two components: a basic atemporal component associated with the state of affairs "itself" — which we will call a *proposition type*, following the terminology of formal philosophers [Sho87] — and other associated with the temporal information. In the sentence "John built a house last year" the *proposition type* will be "John build a house" and the temporal component will represent the information conveyed by the simple past and the adverbial of time "last year".

3 Temporal Model

The temporal model is based on the notion of time interval and relations between intervals. Given an isomorphism between time (set of moments) and the set of real numbers ordered by $\leq$, we define time interval and temporal relations in the obvious way. The initial point a_i (end point a_e) of a time interval $\mathbf{A}$ is the least lower bound (least upper bound) of $\mathbf{A}$, if such a bound exists, and then $A = (a_i, a_e)$. If $a_i = a_e$ then $\mathbf{A}$ is a *moment*. As in [All83,All84], and based on the order relation $\leq$ the following mutually exclusive ordering relations (together with its inverses) are defined between two time intervals, $\mathbf{A}$ and $\mathbf{B}$:

Identity	sim(A,B)	$(a_i = b_i) \wedge (a_e = b_e)$	sim(B,A)
Precedence	pre(A,B)	$a_e < b_i$	pos(B,A)
Contain	inc(A,B)	$(a_i < b_i) \wedge (b_e < a_e)$	dur(B,A)
Overlap	over(A,B)	$(a_i < b_i) \wedge (b_i \leq a_e) \wedge (a_e < b_e)$	over_by(B,A)
Start	ini(A,B)	$(a_i = b_i) \wedge (a_e < b_e)$	ini_by(B,A)
Finish	fin(A,B)	$(b_i < a_i) \wedge (a_e = b_e)$	fin_by(B,A)

The transitive closure of the temporal relations is obtained by computing the possible relations between any two time intervals. For instance, if

$$inc(A, B) \wedge pre(B, C) \quad \Rightarrow \quad pre(A, C) \vee over(A, C)$$
$$\vee inc(A, C) \vee fin\_by(A, C)$$

A time interval $\mathbf{B}$ is a subinterval of a time interval $\mathbf{A}$, iff $inc(A, B) \vee ini(A, B) \vee fin(A, B)$.

These notions of time — totally ordered, dense and unlimited — and time primitives — time periods with some duration — see to be the ones implicit in the temporal references in NL sentences and close to the common sense, and that is why they were adopted here.

4 Proposition Types and Semantic Representation

The meaning of the temporal references in a NL sentence, and mainly tense forms, depends on the temporal properties of its *proposition type*. For instance, the Portuguese present tense can have different meanings according to the proposition type of the sentence (for each sentence its literal rendering in English is given):

a) A Joana gosta de morangos   Joana likes strawberries
b) A Joana chega a casa às 5 horas   Joana arrives home at five
c) A Joana chega amanhã   Joana arrives tomorrow

While a) is only valid in the present, b) can be valid in the future or be a habitual present action, and in c) the adverbial makes it valid only in the future.

We adopt Vendler's classification of verb phrases (and the so called Aktionsart) but our terminology will be different [Mou78]. According to the kind of state of affairs that they describe — static versus dynamic — we can distinguish *proposition types* which are *states* or *occurrences*. The occurrences can be subdivided in *processes, instantaneous events* or *protracted events*.

a) Mary likes strawberries   **state**
b) John ran for an hour   **process**
c) The boy built a boat   **protracted event**
d) The boy found a coin   **punctual event**

This classification is based on the relations between time periods in which the proposition is valid and on its duration. The following definitions could be given:

- *state* – whenever it holds over an interval it holds over all its subintervals:*know, believe, live.*

- *process* – whenever it holds over an interval it holds at least over one of its subintervals:*run, write, wait, walk.*

- *punctual event* – never holds over overlapping intervals or two intervals one of which is a subinterval of the other:*find, arrive, die, notice.*

- *protracted event* – same as *punctual event* but can not occur only in a *moment:build, paint, grow.*

To obtain a temporal value of a given proposition type we first assign a temporal value to the verb lexical entry according to it, as the above examples show. This value can be overridden during the semantic analysis by the verb's arguments and complements:

"John wrote a long book"   *protracted event*
"John write books"(= John is a writer)   *state*
"The turtle ran a mile"   *protracted event*
"John walked *to* the station"   *punctual event*

Notice that we could have assigned a temporal value to the whole sentence instead of only to the proposition type. In that case we would have different values as we add the temporal information. As an example, consider the sentence "John run for an hour". The temporal value of this sentence is *protracted event*, as we cannot say, for instance, that "John run for an hour at the first half of that hour".

4.1 ISR-semantics

The method for building a ISR for a sentence is a bottom-up rewrite process where each step of the semantic representation is made when the syntactic analyser establishes a syntactic function between two constituents [PorFil84], [TomFil89]. The ISR language is intended to represent individuals of some type, set of individuals, properties of individuals and relations between them. We represent the proposition types as terms of the ISR language. The above sentences would have the following ISRs for the proposition types:

```
for(some(1)-book:B!long(B),write(john,B))
writer(john)
for(the(1)-turtle:T,for(one-mile:M,run(T,M)))
for(the(1)-station:S,walk_to(john,S))
```

The association of a time interval to a *proposition type* is defined by the relation:

$$sit(<Type>,<TimeInterval>,<PropositionType>)$$

The <Type> can be: **state,proc** (process), **event** (punctual event) or **pro_event** (protracted event). The <TimeInterval> , to be called the *time of situation* for short, is more difficult to formalise. As the definition of temporal values denote, each state or occurrence does not coincide with a unique, indivisible, and well defined (duration/location) time interval. However a caracterizition of the time interval may be obtained from the temporal value of the proposition type on the one hand and the information conveyed by the temporal references on the other hand. When one says, "I'm leaving tomorrow", it does not mean that "leaving" will take the whole day. In the same way the sentence "I'm reading 'Moby Dick' today", doesn't entail that I must read the whole book today or that I must be reading in all moments of today. Besides if the situation occurs or holds in several disjoint time intervals, several (identical) situations will be considered instead. If we have chosen states and occurrences as time primitives (with some relations of precedence and overlap), [Kam79],[Par84] and then define time instants from them, these problems would be "hidden" but then our system of temporal relations would need to deal with two types of temporal individuals instead of only time intervals.

An arbitrary time interval will be of *type* **time**. The information about its duration or its location can be given by a date system (associated with a system of units of time) or by its temporal relations with other time intervals. Three special types of time intervals were considered corresponding to dates, periods between dates and durations expressed as units of time. This choice is merely a way to improve the calculations of the temporal relations between them. Some examples will be given:

"January 15, 1989"

```
time:I!duration(I,day) & date(I,[year=1989,month=1,day=15])
```

or simplifying

```
date(day,[year=1989,day=15,month=1])
```

"April 5, after 8 o'clock"

```
interval(day,[month=4,day=5,hour=8], [month=4,day=5,hour=24])
```

"Four months and 3 weeks"

```
dur([month=4,week=3])
```

"One day before June"

`some(1)-date(day):I!pre(I,date(month,[month=6]))`

It follows from these examples that given the ISRs corresponding to two time intervals and a time relation between them — normally given by a preposition — the system builds the new ISR (corresponding to the total information), after testing its compatibility — in *date* and *duration* — using the transitive rules of the temporal relations and the date system.

5 Temporal Concepts

To build the temporal semantic representation we rely on the following morphosyntactic forms and syntactic functions,

- Verb tense form and auxiliaries
- Temporal complements: adverbs of time and frequency, PP's, NP's and subordinate clauses
- Other information as: subjects singular or plural; objects definite/indefinite; massive/non massive

These elements will be identified in the functional structures by the semantic analyser. Notice that the verbs forms are completed identified by the lexical and syntactic analysers – including auxiliaries – so we can use them directly.

Some linguistic concepts will be introduced:

Tense Temporal ordering of time intervals with respect to the time of speech or other time of evaluation. It expresses whether the situation described in the sentence occurs or holds in the present, the past or the future. This concept (also called "Deixis") is mainly given by the tense form and locational time adverbial. These can be indexical (*this morning, now, yesterday, three days ago*) or not indexical (*on Monday, in June, at 6 o'clock*), and in last case cannot represent the present.

Aspect Expresses whether the sentence describes a situation as a whole (perfective value) or it refers to the beginning (inchoative value), the middle (durative value) or the end of the situation (conclusive value); if the situation is completed or possible left incomplete. Here we distinguish between perfect and simple verb forms; progressive verb forms; some auxiliary verbs like *finish, continue, remain, begin*; temporal adverbials like *for an hour, during the night, since 1999, until the end of the war*. These adverbials explicitly give the duration or the boundaries of the time of situation.

Duration and Location of the time periods referred.

Iteration The situation can hold or occur in several disjoint time periods. Some verb forms can express an habitual action as "He smokes" and iterative situations are given by adverbs of frequency like *always, never, sometime, every day* or noun phrases with plural nouns as *on sundays*.

6 A temporal representation scheme

In order to express the meaning of temporal references in a sentence as temporal relations between time intervals, some *special time intervals* will be defined. The linguistics concepts will be identified as temporal relations between these time intervals and temporal quantifiers over time intervals. A temporal meaning — concerning tense, aspect, duration and iteration — will be assigned to each temporal reference and the temporal representation for the sentence is built by a rewrite process based on compositionality.

6.1 Time of situation, evaluation and reference

This formalization is based on [Rei47], and followed among others, by [Bru72],[Eyn87]. Three time intervals are considered. The first one is the *time of situation* – type situation:S –, which was defined above. The second one is the *time of evaluation* – type eval:N – which depending on the type of discourse – direct or indirect speech/historical narratives/linear versus non linear discourses – can be the *time of speech* (*now*, *then*) or some other time interval (considered as a moment) given by the context . Notice that in general the *time of speech* is not explicitly referred to within a text sentence and it is supposed to be a *moment*. The third one is the *time of reference* – type reference:R – which connects the time of situation with others time intervals, namely the time of evaluation. It is the temporal view of the situation as described by the NL sentence. As was mentioned above, a sentence can describe - mainly through different verb forms - the whole situation or a particular phase of that situation. The role of this time interval is to capture these differences in the model, as it is implicit in almost all NL sentences. In the sentence "John finishes building a house tomorrow", the proposition type is build(John,house) and, as the whole situation is not supposed to be true in the future, our approach should produce the following ISR: inc(tomorrow,R) & pos(R,N) & fin_by(S,R) & sit(pro_event,S,build(john,house))

where N is the time of evaluation, here the time of speech, and R is the time of reference and S the time of situation. These names will refer to these time intervals henceforth.

6.2 Tense and Aspect

6.2.1 Tense

Tense is defined as the set of the temporal relations between the *time of evaluation* and the *time of reference*. A sentence will have *present* tense if the time of evaluation intersects the time of reference. This would lead to four different hypotheses — $sim(R, N) \lor inc(R, N) \lor fin\_by(R, N) \lor ini\_by(R, N)$ —, but as from a linguistic point of view it seems that there is no difference between them [Eyn87] (the verb forms are the same)[1], only inc(R,N) will be considered, standing for an inclusion relation. The tense will be *future* if the time of evaluation is before the time of reference: pos(R,N); and *past* if the time of evaluation is after the time of reference: pre(R,N). The method used to assign the tense meaning can be illustrated by the following examples, where the proposition type is a *process* and its ISR can be sit(proc,S,work(john))

a) What is John doing now? He is working.

---

[1]However, we can consider that the proposition type and some temporal adverbials can give some extra information in that regard

b) John is working tomorrow

c) John is working on sunday

From these examples it can be noted that the present continuous form can be used to denote present or future tenses. Although, as the proposition type is a process, we have tense(*pres*cont*) = {inc,pos}. In a) the adverb *now* can only be present, so tense(*now*) = {inc}. The intersection of these two sets gives the *tense* of the sentence a): {inc}. In b) the adverb *tomorrow* can only be future, so tense(*tomorrow*) = {pos}, resulting for the *tense* of the sentence b): {pos}. Finally for sentence c) as the noun phrase is not indexical its tense can be future or past, tense(*on sunday*) = {pre,pos}.

Notice that in Portuguese the same analysis holds for the present simple form.

6.2.2 Aspect

Aspect is defined as a set of the temporal relations between the *time of situation* and the *time of reference*. According to the linguistic definition of aspect given above, the following values (used also in [Eyn87]) can occur:

perfective	$sim(S, R) \lor dur(S, R)$
durative	$inc(S, R)$
inchoative	$over\_by(S, R) \lor ini\_by(S, R)$
conclusive	$over(S, R) \lor fin\_by(S, R)$
retrospective	$pre(S, R)$
prospective	$pos(S, R)$

The assignment to the aspectual meaning is analogous of the one used for the tense meaning. Considering these two meanings some sentences will be analysed. An exhaustive analysis of all tense forms and adverbials is beyond the scope of this paper.

1. "Mary has just arrived"

    `inc(R,N) & pre(S,R) & sit(event,S,arrive(Mary))`

    Notice that the translation to Portuguese would be:" A Maria acaba de chegar", where another tense form - present tense plus an auxiliary, that with *events* denotes a retrospective value - must be used.

2. "Mary arrived yesterday"

    `inc(R,yesterday) & pre(R,N) & sim(S,R) & sit(event,S,arrive(mary))`

    where the simple past was used.

3. "Since 1980 Mary has lived in Porto"

    `ini(1980,S) & inc(R,N) & over(S,R) & sit(state,S,live(mary,porto))`

    Once again, in Portuguese another tense form would be used - present simple: "Desde 1980 a Maria *vive* no Porto".

4. "Mary has been sleeping for five hours"

    `sim(dur([hour=5]),S) & inc(R,N) & over(S,R) & sit(proc,S,spleep(mary))`

5. "John had arrived before yesterday"

    `sim(yesterday,R) & pre(R,N) & pre(S,R) & sit(event,S,arrive(john))`

The following table summarizes the possible values for the temporal references used in the above examples:

	Prop. Type	Tense	Aspect
pres*perf	event	{inc}	{pre}
pres*perf	state	{inc}	{over,fin_by}
past*simple	event	{pre}	{dur}
past*simple	state	{pre}	{dur,sim}
pres*perf*cont	proc	{inc}	{over}
since...		{inc,pre}	{pre,over,fin_by}
for...		{inc,pre,pos}	{dur,over,fin_by}
just		{inc}	
yesterday		{pre}	

Adverbials refer also to a certain time interval and provide information on how this interval is related to either R or S. The use of this information is not always simple because of its vagueness.

Although each temporal reference can have several values for tense and aspect, at the end only one must remain, otherwise the sentence will be *temporally ambiguous*.

6.3 Iteration

To deal with quantification over situations another special time interval will be introduced. It concerns the time period that contains the several disjoint time periods where the situation is said to hold or occur. This time interval will play the same role as the *time of situation* before, and following [Eyn87a] it will be called *frame time* — type **frame:F**. We must consider two time intervals of reference: one in relation to the time of speech as before, R and the other, R_q in relation to the time of each individual situation, which will be represented by S^2. It follows that the computation of aspectual values must be different if quantification is present. Notice however that R_q will be used only when there is an explicit reference to some "part" of the situation, as "He always finishes eating at midnight". The main changes will then be in the values of the verb forms, but in general it seems not to be the hardest job. We think that in these cases the aspectual value is always "perfective" and R may be ignored. However for the time being the general representation will be used.

The quantifiers over temporal intervals will be an extension of the usual ones. The quantification is over some period of time that can be explicitly defined (*every day, once a week*), or not (*always, seldom, never*). Moreover if the number of repetitions for each period of time is given, as (*many times a year, most days of the week*) iteration of quantifiers must be used. When dealing with one single situation it could be — and in the current implementation actually is — associated to each time interval an unary quantifier, for instance

"Mary ate a cake yesterday"

```
for(n(1)-reference:R!(inc(yesterday,R) & pre(R,N)),
for(n(1)-situation:S!dur(S,R), sit(event,S,eat(mary,cake))))
```

where the properties of each time interval are connected to their definitions. All the examples above should have had this form, which was not given for the sake of simplicity.

---

[2] Here our approach differs from the one in [Eyn87a].

Some examples on repeated situations follow

1. "Yesterday Mary ate a cake hourly"

```
for(n(1)-reference:R!inc(yesterday,R) & pre(R,N),
for(n(1)-frame:F!dur(F,R),
    for(each-hour:H!dur(H,F),
        for(n(1)-situation:S!inc(H,S), sit(event,S,eat(mary,cake))))))
```

The system must know that "yesterday" is one day long in order to produce the correct ISR for the adverb "hourly" (which implies the temporal relation dur(H,F) via transitiv rules)[3].

2. " In 1899 John went frequently to London"

```
for(n(1)-reference:R!inc(date([year=1899]),R)&pre(R,N),
    for(n(1)-frame:F!dur(F,R),
        for(many-situation:S!dur(S,F), sit(event,S,go_to(john,london)))))
```

Here the adverb is vague concerning the period of repetition, so that one time interval can be omitted and the quantification be made over the time of situation (or, in other cases, the second time of reference).

3. "John smokes"

```
for(n(1)-reference:R!inc(R,N),
    for(n(1)-frame:F!dur(F,R),
        for(most-situation:S!dur(S,F),sit(proc,S,smoke(john)))))
```

In this case the verb form has a habitual reading and therefore the *most* quantifier is used.

4. "John was reading at 6 o'clock"

```
for(n(1)-reference:R!pre(R,N) & sim(date([hour=6]),R),
    for(n(1)-situation:S!inc(S,R), sit(proc,S,read(john))))
```

5. " In June John was frequently reading at 6 o'clock"

```
for(n(1)-reference:R!(pre(R,N) & inc(date([month=6]),R)),
    for(n(1)-frame:F!dur(F,R),
        for(each-reference2:Rq!(dur(Rq,F) & sim(date([hour=6]),Rq)),
            for(n(1)-situation:S!inc(S,Rq),sit(proc,S,read(john))))))
```

The aspectual value of the past continuous is different in the last two sentences: the presence of the adverb of frequency makes the difference.

Finally note that in iterative or habitual sentences one time interval must always contain the repeated ones, so that an abbreviated denotation can be use, e.g freq(R,Q-I,Tp) standing for for(Q-I!dur(I,R),Tp), provided R was defined before.

A difficult problem concerns the scope of quantifiers (including the ones introduced by frequency adverbials) and the occurrence of locational temporal adverbials. We used the linear order of occurrence in the sentence and some inclusion properties (as a month has several time intervals named "6 o'clock") to solve it, although our method does not work in all cases.

---

[3] For instance if "monthly" was used the system will fail to produce a ISR.

7 Some implementation details

The semantic analysis of functional structures of sentences with a main verb must produce the *proposition type* and the temporal information. For the latter we use the same rewrite method of *ISR-semantics*. Some considerations on it and on the basic information needed follows.

Concerning verb forms we have seen that some can be used with adverbials of frequency and others can not, and that some may express habitual situations with some proposition type. Morover, the meaning of the temporal concepts were changed with these facts. So, this information must be available for each tense form and for each language. In Prolog this is defined by a predicate whose arguments are the verb form, the value of the proposition type, the sets of temporal relations for tense and aspect and the information on quantification. Some clauses for some English verb forms would be:

```
tai(pres*cont,event,[pos,inc],[dur,sim],n(1)).
tai(pres*cont,event,[inc],[dur,sim],some).
tai(pres*cont,pro_event,[pos,inc],[inc],n(1)).
tai(pres*cont,proc,[inc],[inc],n(1)).
tai(pres*simple,event,[inc],[inc],most).
tai(pres*simple,state,[inc],[inc],n(1)).
tai(past*simple,event,[pre],[dur],all).
```

where

all	all quantifiers are allowed	some	iterative
n(1)	neither habitual nor iterative	most	habitual

Beginning with the value of the proposition type this information is used to build a first ISR concerning the temporal information. As there are many possible choices, a "practical ISR" carrying along all the pertinent information is produced which in each step can be transformed in the final ISR. This transformation is done when the proposition type is added. This point may be reviewed in future implementations and is related to the criticism made to the Principle of Compositionality as used in *ISR-semantics* in [TomFil89]. In what concerns temporal prepositional phrases, the situation quantification is analysed at first (taking into account the noun determiner and the preposition)[4]. The single cases are treated differently from plural ones. Then the preposition is considered in order to produce new values for tense and aspect and the special time interval is chosen. The preposition and the noun are used to produce an ISR which is added to the old ISR of that special time interval, producing a new ISR. Adverbs are treated in an analogous way, beginning by the analysis of whether they are frequency adverbs, then the temporal values are determined and a new ISR for the special time interval is produced. More details can be found in [Mor88], for a first implementation.

8 Temporal subordinate clauses

As a first step to the temporal treatment of complex phrases and texts temporal subordinate clauses were analysed. The main role of these sentences is to locate the time of reference of the main clause. Essentially the method used is: the subordinate clause is analysed and its time of

---

[4]Prepositions can entail iteration in some contexts; for instance, in Portuguese the use of "desde"(/since) with events

reference is related, by means of the temporal connective, to the time of reference or situation of the main clause. To each connective is possible to associate a unique temporal relation (*after*/pos, *while*/inc,*when*/sim, etc) provided that some deterministic transformations of tense forms were performed and modality is not considered. A first requirement is that the two clauses have the same *tense*. However if the verb form of the subordinate clause is tenseless, its *tense* will be taken as the one of the main clause. Some deterministic syntactic patterns concerning *proposition types, tense forms* and *connectives* can be used to simplify the semantic analysis. In Portuguese, for instance, some uses of the subjunctive forms can be ignored. Another example, both in English and Portuguese, is the use of *when* with events in the simple past, where the connective can be changed to *after*, as the sentence describe successive events. An example taken from [Hei74] is:"When John pushed the button, the bomb exploded".

A detailed analysis of these clauses, in Portuguese, can be found in [Mor88][5]. The main issue here was that the use of *times of reference* allowed a correct temporal relation between the two situations to be find. One example is

"The boat arrived when John was eating"

```
for(n(1) - reference:R!(pre(R,N) &
   for(n(1)-reference:Rs!(pre(Rs,N) & sim(R,Rs)),
for(n(1)-situation:Ss!inc(Ss,Rs), sit(proc,Ss,eat(john))))),
      for(n(1)-situation:S!dur(S,R), sit(event,S,arrive(boat)))))
```

9 Conclusions

We described the main points leading to an implementation of a semantic analyser dealing with temporal references in NL sentences based on time intervals and relations between them.The notion of *proposition type* and temporal concepts were introduced and its representation described. As only single sentences with temporal complements and some types of complex sentences were considered, one line for future work is to test and to extend the scheme used - and the extensions to ISR-language proposed - for dealing with discourse.

10 Acknowledgements

I am most grateful to Miguel Filgueiras for his suggestions and comments on a first draft of this paper.

References

[All83]   James F. Allen. "Maintaining Knowledge about Temporal Intervals". *CACM 26.* 1983

[All84]   James F. Allen. "Towards a General Theory of Action and Time". *Artificial Intelligence 23.* 1984

[Bac81]   Emmon Bach. "On Time, tense and Aspect:An essay in English Metaphysics".*Radical Pragmatics.* 1981

---

[5]Partially based on an English exhaustive analysis made in [Hei74] in a somehow different context

[BenPar78] M.Bennett & B.Partee. *Towards the Logic of Tense and Aspect in English.* 1978.

[Bru72] Bertram C. Bruce. "A Model for Temporal References and its Application in a Question Answering Program". *Artificial Intelligence 3.* 1972.

[Dow79] D. Dowty. *Word Meaning and Montague Grammar.* Reidel. 1979

[Eyn87] F.Van Eynde. "Tense and Time". *Eurotra Reference Manual 4.0.* 1987.

[Eyn87a] F.Van Eynde. "Iteration, Habituality & Verb form Semantics". *Proceedings of 3rd. European Association Conference of the ACL.* 1987.

[Fil84] Miguel Filgueiras. *"Compreensão de Linguagen Natural por Computador: uma Metodologia."* Doctoral dissertation, Universidade Nova de Lisboa, 1984.

[Fil86] Miguel Filgueiras. "Cooperating Rewrite Processes for Natural Language Analysis." *Journal of Logic Programming* vol.3 n.4. 1986.

[Fil87] Miguel Filgueiras. "Genarating Natural Language Sentences from Semantic Representations." *Encontro Português de Inteligência Artificial 87.* APPIA. 1987.

[Hei74] Orvokko Heinämäki. *Semantics of English Temporal Connectives.* PH.D. thesis. University of Texas at Austin. 1974

[Kam79] Hans Kamp. "Events, Instants and Temporal Reference." *Semantics from different points of view.* De Gruyter. 1979.

[Mor88] Nelma Moreira. *Representação Semântica de Referências Temporais em Linguagem Natural.* Essay submitted to the Universidade do Porto. 1988.

[Mou78] A.P.Mourelatos. "Events, Processes and States." *Linguistics and Philisophy* 2. 1978.

[Par84] Barbara Partee. "Nominal and Temporal Anaphora." *Linguistics and Philosophy* 7. 1984.

[PorFil84] A.Porto & M.Filgueiras "Natural Language Semantics: A Logic Programming Approach." *Proceedings of the 1984 International Symposium on Logig Programming.* IEEE. 1984

[Por88] António Porto. "Representação de Conhecimentos e Programação em Lógica". Universidade Nova de Lisboa. 1988.

[Rei47] H.Reichenbach. *Elements of Symbolic Logic.* 1947.

[Sho87] Yoav Shoam. "Temporal Logics in A.I.: Semantical and Ontological Considerations". *Artificial Intelligence* 33. 1987.

[TomFil89] A.P.Tomás & M.Filgueiras. "Some Comments on a Logic Programming Approach to Natural Language Semantics". Centro de Informática, Universidade do Porto.1989.

Extra-sentential dependencies, meaning representation, and generics[1]

Tomek Strzalkowski

Courant Institute of Mathematical Sciences
New York University
715 Broadway, 7th floor
New York, NY 10003
U.S.A.

Abstract

We outline a fragment of the system of semantic rules for computing coherent continuations at any point in discourse by uncovering various links existing between an utterance and its context. In this paper, we describe an extension of this method to handle changes in the level of reference in discourse. In order to accomplish this we develop a multi-level model for representing and manipulating various types of non-singular terms, and define the notion of "remote", inter-level reference. In this context, we discuss a possible representation for selected types of generic sentences.

1. Computing extra-sentential dependencies in discourse

The starting point of this discussion is a language L of regularized parse structures obtained from sentences in a natural language text using some grammar[2]. We are interested in translating some example expressions, sentences and paragraphs of L into well-formed formulas of a λ-categorial language Λ that would give representation of both a sentence's logical form and its cohesive links to the surrounding discourse. In particular, we look closely at the cohesive links created by inter-sentential anaphoric references appearing in different contextual situations. For the purpose of this presentation it is enough to assume that Λ is a predicate calculus language with a λ operator; but see (Strzalkowski & Cercone, 1986) for a formal definition. In (Strzalkowski & Cercone 1986) we described a transformation ISD such that ISD $\subseteq L \times \Lambda$, and whenever a source expression in L consists of more than one sentence, a class of intersentential dependencies within this fragment is identified and resolved, if possible. It must be noted here that ISD represents a semantic process which is

---

[1]This paper is based upon work supported by the Defense Advanced Research Project Agency under Contract N00014-85-K-0163 from the Office of Naval Research.

[2] At present L is identified with the set of phrase-markers that can be generated from English sentences with a categorial grammar CAT (Montague 1974).

entirely independent of any pragmatic or domain related factors. As a result a substantial amount of domain-oriented ambiguity may be left unresolved. In any practical application, this transformation must be accompanied by a pragmatic process, as described in (Strzalkowski 1986). ISD consists of a collection of translation rules $\{R_1, R_2, \cdots\}$, such that each rule is responsible for translating a specific type of dependency. Most of these rules (with the exception of Rule 1 which works directly on expressions of L, translating them into "literal" representations in Λ, independent of one another) are written in terms of two distinguished expressions of Λ, S_1 and S_2, which we call *the context-setting sentence* and *the current sentence*, respectively. Expression S_1 is a Λ-representation of the linguistic context in which the sentence with translation S_2 is to be evaluated. Neither S_1 nor S_2 must correspond to surface sentences, though. S_1 may represent a larger part of discourse, perhaps an entire paragraph; on the other hand, S_2 may constitute only a subclause of S_1 in which case we would talk of intra-sentential dependency. As an example let us consider a two sentence paragraph given below:

S_1: *John interviewed a candidate.*
S_2: *The man had impressive references.*

In the most natural reading of this paragraph, the anaphor of *the man* is resolved against *a candidate* in the first sentence, so that the second sentence actually means: *the man whom John interviewed had impressive references.* This inter-sentential dependency is captured by the translation rule 2, which operates on the "literal" translations of both sentences as delivered by Rule 1.

Rule 2 (Perfect-Context Translation Rule)
If the context-setting sentence S_1 has a referential interpretation $\exists u\,[P(u)\ \&\ F(u)]$, *and the current sentence S_2 contains an unresolved definite anaphor, that is,*

$$S_2 = \exists u\,[C(u)\ \&\ P_1(u)\ \&\ F_1(u)\ \&\ \forall x\,[\{P_1(x)\ \&\ C(x)\} \supset (x=u)]],\ ^3$$

then this anaphor can be resolved against S_1, and the resulting translation of S_2 is obtained as $\lambda C\,[S_2](\lambda u\,[P(u)\ \&\ F(u)])$.

In the example above, the second sentence obtains the desired translation as shown below

$$\exists x\,[man(x)\ \&\ cand(x)\ \&\ int(J,x)\ \&\ had-imp-ref(x)\ \&$$
$$\forall y\,[\{man(y)\ \&\ cand(y)\ \&\ int(J,y)\} \supset (x=y)]]$$

For other studied cases of inter-sentential anaphora, including discourse fragments involving propositional attitudes, attitude report verbs, pronominal anaphors, proper names, and conditionals, see (Strzalkowski 1986a-c) and (Strzalkowski & Cercone 1986)

---

[3] C is a free predicate variable that can be bound by the sentence's context. It has been introduced by Rule 1 with the translation of the definite article.

2. Non-singular terms in discourse

The rules outlined in section 1 cover selected cases of inter-sentential anaphora where the reference level in discourse does not change from one sentence to another. There exists, however, a class of inter-sentential dependencies whereby a reference is made across boundaries of different reference levels in discourse. For example, in

A: *In the zoo John saw an alligator.*
B: *The alligator is a very dangerous animal.*

the alligator in the second sentence most likely refers to a generic object of which the alligator in the first sentence is an instance or extension. Thus we can say that the second alligator is a non-singular *superobject* in which the first alligator somehow participates. To represent this new type of inter-sentential dependency we introduce a multi-level model for interpreting natural language expressions, such that the levels in the model correspond (roughly) to the levels of reference in discourse. For instance, in the example above, the resulting representation would have both alligators placed at different, though related, "object levels". The basic concepts of the approach proposed here are the notions of a singular object and a coordinate, a usually ordered set specifying a type of "dimension" that the object in question spans. The most common of these coordinates are time and space but other more abstract ones are also possible. These two basic concepts are then used to define the notion of the object's *instance* with respect to some coordinate. Thus, the alligator that John saw in the zoo in the example above, is related to the generic concept of alligator by some "species" coordinate that ties (or enumerates?) all alligators around the world.

3. A multi-level model for interpreting natural language terms

A singular object is any entity that can be taken as a coherent whole, in other words, it can be referred to directly using a referring expression of language: a name, a definite description, a pronoun. Thus, at least as far as our ability to refer is concerned, all objects appear singular. Still, it is not the case that all objects are singular in the same way. Take, for example, two persons John and Mary. They are singular objects and they seem singular in the same way, in other words, singular relative to one another. Next take alligator, the species, and the alligator John owns. Although both are singular in their own right, they are not compatible when related to one another: the alligator John owns appears only a manifestation, or extension, of alligator the species at a certain space-time location.

Let us introduce, only intuitively at first, the relation of *relative singularity* among objects, as suggested above. This relation will help us to break down the universe of objects into classes of relatively singular objects, which we call *levels*. The levels can be subsequently partially ordered with *lower than* relation, i.e., $L_1 < L_2$, indicating that level L_1 consists of manifestations (extensions, instances) of objects at level L_2. Let L_0 be an arbitrary level we select as our reference point; if our discourse operates at this level then L_0 defines the current *level of reference* of the discourse. Let L_{+1} and L_{-1} be two other levels different than L_0 and such that $L_{-1} < L_0 < L_{+1}$. At level L_{+1} we place the objects we consider to be generalizations (or abstractions) of some measurable amount of objects from L_0. It is only from the perspective of L_{+1} that we are able interpret *The tiger lives in the jungle*, or *The president is elected every four years*, or *Birds can fly*, or *Tourists start forest fires*. The objects at L_{+1} are singular but only when related to one another within the same level; when viewed from L_0 they appear "generic" or "functional" or the like, in other words, non-singular. Non-singular objects may not have corresponding measurably singular descriptions at L_0 (like *every tiger*, *some president*, etc.), and often it will not be possible to refer to them in the terms of the language available at L_0. Thus, while the statement of *The President lives in the White House* interpreted at level L_{+1} can be argued to be equivalent to the statement *Every president lives in the White House* interpreted at L_0, the same cannot be said of *The tiger lives in the jungle* and *Every tiger lives in the jungle*. We must note that some objects found at L_{+1} could have been placed there by design rather than as a result of generalizing from L_0; an example of such higher-level object may be **The President**.

If level L_{+1} contains generalizations of objects from L_0, then level L_{-1} will contain their specializations or extensions. Descending upon L_{-1} we can see that what we previously considered to be *the atom* actually denotes many different kinds of atoms (H, O, Ca, Fe, etc.), or that *the mail* is not the same every morning. A few definitions will help to put the above intuitions into a more formal setting.

Def. 1. *A use of a description is called singular if it refers to a singular object. A use of a description is called measurably singular if it refers to some measurable quantity of a singular object; otherwise we shall talk of non-singular use.*

Def. 2. *An object level, or simply a level, is an arbitrary collection of relatively singular objects. On the language side, the corresponding reference level encompasses those singular and measurably singular uses of descriptions that refer to the level's objects.*

Def. 3. *For any level L, there are at least two distinct levels L_{-1} and L_{+1} such that L_{+1} contains the non-singular objects as seen from L, and L_{-1} contains the objects for which the objects at L are non-singular.*

Def. 4. *The level L_0 is an arbitrarily chosen level serving as a reference point.*

As described, the structure of levels is not yet adequate to capture the full complexity of the reference structure of discourse. A notion of coordinate has to be introduced along the following lines. We shall call T a *coordinate*, if T is a set of "points" or "locations" at which certain general (or abstract) objects, for example *the president* or *the atom*, are assigned more specific extensions or instances, such as *President Bush* or *H, Fe, Ca, ...* Often, a non-singular object can be decomposed into instances in more than one way, depending which coordinate is used. The U.S. President, for example, is an instance of the president, head of state, and so is President Bush, although different decomposition coordinated are involved in each case. Let $L_{-1}^{N,T}$ be the level where we place the instances of object N decomposed with coordinate T. By analogy, we define $L_{+1}^{N,T}$ to be the level such that for any object M, $M \in L_{+1}^{N,T}$ if $N \in L_{-1}^{M,T}$. In other words, $L_{+1}^{N,T}$ contains the superobject M generalizing over object N with the use of coordinate T.

Suppose that we have an object N called N at level L_0. Suppose further that coordinate T is selected so that for any x, $y \in T$ we have that N-at-$x \neq$ N-at-y. Let us use N_x to stand for N-at-x, where x is an element of T, and let $(N\ x)$ be an expression in our meaning representation language that refers to (or denotes) object N_x, whenever an expression N refers to N. We obtain therefore that

$$\forall\ x,y \in T\ [x{\neq}y \supset (N\ x) \neq (N\ y)]$$

The new objects N_x's cannot be placed at L_0 because, being instances of N, they are not singular relative to N (see Def. 2). Instead, we move them onto a new level $L_{-1}^{N,T}$ leaving the original object N at L_0. We say that the level $L_{-1}^{N,T}$ is lower than the level L_0, and write $L_{-1}^{N,T}{<}L_0$. Often we drop the superscripts N and T over the level symbol, assuming some lower level L_{-1}, whenever it does not lead to ambiguity.

As an example, let us consider a rather naive concept of bird, B, as that of a winged creature that lay eggs, and place it at L_0. Using a genus coordinate, G, we can construct a level $L_{-1}^{B,G}$ containing such objects as **eagle, hawk, goose,** and **penguin**. There is another way of interpreting concept B as well: we introduce a *specimen* coordinate S that allows us to pick up specific birds, such as Opus, the penguin, at level $L_{-1}^{B,S}$. Note that this level is lower than $L_{-1}^{B,G}$ because it contains all levels $L_{-1}^{X,S'}$, where X ranges over objects at $L_{-1}^{B,G}$, and $S'{\subseteq}S$. Now we can attempt to represent meanings of some simple statements about birds. For example, *Birds can fly* is represented at L_0 as can-fly(B), while *Opus is a bird* would translate as $\exists s{\in} S\ [(B\ s) = \text{Opus}]$. We cannot infer from these statements that *Opus can fly*; indeed, *Opus cannot fly*, which translates to $\neg$can-fly(Opus), is not necessarily inconsistent with the above two.

A process reverse to decomposition is that of ascending to a higher level within the level hierarchy. Suppose that for some objects N_1, N_2, $\cdots$, considered distinct at L_0, we discover they share a certain property, such as being an N, so that we need a generalizing concept to talk about them. We select a coordinate T, and climb onto some *higher* level L_1, that is, $L_0{=}L_{-1}^{N,T}{<}L_{+1}^{N_i,T}{=}L_1$, and establish a new object N there, a *superobject*. Now, as viewed from L_1, all N_i's are just the occurrences of N at different values of coordinate T. It is important not to confuse a superobject with a set S of its instances at L_0 that gave birth to this superobject. A superobject N can be identified with a family of functions $\{N_T \mid T$ is a coordinate$\}$ such that each N_T is a function from coordinate T into an appropriate lower level, $L_{-1}^{N,T}$. In particular, a superobject N at L_1 can be viewed from L_0 as a function N_T from T into L_0 such that, whenever $s{\in} S{\subseteq}L_0$, then there is $t{\in} T$ such that $N_T(t){=}N_i{=}s$. The function N_T is then arbitrarily extended beyond the set S. The following definition may be suggested.

Def. 5. *Let L and M be any two distinct levels of relatively singular objects. We say that level L is lower than level M, L < M, iff there exists an object* **P** *at level M and a coordinate T such that* $L \supseteq M_{-1}^{P,T}$.

4. Remote co-references in discourse

We now examine how the foregoing theory of non-singular terms could be utilized to account for some more advanced cases of inter-sentential dependencies in discourse. Let us start with an example and consider the following discourse fragment.

The president$_1$ is elected every four years. Bush is the president$_2$.

Suppose that the president$_1$ and the president$_2$ are interpreted at levels L_1 and L_2, respectively, so that one of the following takes place: either $L_1=L_2$, or $L_1<L_2$, or $L_2<L_1$, where < stands for the *lower-level* relation introduced in Def. 5. Consider first that $L_1=L_2=L_0$. If the two definite descriptions were to co-refer then we would be talking of the same object (individual) in both sentences. That interpretation, although possible, does not agree with our intuition. In this case the conclusion of *Bush is elected every four years* follows immediately. Assume then that $L_2=L_{-1}^{TP,T}<L_1=L_0$ where **TP** is the object at L_1 referred to by the president$_1$, and T is a coordinate. If the president$_1$ is used as a name, we can expect the following translations, respectively:

elected −every −4years (TP)
$\exists t$ [SL(t) & ((TP t)=Bush)]

where $t \in T$ and SL is a selector over T provided by the discourse situation (for example *now, here,* etc.).[4] We summarize the above as follows. In some part of a discourse, a certain (general) object **X** is referred; that is, there is some part, S_1, of the discourse (presented as a single sentence in our examples, for simplicity), such that S_1 predicates something of **X** - that is, $S_1(X)$, where X is a description that refers to **X**. In a subsequent part of the discourse, however, the discourse changes the level of reference and only some instance(s) of **X** with respect to some coordinate T is referred; that is, there is some $t \in T$ such that $S_2((X\ t))$, where S_2 is this new part of the discourse. Apparently, the discourse internal cohesion would be compromised if we did not allow the higher level object **X** be a target of a remote reference by a description (X t) denoting one of its instances. In such a case we say that $S_1(X)$ creates a

---

[4] In a more general case, we would take the phrase *the president$_1$* as an ordinary definite description, assuming some external context C which allows for the use of the definite article (Strzalkowski & Cercone 1989).

supercontext for (X t). We can further say that X and (X t) are *remotely co-referential*. This type of inter-sentential dependency is captured by the translation rule below.

Rule 11 (Supercontext Translation Rule)
If the context-setting sentence S_1 with the translation $\exists x \, [P_1(x) \, \& \, F_1(x)]$ is interpreted at level $L_{+1}^{\xi,T}$, where ξ is an object satisfying sentence S_2 when interpreted at level L_0, and S_2 contains an unresolved remote reference P_2, i.e., $S_2 = \exists y \, [P_2(y) \, \& \, F_2(y)]$, then the full translation of S_2 is obtained by

$$\lambda Q[\lambda C[M_{Q,C}](C_1)](\lambda u[\exists t[\lambda y[P_2(y) \, \& \, F_2(y)]((u \, t))]]),$$

where the supercontext C_1 is $\lambda x[P_1(x) \, \& \, F_1(x)]$, and $M_{Q,C}$ abbreviates the following expression: $\exists x[C(x) \, \& \, \forall y \, [C(y) \supset (x=y)] \, \& \, Q(x)]$.

A similar situation (though not quite just a mirror-image situation) occurs when an expression referring to a higher level object is used to provide an inter-sentential link to a discourse entity that refers to an instance of this object, i.e., when $L_1 < L_2$ (for example, *In the zoo John saw a tiger. Tigers are intelligent animals.*). This is, however, just the tip of an iceberg. One of the important issues which remain to be worked out is how to automatically determine when a change of reference level in discourse takes place. A bare plural, such as *tigers* indicates a higher level reference, especially when co-related with a singular indefinite description, such as *a tiger*. Also, a singular definite description when followed by a co-related indefinite description or a definite plural, would normally indicate transition to a lower reference level (*The tiger has stripes. I saw one in the zoo.*). Another problem is to determine exactly what kind of inferences can be made along a remote co-reference link. At this time we disallow any such inferences whatsoever, to avoid certain unreasonable conclusions. Nonetheless, in many situations inter-level inferences can and should be made, or we risk to forsake our understanding of the discourse. The most obvious cases are those of generic-to-specific inferences, whereby a property attributed to a non-singular generic object (such as in *tigers are dangerous*) is reduced to a form of quantification over instances of this object at a lower level. This latter issue is addressed briefly below (see also, Strzalkowski 1988).

5. Meaning representation for generic sentences

Although the statement *birds fly* is normally understood at some higher reference level, it does appear to convey some information about the concept's instances. Roughly, we would like to build an interpretation along the following lines: *birds fly* is true relative to a coordinate T iff T is decomposing the generic object referred to by *birds* into some lower-level instances in such a way that except for a "negligible" number of exceptions, every instance in this decomposition has the property *flies*. In one possible interpretation, a number of exceptional instances of a concept is called "negligible" if the ratio of this number to the number of all instances of the concept approaches 0 when the number of all instances of the concept is increased. Thus, if we agree that there is no reason to believe that the kind of penguin has at most negligibly many instances, then *birds fly* is false if the decomposition of *birds* is made with respect to the specimen coordinate (i.e., the one which picks up single birds). The statement is true, however, with respect to a different decomposition of *birds*, namely with the coordinate genus, under the assumption that only finitely many elements of this coordinate pick up classes of birds of which we can say that they do not fly. Another possibility emerges when we consider the statement as referring only to a restricted subclass of all birds, and therefore being interpreted in some context: *birds that are so and so fly*.[5] This restrictive context may be provided by a current discourse situation, or it may come from the general knowledge about birds. The coordinate used to define lower-level instances of *birds* remains the same, only now the quantification is narrowed to a subset of it.

The above analysis constitutes just one possible interpretation of a non-singular sentence. Let us call this interpretation *transparently generic*, and let us call a sentence (or utterance) transparently generic if its intended interpretation is transparently generic. Let S be a sentence containing a predicate P with an argument N which refers to a higher-level (non-singular) object ξ, and let P(N) be the translation of S at the corresponding reference level (for example, *fly(birds)*). Then S has a transparently generic interpretation only if there exists a decomposition of the object ξ with respect to some coordinate T, and such that for every instance ξ_t of ξ, for any $t \in T$, if N_t is a description that refers to the object ξ_t, then $P(N_t)$[6] is well-defined (for example *Tweety flies*). This decomposition subsequently serves as the basis for determining the sentence's truth value. In case no well-defined decomposition into a lower level can be found, the truth conditions must be determined within the statement's own level, and no generic interpretation, as we understand it here, will be possible. Examples of such non-generic non-singular sentences involve predications referring to properties of higher-level objects which are not derived from the properties of their instances, such as *being numerous, widespread, frequent, scarce*, or even *extinct*. Thus, *birds are numerous, good Olympic runners are scarce*, or *presidents are elected every four years* are not considered generic. These sentences cannot be interpreted quantitatively with respect to the properties their instances may have.

Let us now consider a quite different example: *physicists win Nobel Prizes*. Is this sentence generic or not? It establishes a meaningful decomposition of the non-singular object denoted by *physicists* into individuals, each of whom can be said, truthfully or not, to win

---

[5] For example: *here; in the moderate climatic zone*, etc.

[6] P may need to be adjusted for tense and/or plurality of object NP's (if any).

some Nobel Prizes. [7] And yet, it is not true that *nearly all physicists win Nobel Prizes*. It is also pointless to look for some restricting context that would allow us to understand this statements in some narrower sense. Instead of looking at the set of physicists, however, we may turn our attention to the set of individuals who win Nobel Prizes. How many physicists are among them, do they create a significant, non-negligible group? If so, then our claim that physicists win Nobel Prizes is justified, provided that they will remain a non-negligible group as the set of Nobel Prize winners is expanded. In this way we obtain another decompositional interpretation of non-singular sentences, which we would like to call the *opaquely generic* interpretation, because of a certain similarity between this interpretation and opaque readings of some class of universal statements (see, for example, Partee 1978).[8] Therefore, a non-singular sentence N(P) is true in its opaquely generic interpretation just in the case when, among all lower level objects that have the property N (i.e., Nobel Prize winners) and are of the same singularity as the instances of the object denoted by P, the instances of the object denoted by P (i.e., single physicists or groups of physicists) create a non-negligible subclass. In other words, as we grow the set N, its intersection with P will grow at a comparable pace. An interesting thing to note is that generic sentences usually assume either transparent or opaque reading as the preferred one. There seem to be situations, however, where both interpretations are equally possible, for example *birds fly*: either nearly all birds fly (in some context), or birds are non-negligible among those vertebrates (all animals, things, etc.) that fly. This may be the reason why the transparently generic interpretation of this sentence does not always appear satisfactory.

We propose that two new quantifiers be introduced into the predicate calculus. These are $\overset{\circ}{\forall}$ and $\overset{\circ}{\exists}$ which should be read, respectively, as *all except for a negligible number of exceptions*, and *a non-negligible amount*. These quantifiers are well-defined only if the immediate context on which they operate is known. Thus, it is more appropriate to consider these symbols together with a context-setting set, that is $\overset{\circ}{\forall}\{x \in P\}$. For example, the transparently generic representation for *birds fly* would be

$$\overset{\circ}{\forall}\{x \in \text{Birds}\}[\text{fly}(x)]^9$$

Similarly, *physicists win Nobel Prizes* receives the opaquely generic interpretation as

$$\overset{\circ}{\exists}\{x \in \text{Win-NP}\}[\text{physicist}(x)]$$

---

[7] The predicate *win Nobel Prizes* takes one of the two possible decompositions, as we decompose physicists into lower-level instances (individuals or groups). It may be either *win(s) Nobel Prizes*, a habitual, or *win(s) some Nobel Prize(s)*. We assume the second of these possibilities here. Habituals are not discussed here.

[8] These similarities have chiefly to do with the quantifier scoping.

[9] Or, more appropriately, $\exists T_B \overset{\circ}{\forall}\{t \in T_B\}[\text{fly}(B_t)]$ where T_B is a coordinate decomposing **B**, the object denoted by *birds*.

where Win-NP denotes the higher-level concept of *Nobel Prizes winners*. Of course we need to define the semantics of the new quantifiers and establish some of their logical properties. One possible interpretation of the new quantifiers could be built along the following lines.

Let $P = \{x|p(x)\}$ and $Q = \{x|q(x)\}$ be discrete sets. Let $|X|$ denote the cardinality of set X. Then we shall consider the formula $\overset{\circ}{\forall}\{x \in P\}[q(x)]$ as being true iff the ratio $\dfrac{|P \cap Q|}{|P|}$ approaches 1 when $|P|$ is increased; otherwise the formula is false. Similarly, we shall consider the formula $\overset{\circ}{\exists}\{x \in P\}[q(x)]$ as true iff the ratio $\dfrac{|P \cap Q|}{|P|}$ does not approach 0 when $|P|$ is increased; otherwise the formula is false. The above could be restated formally in terms of limits, but there seem to be several problems with such interpretation. For one thing, generic interpretations could not be assigned to sentences referring to large but finite sets (*NYU undergraduates like pizza*). On the other hand, we do not have to take limits literally, but merely as a convenient way of expressing a certain noticeable general *pattern*, as we examine given evidence, piece by piece. Another problem is that the ratio of 1 may be too stringent a criterion for the truth of a transparently generic statement. Some people feel that generics are *fuzzier* than that. This may have to do with the problem of finite sets, or with logical properties of generics more generally. These problems notwithstanding, we may note that the new quantifiers are duals with respect to negation (Barwise & Cooper 1981), which is intuitively correct.

$$\neg\overset{\circ}{\forall}\{x \in P\}[q(x)] \text{ iff } \overset{\circ}{\exists}\{x \in P\}[\neg q(x)]$$

$$\neg\overset{\circ}{\exists}\{x \in P\}[q(x)] \text{ iff } \overset{\circ}{\forall}\{x \in P\}[\neg q(x)]$$

Thus, *birds fly* is false in its transparent reading just in the case when the number of birds that do not fly is non-negligible among all birds. Note that the negation of *birds fly* is a weaker statement than *birds do not fly*. Indeed, *birds do not fly* implies falsehood of *birds fly*, but not vice versa. Similarly, *Physicists win Nobel Prizes* is false in its opaque reading when among all Nobel Prize winners all but a negligible number are not physicists.

Another possible interpretation for the new quantifiers could be given within a standard modal logic[10] (Hughes&Cresswell 1978), with $\overset{\circ}{\forall}$ and $\overset{\circ}{\exists}$ understood as the possibility operator M and the necessity operator L, respectively. Specifically,

$$\overset{\circ}{\forall}\{x \in P\}[q(x)] \text{ iff } M(\forall x[p(x) \supset q(x)])$$

$$\overset{\circ}{\exists}\{x \in P\}[q(x)] \text{ iff } L(\exists x[p(x) \& q(x)])$$

---

[10] The access relation between possible worlds should be at least reflexive and transitive, and thus we are looking at systems S4 and up.

Thus, *birds fly* is true in the transparent reading iff it is possible that all birds fly. On the other hand, *physicists win Nobel Prizes* is true in the opaque reading iff it is necessary that some physicists win some Nobel Prizes. With this new interpretation we escape some of the difficulties of the interpretation based on limits, but we get some other instead. For instance, the transparently generic statement, such as *New York taxicabs are yellow*, is considered true only if we can explain away *all* exceptions, that is, if we can find a possible world in which no exceptions exist. We do not have any room left for some rebel red cab.

Apart from the problem of finding the appropriate interpretation for the new quantifiers, we have to find some way to determine, for each generic statement, how it is supposed to be understood: transparently, opaquely, or in some other way? It should be clear by now that such a decision cannot be made on the sentence by sentence basis and that the linguistic and extra-linguistic contexts need to be examined. Let $Q(P)$ be an L_{+1} translation of some generic statement, where Q is a predicate and P denotes an object at L_{+1}. We propose that the following procedure is adopted for interpreting $Q(P)$ at the level L_0.

(1)   If it is consistent with the way the world is believed to be, assume the transparent reading, i.e., $\overset{\diamond}{\forall} \{x \in P\}[x \in Q]$.

(2)   Otherwise, if the transparent reading is explicitly known not to be true (cf. *Frenchmen eat horsemeat*), then use a currently available context C and assume the restricted transparent reading, i.e., $\overset{\diamond}{\forall} \{x \in P \cap C\}[x \in Q]$.

(3)   Otherwise, if no such context can be found, or if the restricted transparent reading is known to be false for any available context (cf. *physicists win Nobel Prizes*), then assume the opaque reading, i.e., $\overset{\diamond}{\exists}\{x \in Q\}[x \in P]$.

(4)   Otherwise, if the unrestricted opaque reading is known to be false (cf. *teams of huskies are used for transportation*), then use a currently available context C and assume the restricted opaque reading, i.e., $\overset{\diamond}{\exists}\{x \in Q \cap C\}[x \in P]$.

(5)   Otherwise, the statement is not generic in the usual sense, or else it is false.

6. Conclusion

The problem of inter-sentential dependencies in discourse has been given varying degrees of attention in linguistics, philosophy of language and in artificial intelligence research, see, for example, (Partee 1978), (Sidner 1979), (Webber 1979), (Grosz 1977), (Hirst 1981), (Brown and Yule 1984) and (Hinrichs 1986). Formal linguistic and philosophical approaches to discourse analysis, while usually aiming at broader description of linguistic phenomena, normally are not directly suitable as a basis for a computational theory of natural language processing. Computational linguistic research, on the other hand, remained mostly application oriented and thus offered a limited range of solutions. In general, we observe that the research in the field of inter-sentential dependencies in discourse has not gone far beyond a limited domain of anaphoric in-text references. Even in this limited domain, however, there is a tendency to disregard cases where utterances have other than singular and extensional readings. Thus it comes as no surprise that various proposed representations are not as adequate and accurate as they should be. The research presented here seeks to avoid some of the above problems by a more careful selection of the meaning representation language, as well as by taking a broader, more comprehensive approach to the problem of inter-sentential dependencies.

7. References

Brown, G., G. Yule (1984). *Discourse Analysis*. Cambridge Textbooks in Linguistics. Cambridge University Press.

Carlson, G. N. (1982). "Generic Terms and Generic Sentences." **Journal of Philosophical Logic. 11** pp. 145-181.

Grosz, B. J. (1977). "The representation and use of focus in a system for understanding dialogues." Proceedings of the *Fifth IJCAI*. Cambridge, Mass. pp. 67-76.

Hinrichs, E. (1986). "Temporal Anaphora in Discourses of English." *Linguistics and Philosophy*. 9 (1). pp. 63-82.

Hirst, G. (1981). *Anaphora in Natural Language Understanding: A Survey*. **Lecture Notes in Computer Science.** vol. 119. Springer.

Hughes, G. E., M. J. Cresswell (1978). *An introduction to Modal Logic*. Methuen and Co., Ltd. London.

Montague, R. (1974) *Formal Philosophy. Selected Papers of Richard Montague*. R. H. Thomason (ed), Yale University Press.

Partee, B. H. (1978). "Bound variables and other anaphors." In D. L. Waltz (ed.), *TINLAP-2: Theoretical Issues in natural language processing*. pp. 79-85.

Sidner, C. L. (1979). "The role of focusing in interpretation of pronouns." Proceedings of the *17th Annual Meeting of the ACL*. pp. 77-78.

Strzalkowski, T. (1986a). "Representing Contextual Dependencies in Discourse." *Proc: Canadian Conference on Artificial Intelligence (CSCSI/SCEIO)*. Montreal.

Strzalkowski, T. (1986b). "An Approach to Non-Singular Terms in Discourse." *Proc: 11th Int. Conf. on Computational Linguistics (COLING)*. Bonn, Germany.

Strzalkowski, T. (1986c). *A Theory of Stratified Meaning Representation*. Doctoral Dissertation. Simon Fraser University, Burnaby, B.C.

Strzalkowski, T., N. Cercone (1986). *A Framework for Computing Extra-sentential References*. **Computational Intelligence.** 2(4). pp. 159-179.

Strzalkowski, T., N. Cercone (1989). "Non-singular Terms in Natural Language Discourse." To appear in **Computational Linguistics.**

Strzalkowski, T. (1988). "A meaning representation for generic sentences." Tech. Report #423. Courant Institute of Mathematical Sciences, New York University.

Webber, B. L. (1979). *A Formal Approach to Discourse Anaphora*. Doctoral Dissertation. Harvard University.

Enhancing Text Quality in a Question–Answering System

Clarisse Sieckenius de Souza [§]

Donia R. Scott [†]

Maria das Graças Volpe Nunes [‡] [§]

[§] Dept. de Informática, PUC/RJ
R. Marquês de São Vicente, 225,
22453 Rio de Janeiro / RJ – Brasil

[†] Philips Research Laboratories,
Cross Oak Lane, Redhill,
Surrey RH1 5HA, U.K.

[‡] ICMSC – Universidade de São Paulo,
R. Carlos Botelho, 1465,
13560 – São Carlos / SP – Brasil

1. Introduction

Cooperativity has been extensively declared to be a necessary feature of intelligent interactive systems. A cooperative response is one which optimally achieves the responder's communicative goal, which is to change the questioner's mental state from one of not knowing to knowing the facts questioned [1]. To achieve this goal in an optimal way, the responder should not only provide the appropriate information, but do so in a manner which ensures that it will be easily understood. Leaving aside issues of information content, it is clear that grammaticality is a necessary but not sufficient criterion in this context for judging the quality of a response. We will assume for the sake of discussion that in conversational systems which involve text output, text that is 'good' according to the writing conventions of the language in question is adequate for the situation.

This paper describes some methods of enhancing the textual quality of responses generated within the framework of Rhetorical Structure Theory [2,3], a framework that is currently being explored by the authors for producing textual responses in Brazilian Portuguese [4,5,6] and by others for English [7]. It is clear that although there are general criteria for good text that hold across languages, fine-grained tuning is required for each language. Our methodology addresses the general problem of producing good-quality textual responses, with particular reference to Brazilian Portuguese.

Rhetorical Structure Theory (RST) is a theory of text organization in which spans of text are described according to the rhetorical relations that hold between them. Elements of a relation are referred to as nuclei and satellites, with nuclei being more semantically primary to the text than satellites. Relations hold between elements of a text at a number of levels (ie. a RST structure is essentially hierarchical). Text coherence is defined by the existence of a rhetorical relation between each part of the text and at least one of its neighbours, and cohesion as the existence of a relation that holds over the entire text.[1]

Each RST relation is defined by the constraints that hold on the content of its elements and on their combination and by a statement of what its impact should be on the reader. This characteristic is especially important in question-answering systems, where beliefs play a major role in the design of cooperative responses.

Although RST is essentially a descriptive theory of text structure, it is particularly attractive for text generation since it encompasses criteria by which a piece of text can be judged as good on both linguistic and cognitive grounds. In a generative process, however, the step between the planning and realisation phases must involve some sort of linguistic strategy for the mapping of structure onto text. Such a strategy would direct the syntactic and lexical choices available for expressing the relations that hold between the information units that form the terminal elements of the structure. Previous research [8] has pointed to what some of these mapping elements would look like.

LETTERA is a program that uses RST as a basis for generating textual responses in Brazilian Portuguese to Yes/No questions about crimes and criminology [5]. The input to LETTERA is an RST schema, the construction of which is guided by focus considerations [4,6]. These schemas keep intact the original specifications of RST relations. The generation of text involves a mapping between RST relations and linguistic markers, and the use of a generative grammar of Portuguese. The grammar operates in two steps: (a) generating basic sentences from clause-sized knowledge-representation structures

---

[1.] The JOINT schema is an exception to this.

(first–order predicates) and (b) performing transformations on these to produce the final text. A typical output of LETTERA would be:

> *Question:* Pedro foi ferido?
> *Was Peter hurt?*

> *LETTERA:*
> Sim, com facadas. O autor do crime é desconhecido e fugiu.
> O local do crime é o Leme e a data é dia 21 de junho.
> *Yes, with stabs. The author of the crime is unknown and has*
> *fled. The location of the crime is Leme and the date is June 21.* [2]

Although correct in essence, this response is stylistically inadequate. A much better text in Brazilian Portuguese would be:

> *LETTERA:*
> Sim, com facadas. O autor do crime, ocorrido no Leme no
> dia 21 de junho, é desconhecido e fugiu.
> *Yes, with stabs. The author of the crime, which occurred in*
> *Leme on June 21st, is unknown and has fled.*

where the second sentence contains an embedded clause. It is indisputable that although the meaning of the first text is absolutely clear, the second is much more acceptable as 'fluent' Brazilian Portuguese. A similar problem, which Hovy [7] refers to as one of sentence scoping, occurs in PENMAN.

In the rest of this paper, we describe the technique we have developed for improving the quality of text generated by LETTERA so that it is more like the second than the first example.

2. Expanding RST–based Planning Capabilities

The responses LETTERA produces to Yes/No questions all conform to one of the general schemas shown in Figures 1 and 2. The organisation of these schemas is guided by focus considerations and by general principles of cooperativity. As shown in the figures, degrees of cooperativity vary as one moves through the regions of a schema. Each node in the schema is a relation, with the heavy branches pointing to Nuclei and the light ones to Satellites. The variables x and y correspond to the focussed elements of the reponse; p_i and p_i' correspond to predicates, where p_i' is related, but not equivalent, to p_i .

---

[2] The English translations given throughout are more–or–less literal ones.

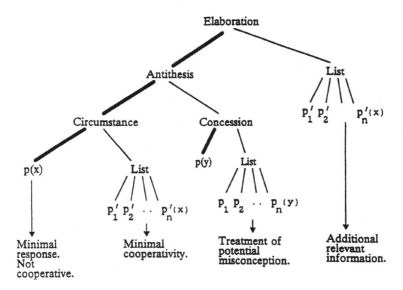

Figure 1: Yes Schema

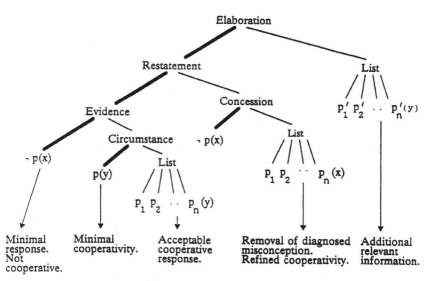

Figure 2: No Schema

Response schemas represent the upper limit on what a response can contain. Responding to Yes/No questions, the output of the planner (the input to LETTERA) is one of the above schemas to which terminal clause–sized elements (first-order predicates) have been added. Realising these schema by traversing them in a depth–first manner, transforming each terminal element into an S–bar with accompanying lexical markers of relations and with anaphoric reference could result in text such as: [3]

Example 1: Yes Schema

Question: Pedro foi atacado?
Was Pedro attacked?

Response:

1. $\{p(x)\}$ Sim.
Yes.

2. $\{p1(x)\}$ Pedro foi atacado com um guarda-chuva.
Pedro was attacked with an umbrella.

3. $\{p2(x)\}$ Ele foi atacado com uma bolsa.
He was attacked with a handbag.

4. $\{p(y)\}$ Não foi Paulo a vítima,
Paulo wasn't the victim,

5. $\{p_1(y)\}$ embora ele tivesse roubado a carteira de um pedestre.
although he had stolen a pedestrian's wallet.

6. $\{p_1'(x)\}$ Pedro costumava roubar as pessoas na rua.
Pedro is known to have robbed people on the street.

7. $\{p_2'(x)\}$ Ele tinha estado preso várias vezes.
He has been imprisoned many times.

8. $\{p_3'(x)\}$ Ele tinha sido condenado por pequenos furtos.
He has been convicted for petty theft.

Example 2: No Schema

Question: José foi suspeito de ter ferido Pedro?
Was Jose suspected of having injured Pedro?

Response:

1. $\{\neg p(x)\}$ Não.
No.

2. $\{p(y)\}$ José foi testemunha do crime,
Jose was a witness to the crime,

3. $\{p_1(y)\}$ Uma vez que ele viu o crime.
since he saw the crime take place.

4. $\{\neg p(x)\}$ Ao passo que José não foi suspeito,
Even though Jose was not suspected,

5. $\{p_1(x)\}$ se bem que ele esteve no Leme no dia 21.
even so he was in Leme on the 21st.

---

[3] Information on how the content of responses is determined is given in [4] and [6].

6. {pɪ'(y)} José era primo de Pedro.
   Jose was Pedro's cousin.

For purposes of explication, we show the focus tag and number associated with each clause. Of course, the final output of the generator will be rather better presented.

It is fairly apparent from these examples that the set of transformational operations used to produce them is not sufficient to render a stylistically pleasing text. An obvious solution would be expanding the realisation component to allow it to perform more sophisticated syntactic operations for clause–combining. It is clear, however, that such enhancements must be sensitive to the structural context in which terminal elements occur and not simply to the immediate (low–level) context of the neighbouring elements.

For example, from the point of view of style, clause 6 in Example 2 should be embedded in clause 2 but not in clauses 3, 4 or 5. Similarly, it would make good stylistic sense for embedding to operate between clauses 6 and 2, but not coordination. Example 2 also indicates the types of stylistic blunders that can occur when the realiser does not have access to information about the constraints that apply to the markers of a relation: those used for clauses 4 and 5, although appropriate for the relation, should not occur together.

In addition to structure–sensitive syntactic realisation rules, some sort of interaction with linguistic information will be desirable at the planning stage. That is, the rhetorical relations, the elements on which the planner operates to produce the RST structure, must contain as part of their definition a specification of the linguistic operations that can be applied to them.

3. Adding Linguistic Information to RST Relations

We propose that the specifications of RST relations should include the information outlined below. The items presented here are not intended to comprise the full set of information required for the production of stylistically adequate text. Rather, they comprise the minimal set required to produce stylistic enhancements of the type discussed above.

1. A specification of the permissible syntactic structures in which the relation's Nuclei and Satellites can be linguistically realised.

The default syntactic realisation of all structure–terminal elements is a sentence (S–bar). However, whereas Nuclei are only realisable as S–bars, Satellites may also be realised as sub-sentential structures (e.g. adjectives, noun-phrases or prepositional phrases). In this respect we depart from the clause-combining proposal of [8], which suggests that satellites should also be realised as S-bars. Instead, we take the view that the semantic subordination of Satellite to Nucleus should be expressible syntactically as embedding. This point is discussed in greater detail below.

2. A specification of the lexical or phrasal markers that apply to the relation, under what conditions and with attachment to which element.

Although the rhetorical relations between two text spans are sometimes retrievable from the mere juxtaposition of the two, this is often not the case. When it is not, then explicit signals of the relation must be given. The more syntax and semantics interact to produce the meaning of a relation, the greater the need will be to explicitly mark that relation.

3. A specification of the permissible permutations of a Nucleus and a Satellite, and the conditions under which they may occur.

As a general principle of RST, there are no constraints on the order in which the elements of a relation can occur. However, a 'Nucleus before Satellite' order is most prevalent in natural text, presumably due to cognitively-motivated factors related to the primacy of Nuclei over Satellites to the text. A 'Satellite before Nucleus' order tends to coincide with the presence of explicit lexical or syntactic markers of the semantic subordination of Satellite to Nucleus.

4. Structure-sensitive Syntactic Rules

Rhetorical relations can be signalled syntactically through subordination and coordination. In general, syntactic subordination reflects the presence of semantic subordination of Satellite to Nucleus, whereas coordination reflects the linking of independent elements — that is, Satellites with other Satellites and Nuclei with other Nuclei (see e.g. [9]). Exceptions to this rule involve cases where coordination reflects semantic subordination, and where subordination is temporal or causal. For example:

Eles não estão se dando bem, e ela decidiu sair de casa.
They're not getting along, and she's decided to move out.

For reasons of simplicity, we have chosen to use the general rule for making the choice between applying syntactic subordination or coordination and to deal with the exceptions within the specification of relations by treating the coordinating conjunction as a lexical marker. For example, "and" will appear as a lexical marker in the specification of SEQUENCE and relations in the CAUSE cluster.

4.1 Embedding Environments

The semantic subordination of Satellite to Nucleus will be syntactically marked by embedding. Although research on text analysis using RST suggests that embedding will be undesirable, or at the very least that its frequency should be restricted [8], our experience has shown this not to be the case. LETTERA presents a number of situations which favour embedding, most noticeably when the response contains information that is supplementary or complementary to the main idea that it is attempting to convey to the reader. These situations tend to involve the ELABORATION, CONCESSION and CIRCUMSTANCE relations. Given that LETTERA uses only a reduced set of RST relations, it may well be the case that general embedding rules involving all 20 RST relations will be required, but this is outside the scope of the present paper.

Rule 1: A Satellite can only be embedded in its Nucleus.

This restriction on which of the Nuclei of a schema can be a candidate home for an embedded Satellite ensures that embedding does not disturb the hierarchical relationships of the RST structure.

Rule 2: Embedding can be realised as an adjective, appositive noun phrase (*predicativo*), prepositional phrase or relative clause and should be realised in that order of preference.

This rule provides for subordinate structures that do not impair the style of the main clause. Although psycholinguistically motivated, the specification of preferred constructions is to some extent language dependent. The order given in the rule is that which is most appropriate to Brazilian Portuguese, and will require fine-tuning when applied to another language.

Rule 3: Embedding can occur within the left-most nuclear clause in the structure bearing the same focus value as the candidate clause.

Exceptions to the rule will be expressed as syntactic constraints in the specification of relations. For example, Satellite elements of CIRCUMSTANCE and CONCESSION can only be embedded in their immediate Nucleus, and embedding cannot occur across Nucleus and Satellite of RESTATEMENT.

To maximize stylistic effects, these three rules are applied in the order in which they are presented here. In addition to them, another more global structure–related embedding rule is required:

Rule 4: Satellites in a LIST schema of ELABORATION should (where possible) be embedded, provided that the number of remaining clauses is 0 or greater than 1.

This rule prevents the appearance of 'dangling' sentences in the text. ELABORATION is perhaps the weakest relation, in that the content of its Satellite is less strongly related to that of the Nucleus that in other relations. When there is only one clause in the Satellite of ELABORATION, the effect on the reader is of it being included as an after–thought. This effect increases in proportion to increases in the size of the Nucleus and decreases in the size of the Satellite.

4.2 Coordination Environments

As mentioned before, coordination will be applied as a syntactic marker of the absence of semantic subordination. It appears to be the case that, at least for Brazilian Portuguese and English, elements of a text that bear different rhetorical relations to the rest of the text are not suitable candidates for coordination.

The only structural configurations in RST which do not involve subordination are multi–nuclear schemas (CONTRAST, JOINT and SEQUENCE) and multi-satellite ones (LIST and MOTIVATION/ ENABLEMENT). In the light of the above constraints on coordination, only three of these support coordination, leading to the rule:

Rule 5: Coordination can only occur between elements of LIST, SEQUENCE and CONTRAST. [4]

There are a number of other aspects of coordination which affect style and which are rather more related to psycholinguistic than structural factors. These lead to two more global coordination rules which reflect psycholinguistic evidence [10] on the facilitation effects of syntactic factors on sentence processing.

---

[4] JOINT is not included here since it does not lead to coherence.

Rule 6: The greater the number of shared parameter values between clauses, the more desirable it is to coordinate them.

Rule 7: It is more desirable to coordinate Noun Phrases before Prepositional Phrases, which in turn are more desirable candidates for coordination than Verbs or Verb Phrases.

4.3 Heuristics for Sentence Complexity and Rule Ordering

In addition to the above structure–related rules for combining terminal clauses, there are a number of more general ones that are required for the production of stylistically good text. These rules guarantee that the filtering of the number of embedded and coordinated clauses, and the number of levels of embedding, does not degrade the clarity of the derived text. They are:

Rule 8: Sentences should contain no more than 3 clauses, including embedded ones.

Rule 9: Sentences should contain no more than 1 level of embedding.

Rule 10: Embedding should occur before Coordination.

Rule 11: Embedding should occur before focus transformations.

Rule 12: Clauses with time and place predicates should not be coordinated.

These rules are the result of applying native intuitions on the effect of sentence complexity on style (8 and 9), and of the effect of implementations of partial algorithms in LETTERA of the embedding and coordination rules discussed above (10 and 11). Finally, cognitive factors appear to favour time and place as a single predicate when related to the same event. Exceptions to this appear to occur only for reasons of emphatic stress for argumentative purposes.

5. Discussion:

This paper addresses the problems that arise when text is generated by realising the terminal elements of a hierarchical plan in a strictly bottom–up way. It argues, as we have argued elsewhere [11], that the generation of good quality text can only be achieved if the realisation process is sensitive to the structure of the plan and to psycholinguistic factors. We have suggested here some methods of achieving this within the framework of Rhetorical Structure Theory. Applying them to the text plan for Examples 1 and 2 above, we now get:

Example 1:

Sim.   Pedro, que costumava roubar as pessoas na rua, foi atacado com um guarda-chuva e uma bolsa.   Não foi Paulo a vítima,   embora ele tivesse roubado a carteira de um pedestre. Pedro   tinha estado preso várias vezes, e sido condenado por pequenos furtos.

Yes.   Pedro, who is known to have robbed people on the street, was attacked with an umbrella and a handbag.   Paulo wasn't the victim,   although he is known to have stolen a pedestrian's wallet. Pedro has been imprisoned several times, and has been convicted for petty theft.

Example 2:

Não. José, primo de Pedro, foi testemunha do crime, uma vez que ele viu o crime. José não foi suspeito, embora tivesse estado no Leme no dia 21.
No. Jose, Pedro's cousin, was a witness to the crime, since he saw it take place. Jose was not suspected, even though he was in Leme on the 21st.

The addition of linguistic information to the specifications of the rhetorical relations and the application of our structure-sensitive syntactic rules clearly result in a significant improvement in text quality.   Although this can be seen in the English translations, the extent of the improvement in our examples is much more obvious to readers unfamiliar with Portuguese.

Of course, a number of other, non-structural, considerations will also need to be taken into account for further improving the text style. For example, there is the general problem of reference. The improved version of Example 2 would be much better, in the sense of being more easily understood, if "in Leme on the 21st" were replaced with "present at the crime". Just when replacements of this type are required and what they should look like remains to be solved. Similarly, there is the problem of synonymy. It is a basic rule of good text that the same word or marked syntactic construction must not be repeated too often or too closely together. This is extremely important for Portuguese and, to a somewhat lesser   extent, for English.   Although LETTERA deals with this problem, it does not do so in a theoretically motivated way. General solutions must necessarily involve theoretically inspired rules for determining just what "too often" and "too close" really mean.

The generality of our rules to the full set of RST relations is not yet known since they have only been tested with the subset of relations used in LETTERA. Our examination of other relations leads us to believe that they have a wider application, but this issue will only be resolved by an in-depth study of all relations. This is the subject of ongoing research.

Finally, this work raises a theoretical point with respect to RST, in that applying RST as an analysis technique to the resulting text will not produce a

A KNOWLEDGE-BASED SYSTEM TO

SYNTHESIZE FP PROGRAMS FROM EXAMPLES

Zhu Hong & Jin Lingzi
Computer Science Department
Nanjing University
Nanjing, P.R.China

Abstract

This paper describes a knowledge-based system to synthesize functional programs of Backus' FP system [1,2] from input / output instances. Based on a theory of orthogonal expansion of programs [3,4], the task of program synthesis is expressed in program equations, and fulfilled by solving them according to the knowledge about the equivalence between programs. Examples are given in the paper.

1. Introduction.

By program synthesis, we mean the derivation of programs from incomplete specifications, such as a finite set of input / output pairs of the intended programs. Such specifications have the advantages of readability, and do not need much training to write and understand specifications. However, the synthesis of programs from them means to find the regularity in and between the examples. The nature of incompleteness results in the existence of more than one programs with different functions satisfying the same specification. What is really required depends on the knowledge in the specifier's brain. Hence, to synthesize the 'correct' program the machine should use the same knowledge as that of specifiers.

In this paper, we describe a knowledge-based system for synthesizing recursive functional programs of Backus' FP system[1] from input/output examples. The method is based on the algebra of programs [1,2] and a theory of orthogonal structure that is identical to that produced by the planner. The question arises as to what this phenomenon really means. The answer to this revolves around the issue of what is the status of the planner's RST structure. We would want to claim here that the structure produced by the text planner reflects the relations that hold between the information elements of the text to be produced and that although this must be related to the discourse structure of the text, it is not equivalent to it. The crucial test of the compatibility of the two structures rests on whether the second retains the hierarchical relations of primary and secondary information of the first. In this sense the planner's structure can be considered as the mental model we want the reader to have of the text content, a model which can be expressed in a number of ways.

References

[1] Grice, P. (1975). 'Logic and Conversation'. In P. Cole and J. Morgan (Eds.), *Syntax and Semantics 3: Speech Acts*, Academic Press.

[2] Mann, W.C. and Thompson, S.A. (1986). 'Rhetorical Structure Theory: Description and Construction of Text Structures'. Technical Report ISI/RS-86-174, Information Sciences Institute, University of Southern California.

[3] Mann, W.C. and Thompson, S.A. (1987). 'Antithesis: A Study in Clause Combining and Discourse Structure'. In R. Steele and T. Threadgold (Eds.), *Language Topics: Essays in Honour of Michael Halliday*, Vol. 2, John Benjamins Publishing Company, Philadelphia.

[4] Nunes, M.G.V. (1988). 'Deep Generation in a Crime Knowledge-Based System'. Series Monografias em Ciencias da Computacao, Dept. de Informatica, PUC/RJ.

[5] Nunes, M.G.V. (1989). 'LETTERA: um Gerador de Texto em Portugues'. Series Monografias em Ciencias da Computacao, Dept. de Informatica, PUC/RJ.

[6] Nunes, M.G.V. and Scott, D.R. (1988). 'O Componente Estrategico de um gerador de respostas para um sistema baseado em conhecimento criminal', Anais do 5 Simposio Brasileiro de Inteligencia Artificial, Natal.

[7] Hovy, E. (1988). 'Planning Coherent Multisentential Text'. *Proceedings of the 26th Meeting of the ACL*. Buffalo, New York.

[8] Matthiessen, C. and Thompson, S.A. (1987). 'The Structure of Discourse and "Subordination" '. In J. Haltman and S.A. Thompson (Eds.), *Clause Combining in Discourse and Grammar*, John Benjamins Publishing Company, Amsterdam.

[9] Lyons, J. (1968). *Introduction to Theoretical Linguistics*, Cambridge University Press, Cambridge.

[10] Frazier, L., Taft, L., Roeper, T., Clifton, C., Ehrlich, K. (1984). 'Parallel Structure: a Source of Facilitation in Sentence Comprehension', *Memory and Cognition*, 12.

[11] Scott, D.R. and de Souza, C.S. (1989) . 'Conciliatory Planning for Extended Descriptive Texts', Series Monografias em Ciencias da Computacao, Dept. de Informatica, PUC/RJ.

program expansion [3,4]. A finite set of input / output pairs are transformed into a set of simple programs according to the knowledge of the relationship between input / output pairs and simple programs computing them. The set of simple programs are considered as terms in an orthogonal expansion of the intended program. By a theorem of program expansion, we can obtain a set of program equations that determine the program to be synthesized. Finally, these equations are solved according to the knowledge of the equivalence between programs, and fulfill the task of synthesis. Therefore, the most distinguish feature of our synthesis method is to detect regularities by solving equations instead of by pattern matching and other general induction mechanisms.

The paper is organized as follows. Section 2 outlines the synthesis method by a simple example. Section 3 describes the structure of the system and its implementation. Section 4 gives some typical programs synthesized by the system. Finally, section 5 compares our approach with some related work. The algebra of functional programs serves as the common knowledge of the equivalence between programs. Readers should refer to [1,2] for details about FP system and its algebra of programs.

2. Overview of The Synthesis Methodology.

The program we are going to synthesize is assumed to be in the form of
$$f = p \to q ; h \circ [e , f \circ d].$$
We make the choice for the following reasons :
(1) It is a generalization of the standard form of general recursive functions
$$\begin{cases} f(u,0) = A(u) \\ f(u, x+1) = B(u,x,f(u,g(x+1))). \end{cases}$$
Moreover, the canonical form [5] of linear functional forms
$$p \to q ; h \circ [id, f \circ d]$$
is a special case of the left hand side of the equation. So it is general enough that every computable function is expressible in the form.
(2) It is not too general to cause too many technical difficulties. In fact, it is a linear recursive function. We know well about its execution behavior and its orthogonal expansion. We have that [3,4]

Theorem 1. (Orthogonal Linear Expansion Theorem)
A linear recursive program
$$f = = p \to q; h \circ [e, f \circ d]$$
can be expressed as

$$f = \sum_{i=0}^{\infty} p \ o \ d^i = = > (h \ o \ [e, \ x \ o \ d])^i(q)$$

provided that $p \ o \ d^n = > - p \ o \ d^m, n > m$, where $P = = > Q = P -> Q; \perp$.

Now, let us explain the method by a simple example. Consider the following set of input / output instance pairs of a program which reverses the elements in a sequence.

$$\{ < a > \quad = > \quad < a > \ ,$$
$$< a, b > \quad \quad = > \quad < b, a > \ ,$$
$$< a, b, c > \ = > \quad < c, b, a > \ \}.$$

Since a, b, and c are considered as arbitrary objects, we transform the input / output pairs into the following simple programs which only compute the outputs from the corresponding inputs.

length= 1 = = > [1]

length= 2 = = > [2, 1]

length= 3 = = > [3, 2, 1]

Notice that for every object x, (length= 2):x = true if and only if x is in the form of < a,b> . Moreover, for every object x, if x is in the form < a,b> , then [2,1]:x will be in the form of the output term < b,a> , otherwise [2,1]:x will be undefined. So (length= 2)= = > [2,1] only computes the outputs from inputs. (length= 2) is called a characteristic predicate of the term < a,b> , and [2,1] is called a simple function. The other two simple programs have similar properties. These programs are then regarded as terms in the expansion of the intended program REVERSE. So we have that

$$\text{REVERSE} >\_ \text{length}= 1 = = > [1]$$
$$+ \ \text{length}= 2 = = > [2, 1] \quad \quad (2.1)$$
$$+ \ \text{length}= 3 = = > [3, 2, 1].$$

Recall that the program to be synthesized is assumed to be in the form of

REVERSE = = p -> q; h o [e, REVERSE o d]

and is expanded into

REVERSE = = p = = > q

+ p o d = = > h o [e, q o d]

+ p o d o d = = > h o [e, h o [e, q o d] o d]

...

Compare the inequality (2.1) with the expansion, we will get the following equations:

p = (length= 1)

p o d = (length= 2)

p o d o d = (length= 3)

q = [1]

h o [e, q o d] = [2, 1]

h o [e, h o [e, q o d] o d] = [3, 2, 1] .

From them, we can derive that

p = (length= 1)

q = [1]

(length= 1) o d = (length= 2)

(length= 2) o d = (length= 3)

h o [e, [1] o d] = [2, 1]

h o [e, [2, 1] o d] = [3, 2, 1]

The solution is

p = (length= 1)

q = [1]

d = taill

e = 1

h = apndr o [2, 1]

Hence, the result program is

REVERSE = = length= 1 -> [1] ;

apndr o [2, 1] o [1, REVERSE o taill]

According to the algebra of programs, this is equivalent to

REVERSE = = length= 1 -> [1] ;

apndr o [REVERSE o taill, 1].

In general, let $\{ x_0 => y_0 , x_1 => y_1 , ... , x_n => y_n \}$ be a set of input /output pairs, $x_0 , x_1 , ... , x_n$ be listed from a simple case to complex one in some sense, and x_0 be the simplest case the program will deal with. If the programs

$$P(x_i) = = > F(x_i,y_i)$$

only compute output y_i from input x_i for $i = 0,1,...,n$, we can obtain the following systems of equations of programs.

$$\begin{cases} p = P(x_0) \\ q = F(x_0,y_0) \\ P(x_i) = P(x_{i-1}) \text{ o d} \qquad i = 1,2,...,n \\ F(x_i,y_i) = h \text{ o } [e , F(x_{i-1},y_{i-1}) \text{ o d}] \quad i= 1,2,...,n \end{cases}$$

The programs p, q, d, e and h satisfying the equations determine the intended recursive program.

To summarize, the synthesis process can be divided into two phases. The first phase transforms input / output pairs into simple programs which only compute outputs from inputs. This is done by using the knowledge about relationship between I/O pairs and programs computing them. The second solves equations of programs according to the knowledge about equivalence between programs. The laws of the algebra of programs may serve as such knowledge. An elaborate knowledge base is constructed to solve program equations. Some experiments with it show that it is satisfactory. Only a little search is needed. More details about the synthesis method can be found in [6].

3. The Structure of the System.

3.1. The Organization of the Knowledge Base.

For the limitation of space, it is impossible to give details about the knowledge used in the system. We only describe its structure and main functions here.

The knowledge base is divided into several groups. They are

* *Laws of Algebra of Programs:*
    Its main functions are
    (1) Simplifying equations to be solved;
    (2) Checking whether a solution of a single equation is also that of the whole system;
    (3) Optimizing result programs.

* *Transformations of I/O Pairs into Simple Programs:*
    It is further divided into two subgroups according to their functions.
    (1) Transformations of input terms into their characteristic predicates;
    (2) Transformations of output terms into simple functions. Here, simple programs are those constructed from primitives, constants and selective functions by composition and construction functionals.
    Under the conditions that
    (1) input terms do not overlap;
    (2) output terms have no extra variables that do not occur in input terms; and
    (3) finally, input terms are linear, i.e. no variable occurs more than once,

the groups of rules constitute a function that maps I/O pairs into simple programs computing them. The correctness of the rules has been proved [6].

Knowledge about Solutions of Program Equations.

Three kinds of simple equations are involved in synthesis of linear recursive programs. They are simple left linear equations
$$x \circ R = S,$$
simple right linear equations
$$R \circ x = S$$
and simple nested left equations
$$x_1 \circ [x_2, D] = S.$$
The programs R, S and D are simple programs. Three groups of rules are used to solve these equations. They are

(1) rules solving simple left linear equations;

(2) rules solving simple right linear equations;

(3) rules deriving left adjunctions of simple programs.

A left adjunction of a program D is a program A such that A and D have the same domain, and [A,D] is partially left invertible. The most important property of left adjunctions is that [6]

Theorem 2.

For every program A', if the equation
$$x \circ [A', D] = S$$
has solutions, so does the equation
$$x \circ [A, D] = S,$$
where A is a left adjunction of D.

Therefore, simple nested left equations can be solved by first deriving a left adjunction of D and then solving a simple left linear equation.

The main properties of the rule sets about solutions of simple equations are that they are locally confluent and noetherian [6]. This means that the solution of equations can be done merely by rewriting equations into equations until canonical forms appear. The correctness of the rule has also been verified [6].

3.2. About The Implementation.

The system is written in a metalanguage TrapML designed for transformational programming[7]. It provides three kinds of module facilities to describe the syntactical structure of objects, transformation rules and strategies. The metaprograms are used to equip an abstract transformation system NDTPS[8]. It provides man_machine interface and various other functions of transformation systems such as recording transformation process, controlling intermediate versions and displaying information about knowledge base and results.

The syntax of FP system and input / output pairs are described by syntax modules. Each group of knowledge is described by a rule set module. The synthesis strategy is defined in a strategy module. The powerful expressiveness makes knowledge base quite compact. Many rules which are usually defined recursively, say, the algebraic law of FP system

$$[f_1, \ldots, f_n] \text{ o } g = [f_1 \text{ o } g, \ldots, f_n \text{ o } g]$$

can be written in a single rule of TrapML. There are about one hundred rules totally.

Although the emphasis of the implementation is mainly on the logical clarity, the efficiency of the system is still satisfactory. When executed on a personal computer IBM_PC/AT, it takes about a dozen of minutes to automatically synthesize the programs listed in the paper, e.g. the synthesis of the REVERSE program takes about 3 minutes, the inner product described below 13 minutes. More details about the synthesis system can be found in [9].

4. Some Experiments With The System.

This section will give more example programs that have been synthesized by the system.

Example 1.
Given the set of I/O instances
    { < a> = > a, < a,b> = > a + b, < a,b,c> = > a + b + c },
it is intended to synthesize a program that sums up a list of numbers. The system first derives the following simple programs:
    length= 1 = = > 1
    length= 2 = = > + o [1, 2]
    length= 3 = = > + o [1, + o [2, 3]],
then solves the equations and gives that
    p = length= 1
    q = 1

```
        d =  taill
        e =  1
        h =  +
```
The result program is
```
      SUM =  (length= 1) ->  1; +  o [1, SUM o taill ]
```

Example 2.

To synthesize a program computing the maximal element of a list of numbers, we deliver the following set of I/O pairs to the system :
```
  { < a>  = >  a,
    < a,b>  = >  if a >  b then a else b,
    < a,b,c>  = >  if b >  c then ( if a >  b then a else b )
                          else ( if a >  c then a else c )  }
```
The simple programs derived by the system are
```
            length=  1 = = >  1
            length=  2 = = >  >  o [1, 2] ->  1; 2
            length=  3 = = >  >  o [2, 3] ->
                              ( >  o [1, 2] ->  1 ; 2);
                              ( >  o [1, 3] ->  1 ; 3)
```
The solution is
```
            p =  length=  1
            q =  1
            d =  taill
            e =  1
            h =  >  o [ 1, 2 ] ->  1; 2.
```
The result program is
```
        MAX =  (length= 1) ->  1;
            (>  o [ 1, 2 ] ->  1 ; 2 ) o [ 1, MAX o taill ]
```

Example 3.

A program computing the inner product of two vectors is synthesized from the set of input / output pairs
```
    { < < a1 > , < b1 >  >  = >  a1 x b1 ,
      < < a1, a2 >  , < b1, b2 >  >
                = >  (a1 x b1) +  (a2 x b2),
      < < a1, a2, a3 > , <  b1, b2, b3 >  >
                = >  (a1 x b1) +  (a2 x b2) +  (a3 x b3) }.
```
The simple programs only computing these examples are
```
      (length= 2) & / and o [(length= 1) o 1,(length= 1) o 2]
```

$$= = > \quad * o \, [1 \, o \, 1, \, 1 \, o \, 2],$$
$$(\text{length}= 2) \& / \text{and} \, o \, [\, (\text{length}= 2) \, o \, 1, \, (\text{length}= 2) \, o \, 2]$$
$$= = > \quad + \, o \, [* o \, [1 \, o \, 1, \, 1 \, o \, 2], \, * o \, [2 \, o \, 1, \, 2 \, o \, 2]],$$
$$(\text{length}= 2) \& / \text{and} \, o \, [\, (\text{length}= 3) \, o \, 1, (\text{length}= 3) \, o \, 2]$$
$$= = > \quad + \, o \, [* o \, [1 \, o \, 1, \, 1 \, o \, 2],$$
$$+ \, o \, [* o \, [2 \, o \, 1, \, 2 \, o \, 2],$$
$$* o \, [3 \, o \, 1, \, 3 \, o \, 2]]]$$

The solutions are

$$p = \quad (\text{length}= 2) \, \&$$
$$/ \text{and} \, o \, [(\text{length}= 1) \, o \, 1, (\text{length}= 1) \, o \, 2]$$
$$q = \, * o \, [1 \, o \, 1, \, 1 \, o \, 2],$$
$$d = \, [\text{taill} \, o \, 1, \, \text{taill} \, o \, 2],$$
$$e = \, [\, 1 \, o \, 1, \, 1 \, o \, 2 \,].$$
$$h = \, + \, o \, [* o \, 1 \, , 2].$$

After simplification the system outputs the result program

$$IP = \quad \text{length}= 2 \, \& \, \text{and} \, o \, [\, (\text{length}= 1) \, o \, 1 \, , \, (\text{length}= 1) \, o \, 2 \,]$$
$$\text{->} \, * o \, [\, 1 \, o \, 1 \, , \, 1 \, o \, 2 \,];$$
$$+ \, o \, [\, * o \, [1 \, o \, 1, \, 1 \, o \, 2 \,],$$
$$IP \, o \, [\text{taill} \, o \, 1, \, \text{taill} \, o \, 2 \,]]$$

Example 4.

To synthesize a program of matrix multiplication, we first derive an auxiliary program that multiplies a matrix by a vector and outputs a vector. Let us specify the program by a set of input / output pairs.

$$\{ < \, a \, , < \, b1 \, > \, > \, = > \, < \, a \, V*V \, b1 \, > \, ,$$
$$< \, a \, , < \, b1, \, b2 \, > \, > \, = > \, < \, a \, V*V \, b1, \, a \, V*V \, b2 \, >$$
$$< \, a \, , < \, b1, \, b2, \, b3 \, > \, > \, = > \, < \, a \, V*V \, b1, \, a \, V*V \, b2, \, a \, V*V \, b3 \, > \, \}$$

where V*V is the inner product of two vectors, a, and bi are vectors, and bi is the i'th row of the matrix. The symbol V*V is a user-defined binary operator. How to understand such symbols can be described by user in additional rule set modules. In case of V*V, it is considered as the IP program given in the example 3.

The simple programs derived by the system with the help of such knowledge are

$$\text{length}= 2 \, \& \, (\text{length}= 1) \, o \, l(2)$$
$$= = > \, [\, IP \, o \, [\, l(1), \, l(1) \, o \, l(2) \,] \,]$$
$$\text{length}= 2 \, \& \, (\text{length}= 2) \, o \, l(2)$$
$$= = > \, [\, IP \, o \, [\, l(1), \, l(1) \, o \, l(2) \,],$$

IP o [l(1), l(2) o l(2)]]

length= 2 & (length= 3) o l(2)

= = > [IP o [l(1), l(1) o l(2)],

IP o [l(1), l(2) o l(2)],

IP o [l(1), l(3) o l(2)]]

The solution is

p = length= 2 & (length= 1) o l(2)

q = [IP o [l(1), l(1) o l(2)]]

d = [l(1), taill o l(2)]

e = [l(1), l(1) o l(2)]

h = apndl o [IP o l(1), l(2)]

The result program is

VM = = length= (2) & (length= (1) o l (2))

-> [IP o [l(1), l(1) o l(2)]];

apndl o [IP o [l(1), l(1) o l(2)],

VM o [l(1), taill o l(2)]]

The matrix multiplication program can be synthesized from the following input / output pairs.

{ < < a1 > , b > = > < a1 V*M b > ,

< < a1, a2 > , b > = > < a1 V*M b , a2 V*M b > ,

< < a1,a2,a3> , b> = > < a1 V*M b, a2 V*M b, a3 V*M b> }

where V*M is a user-defined binary operator regarded to be the program VM. The result program is

MM = = length= 2 & (length= 1) o l(1)

--> [VM o [l(1) o l(1), l(2)]];

apndl o [VM o [l(1) o l(1), l(2)],

MM o [taill o l(1), l(2)]]

More examples can be found in [6].

5. Related Work.

There are several methods to synthesize LISP programs from input / output examples. However, almost all of them were based on the Summers' Basic Synthesis Theorem[10], which gives the relationship between recurrence relations and recursive programs. One of the characteristics of these methods is the need of discovery of a recurrence relation between semitraces which are functional expressions correctly computing the example output from the input while allowing several different orders of evaluation. Semitraces are created from input / output pairs by an algorithm. As D.R.Smith pointed out [11], perhaps the most striking point of contrast between these methods lies in their approaches of finding recursive loops. Summers' and Kodratoff's method [10,12] detects recurrence patterns by matching the semitraces obtained from different example outputs. By Biermann's and Smith's method [13,14] it is detected by matching or folding a semitraces into itself. The Jouannaud and Guiho's [15] is by matching an example input with its corresponding output. Therefore, the syntactical structure of the semitraces is of particular importance. This is the bottle neck of the capability of the methods. And perhaps it is why almost all of the methods deal with list processing programs and none of them treat numerical problems. In our approach, the syntactic structure of the simple programs obtained from input / output pairs are not so important since the recursion is detected and generated by solving equations instead of pattern matching. Solving equations is mainly a semantic task. It depends on the knowledge of the equivalence between programs.

The synthesis of Backus' FP program is also discussed in [16]. A set of linear functionals are proved to be synthesizable. But how to detect and generate recursive programs is assumed to be solved by the methods mentioned above. As shown by the example, our system can synthesize not only programs definable by a single linear recursive equation, but also programs defined by several linear recursive equations.

References

[1]. J.Backus, Can programming be Liberated from von Neumann Style? A Functional Style and Its Algebra of Programs, CACM. 21:8 (1978) 631-641.

[2]. J.Backus, The Algebra of Functional Programs, in Formalization of Programming Concepts, J.Diaz, & I.Ramos, eds., LNCS 107, Springer_Verlag, 1981, 1-43.

[3]. Zhu Hong, A Theory of Program Expansion and Its Application to Programming, Ph.D Thesis, Nanjing University, Aug. 1987.

[4]. Zhu Hong, A Theory of Program Expansion, Scientia Sinica (Series A), 8(1988), 887-896.

[5]. U.S.Reddy,& B.Jayaraman,Theory of Linear Equations Applied to Program Transformation, Proc.8'th IJCAI, 1983, Vol.1, pp10~16.

[6]. Zhu Hong & Jin Lingzi, A Knowledge_Based Approach to Program Synthesis from Examples, Journal of Computer Science and Technology, (in press).

[7]. Jin Lingzi, Researches on Metalanguage for Transformational Program-

ming, Ph.D. Thesis, Nanjing University, December, 1987.

[8]. Jin Lingzi, Zhu Hong & Xu Jiafu, NDTPS -- An Experimental Metalanguage Transformational Programming System, Proceedings of the International Conference on New Generation Computer Systems, April, 1989, Beijing.

[9]. Jin Lingzi & Zhu Hong, Metaprogramming -- Applications to Program Synthesis from Examples, Beijing International Symposium for Young Computer Professionals, Aug. 1989. (in press).

[10]. P.D.Summers, A Methodology for LISP Program Construction from Examples, J.ACM, 24:1 (1977), 161-175.

[11]. D.R.Smith, The Synthesis of LISP Programs from Examples:A Survey, in Automatic Program Construction Techniques, A.W.Biermann, G.Guiho, & Y.Kodratoff,(eds.) Maclillan Publishing, 1984, 307-324.

[12]. Y.Kodratoff,& J-P.Jouannaud, Synthesizing LISP Programs Working On the List Level of Embedding, in Automatic Program Construction Techniques, 325-374.

[13]. A.W.Biermann, Dealing With Search, in Automatic Program Construction Techniques, 375-392.

[14]. A.W.Biermann, The inference of Regular LISP Programs from Examples, IEEE Transactions on Systems, Man, and Cybernetics, SMC-8:8(1978), 585-600.

[15]. J-P.Jouannaud, & G.Guiho, Inference of Functions with an Interactive System, in Machine Intelligence 9, D.Michie, (Ed.) Ellis Horwood, 1979, 227-250.

[16]. D.Banerjee, A Methodology for Synthesis of Recursive Functional Programs, ACM TOPLAS 9:3 (1987), 441-462.

A PATH PLANNER FOR THE CUTTING OF NESTED IRREGULAR LAYOUTS

José Távora and Helder Coelho

LNETI-DEE
22, Paço do Lumiar
1699 LISBOA Codex, Portugal

LNEC
101, Av. Brasil
1789 LISBOA Codex, Portugal

ABSTRACT

A combinatorial path planning problem arises when trying to cut optimally a layout of nested irregular forms. Heuristic search techniques coming from AI and OR are applied to build an approximate resolution method. Results for "real-life" instances (clothing layouts in the apparel industry) are presented and evaluated.

INTRODUCTION

Automatic cutters used in the apparel industry are big plotter-like machines moving a tool (knife, laser beam or waterjet) to process large rectangles of fabric where many contours representing cloth pieces are layed out in a waste-minimizing nested way.

Due to irregularity, orientation and other process constraints, contours do not share its frontiers, thus forbidding common-line cutting. Each piece is detached in a continuous contour-following operation beginning and ending on a single entry point, followed by a straight-line inactive-tool transport movement towards a new contour. For a whole layout the tool's travel can thus be divided into a **cutting path** and a **no-load path**. The latter is a broken line formed by all no-load movements, its total length depending on the chosen piece sequence and entry points.

This cutting strategy minimizes the tool's on-off transitions and associated delays while reducing positioning errors. It may, however, produce long no-load paths if a bad piece sequence or unconvenient entry points are chosen. With cutting and no-load speeds having similar fixed values, the total time it takes to process a layout (global cutting time) depends strongly on the length of the no-load path. Minimum cutting times will thus be obtained by minimizing this length.

Under the above goal lies the resolution of a **combinatorial optimization** problem (to be called the No-Load Path Problem) which is simultaneously complex and has big dimensions for "real-life" instances. These characteristics point out to the use of abstraction and **heuristic search** techniques capable of breaking down complexity and providing good (even if not optimal) solutions at an acceptable computational cost.

Following these principles, an approximate resolution method was developed and implemented as a **path planner**. The planner, written in **LISP** and running on a personal computer, searches for a set of no-load movements minimizing the global cutting time and thus increasing the cutter's throughput. Although tested with clothing layouts, the planner (or its underlying method) are applicable to other nested layouts where common-line cuts are not possible or the described cutting technique is preferable.

In the following, the minimum no-load path problem is briefly formulated and the resolution strategy outlined (sections two and three). Main modules of the resolution method are detailed in the next three sections. Finally, results are discussed and future work directions pointed out.

FORMULATING THE PROBLEM

The No-Load Path Problem (**NLPP**) is now informally stated:

Given a set of polygons (representing pieces to cut) layed on a rectangular surface without mutual overlap or common edges, find a minimum-length broken line (a no-load path) which visits them all without exclusion nor repetition. The line must begin in one of the rectangle's corners (the origin), break on one and only one vertex of each polygon and end in a vertex of the last visited one.

The problem's combinatorial-optimization nature is apparent from this formulation. Even for a small number of simple polygons the optimal no-load path must be searched between a great number of vertex combinations. Moreover, the set of possible solutions (solution space) grows explosively with the dimensions of the problem's instances. In fact, if **n** stands for the number of polygons and m_k for the number of vertices on the **k** polygon, the number **P** of candidate no-load paths where to search for the optimum is given by

$$P = n! \ (m_1 \ m_2 \ .. \ m_n) = n! \ m^n \qquad (1)$$

with **m** being the geometrical mean of the m_k.

A **graph model** of the **NLPP** is readily defined by associating polygon vertices and the origin with graph **nodes** and possible no-load movements with **arcs**. Most of the arcs connect every polygon node with all nodes in all other polygons (forming bidirectional links); the rest unidirectionally connect the origin with all polygon nodes. All arcs are weighted by the euclidean distances between the vertices represented by the nodes they connect. An alternative **integer programming** formulation can be found in [1][2].

The **NLPP** is not easily classified among known combinatorial optimization problems. A near relative seems to be the Clustered Travelling Salesman Problem (**CTSP**) [3][4][5][6] where points (cities) are total or partially organized in clusters, the ultimate goal being (like in the standard travelling salesman problem (**TSP**)) to find a minimum-length tour visiting them all. However, points belonging to clusters must be visited continuously in the **CTSP** and so local and global optimization goals interact. On the contrary, the **NLPP** disregards visits inside each cluster (set of a polygon's vertices) and requires a single input-output point. Both **NLPP** and **CTSP** can anyhow be considered as **TSP** generalizations in the sense that both tend to this problem if clusters are "shrinked" to the dimensions of a point. The **NLPP** is further analysed in [2] where it is proved that it belongs to the **NP-complete** class of problems.

The **NNLP** has never (to the authors' knowledge) been treated in published litterature prior to [7]. Nevertheless, manufacturers of **CAD-CAM** systems for the apparel industry address the problem, either including very simple no-load path optimizers in their machines' controllers [8] or by selling software packages where the manual modification of the cutting sequence can be done [9].

RESOLUTION METHOD

Real clothing layouts can have up to several hundred pieces described by up to thirty or even more vertices. As a result, big **NLPP** instances may have more than one thousand points. Exact resolution methods (v.g. using branch-and-bound techniques) were therefore excluded as they are not compatible with the cutter's computing environnment and allowable computing times. Instead, an **heuristic** method producing approximate sub-optimal solutions with limited computacional ressources was prefered.

The resolution strategy relies on a <u>decomposition heuristic</u> and an <u>iterative improvement scheme</u>. Using the decomposition rule, the **NLPP** is broken in two subproblems to be solved separately and in sequence. The first subproblem requires that all polygons (abstracted by "central" points) are visited with minimum travel mileage. The second requires that a minimum-length no-load path be chosen between the vertex combinations <u>allowed</u> by the first sub-problem's result (a piece/polygon sequence). As can be readily seen, the first sub-problem is a <u>Travelling Salesman Problem</u> **TSP**, the second being a case of the <u>Shortest Path Problem</u> (**SPP**). Thus, the decomposition produces two well-studied problems for which many approximate or exact resolution methods are known.

Solving the subproblems by **TSP** and **SPP** algorithms provides no-load paths too crude to serve as solutions to the **NLPP**. However, if a no-load path is improvable by a reordering of its vertices, the resulting new underlying <u>polygon sequence</u> can be fedback to the **SPP** solver, producing eventually a better new no-load path. The process can then be recycled until no further improvement is observed, defining an iterative improvement scheme. The resolution method can be further extended by a <u>vertex insertion algorithm</u>, to be applied after the iterative improvement scheme blocks. This final module finds its uses on some difficult instances or in case more accurate results are required.

TSP SUBPROBLEM

The **TSP** subproblem needed a single-point representation for each polygon. Ideally, these points should be "central", insensitive to small-area border details and invariant with translations and rotations. These items are fullfilled by the **centroid** (center of gravity) of each polygon, which was computed using an exact iterative area-decomposition algorithm. For clothing layouts however, much simpler centroid approximations are as efective, many piece shapes being grossly rectangular and vertically or horizontally aligned. In this case, computing the center of each polygon's **bounding box** provided good and fast-obtained centroid approximations.

For the **TSP** subproblem several known approximate resolution methods were tried. The selection criterion was to use lowest-complexity [$O(n^2)$] yet effective algorithms. In fact, although the optimum polygon sequence rarely defines the optimum no-load path, best solutions to the **TSP** sub-problem were seen in many cases to produce the best final results (in spite of considerable path changes during the resolution process). Selected methods were the **nearest-neighbour (NN), nearest-insertion** (NI) and **farthest-insertion(FI)** algorithms [10] [11]. Complementing these so-called insertion heuristics the **two-optimal (2OPT)** [12] edge-exchange improvement heuristic used in this case to improve results coming from the insertion heuristics. All algorithms were slightly modified to reflect the kind of **TSP** to be solved (no return to the origin is required).

In addition to the above methods, two new algorithms were designed to exploit the problem's particular domain. In fact, many clothing layouts are formed by "big" and "small" pieces; big pieces occupy most of the layout (setting its main structure) while little ones are inserted mainly in small spaces left. The new algorithms, to be called **nearest-neighbour farthest-insertion** (NNFI) and **double farthest insertion** (DFI), handle big and small polygons separately, being (as their names indicate) combinations of already refered methods. **NNFI** forms a first sequence with only big polygons using the simple **NN** algorithm and then inserts the rest with the **FI** heuristic. **DFI** doubles the application of the **FI** method, first to the big polygons and next to the small ones.

Results produced by all algorithms for a set of eleven **TSP** subproblem instances (including real clothing layouts and test maps) are detailed in [2] and summarized in [1]. The results showed that **FI** is the best algorithm to use alone, strongly outperforming **NI**. When combined with **2OPT**, algorithm **NN** makes a strong improvement (outperforming **NI**) and the two special algorithms **NNFI** and **DFI** produce the best final performances. Note however that these conclusions refer to average values. A close examination of **NNFI** and **DFI** shows that they perform less robustly than **FI** for a large spectrum of layout types. Actual running-times are also very different for all algorithms. For instance, for a fifty-five (sixteen big) piece layout, **NN, 2OPT, NNFI** and **DFI** respectively take about **6, 10, 83** and **86%** of the **FI** running-time.

SPP SUBPROBLEM

As a **P**-class problem, the **SPP** on the polygons' vertices can be efficiently solved by known exact algorithms. Although interesting (or necessary) for some difficult small **NLPP** instances, this approach fails for medium and big industrial layouts, for which even $O(n^2)$ running times are too long. The repeated use of the **SPP** solver in the iterative improvement scheme also emphasizes the need for a fast and effective approximate algorithm for this subproblem.

The **VT** algorithm was designed to fullfill these requirements. Using information obtained with the **TSP** subproblem (namely the centroids' coordinates), **VT** is a two-pass heuristic using a 'greedy' approach and memorizing only the current state of the computation (thus being a hill-climbing method). To formulate **VT**, consider a sequence $(p_1, p_2,...p_i...p_n)$ of polygons produced by the **TSP** subproblem. Let each polygon p_i be characterized by its centroid c_i and its vertices $v_i(k)$ with $k=1..m$ (from now on will consider a constant number of vertices for all polygons). Let **prev**(ious) and **best** be variables for vertex coordinates and let **target** store centroid coordinates. Let **res**(ult) be an initially empty data-structure from which the final result (a list of vertices defining a no-load path) is obtained.

<u>Algorithm **VT**</u>:

1. (First pass)
    prev <-- v_0
    res <-- insert v_0 in **res**
    FOR i=1 **TO** n-1
        target <-- c_{i+1}
        best <-- find $v_i(k)$ minimizing {dist [**prev**, $v_i(k)$] + dist [$v_i(k)$, **target**]}
        prev <-- **best**
        res <-- append **best** to **res**
    best <-- find $v_n(k)$ minimum {dist [**prev**, $v_n(k)$]}
    res <-- append **best** to **res**
2. (Second pass)
    Repeat first-pass procedure using vertices in **res** as targets.

Many <u>exact</u> algorithms are useful for the **SPP** sub-problem, the most famous being the **Dijkstra algorithm** [13]. A better alternative seems however to be found in the **proportional cost algorithm** (**PC**) proposed by Nilsson [14]. Although based on Dijkstra's method [14], the **PC** algorithm does not require an explicit input graph and adopts adaptive dynamical data-structures. The first of these features is important to the **SPP** sub-problem due to the particular nature of its underlying graph. In fact, once a polygon sequence is fixed (by the **TSP** sub-problem) the allowed arcs connect every polygon node (vertex) to every node in the <u>next</u> polygon (thus defining a <u>layered</u> graph). These arcs are a very small fraction of the corresponding set in a complete graph linking all vertices. Explicitly defining the **SPP** graph by a cost matrix would therefore produce a storage-wasting very sparse array.

The **PC** algorithm was applied to the **SPP** as a special case of the more general **A*** **algorithm** [14][15]. To exploit **A***, three different <u>heuristic information functions</u> (**h'**) were tried. The first one (**h'$_1$**) measured the straigth-line distance from the current vertex (in expansion) to the <u>nearest</u> vertex in the <u>last</u> polygon. The second (**h'$_2$**) gave the straigth-line distance to the centroid of the last polygon. Finally, **h'$_3$** was the length of the broken-line beginning in the current vertex and touching all centroids in sequence up to the last polygon. Note that **h'$_1$** produces an <u>admissible</u> algorithm, while **h'$_2$** and **h'$_3$** do not.

PC, **A*** and **VT** algorithms were tested with a set of five small and medium maps (four of them being clothing layouts in amputated form). Detailed results are discussed in [2] and summarized in [1]. A comparison of the methods' average accuracy shows that **VT** clearly outperforms **A*** the non-admissible heuristics **h'$_2$** and **h'$_3$** are used (error span is also much better in **VT**).

Analysis of execution times for **PC** and **A*** algorithms [2] indicates there's little interest in using **h'** functions like those which were tested. In fact, **A*(h'$_1$)**, while being admissible, takes much more time than **PC** due to the heuristic's computing load; **A*(h'$_2$)**, while executing faster than **PC** (varying between **75%** to almost **100%**) produces errors for some layouts; finally, **A*(h'$_3$)** shows a very irregular performance either executing appreciably faster than **PC** either much more slower. On the contrary, with its **O(n.m)** time-efficiency, **VT** takes only a small fraction of **PC**'s execution time (tipically less than **10%**), in exchange for an acceptable error level. Note that in spite of its good performance with normal layouts, **VT** can produce poor results in some situations, namely when there are long and thin protuberances in the polygons.

ITERATIVE IMPROVEMENT

As said in the third section, iteratively improving a no-load path and feeding-back its new polygon-sequence information generally refines the crude solutions given by the simple series combination of **TSP** and **SPP** solvers. To act as an improvement module, the already cited **2OPT** algorithm (modified to handle vertex rather than polygon sequences) was chosen and included in the resolution method.

The iterative-improvement scheme is illustrated in figure **1**, which also shows the application of the whole resolution method to a small test map. The process begins with a two-step resolution of the **TSP** subproblem (figs. **1a** and **1b**) using the **NN** and **2OPT** heuristics. Next, the **SPP** subproblem is solved for the first time using **VT** (fig. **1c**). Finally, the (vertex adapted) **2OPTv** algorithm and **VT** alternate to produce the best-found path for this process (figs. **1d** to **1f**). Note that with other algorithms (like **FI** and **PC**) convergence would be faster to a (slightly better) solution.

To further refine paths produced by the described strategy, a final improvement module can be added after the **SPP** solver's output. A new heuristic algorithm, to be called **INS**, was designed for this purpose. The **INS** heuristic takes each vertex of each polygon and sees if it can be inserted (with a cost advantage) in any other point on the no-load path. In the affirmative case, the current no-load path vertex of the polygon under test is deleted and the new one inserted.

To formulate **INS**, consider a sequence of polygons $(p_0, p_1, p_2,...p_i...p_n)$ where p_0 stands for the origin. Each p_i contributes a vertex vp_i for the corresponding no-load path; $v_i(k)$ stands for a generic p_i vertex while vp_h and vp_n represent generic no-load path vertices. Let **gain** and **loss** be numeric variables. Let **path** be a data-structure for the changing no-load path, from which the improved path can be found.

Algorithm **INS**:

path $\leftarrow$ $(vp_0, vp_1, vp_2,....vp_i,....vp_n)$
FOR i=1 **TO** n
    gain $\leftarrow$ {dist $[vp_{i-1}, vp_i]$ + dist $[vp_i, vp_{i+1}]$ - dist $[vp_{i-1}, vp_{i+1}]$}
    Find $v_i(k)$ on p_i and vp_h on **path** minimizing {dist$[vp_h, v_i(k)]$+dist$[v_i(k), vp_{h+1}]$}
    loss $\leftarrow$ minimum {dist $[vp_h, v_i(k)]$ + dist $[v_i(k), vp_{h+1}]$}
    IF gain > loss THEN
        path $\leftarrow$ a modified **path** with vp_i eliminated and $v_i(k)$ inserted after vp_h.

Note that whenever an insertion can be made, it will, so **path** may be continually changing. In any case, without regard to the polygon's current position, each of its vertices will be tested for insertion. Note also that several details were ommited in the formulation: (**1**) **gain** must receive {dist $[vp_{i-1}, vp_i]$} when the last polygon is considered (i=n); (**2**) vertex vp_i must be removed from **path** when testing $v_i(k)$ insertions; (**3**) **loss** must receive {dist $[vp_h, v_i(k)]$} if vp_h happens to be the last element of **path**.

Applying **INS** is important when a "too-flat" no-load path is produced early preventing **2OPT** from improving it and thus blocking the resolution process. In alternative it can be used to further refine already acceptable solutions. In both cases, **INS** will generally provide better solutions and even permit <u>several applications of itself</u>. The price to pay can however be high, as **INS** takes $O(m.n^2)$ time-consuming dist(ance) operations. An interesting modified version could restrict the insertion tests to each polygon's near neighbours.

This approach would require the classification of typical instances in order to determine a convenient neighbourhood level.

RESULTS

Figure **2** shows the final results after applying the complete resolution method to two clothing layouts. The instances were chosen from about twenty different maps and layouts whose detailed study for several resolution alternatives is done in [2]. The **a** and **b** maps are clothing layouts of medium-to-big dimensions (the original **b** map had five pieces amputated due to storage limitations). The results shown in figs. **2a** and **2b** have been obtained with a **FI-2OPT** compound method for the **TSP** subproblem and several applications of **VT**, **2OPTv** and **INS** for the rest of the resolution process.

To evaluate the whole method's performance as far as the deviations from the optimum were concerned, an empirical analysis [16] (based on computational experience) was used. However, the technique requires finding or estimating the optimum solution values for the **NLPP** instances, which is a difficult task due to the lack of exact resolution methods for the problem, other bibliographic references and the "real-life" dimensions of many maps.

A multiple approach has been used for this question, combining exaustive evaluation (for very small instances), manual estimation (improving machine solutions) and qualitative appraisal. For the bigger instances an empirical statistical approach [16] [17] was tried. The chosen method is based in one of the point estimators (O_{avg}) proposed in [17] for estimating the optimum of combinatorial optimization problems. Prior to application, the estimator was tested with small-size problems where the optimum was known providing good estimates of the optimum solution values. The errors indicated for maps **a** and **b** were estimated with the method. Note however that O_{avg} is sensitive to heuristic error [17], artificially improving less good solutions. Thus, although intensive testing on the instances made these estimates relatively reliable, they need eventually to be reviewed when a better way to determine or estimate the optimum is available.

The **NLPP** resolution method was implemented as a prototype computer program running on a Macintosh Plus® computer. Knowledge representation was purely procedural, due to the problem's algorithmic nature and the need to closely control the reasoning process.

For the program's development which was done in the same computer, a **LISP** interpreter (Le-Lisp®) was used. **LISP** was chosen for its easy-to-use dynamical data-strucures and general flexibility, which favoured a high development efficiency. The price to pay (as expected) was a weak computational efficiency.

The biggest instance to be solved was map **b** (fig. **2b**). For this layout, about 60 minute are necessary for a 6% error solution (without the **INS** trials) and 4 additional hours for the best-found solution (2.1% error). These times are in many cases too big for practical application. Note however that a **LISP** interpreter was used and that the program (in its first version) is not particulary optimized. With a **LISP** compiler, running times are expected to be reduced by a 5 to 10 factor, quite acceptable for the application. In alternative, a target program could be rewritten in a time-efficient language (like **C**, for instance). Finally, note that due to the method's modular and iterative nature, the optimization effort can be tailored to produce higher albeit acceptable errors (by limiting the number of iterations in the improvement cycle).

CONCLUSIONS

Results obtained for real-life instances show that the resolution method can produce good sub-optimal solutions even with limited computacional ressources. However, more work must be done. From the theoretical point of view a better way of finding or estimating the optimum is needed. From the application point of view several developments are already in progress including a much simpler planner for the plotting of clothing layouts [18] and a generalization of the method to accept mixed common-line and contour cutting.

ACKNOWLEDGEMENTS

The authors wish to thank prof. Maria Teresa Almeida from Instituto Superior de Economia in Lisbon for encouragment and helpfull discussions.

REFERENCES

1. J. Távora, "Path planning for a class of cutting operations," Applications of Artificial Intelligence VII, Mohan M. Trivedi (ed.), Proc. SPIE 1095, pp 404-415, (1989).

2. J. Távora, "Tool-path planning in textile cutters: heuristic methods for a new combinatorial optimization problem," Thesis for a Researcher Degree, LNETI, March 1989 (in portuguese).

3. J.A. Chisman, "The Clustered Travelling Salesman," in Computers and Operational Research, Vol. 2, pp. 115-119, Pergamon Press, UK (1975).

4. F.C.J. Lokin, "Procedures for Travelling Salesman Problems with Aditional Constraints," European Journal of Operational Research 3, pp. 135-141 (1978).

5. K. Jongens and T. Volgenant, "The Symmetric Clustered Travelling Salesman Problem," European Journal of Operational Research 19, pp. 68-75 (1985).

6. M.T. Almeida and L. Brum, "Heuristic methods for the Clustered Travelling Salesman Problem," work doc. n. 43, CEMABRE, Instituto Superior de Economia, Lisbon (1988) (in portuguese).

7. J. Távora, "Optimizing tool-path when cutting pieces of fabric," Proceedings of the Third Portuguese Meeting on AI (EPIA-87), 7-9 October 1987, Braga, Portugal (in portuguese).

8. LECTRA Systèmes, Cestas Bordeaux, France; personal communication (1986).

9. GERBER (GGT), Tolland CT, USA; catalog 10057.

10. D.S. Johnson and C.H. Papadimitriou, "Performance guarantees for heuristics," in E.L. Lawler et al. (ed.) The Travelling Salesman Problem, John Wiley & Sons, Chichester, UK (1985).

11. Golden et altri, "Approximate Travelling Salesman Algorithms," Operations Research, Vol. 28, No. 3, Part II, May-June (1980).

12. S. Lin, "Computer Solutions of the Travelling Salesman Problem," Bell System Technical Journal 44, pp. 2245-2269 (1965).

13. E.W. Dijkstra, "A Note on Two Problems in Connection with Graphs," Numer. Math. 1, pp. 269-271 (1959).

14. N.Nilsson, Problem-solving Methods in Artificial Intelligence, McGraw-Hill, NY (1971).

15. J.Pearl, Heuristics, Addison-Wesley Pub. Co. Reading MA (1984).

16. B.L.Golden and W.R. Stewart, "Empirical analysis of heuristics," in E.L. Lawler et al. (ed.) The Travelling Salesman Problem, John Wiley & Sons, Chichester, UK (1985).

17. D.G. Dannenbring, "Procedures for Estimating Optimal Solution Values for Large Combinatorial Problems," Management Science Vol. 23 No. 12, pp. 1273-1283, Aug. (1977).

18. F. Janeiro, J. Jorge, J. Távora, "Optimizing the plotting of clothing pieces," Proc. PPP/AC-89, 10-12 May 1989, Lisbon (in portuguese).

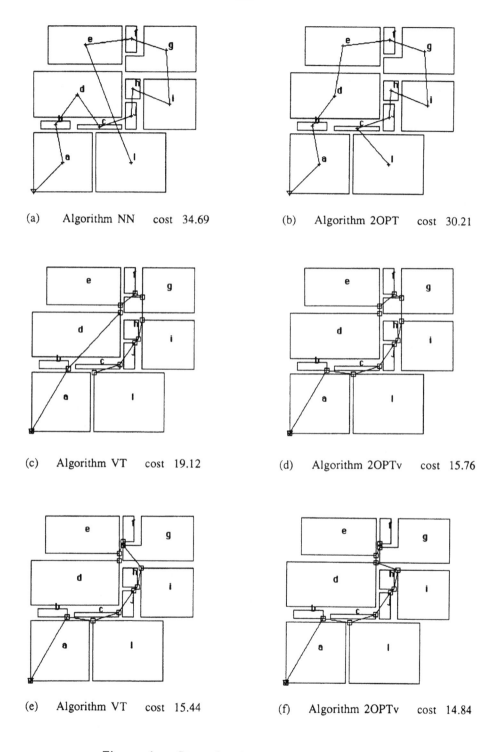

(a)　　Algorithm NN　　cost　34.69

(b)　　Algorithm 2OPT　　cost　30.21

(c)　　Algorithm VT　　cost　19.12

(d)　　Algorithm 2OPTv　　cost　15.76

(e)　　Algorithm VT　　cost　15.44

(f)　　Algorithm 2OPTv　　cost　14.84

Figure 1:　Steps in the resolution process

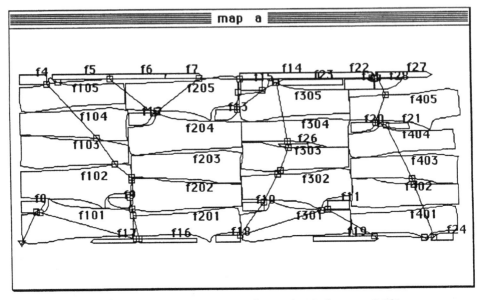

(a) Clothing layout (45 pieces)   estimated error 3.7%

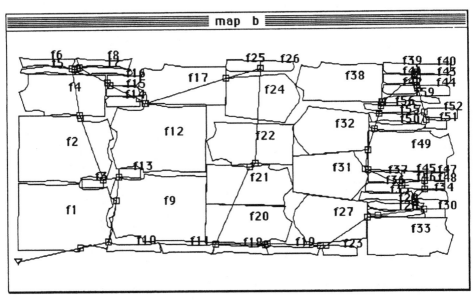

(b) Clothing layout (55 pieces)   estimated error 2.0%

Figure 2: Final no-load paths for two clothing layouts

Reasoning Objects with Dynamic Knowledge Bases

Christoph Welsch

Universität Stuttgart
Institut für Informatik
Azenbergstr. 12
D-7000 Stuttgart 1

Gerhard Barth

DFKI, Deutsches Forschungszentrum für
Künstliche Intelligenz
Erwin-Schrödinger-Straße
D-6750 Kaiserslautern

Abstract

Object-oriented programming has proven its appropriateness for simulating real wolds, in particular for imitating human societies and their ability to solve problems. Object-oriented software is easy to modify and to extend, a property of great importance for AI applications. Logic programming on the other hand stands out for its declarative specification language, built-in inference capabilities and clear theory. A well known feature of logic programming is the separation of knowledge representation and inference method.

We present a framework which amalgamates object-oriented and logic programming. It combines the object-oriented view with the logic formalism. Objects are considered as reasoning entities whose knowledge bases may change over time. They communicate via messages in order to ask for or to provide information. In response to new information, an object may have to update its knowledge. Operationally, reactions to messages are inference processes based on Prolog's inference by resolution mechanism. Great importance is devoted to simple and intelligible semantics of knowledge base alterations being the only way to change states. To this end, an object's knowledge base is divided into three parts: assumptions, reflections and reactions, each consisting of Horn clauses. Only assumptions are allowed to be altered. Knowledge can not be modified while an inference process is going on, resulting in easy-to-understand and easy-to-formalize semantics.

1 Introduction

Object-oriented programming is recognized as an excellent vehicle to simulate physical worlds since physical entities and mental concepts can be directly represented as objects. Knowledge about a concept is locally concentrated at one place. Interactions among objects are modelled by messages. The capability of changing state which is essential for objects allows to model the inherent dynamics of physical entities as well as the ability of intelligent units to learn over time. The object-oriented view of communicating objects is often found to be natural since it closely resembles human societies. This makes it possible, to imitate problem solving in human societies by object-oriented systems. Also, the well-known virtues of object-oriented programming with regard to software evolution – which is of particular importance for rapidly evolving AI software – stem from the decentralized view.

The outstanding benefits of object-oriented programming have motivated a lot of efforts to bring object-oriented features into other programming methodologies, e.g. into applicative [10] or logic programming [1,5,11]. Our work deals with an integration of object-oriented and logic programming. The strengths of logic programming are its separation of knowledge representation from inference strategy which allows for a declarative style of specifications, and its solid theoretical basis. Beyond that, the concept of mathematical variable together with unification, and the concept of non-determinism together with backtracking have proven to be very useful for many AI applications.

Instead of a pragmatic coupling of both methodologies, as e.g. in [6], we have aimed at a system which amalgamates the most powerful elements of object-oriented and logic programming within one computational model. We have expected thereby not only to open new application areas, but also to enrich both paradigms in a natural way by useful new concepts, while remedying their shortcomings.

We have taken from object-oriented programming the view that any discourse area consists of communicating objects with changeable states, and from logic programming the language which allows to specify relations in a declarative style, thereby abstracting from inference method.

Some work related to ours has already been done. The proposal in [8] deals with communicating Prolog units, where communication and inheritance patterns are specified on a meta-level. The language presented in [9] emphasizes concurrency and software engineering support; [4] offers Smalltalk-like concepts (classes, instances, methods) within a Prolog-like representation scheme.

These approaches, however, suffer from ignoring changeable states as a vital issue of object-oriented programming. In a system where objects are composed of pieces of logic programs, changeable states demand for changeable knowledge bases which seem to be incompatible with first-order logic, being the basis of Prolog. We claim that dynamic knowledge bases are fundamental for simulating real worlds, and thus are one of the key problems of object-oriented/logic integrations. It has to be well considered and must influence the design of the target system right from the beginning. We have not been satisfied with Prolog's approach to allow for changing states, where knowledge bases can be dynamically altered by pseudo predicates assert and retract during inference processes. This is disastrous from a theoretical point of view and dangerous from a practical one, because code is modifying itself. Our way out is to distinguish between reasoning and state changing as two non-interfering activities.

To simplify matters, we ignore inheritance issues in the sequel. Nevertheless, we consider inheritance as an extremely important feature of object-oriented programming which should also be very useful for logic programming

2 Basic Model

We have integrated object-oriented and logic programming in a prototypical language called logObjects. The domain of discourse is viewed as a universe of reasoning objects which communicate by sending messages. Each object owns a piece of knowledge, specified in a Prolog-like syntax, and inference capabilities, being Prolog's SLD-resolution (s.[7]).

While messages in conventional object-oriented systems are imperative in nature and can be considered as requests for performing certain tasks, we assume that objects are quite intelligent units (in a very restricted sense, though), so communication might be more "civilized" than mere requests. In our model, communication serves the purpose of information exchange. Why should an object initiate communication? Either it needs information or it wants to notify interesting news. Thus, we distinguish two message types:

1. **Inquiries** – sent in order to *get* information.

2. **Notifications** – sent in order to *give* information.

Both trigger resolution proofs within the receiver. Yet depending on the message type, different parts of an object's knowledge are used. While inquiries refer to the current situation, notifications make receivers reason about the future, more precisely: about how to change their knowledge in order to account for the given information. But a receiver doesn't actually alter any consulted knowledge base parts in response to a notification, but merely "plans" the alteration. Thus, reasoning does not interfere with modifying knowledge bases.

As figure 1 illustrates, the knowledge base of any object consists of three parts: Assumptions, reflections, reactions.

Assumptions: The assumption part contains the changeable portion of an object's knowledge. Typical assumptions are properties varying from time to time as e.g. the location of a robot's arm. It is the assumption part which constitutes an object's state. This is the only component that ever may be altered.

Reflections: While the assumptions form the dynamic component of an object's descriptive knowledge, the reflections are its static one. They are rules, or "natural laws", which are assumed to be stable. For instance, the rule that a robot may begin varnishing if its arm is in a certain position, such a rule might be placed in the robot's reflection part. As shown in figure 1, reflections together with assumptions are all that an object needs to react upon inquiries.

Reactions: The reaction part contains an object's behavioral knowledge. It is made up of productions similar to those of production-oriented programming languages like OPS5 [2]; they state what to do upon receiving notifications. Such a production could

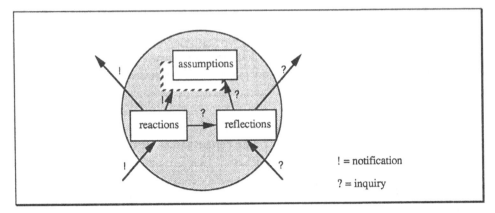

Figure 1: The logObject model

e.g. express that a robot, when notified of an object being completely varnished, should stop varnishing.

The difference between the rules in the reflection and those in the reaction part is that the former are deduction rules while the latter are conceived as action rules, i.e. they say what to do rather than what is true. In our model however, actions are not performed immediately since this would interfere with on-going inferences. Rather, they are carried out only when the inference process terminated successfully.

From the receivers' point of view, the process triggered by a notification serves the purpose of computing a consistent set of future assumptions, pictured in figure 1 as dotted box. The meaning of consistency in that context will be explained later. Notifying doesn't actually alter any valid assumptions, but merely "suggests" future ones. To accomplish changes, the originator of notifying has to send the special instruction `accept`, which can be considered as a third message type in addition to inquiries and notifications. When sent, `accept` is broadcasted to all objects involved in the preceding notification process, causing them to substitute their future assumptions for their current ones. Thus, `accept` is a very simple operation with no reasoning involved. Unlike valid assumptions, future assumptions persist only for the period of one computation, like the run time stack of procedural languages.

3 Inquiries

The language for specifying objects has been adapted from Prolog. A Prolog program is a collection of Horn clauses which have the general form

$$L :- R_1, ..., R_n.$$

L is called the clause's left hand side (lhs), $R_1, ..., R_n$ its right hand side (rhs). L and R_i are atomic formulas, each made up of a prefixed predicate symbol, and functional terms or variables as arguments. Variables are implicitly all-quantified and written with beginning upper-case, predicate and function symbols with beginning lower-case letter. Prolog's built-in inference machine, based on SLD-resolution with term unification, is capable of deriving whether a conjunction of atomic formulas – called the inference goal – is logically implied by the program.

In principle, inquiries are nothing but Prolog goals. They trigger resolution proofs, taking the receiver's reflections and assumptions as knowledge base.
Syntactically, an inquiry is a message

receiver : goal

receiver stands for an object's name or a variable; *goal* is an atom, called *message selector*, or conjunction of atoms, written {*atom_1, ..., atom_n*}.

As a concrete example for an object's definition, figure 2 shows the partial description of a taxi. An object is named by a Prolog constant, here taxi266, which by unification is treated as any constant, i.e. only identical names unify.

```
taxi266 =      assumptions
                   loc(station).
                   state(free).

               reflections
                   isa(taxi).
                   distance(FromHere, 0)  :- loc(FromHere).
                   distance(To, Dist)
                      :- loc(From),
                         citymap: distance(From, To, Dist),
                         To: isa(address).
               end
```

Figure 2: An Object with assumptions and reflections.

The assumption part contains object features of temporary nature such as the current location of taxi266. These are facts which may change as time progresses, but they remain stable for the full period of any reasoning process, no matter whether reasoning is involved in an inquiry or – as will be seen shortly – in a notification.

The clauses of the reflection part differ only slightly from ordinary Prolog clauses: the subgoals on the right hand sides are considered to be messages. For example, the subgoal

```
citymap:distance (From, To, Dist)
```

in figure 2 asks citymap whether it knows about the distance Dist between From and To. If so, it returns success together with the computed variable bindings; otherwise the inquired object answers with failure, thereby triggering the backtracking mechanism. Messages without receiver are assumed to be addressed to the sender itself, comparable to self-messages as e.g. in Smalltalk-80.

The sub-inquiry

```
To: isa(address)
```

in figure 2 shows that also a variable is a valid receiver which is not required to be a ground variable when sending the message. In this case, the message is broadcasted to all objects in the universe. It fails if no object can prove the goal.

4 Notifications

An object's assumptions remain unchanged as long as there is no reason to change them. But the necessity of updating assumptions may arise when something relevant is occurring. For example when a free taxi has been ordered by a passenger, the taxi should no longer assume to be free. Events such as "taxi being ordered" are communicated among objects via notifications. A notification shares its syntax *receiver:selector* with inquiries, but unlike them, the message selector here doesn't denote a relation whose validity is to be verified, but rather represents a piece of information supplied by the sender and to be reacted upon by the receiver.

The rules on how to react are comprised in the receiver's reaction part and called *productions*. They are Horn clauses with add-on semantics giving them two different interpretations. Productions have the form:

$$
\begin{aligned}
key \ &\Rightarrow \ [messages] \\
&:- \ prerequisites
\end{aligned}
\tag{1}
$$

Here, *key* is a Prolog term, *messages* are notifications. The *prerequisites* consist of inquiries, thus correspond exactly with the body of a reflection clause. Figure 3 shows an example. Remember that messages without receiver are assumed to be self-addressed.

The syntax (1) obviously matches the pattern of a clause with the two-valued predicate "=>" on the lhs and prerequisites as rhs. Thus, it is perfectly feasible to use it as a reflection clause, and to send e.g. the inquiry

```
?- taxi266: calledBy(Somebody)
   => WhatWouldYouDo.
```

However, productions are primarily conceived as behavior patterns. As such they prescribe how to react on notifications such as[1]

```
!-  taxi266: calledBy(harold).
```

---

[1]In order to distinguish between user sent inquiries and notifications, the former are marked as in Prolog by preceding "?-", the latter by "!-".

```
taxi266 = assumptions
                ... assumptions and reflections as in figure 2 ...
           reactions
             calledBy(Passenger)
                => [assume(client(Passenger),
                    loc(WhereHeIs),
                    state(busy))]
                :- state(free), Passenger: beingAt(WhereHeIs).
             drivenTo(Target)
                => [assume(dest(Target)),
                    Passenger: beingAt(Target)]
                :- client(Passenger),
                    Passenger: desiredPlace(Target).
           end
```

Figure 3: Augmenting the object of figure 2 by reactions.

which informs taxi266 of being called by someone named Harold.

As behavior pattern, the syntax (1) reads operationally as "if the message selector unifies with *key*, and *prerequisites* hold, then send *messages*".

Like inquiries, notifications either succeed or fail. In the case of success, they convey the computed variable bindings. A notification succeeds if

1. there is a matching production within the receiver's reaction part, i.e. a production whose key unifies with the message selector, and

2. the prerequisites of that production hold, and

3. the messages to the right of "=>" within that production succeed.

These tests are chronologically checked in the above order. If during phase (2) or (3) a sub-inquiry or sub-notification fails, computation backtracks by trying the preceding message again.

As the reader might have realized, the computational treatment of a production as behavior pattern is again that of a Prolog clause. But in contrast to the above mentioned interpretation for inquiries, the clause's lhs now solely consists of the production key while the sub-notifications are considered as part of the rhs. Thus, a production can be interpreted in two different ways, depending on its context of usage. This has the nice consequence that the same inference procedure can be used for inquiries as well as notifications.

There are basically two possible activities upon notifications: the receiver may (a) propagate notifications to other objects and/or (b) compute a private set of future assumptions. But keep in mind that reaction processes don't actually alter valid assumptions. The alteration, which indeed is assumption replacement, must be explicitly initiated by accept.

In the following section, we discuss how sets of future assumptions are constructed by means of the reserved symbol assume (see figure 3). One can consider assume as a primitive built-in message, understood by all objects.

5 Assumptions

Before discussing assume-messages, we have to clarify the concept of assumptions. Remind that assumptions stand for temporary knowledge. Since needed for reflections, an object's assumptions should be a set of Horn clauses. But in favour of efficient computations and a simple theory, we postulate that only facts are allowed as assumptions with exactly one argument, and that at most one fact for any predicate symbol may exist in an assumption set.

By now, the semantics of assume-messages can be intelligibly and accurately explained as a special variant of the so called feature unification (see e.g. [1]) which we like to call *assumption unification*[2]. The idea is to merge two sets of assumptions as follows:

1. *"Specialization"*: Unify those assumptions with equal predicate symbols by ordinary first order term unification.

2. *"Enlargement"*: Take over the remaining assumptions literally into the resulting set.

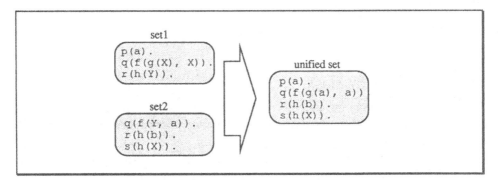

Figure 4: Assumption unification.

Figure 4 illustrates the concept. Assumption unification fails, if at least two assumptions with the same function symbol cannot be unified by means of ordinary first order term unification.

During a reactive inference, assumption unification is repeatedly applied in order to construct the future assumptions step-by-step. Initially, when such an inference takes off – originated by the user sending some notification – the future assumption sets of all

---

[2] Compared to the cited references, we can ignore a partial order on symbols as well as coreferences between arguments.

objects are empty. Every assume-message causes the current future sets of the active object to be unified with the set of assume's arguments, producing the object's next future assumption set. If unification fails, backtracking is performed.

The following example is intended to clarify matters. Imagine two objects, taxi266 and harold, the latter being described in figure 5. Additionally, let user have sent the notification

```
!- harold: left.
```

Then, upon failure of the first production in figure 5, production 2 is tried. Let SomeTaxi be bound to taxi266 after successful processing of the inquiry part. Two notifications to taxi266 and one assume-message have now to be executed. Figure 6 shows how the future assumption sets to taxi266 and harold evolve by these messages. The reader is encouraged to verify it on his own by tracing the computation.

After all, the reaction has successfully terminated, and the user may subsequently send accept. Then both objects – in general: all objects involved in notifying – overwrite their old assumptions by their future ones in such a way that assumptions with the same predicate symbol are replaced, while those without a substitute in the future set are left unchanged.

```
harold =  assumptions
              beingAt(parkAve(13)).
              nextPlace(school).
              favoritePlace(cemetery(C)).

          reflections
              desiredPlace(P)  :- nextPlace(P).
              desiredPlace(P)  :- favoritePlace(P).

          reactions
              left  % Production 1
                => []
                :- beingAt(P), desiredPlace(P).
              left  % Production 2
                => [SomeTaxi: {calledBy(harold), drivenTo(P)},
                    assume(beingAt(cemetery(east)))]
                :- SomeTaxi: isa(taxi).
          end
```

Figure 5: A second example of an object.

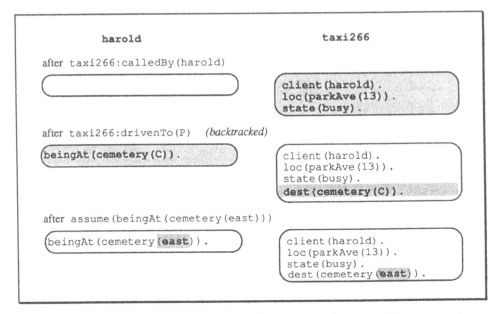

Figure 6: Evolution of future assumption sets in the example.

6 Implementation

We have just completed the first prototype implementation of logObjects. It has been implemented in an object-oriented language similar to Objective-C [3]. We have decided in favour of an object-oriented language for two reasons. To begin with, we have felt that object-oriented programming is extremely useful in developing experimental prototypes like ours, where emphasis lies on clarity rather then efficiency. Secondly, we have seen it as a welcome opportunity to gain valuable experiences with object-oriented software construction.

We began the implementation by embedding a working Prolog interpreter into the existing object-oriented system. The primary result of this has been the class `Prolog` which allows to create ordinary Prolog systems and to send them goals to be proved. Next we have made Prolog modular by introducing names for programs together with inquiries as a new kind of subgoals. This phase has eventually lead to the class `ModProlog`, a subclass of `Prolog`. See figure 7 for illustration. Finally, `ModProlog` has been augmented by assumptions and productions, with the subclass `LogObjects` as the ultimate goal.

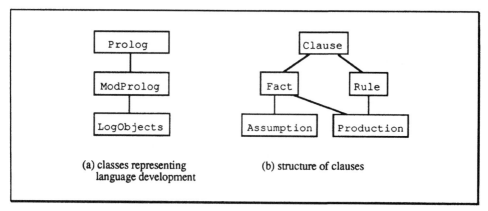

(a) classes representing
language development

(b) structure of clauses

Figure 7: **Parts of the implementation class hierarchy.**

7 Conclusion

We have presented an integration of logic and object-oriented programming which combines fundamental features of both, taking the object-oriented view to model the discourse area, and logic programming to describe the entities and to provide the calculus. The resulting system, logObjects, seems to be a promising basis for further integrations of the object-oriented and logic programming paradigm. It overcomes the imperative flavor usually associated with messages, and gives objects a more "intelligent" appearance. The separation of logic and control, peculiar to logic programming, is carried over to the object-oriented model, thereby increasing the abstraction level of specifications. The simple and theoretically sound semantics of logic programming are preserved as far as possible by strictly separating inference processes from those that alter clauses. As a result, the language outline presented here is very amenable to a formal treatment.

However, we have to get more experience with this new style of programming in order to improve its applicability. It seems by now that, beside some syntactic sugaring, temporally ordered collections of future assumption sets instead of only one such set might be useful since they would allow to reason not only on the present and the ultimate future situation, but also on intermediate ones. Such an extension however might substantially complicate computation and must be well considered. In addition, we are exploring an appropriate notion of inheritance to be incorporated into logic programming and the logObjects model.

References

[1] H. Ait-Kaci and R. Nasr. LOGIN: A Logic Programming Language with Built-In Inheritance. *Journal of Logic Programming*, vol. 3, pp. 293–351, 1986.

[2] L. Brownston et al. *Programming Expert Systems in OPS5*. Addison-Wesley Publishing Company, 1986.

[3] B. J. Cox. *Object Oriented Programming: An Evolutionary Approach*. Addison-Wesley Publishing Company, 1986.

[4] K. Fukunaga and S. Hirose. An Experience with a Prolog-based Object-Oriented Language. In *Proc. OOPSLA'86*, pages 224-231, SIGPLAN Notices vol. 21, no. 11, November 1986.

[5] K. Kahn, E. D. Tribble, M. S. Miller, and D. G. Bobrow. Vulcan: Logic Concurrent Objects. In B. Shriver and P. Wegner, editors, *Research Directions in Object-Oriented Programming*, The MIT Press, 1987.

[6] T. Koschmann and M. Walton Evens. Bridging the gap between object-oriented and logic programming. *IEEE Software*, 5(4):36-42, July 1988.

[7] J. W. Lloyd. *Foundations of Logic Programming*. Springer-Verlag, 1987.

[8] P. Mello and A. Natali. Objects as Communicating Prolog Units. In *Proc. ECOOP'87*, pages 181-191, LNCS, no 276, Springer-Verlag, 1987.

[9] J. Vaucher, G. Lapalme and J. Malenfant. SCOOP: Structured Concurrent Object Oriented Prolog. In *Proc. ECOOP'88*, pages 191-211, LNCS, no 322, Springer-Verlag, 1988.

[10] D. Weinreb and D. Moon. *Lisp Machine Manual*. Chapter 20, page 279. Symbolics Inc., 1981.

[11] C. Zaniolo. Object-oriented Programming in Prolog. In *Proc. of the International Symposium on Logic Programming*, pages 265-270, Atlantic City, N.Y., USA, 1984.

PROSE : A CONSTRAINT LANGUAGE WITH CONTROL STRUCTURES

Pierre Berlandier

INRIA Sophia Antipolis
2004 Av. Emile Hugues
F-06565 Valbonne

Abstract

Constraint languages tend to lack some computational capabilities that are crucial to any programming language. Those capabilities range from control structures such as conditionals or iteration to recursive constructions.

We propose here the constraint programming language PROSE which allows a natural implementation of such structures without resorting to any external language. An important contribution of this self–contained approach is to preserve the declarative semantics of the constraints. The language characteristics follow on the one hand from the uniform representation we give to the constraints and the constrainable objects and on the other hand from the ability to refer to the value history of the constrained variables.

1 Introduction

Constraints are getting more and more considered as an interesting paradigm for knowledge representation as well as a helping tool to free the programmer from consistency checking and enforcement matters. Indeed, the constraint formalism significantly adds expressiveness to other knowledge representation formalisms as shown in [17], [13], [12] or [4]. By another way, as remarked in [14], constraint solvers are efficient systems to which delegate some low level problem–solving tasks. Logic programming languages like PROLOG III [8] tend now to embody packages dedicated to constraint management in order to enhance the power of their resolution mechanism.

Nevertheless, the programming language aspects of constraint systems are often neglected to the benefit of other ones, principally the efficiency of the satisfaction process. This leads constraint systems to be used far below their potential capabilities. As a matter of fact, as soon as one wants to capture the semantics of a constraint problem that involves conditionals or loops, he (or she) gets stuck or in best (or maybe *worst*) cases, has to resort to some imperative construction belonging to the language that underlies the constraint system.

The work presented here focuses on the means to enlarge the range of computational capabilities for constraints. We propose a constraint language that enables, under very few assumptions and in a natural way, the expression of conditional, iterative and recursive constraints. This language has been built on Le_Lisp [7] that supplies us with the object environment we need. Its satisfaction algorithm is based on the local propagation principle [6,18,10,11,16]. The whole system is presently used as a data–base consistency maintenance system in the SMECI [1] expert system shell.

In the ensuing sections, we shall first present the details of the syntax and semantics for the constraint definition in PROSE. This presentation is rather informal and relies on examples. We will then show how constraints issued from those definitions can be grouped to make up a constraint program with control structures.

2   Constraints Definition

2.1   Simple Constraints

A constraint states a relationship between a set of attributes. It refers to a constraint type that describe its structural and behavioral semantics. Constraint types are described by the user in a quite standard way, derived from the descriptions proposed in some well known constraint languages such as [6], [18] or [10]. The structural semantics is defined by a Lisp evaluable predicate that expresses the relationship that must hold between the attributes. The computational part of the constraint is defined by a set of methods that specify the alternate ways to reenforce the constraint when it is violated. For example, we define the constraint type *sum* that implements the relation

$$x = y + z$$

by the following declaration:

```
relation sum
on some integers x,y,z
is (= [x] (+ [y] [z]))
holds-after
    [x] ← (+ [y] [z]) or
    [y] ← (− [x] [z]) or
    [z] ← (− [x] [y])
end-relation
```

If the value of an attribute can not be uniquely determined by the value of the other attributes of the constraint, the constraint has no inferential capabilities (at least for *value inference*[1] type constraint languages). The set of methods of its constraint type is therefore empty. This is the case, for example, of comparison constraints. The relation

$$x > y$$

is thus defined by:

```
relation greater-than
on some integers x,y
is (> [x] [y])
end-relation
```

The purpose of such constraints is limited to the detection of contradictory environments during the execution of the satisfaction process.

---

[1] The nomenclature is from [9]

2.2   N–ary Constraints

Let's now suppose that one wants to express a constraint which involves an undefined albeit finite number of attributes, all belonging to the same set. This is the case for the following n–ary sum relationship:

$$y = \sum_{x_i \in s} x_i$$

We want the constraints issued from this relationship to behave just like the binary sum constraints, that is to say that each attribute can be separately referenced and computed to enforce the constraint. Therefore, the variable to constrain should not be the set itself but instead, each element of the set. To this end, we provide *set variables*. Those variables will match, at instanciation time, any list of attributes, including the null list. Set variables are explicitly declared as such and each member of this set is assumed to play the same role in the constraint. For example, the *n–ary sum* constraint type can be defined by the following declaration:

> *relation nary-sum*
> *on an integer y and*
> *   a set of integers s*
> *is (= [y] (apply '+ [s]))*
> *holds-after*
> *   [y] ← (apply '+ [s]) or*
> *   [i/s] ← (− [y] (apply '+ [s\i]))*
> *end-relation*

In order to ease the description of methods involving set variables, we provide the notations [elt/set] and [set\elt] that mean respectively "any element *elt* of *set*" and "every element of *set* except *elt*". The method

$$[i/s] \leftarrow (− [y] (apply \; '+ [s\backslash i]))$$

therefore applies symmetrically for every element of the set *s*.

2.3   Temporal Constraints

Time is an important feature to take into account in reasoning systems. We often need the ability to describe the evolution of a variable with respect to its previous values. This will appear as an essential prerequisite to the non–procedural expression of iterations.

On top of the object environment we are working in is a mechanism that maintains a sequence of snapshots of the object values. Those snapshots are taken according to a referential clock ticking. A clock is represented by a usual object of the environment. Its ticking is guided by any arbitrary event such as the single modification of an object slot, the application of an inference rule, the initiation of a new simulation cycle, depending on the context where the system is used.

Each variable has, hence, an history of its previous values that can be referred to, specifying an amount of time. In order not to limit ourselves to a single time, new clocks can be created by defining both the semantics of their ticking w.r.t the environment and a method to retrieve past values w.r.t this clock.

Suppose we want to define the relation

$$x_{t_i} > x_{t_{i-1}}$$

that will ensure that some variable is increasing along with a given time. This can be done in PROSE by the following declaration:

```
relation increase
on an integer x and
    a clock t
is (> [x] [x(t−1)])
end-relation
```

As shown in the above definition, the syntax of a temporal reference to a variable *var* is [var(clock-amount)] where *amount* is a constant integer or an integer variable.

Note that several clocks can be used at the same time for the temporal references in a single constraint type declaration. The *current* value of a variable *var* being independent from time, the reference [var] that doesn't specify any clock presents no ambiguity.

The next temporal constraint is derived from an example found in [2]. The *fibonacci* constraint type described below states that an integer x is linked with its previous values by the relationship:

$$x_{t_i} = x_{t_{i-1}} + x_{t_{i-2}}$$

The history of the variable thus represents the sequence of Fibonacci numbers.

```
relation fibonacci
on an integer x and
    a clock t
is (= [x] (+ [x(t−1)] [x(t−2)]))
holds-after
    [x] ← (+ [x(t−1)] [x(t−2)])
end-relation
```

Problems arise in PROSE as they arose in Lucid [3] when variables are defined in terms of their own future. It would be the case, for example, if the previous constraint type would define the following method:

$$[x(t−1)] ← (− [x] [x(t−2)])$$

To avoid such problems, the constraint type definition syntax simply disallows any temporal reference in the left hand side of a method.

2.4   From constraint descriptions to constraint classes

PROSE has got a uniform approach to constraints and constrained objects. Descriptions of constraint types are thus compiled, resulting in object class definitions. Constraint programs are simply written by creating instances of those classes with the constraint–type variables corresponding to slots of the objects in the environment. For their part, the compiled classes are made up of the following slots:

- a class–slot that holds the predicate of the constraint

- a class–slot that holds the set of methods

- as many instance–slots as variables for the relationship, bearing the same name as their corresponding variable. Those slots will hold the pointers to the object slots involved by the constraint instances.

- an instance–slot called *existence*, who will tell if the constraint instance is currently active or not. When its value is *false*, the constraint is not taken into account by any satisfaction mechanism. In [18], constraints are compared to little autonomous devices like digital integrated circuits. In this metaphor, the *existence* slot might represent the "control line" of such circuits.

Representing constraints as usual objects of the environment is a key feature of the language as every constraint can be treated as a full–fledged constrainable object. Such meta–circular architecture are known to ease the implementation of control activities [15]. We are now in possession of all the ground materials of the language that will allows us to express control structures with constraints.

3 Implementing Control Structures

3.1 Conditionals

The *existence* attribute of the constraints will clearly serve us implementing conditional constraints. A constraint is made conditional by relating the value of its *existence* attribute with the boolean value returned by a predicate expressing the desired condition. Of course, the equation between the *existence* and the predicate is represented by another constraint.

For instance, to implement a constraint program representing the following relationship:

$$x = (if \ \ u < v \ \ then \ \ y + z \ \ else \ \ x)$$

we first decompose the latter into the elementary relationships

$$\mathcal{R}_1 : x = y + z$$
$$\mathcal{R}_2 : test = (u < v)$$

From two constraints C_1 and C_2 respectively instances of the constraint types representing $\mathcal{R}_1$ and $\mathcal{R}_2$, the program is built by assigning to the *"test"*-slot of C_2 the pointer to the *existence* slot of C_1. The constraint C_2 acts here as a meta–constraint on C_1 and will perform reflective activities during the satisfaction process.

One should be aware that relationships like:

$$x = (if \ \ x < v \ \ then \ \ y + z \ \ else \ \ x)$$

has no behavioral semantics for the variable x. Indeed, the constraint types corresponding to the relationships $x = y + z$ and $test = (x < v)$ define respectively the methods $[x] \leftarrow (+ \ [y] \ [z])$ and $[test] \leftarrow (< \ [x] \ [u])$. Thereafter, instanciating the variable x of the two constraint types with the same object slot induces a circularity in the computation flow for this slot. This can be detected dynamically at the time the program is constructed (but is not in PROSE for efficiency purposes).

3.2 Iteration

As shown in [3], loops can be described using a non–procedural semantics. With respect to the variables that are modified at each iteration, a loop establishes a relationship between the current value of those variables and their value in the *next* iteration. Here takes place the temporal expressiveness of constraints. For example, the relationship corresponding to the statement "x is incremented by 1 until its value is greater than y" may be

$$x_{t_i} = (if \ \ x_{t_{i-1}} < y \ \ then \ \ x_{t_{i-1}} + 1 \ \ else \ \ x_{t_i})$$

This can be decomposed into the temporal relationships "x is incremented by 1"

$$x_{t_i} = x_{t_{i-1}} + 1$$

and "*test* watches : is the former x greater than y ?"

$$test_{t_i} = (x_{t_{i-1}} < y_{t_i})$$

that will be used to condition the former one in the same way as in the previous section.

A language with a general concept of iteration must support the nesting of loops. Nested loops can be expressed in PROSE, even though it is not as straightforward as it is for one–level loops. This comes from the fact that the use of a single time reference is not sufficient to reflect the nesting concept. Indeed, two independent relationships expressing loops become nested by giving them two *distinct* but *wisely related* time references (clocks). Therefore, expressing nested loops involves the creation of new clocks and the mutual constraining of their ticking.

4 Conclusion

We've been describing the constraint expression capabilities of PROSE. The main goal of this research is to enlarge the range of problems a constraint language can cope with, while preserving its declarative semantics. We now plan to investigate further the integration to the language of usual temporal logic operators such as *always* and *eventually* as well as a mean to introduce some kind of fuzziness in constraint expressions.

From the point of view of constraint satisfaction, PROSE uses a local propagation algorithm to make its value inferences in the constraint network. The algorithm executes a depth first traversal of the constraint graph and resort to dependency directed backtracking when a contradiction occurs. We integrated PROSE's functionalities in an expert system shell (see [4]), inside which it is in charge of maintaining the consistency for the data–base after this latter was modified by the application of an inference rule. The elementary grain of time for this application is therefore the lifetime of a state of the expert system reasoning.

As a final comment, we shall outline that, aside from the expression of conditional constraints, the meta–circular representation of constraints solves problems that are inherent to constraint expression in object environments (see [5]), one of these problems is the maintenance of constraint parallel to the evolvement of a constrained object part–hierarchy [13].

References

[1] *Smeci Version 1.3, Users' Reference Manual.* ILOG, 2 Av. Galliéni, F-94253 Gentilly, 1988.

[2] M. Abadi. *Temporal-Logic Theorem Proving.* PhD thesis, Stanford University, 1987.

[3] E. Ashcroft and W. Wadge. Lucid, a nonprocedural language with iteration. *Communications of the ACM*, 20(7), 1977.

[4] P. Berlandier and S. Moisan. Dynamic constraint management in expert systems. In *Proceedings of the 3rd international symposium on knowledge engineering*, Madrid, October 1988.

[5] P. Berlandier and S. Moisan. Reflexive constraints for dynamic knowledge bases. In *Proceedings of the 1st international computer science conference '88*, Hong-Kong, December 1988.

[6] A. Borning. *ThingLab : A Constraint-Oriented Simulation Laboratory.* PhD thesis, Stanford University, 1979.

[7] J. Chailloux. *Le_Lisp Version 15.22, Users' Reference Manual.* ILOG, 2 Av. Galliéni, F-94253 Gentilly, 1989.

[8] A. Colmerauer. Une introduction à prolog III. In *Actes de la journée : Etat de l'art et perspectives en programmation en logique*, AFCET, 1989.

[9] E. Davis. Constraint propagation with interval labels. *Artificial Intelligence*, 32:281–331, 1987.

[10] J. Gosling. *Algebraic Constraints.* PhD thesis, Carnegie–Mellon University, 1983.

[11] H. Gusgen. *Foundation of a System for Constraint Satisfaction:* CONSAT. Technical Report, GMD Sankt Augustin, 1986.

[12] H. Gusgen, U. Junker, and A. Voss. Constraints in a hybrid knowledge representation system. In *Proceedings of the IJCAI 87*, 1987.

[13] D. Harris. A hybrid structured object and constraint representation language. In *Proceedings of the AAAI 86*, 1986.

[14] W. Leler. *Specification and Generation of Constraint Satisfaction Systems.* PhD thesis, University of North Carolina at Chapel Hill, 1987.

[15] P. Maes. Issues in computational reflection. In P. Maes and D. Nardi, editors, *Meta-Level Architectures and Reflection*, North–Holland, 1988.

[16] J. Maleki. *ICONStraint : A Dependancy-Directed Constraint Maintenance System.* PhD thesis, Linkoping university, 1987.

[17] M. Morgenstern. Constraint equations: a concise compilable representation for quantified constraints in semantic networks. In *Proceedings of the AAAI 84*, 1984.

[18] G. Steele. *The Definition and Implementation of a Computer Programming Language Based on* CONSTRAINTS. PhD thesis, MIT, 1980.

An External Database for Prolog

José Paulo Leal

Centro de Informática da Universidade do Porto

R. das Taipas 135 / 4000 Porto

Portugal

Abstract

This work describes a disk-resident database for Prolog which uses mechanisms similar to the ones used by the clausal database for recording and retrieving terms. It is intended to be used by applications requiring a flexibility greater than that provided by an interface to traditional database system. There is almost no restriction on the terms stored in the database and the retrieval mechanisms produces terms in the order they were recorded. To enhance the performance of the system, the database organization provides an access mechanism using hash-codes on "key" arguments of the recorded term. The database also provides basic support for multi-user access.

Area : Architectures and Languages / Logic Programming

1 Introduction

Although many Prolog implementations provide mechanisms for interfacing with classic database systems, in some situations those systems are not suited to store the kind of data needed by the applications. This is the case of applications where the data takes the form of complex Prolog terms representing, for instance, expert system rules, natural language grammar rules or dictionary entries.

Such systems are implemented, at least in a first stage, using the clausal database or, if one exists, an internal database. When a great amount of data is needed the choice is usually a relational database system. A certain relationship between the relational model and Prolog is then assumed:

relation	$\longrightarrow$	predicates
tuple	$\longrightarrow$	clause
attribute	$\longrightarrow$	argument

This relationship enables the implementation of relational databases in Prolog. On the other hand, due to some of the characteristics of the relational model the arrows cannot be reversed:

	Relational Model	Prolog
data structure		
domains	atomic values	all kinds of terms
	(and NULLS)	(including list, functor-terms and variables with multiple occurrences)
n-ary relations	$n > 0$	$n \geq 0$
	set of unordered tuples	set of ordered tuples
data integrity constrains		
keys	primary keys cannot	no restrictions on
	be NULL	particular arguments
data manipulation		
	quéries return a table	a clause at a time is returned trough backtrack

The use of clauses (or the internal database) to store the data. has, however, the following drawbacks: all the data must be resident in memory, there is no persistence, and no mechanisms for multi-user access are provided.

This work describes an external database, which aims at overcoming the inconvenients mentioned above, for the YAP Prolog system [Damas et al.]. YAP is based on a portable Prolog compiler compatible with C-Prolog. Like the YAP compiler, the external database is written in C and runs at present under the UNIX operating system. It was developed in a SUN3/60 workstation.

The external database began originally as a permanent (i.e. disk resident) version of the internal database. In the sequel, features were included to make multi-user access possible.

No restrictions are imposed on the terms stored in the database. They may contain variables with multiple occurrences, and may have any size or depth. Thus any kind of information representable by a Prolog term may be recorded.

Simultaneous use of the same database file by several Prolog programs is supported through predicates for modifying a term while guaranteeing exclusive access to it so that database consistency can be kept.

It should be stressed that the aim of this work was to implement a tool for Prolog applications that need to store a great amount of data using all the flexibility of the clausal database. It is, by no means, intended to produce a full-fledged relational database system using Prolog as a query language or as an host programming language. Therefore, only the basic aspects of database access and control are addressed. Some functions usually found in conventional database management systems, such as query optimization, integrity constrains, security, and views were totally ignored. They can be implemented, in Prolog, using well known techniques [Parsaye].

2 Conceptual Architecture of the Database

As mentioned in the introduction, the database was originally modeled on the clausal database of Prolog systems, and so it can be seen, in a simplistic way, as an ordered collection of Prolog terms which is accessed and modified through the following kinds of primitives:

recorded_db(X)   for querying the database
erase_db(X)   for removing a term from the database
record_db(X)   for inserting a term a the the end of the database

In clausal database unification is the matching mechanism beetwen clauses and goals. Following the same paradigm the external database is searched for terms unifying with the argument of the recorded_db(X) predicate. We also include two other forms of this predicate. They use, as a matching criteria, the term stored in the database being an instance of the argument, and equality of terms modulo variable names. Note also that this predicate is backtrackable and, thus, can be used to access, by backtracking, all the terms matching its argument.

The erase_db(X) predicate removes the first term matching its argument from the database. As with the recorded_db/1 predicate, there are two other forms of this predicate with different matching criteria.

Although the outlined above was a starting point for the design of the conceptual architecture of the external database, it is obvious that, in order to achieve efficiency and multi-user support, same changes were required.

Firstly, most of the applications organize data around classes of terms similar to the notion of *relation* in the conventional database systems. This led us to change our view of the database as an ordered set of terms with the same functor. Since the only Prolog terms with no functor are the atomic ones, they are collected in a "functor-less" relation. This forced us to restrict the arguments of the basic access predicates described above to be non-variables. In order to improve the efficiency of the access for a given relation, the programmer can use the predicate

relation_usage(Name,Arity,Indices)

to specify indexing information for the relation name Name with arity Arity. This does not impose any restriction on the terms used as arguments of the basic access predicates as it only conveys some pragmatic information for speeding up database look up. This predicate can also be used to retrieve information about the indices currently used by a relation (for instance, to be used in query optimization).

Secondly, in certain uses of the database system updating is very frequent. To cater for this in an efficient way, instead of deleting and recording the modified term, the predicate

```
modify_db(T,UpdateGoal,NewT)
```

was introduced. It replaces a term T with the term NewT after executing the Prolog goal UpdateGoal. Note that this predicate is applied only to the first term matching T for which the update goal succeeds. It fails when no such term is found. A similar predicate is available to modify all terms matching the specification. Again, variations of this predicates, using different matching criteria, are provided.

The database integrity can be kept in multi-user applications by using the modify_db/3 predicate since it guarantees exclusive access to the term being modified. To see how this predicate works, consider the case where we want to interchange the second argument (the first is the key argument and cannot be changed) of two terms with the main functor income/2. This can be achieved through the following code using two nested calls of the modify_db/3 predicate.

```
modify_db( income(zp,X),
           modify_db(income(pr,Y),true,income(pr,X)),
           income(zp,Y))
```

3   Implementation Decisions

A database with the characteristics described in the previous section must have certain restrictions in the choice of the access mechanisms:

1) Apart from the indexed access that is naturally expected, the database must provide a default search, to guarantee, in all cases, the order of recovery.

2) In the indexed access:

a) - No requirement on the uniqueness of the key (as they are not required for Prolog clauses).

b) - The terms with the same key arguments must be *sorted* by their recording order.

c) - Variables can occur in terms in arguments used as keys. The search method must allow it and garantee that terms are recovered in the correct order.

3) The search method must be compatible with backtracking and consistent when used with it.

The methods used in the first versions of the database are the hash addressing in its basic form, combined with linear search as default. They were chosen for their simplicity and comparative efficiency when used with medium sized stable relations. As we shall see, they meet all the previous specifications.

Other index addressing methods with the characteristics discussed above could be implemented, in particular to deal with large or dynamic relations. A method of the B-Tree family seems to be particularly recommended for this purpose and its implementation is expected in future versions.

The type of applications for which this database was designed will generally need a fast access to the recorded data. With this system we expect to have an access time of the same order of magnitude of the memory resident databases, i.e. databases using clauses or an internal database; at least with small and medium sized relations. To achieve this goal, it is necessary not only to have a fast access method but also to use a caching mechanism to maintain the information in memory as long as possible.

The UNIX file system offers a service of that kind that could partially solve this problem, but we have found it inappropriate for our purposes.

In the remainder of this section the implementation of this topics will be discussed in more detail.

3.1 General access mechanism

The fact that the database must provide an access to terms through unification and must retrieve terms in the order in which they were recorded, precludes, in general, the use of the traditional database access mechanisms. It is obvious that, in general, we must resort to a linear search method to retrieve the terms that match a given term. Since unification is an expensive operation we use a technique known as "pre-unification" that speeds up linear search by avoiding the need to access the complete representation of terms within a relation. This technique, which is also used in the internal database of YAP, and was previously described in [Futo et al.], works as follows.

We associate with each term recorded in the database two codes. One is based on the concatenation of the hash codes of up to the first 8 arguments of the term. The hash code for each argument takes into consideration the type and value of the argument. The second code is a binary number with zeros on positions corresponding to variables.

These codes can be used as a very fast test to decide whether or not two terms are unifiable. For that purpose, the bitwise conjunction of the arguments code of the first term and the variables code of the second term, and vice-versa are compared. The terms can not unify if the results are not the same.

The pre-unification test is used as follows.

For each relation, we keep a linear table at the end of which we add, every time a term is recorded, a pointer to the representation of the term, and the codes described above.

When searching for terms pre-unifying with a given term we compute two similar codes for that term, and make a linear scan of the table for those entries for which the unification test succeeds. Only after the test succeeds we fetch the term from the disk and perform the unification. This process reduces both the number of unifications and accesses to disk.

3.2   Index Access Mechanism

In the current database implementation the index access mechanism is based on hashing. We shall see that this method meets all predefined specifications.

It is trivial to verify that this method accepts more than one term with the same key.

The term insertion order is preserved, provided the terms in each hash-bucket are maintained in the same order in which they were recorded. Note, in passing, that methods closely related to this one for partial-match retrieval, such as those proposed in [Chomicki et al.] , could not be used directly as a general access method, since they would not respect the order in which the terms were recorded, and would require the uniqueness of the key arguments.

Terms with variables in the key arguments have a replica in every bucket. In this way, not only a certain locality of the search - which increases its efficiency - results, but also the appropriate order of retrieval is ensured. It can be assumed that there will not be too many terms with variables in the key arguments, so that the cost of this redundancy is not expected to be very high.

As mentioned in the previous section the user can employ the `relation_usage/3` predicate to specify one or more sets of arguments to be used as (ground) indices. If none is specified by the user the system will use the set consisting of just the first argument.

Of the several indexing sets specified for a relation, we will distinguish one as the preferred indexing set and will refer to the others as the secondary indices.

The tuples of a relation are divided into buckets using an hash function on the arguments specified by the preferred indexing set. In a bucket directory we will find, for each possible hash-code, a pointer to a sequence of disk pages containing the representation of the terms having that particular hash-code. Note that under each hash bucket, the terms are kept in the order in which they were recorded.

A similar organization is used for secondary indices but the information under each bucket consists of pointers to the representation on the terms instead of the terms themselves.

To look up a term we start by checking if, for any of the indexing sets, all the relevant arguments are non-variables. If is not the case we use the general access method previously described.

Then, an hash function is applied to the key arguments in order to compute the bucket's number and the bucket directory is consulted to find the sequence of terms with that particular hash-code. Finally every term in that sequence is checked for a matching with the initial term.

The hash function of a term is computed from the partial hash functions of each key argument. The hash value is the remainder of the division of the sum of those values by the number of buckets. In a numerical argument, the partial hash function result is its value. In all other cases the partial hash function is computed from the string of characters of the argument external representation. The sum of the characters code shifted to the left by their position in the string has been found to be a well distributed hash function for a wide range of applications.

When a new relation is created a certain number of hash-buckets is assigned to it. If the number of tuples of a relation grows so much that the number of pages of an hash-buckets exceeds a pre-defined value – usually 1 – the number of buckets in the bucket directory will be doubled in order to keep the average number of terms in each bucket within reasonable bounds.

3.3 Backtracking

As we have seen in the introduction, the backtracking mechanism will access a database term at a time. The information needed to handle backtracking is maintained in the execution stack: as records (or pointers to them) are clustered by their insertion order it is enough to save in the stack the position of the record (pointer) where the last matching term was found. Actually more information is kept in stack to avoid unnecessary calculations and searches during backtracking.

We had a special concern about the consistence of backtracking when a relation is updated before the next backtrack. A particular problem could arise in the indexed search. Consider the execution of a goal were `recorded_db/1` predicate has succeeded n times and the subsequent insertion of a new term causes an automatic relation restructuring before the next backtracking, possibly moving all terms with the relevant key value to another page. For instance, the execution of the goal

```
:- recorded_db(f(a,X)), record_db(f(b,X)), fail.
```

could lead to an inconsistency of that kind.

To avoid this kind of inconsistency, when a relation restructuring has occurred before the next backtrack, the search will continue in the new page and the first n matching terms will be skipped.

3.4 Buffering Mechanism

To improve the database efficiency and reduce the number of disk accesses, the system uses a pool of buffers as a cache mechanism for disk pages.

All the access to database pages is done through these buffers which are kept in memory as long as possible. When a buffer is needed to access a database page and there is none free, the database releases the least recently used one. This decision is made taking into account both the number of accesses to the pages and the "time" of the last access.

Even with this mechanism a page that is currently buffered may have to be re-read. If the database file is in use by several users and is updated then all other users having a private copy of the updated page must refresh their buffers.

In this situation (multi-user access) the database must be locked to prevent the introduction of inconsistency when different processes are updating the same relation simultaneously. Locks are maintained over file pages.

3.5 Physical organization of the Database

The database is stored in a single file. The file is organized in pages of a fixed size, which is currently 4K.

The first page of the file is used to keep global information. In particular, it contains the following information:

- The chain of free pages.
- The location of the atom table.
- The location of the relation directory.

The atom table contains an hash table, giving, for each possible hash code, the address of the first of the sequence of linked pages where the actual ASCII representation of the atoms with that particular hash code are stored.

The relation directory contains the following information for each relation present in the database:

- The name and arity.
- The location of the chain of pages containing, for every term of the relation recorded in the database, the pre-unification codes for the term and pointers to the actual representation of the term.

- The location, for each indexing set in use for the relation, of the chain of pages containing the hash buckets for the indexing set in question.

Each chain of data pages is used in a linear fashion and can grow as needed. All the data pages provide a field for linking to a continuation page. The actual information stored in a chain, such as the representation of a recorded term, can be split among several continuation pages.

3.6 Representation of terms

Prolog terms are encoded as sequences of 32-bit cell in prefix form. Atomic terms (numbers and atoms) and variables are encoded using only one cell while structured terms (functor-terms and lists) use a sequence of contiguous cells.

In a cell encoding an atomic term as well as in the first cell of a sequence encoding a structured term, the 4 leftmost bits determine the type of the term. The remaining bits, or the following cells, record the term itself.

When encoding an atom the remaining bits record a pointer to an entry in the atom table were the atoms external representation (a string of characters) is kept. The unification process is more efficient using this method and the redundancy of recording repeatedly used names is avoided.

Variable terms are encoded as an offset to their previous occurrence in the sequence of cells, or a special value in their first occurrence. Note that variables will only appear in structured terms, a variable alone cannot be saved in the database.

The rightmost bits of a functor term record its functor - name and arity - and the following cells record its argument in order.

In general a list of terms is implemented as a list of pairs where each pair is a special functor (the dot) with arity 2. For lists with only atomic elements - string lists - is used a special compacted format: the first cell will record the size of the list and the following cells will record the elements in order. The general case has to be kept to allow an efficient unification in all circumstances.

4 Conclusion

The value of this work can only be fully appreciated after a good number of realistic applications having used it, specially those with large knowledge bases or dictionaries - the kind of applications this database was written for.

For the moment, this database was used with SPIRAL, a natural language interface to databases [Filgueiras]. This kind of application need to store two kinds of information: the database itself and the dictionary used for lexical analysis. The former kind of predicates could belong to a relational database as they possess all the characteristics of the relational model. The latter kind uses more complex predicates that do not fit well in the relational model: predicates with linked variables, fields with different kinds of structures, more then one tuple with the same primary key (the same word may have different meanings).

Since the characteristics of this database are very similar to those of the clausal database of Prolog, which was previously used to store all relations, this adaptation was very straightforward.

5 Acknowledgements

The work described in this paper was partially supported by Junta Nacional de Investigação Científica, under contract no. 87.366, and by Instituto Nacional de Investigação Científica.

References

[Chomicki et al.] J. Chomicki, Wlodzimiers Grudzinski "A Database Support System For Prolog", in L. Moniz Pereira, L. Monteiro, A. Porto, M. Filgueiras (eds.), Proceedings of the Logic Programming Workshop 83, Universidade Nova de Lisboa, 1983.

[Damas et al.] L. Damas, V. Costa, R. Azevedo, R. Reis, "Yap Reference Manual", Centro de Informática, Universidade do Porto.

[Date] C. J. Date, "An introduction to Database Systems", Addinson-Wesley Publishing Company, 1986

[Filgueiras] M. Filgueiras, "Cooperating Rewrite Process for Natural Language Analysis", Jornal of Logic Programming, vol 3 no. 4, 1986.

[Futo et al.] I. Futo, F. Darvas and P. Szeredi, "The Application Of Prolog to the Development of QA and DBM Systems", Logic and Databases.

[Parsaye] K. Parsaye, "Database Management, Knowledge Base Management and Expert System Development in Prolog", in L. Moniz Pereira, L. Monteiro, A. Porto, M. Filgueiras (eds.), Proceedings of the Logic Programming Workshop 83, Universidade Nova de Lisboa, 1983.

[Robinson] J. A. Robinson, "A Machine-Oriented Logic Based on the Resolution Principle", JACM, Vol 12, No 1 (January 1965), pp. 23-41.

[Ullman] J, D. Ullman, "Database Systems", Pitman Publishing Limited, 1980.

Non-Exact Matching

Harald Kjellin
Bassam Michel El-Khouri

Department of Computer and Systems Sciences
University of Stockholm
S-106 91 Stockholm, Sweden
Phone: 46-8-16 35 77
Telefax: 46-8-15 97 26
Email: hk@dsv.su.se
Email: bassam@dsv.su.se

Abstract

We suggest a method that utilizes relations of relevance between attribute-value pairs to derive importance measures on the attribute-value pairs describing a target object. The intention with using weighted attribute-value pairs is to improve information retrieval by giving a search process an opportunity to select or reject attribute-vectors describing source targets stored in a knowledge-base.

The method presupposes a matching process that considers the relative importance of attribute-value pairs when it compares two attribute vectors. Such a matching process can dynamically establish this relative importance of attributes-value pairs by letting some of a specific vector's attribute-values assign weights of importance to other attributes-value pairs in the vector. The assigned weights reflects the importance of the attribute-value pairs in relation to some desired analogy or similarity. We illustrate this weight assignment process with the help of some examples. The examples indicate that the performance of the matching process can be improved when it utilizes weighted attribute-value pairs. Especially when the similarity between attribute vectors depends on the problem solving context. The method has been tested in real life domains and was found to perform satisfactory.

Introduction

In many case-based reasoning systems featuring analogical problem solving, the retrieval process constitutes a corner stone in the architecture of the system. The problem is often to find among a store of base cases or potential source cases one (or some) that mostly shares in the description of the target case. When an analogous case is thus found, a mapping process from the source case to the target case projects a solution in the form of unshared base attributes, relations, and causal chains to the target case. Subsequently, a justification as to the validity of the performed inference is attempted and a confirmation of the solution may be requested.

The resulting match between the target case and the source case may be total but more often than not is partial. To find the best partial match in such systems may be a bottle-neck in the retrieval process and as such is worth a closer investigation. In this paper we discuss the result of considering partial matching as an asset and give some suggestions on how to improve the performance of the retrieval process by allowing partial match on some attribute-value pairs that are judged to be important or relevant. The intuition is that matching will gain in effectiveness and precision if a prior knowledge exists about which subset of attribute-value pairs are more essential or relevant for the solving of some analogical problem. The gain in effectiveness should result as a spinoff product from pruning the number of cases to be searched in the store of base cases. Whereas the gain in precision is accommodated for by the loss of all the cases that are judged to be irrelevant.

The idea of influencing the retrieval process by the use of importance or relevance factors is not entirely new. For instance, goals were argued to be important (Carbonell 85) especially when used as a controlling mechanism to focus the attention of the retrieval system on particular features (Seifert 88). The importance of the role that causal relations (Winston 80) predictive relations (Kolodner 87) and higher order relations (Gentner 83) play in the matching process has also received a considerable attention. Salience and diagnosticity of attributes were emphasized by Tversky (Tversky 77) when measuring the similarity between two objects.

However, a common feature to all of the above mentioned factors is the fact that they are predefined prior to the problem solving process. This may well be adequate in small and strictly specialized domains. But in larger and less specialized ones, the above mentioned approach is problematic. Attribute-value pairs that are used in defining a problem might be more or less important depending on the context in which the system is trying to reason.

As a tentative solution to the problem of relative relevancy or importance, we argue for a dynamic generation of weights on attribute-value pairs.

The importance or relevancy of attribute-value pairs as reflected by their weights is directly reflected by the type of problem at hand and will vary with the context in which the problem is defined. This context is captured by analyzing the problem description through allowing the existence of some attribute values in a target case to assign weights to other attribute-value pairs in the target case. This aspect of weight assignment will hopefully result in a description where all the attribute-value pairs that are necessary and sufficient for the matching process to function satisfactorily, are covered by those attribute-value pairs in the problem description that emerge with the highest weights.

A direct consequence of this approach of dynamically assigning importance to features is that it is not necessary for the user to have a complete comprehension of the importance of features when giving them as input to the system.

Relations of relevance

The importance of features described above can be represented as relations of relevance between attribute value pairs. To establish weights as simple functional dependencies, between attribute-value pairs may be easier for the system developer to implement than to construct a complete and coherent model for the problem domain. Moreover, some of the problems that arise in connection with knowledge acquisition, such as maintaining rule consistency in rule-based systems, may be solved if parts of the domain knowledge are represented on a low level of abstraction (Schank 82).

Consequently, we propose, that useful domain knowledge can be represented as relations of relevance between attribute-value pairs, where by relevance we mean that an attribute-value pair value can determine the importance of other attribute-value pairs. Relations of relevance between attribute-value pairs are examples of partial and elementary domain knowledge (Michalski 85) whose representation and implementation are easy to accomplish without an especially deep or profound understanding of the problem area.

Illustrative examples

We will now elaborate on these ideas by showing how some attribute-value pairs in a target case can determine the weights of other attribute-value pairs in the same target case by the use of relations of relevance. This weight assigning process and the representation that we adopt are illustrated in the sequel:

Ideally, for each value of an attribute in the language that is used to define cases, we want to have a parameter that defines the relationship of this attribute-value pair to all the other attribute-value pairs. A parameter is then a weight that determine the strength of the relationship between one attribute-value pair and some other attribute-value pair (that includes all attributes other than the former) and should be conceived of as a quantified measure of the relevance of the second attribute-value pair to the first one. A positive measure, then, represents the strength in the belief that one attribute-value pair is semantically related to another, while a zero measure indicates an absence of such a belief; that is that the two pairs are semantically independent of each other. We call a perspective a conceptual structure that for some given attribute-value pair has represented in it the weights of the relationships between this attribute-value pair and all the other pairs. However, in practice, there is no need to represent, in a perspective, relations that are assigned a zero measure.

We will now use a simplified example for the purpose of illustrating the above mentioned assignment process. Suppose that we have target case described as follows:

{attribute(instrument,knife),attribute(action,eating),
attribute(part_of_body,mouth),attribute(sensation,hungry)}.

Also, and in the purpose of demonstrating how the attribute "action" is assigned a sum of weights found in the perspectives that are triggered by the remaining three attributes, let these perspectives look as follows:

perspective(inskni,instrument,knife,[rel(action,eating,2),
        rel(action,cutting,3)]).

perspective(parmou,part_of_body,mouth,[rel(action,eating,3),
        rel(action,kissing,4)]).

perspective(senhun,sensation,hungry,[rel(action,eating,4),
        rel(action,cooking,3)]).

Note that in these specifications, there are weights associated with the action of eating in all three perspectives. If these three weights are added together the attribute-value pair (action,eating) from the target case would receive the weight 9 (2 +3 +4 = 9) which if higher than the resulting weights for the other attribute-value pairs would indicate that it is an important attribute-value pair.

As stated before, weights can be either positive or null. Neutral values are never considered in the perspectives. Positive relations between attribute-value pairs are only represented in the perspectives if they are considered obvious or if they could pass the common sense constraint that persons with different backgrounds would also classify them as positive.

It may, however, still be difficult to establish the correct type of relations between attribute-value pairs. Even seemingly obvious relations can be viewed differently by different experts, which creates a need for a sufficient amount of "expert" knowledge about these relations. When building the prototypes referred to later in this paper, we utilized the strategy of first collecting examples of how "experts" would define the problems represented as attribute vectors. Then we applied statistical calculations on the data-base of such attribute vectors, in order to establish obvious functional dependencies between the attribute-value pairs. We mainly used a probability calculus in order to establish how well the existence of one attribute in a problem description can predict the existence of another attribute in the same problem description. Finally we analyzed and edited the functional dependencies manually in order to arrive at a limited amount of useful weighted relations. An advantage of using information inherent in the stored cases when establishing the weighted relations, is that the larger the data-base of stored cases during the development of the prototype, the better the relations will represent general expert knowledge.

Different combinations of attribute values in a problem produce different weight profiles in the problem. A problem with weights on its attribute-value pairs is assumed to find more relevant matches than a problem without weights, because added problem-specific domain-knowledge (as weights) will assist the matching process in acknowledging the relative importance of the attribute values and thus will help prune the search space substantially. Needless to say that the choice of how a certain perspective should look like, is crucial to the proper functioning of the process.

Evaluating the methods

Previously in the text simplified examples have been demonstrated. It is known to many AI-researchers that even if a method seems to function well in limited examples it might still be difficult to implement it in real world systems. This suggests that there is a need for further evaluations of the described methods before determining their usefulness.

The techniques advocated in this paper describe weak heuristics to be used in systems that utilize a vague or limited domain knowledge. Systems whose performance depends on vague domain knowledge are difficult to analyze from a logical viewpoint. It is difficult to establish whether an analogy is logically correct or not unless one uses variations of the determination rules that are proposed by Davies (Davies 88). Such difficulties have inspired an ambition to experiment with the proposed methods in extensive applications, and then evaluate their performance through subjective estimations of how well the matching process selects a source case from the knowledge base. As such, the methods advocated in this paper may very well be considered as ad hoc methods that have been proven (as in many other celebrated systems) to work well in real life domains.

The first prototype that was implemented with these ideas in mind, was a support system for an unemployed person looking for a suitable work. The prototype asked the user about his intentions, hobbies, desires and his outlook on life. From the answers to the questions the system constructed a profile of weighted attribute-value pairs representing the persons talents and interests. This profile was then matched with stored profiles, each coupled with a description of an occupation. Finally the system showed the unemployed person all occupations that matched his answers to the questions.

According to comments on the demonstration of the system, it performed surprisingly well. Presently, arrangements are made to confront the performing system with professional employment counsellors who will hopefully be able to make a more precise evaluation of the systems performance.

Presently conducted experiments

Four more experiments have been initiated. The intentions with the projects are to refine and evaluate the weight assigning algorithms and also to determine what kind of problems and domains are suited for the suggested methods. The projects are carried out in the following areas:

1: Choice of media when marketing a product.

An attribute vector representing potential consumers, classifications of a product and marketing information is matched with analogue stored attribute vectors where each stored attribute vector is coupled with information about how the product was advertised.

2: A support system for analyzing psychological test results.

An attribute vector representing the output from a Rorschach test is matched with analogue attribute vectors coupled with an experts interpretation of the test results.

3: Business analysis.

An attribute vector representing representing the basic economic figures of a private company is matched with similar stored attribute vectors where each stored attribute vector is coupled with advice from a business analyst, giving information about the status of the company and recommending strategies for improvement.

4: A knowledge base of administrative routines.

A user with fragmented knowledge about an administrative routine can match this knowledge with stored analogue routines in order to get inspiration from the analogies made.

Common features of the described systems

These described ongoing projects use the same problem-solving strategy. First, domain knowledge that is consisting of "hard facts" is the input to the system. These facts are processed into a profile describing of the problem. Hard facts can here be defined as non ambiguous domain knowledge represented as rules. Secondly the profile is matched against stored profiles that are coupled together with an experts solution to the interpretations. This second stage utilizes vague domain knowledge that reflects the experts experience and intuition.

Future research

Given the assumption that the relative frequency of combinations of attribute values in the knowledge-base can determine the predictability of one attribute value in relation to other attribute values, it is possible to use conventional statistical methods to determine to what degree the existence of one attribute value pair can predict the existence of another attribute-value pair. The predictability of attribute values, could then be used as a measure of the importance of this attribute value in the case.

Future research will involve applying more sophisticated statistical computations to the prototypes that are under construction. These statistical modules will establish functional dependencies between attribute-value pairs from the information inherent in the stored cases of a system. The functional dependencies can then be utilized by the matching process when it assigns weights to attribute-value pairs in a target case.

Conclusion

We have argued that weights on attribute-value pairs in a target case can help a matching process to select the most relevant source case.

Such weights can be manually established or statistically derived. There exist well known systems who have assigned a fixed importance to the attributes of a target case in the matching process, Carbonell's system Aries (Carbonell 83), Lebowitz system GBM (Lebowitz 83), Kolodner's system Mediator (Kolodner 87) and Winston's system Macbeth (Winston 80). These weights are established only once by the system developer and cannot be modified during the life time of the system.

Such solutions can be useful when the purpose of the system is to solve one specific kind of problem, where the problem is perceived from the same point of view each time the system tries to solve it.

The weights can also be manually determined by the user when the case is given as an input to the system (Kodratoff 87). This method presupposes high expertise knowledge from the user, and can be recommended when creating new cases while developing the system.

This paper suggests that dynamically assigned weights to attribute-value pairs can be used to improve the matching process. So far the performance of the implemented methods have been promising. A further evaluation is needed before it is possible to fully asess the usefulness of the methods.

We have seen how information inherent in the attribute-value pairs of a case can be utilized in order to assign weights to other attribute-value pairs in the case. However, in such a weight assigning strategy we can establish the importance of an attribute-value pair from the sum of all weights it achieves from the other attribute-value pair in the case.

Further research will involve the utilization of functional dependencies between attributes as advocated by Davies(1988) and Russel(1988).

References

[Carbonell 86]   Carbonell, J.G.
Derivational analogy:A theory of reconstructive problem solving and expertise acquisition,
In Machine learning:An Artificial Intelligence Perspective, vol. II, (Eds) Michalski, R. S.,Carbonell, J.G. and Mitchell,T.M.,
Tioga Publishing Company, Palo Alto, CA, 1986.

[Carbonell 85]   Carbonell, J.G.
Learning by analogy: Formulating and generalizing plans from past experience.
Machine learning:An Artificial Intelligence Perspective, (Eds) Michalski, R.S.,Carbonell, J.G. and Mitchell,T.M.,
Tioga Publishing Company, Palo Alto, CA, 1985.

[Davies 88]   Davies, T.R.
                       Determination, Uniformity, and Relevance:
                       Normative criteria for generalization and reasoning by
                       analogy,
                       In Analogical Reasoning,
                       (Ed) David H. Helman,
                       Kluwer Academic Publishers,
                       Dordrecht, The Netherlands

[Gentner 83]   Gentner Dedre.
                       Structure-Mapping: A Theoretical Framework for Analogy.
                       Cognitive Science 7, 155 - 170, 1983.

[Kodratoff 87]   Kodratoff Yves
                       Learning Based on Conceptual Distance
                       Proc. of IEEE Transactions on Pattern Analysis and Machine
                       Intelligence, 1987.

[Kolodner 87]   Kolodner, Janet. L.
                       Extending Problem Solver Capabilities Through Case-Based
                       Inference,
                       Proceedings of the 4th International Workshop on Machine
                       Learning, Morgan Kaufmann,Los Altos,Ca,1987

[Lebowitz]   Lebowitz, M.
                       Generalization from Natural Language Text,
                       Cognitive Science, No. 7, page 1-40, 1983.

[Michalski 85]   Michalski, Ryszard S.
                       A theory and methodology of inductive learning
                       In Machine learning:An Artificial Intelligence Perspective,
                       (Eds) Michalski, R.S.,Carbonell, J.G. and Mitchell,T.M.,
                       Tioga Publishing Company, Palo Alto, CA, 1985.

[Russel 88]   Russel Stuart
                       Analogy by Similarity
                       In Analogical Reasoning
                       (Ed) David H. Helman
                       Kluwer Academic Publishers
                       Dordrecht, The Netherlands

[Schank 82]   Schank, R. C.
                       Dynamic Memory
                       Cambridge University Press, Cambridge,England,1982.

[Tversky 77]   Tversky, Amos.
                       Features of similarity.
                       Psychological review, 84, 1977.

[VanLehn 80]   Van Lehn, K. and Brown, J. S
Planning nets
in Aptitude learning and Instruction,
(eds.), Snow,R.E,Frederico, P.A. and Montague, W.E.
Volume: Cognitive Process analyses of learning and
problem solving, 1980,.

[Winston 80]   Winston, P. H.
Learning and reasoning by analogy.
CACM, vol 23, no 12, 1980.

RAD: The Risk Advisor Expert System

George C. McGregor

European A.I. Technology Centre,

Digital Equipment Corporation,

Valbonne, France

The Risk Advisor (RAD) is a decision support expert system which supports Sales and Project Managers involved in the pre-sales activities of large customer projects. The system gives advice on financial, organisational, contractual and management aspects of the project. The user responds to questions, and the system creates a report which is used in the decision-making process. This paper describes the system, and the development method, and concludes that there are many areas in the business domain where this type of advisory system would be useful .

1 Introduction

Digital is involved more and more in selling "projects" to external clients; solutions to specific business problems. This usually involves the design of special purpose hardware or software, not just the supply of "off-the-shelf" hardware or software products. Because Digital must perfectly understand the business needs of the client, the relationship between Digital and the client must be very good.

The environment around such a project can be very complex, particularly if external consultants and third-parties are involved. For the benefit of both the client and Digital, it makes sense to assess any potential projects very carefully before a large amount of effort is expended.

This process of assessment is called "project qualification" or "project risk assessment" and takes place continuously throughout the period between the initial "lead" (the initial idea for the project) and the formal bid for the project. It is important to keep evaluating the risks and opportunities presented by the project throughout this period.

There was no formal method of performing this task of project qualification, but there were experts who performed the task, and whose expertise was recognised throughout the company. Because these experts were scarce, and the business was growing, it was evident that some other means of transmitting the project-qualification knowledge to all Digital offices was becoming necessary.

2 Previous Attempts

There was already a project qualification check-list on paper, which was used intermittently across the company. This had been developed as part of a project development methodology, and consisted of about forty YES/NO questions. The results were summed to come to some conclusion about the risk associated with the project.

This was not widely used for a number of reasons. Among them:

- The check-list had been developed centrally, and didn't take into account local variations in the method of qualification. Some questions were therefore irrelevant in certain cases, and this threw the whole result into doubt. This inflexibility caused a certain degree of rejection.

- There was neither help available in responding to questions, nor in interpreting the result: The knowledge which had been used in the process of developing the check-list was no longer present when it was being used.

- The result was given as good, medium or bad. This information was by itself, insufficient. What was required was some advice on how to improve the situation if it was not good.

3 The Nature of the Knowledge

The knowledge used by the experts had certain characteristics which were clearly of importance. These were as follows:

- THEY KNEW WHAT TO ASK AND WHEN:
  A project is a large and complex entity, and there are many areas which need to be investigated, such as the financial issues, the legal terms of the contract, the management structure of the client, and the technical complexity of the project. Experts asked a small number of key question. They never forgot to ask important questions, but knew when answers were urgently required, and knew when they could wait. For example, right at the beginning of the pre-bid phase, one might not be too concerned about the clarity of the requirements, since this should become clearer before the bid. Just before the bid however, the absence of a good spec. would be disastrous.

- THEY ASSESSED:

  The experts gave clear indications of the potential risks to a project; estimating where the project could go wrong, and the impact to the business if it did. These assessments were constantly updated as a result of changing circumstances during the pre-bid period.

- THEY GAVE ADVICE:

  Not only did the experts assess the (potential) project, but they also suggested ways in which it could be improved. These pieces of advice were often assigned levels of urgency. "Find out urgently who is in charge of the project budget!"; "Inform other groups in Digital that we will need their support", are examples of the kind of recommendations they made.

- THEY COULD WORK WITH MISSING DATA:

  Even with responses to only a fraction of their questions, experts could make assessments and give advice.

- THEY APPLIED POLICY:

  The experts knew the "rules": they knew who in Digital should approve what, and understood the policies with respect to certain types of project. After investigating a project, they would say things like "This must be approved by X and reported to Y because it involves several groups, and is greater than Z million dollars".

- THEY COPED WITH LOCAL VARIATIONS:

  They took into account local variations when giving assessments and advice. For example a "very large" project in one country could be a "small" project in another.

4 System Requirements

The RAD system had therefore to represent the content of the experts knowledge, and the form in which it was applied (see Section 3). There were also some specific interface requirements:

- The system would be used by non-technical users, and only periodically. This meant that the user-interface had to be extremely simple to use, and that context sensitive help had to be constantly available.

- It had to be possible to modify previous runs, as a result of a change in the situation (for example after something had been re-negotiated), but without having to re-answer all the questions.

- Because previous responses can be changed, the system has to maintain consistency. For example, there may be several questions concerning an external consultant, which are dependent on such a consultant being present. If the user modifies the response to the consultant question, from "no consultant present" to "consultant present" the system must ask the questions about the consultant. If the value is modified in the other direction, the system must reset the questions about the consultant.

5 The RAD System

The goal was therefore to produce a system which satisfied the requirements of sections 3 and 4. The basic function of the system is to ask questions and to create a report. Figure 1 shows RAD running, and Figure 2 and Figure 3 show parts of a report created by the system. The system is designed to operate on any VT100 compatible terminal.

The system presents a menu-driven interface to the user. By default, the system will run through all the questions in order, unless the system is started with a previously saved run.

Figure 1: RAD Running

This can be interrupted at any time to move to the system menu (see Figure 1) from which the current advice can be inspected, or a report created, among other functions. One key moves between the dialogue window, and the menu. The question session can be resumed where it was left off, by using the same key to return to the dialogue window. Context sensitive help is available for every question.

It is also possible to use the QUESTIONS item on the top-level menu to focus on specific areas. Using this, for example, the user can focus directly on the questions concerning the market, or the external consultant, to modify previous values.

It is important to note that the system is in a stable state when the top-level menu is available. The user controls how the system behaves next by, for example, proposing to inspect the systems recommendations, or proposing values or modifications to questions.

A report can be created at any time, even if no questions have been answered. Default values will be used however, and the report will be most unfavourable in this extreme case. Uncertainty is explicitly dealt with in the system. Each question has a possible "not sure" answer. This can be clearly seen in the example method given in Section 6 below

```
            RAD test_proj 27-jan-1989 run by GMCG



    3   TECHNICAL RISKS


    test_proj 27-jan-1989 RAD REPORT
    ----------------------------
    TECHNICAL RISKS :

    Most Important Technical Risks
    ----------------------------


    The Technical Risk is assessed to be medium

    There will be new products/techniques used in the project


    There are performance clauses in the contract (guarantees,
    warranties or penalties)

    You don't intend to prototype

    There is no good Requirements Specification
```

Figure 2: RAD Report Fragment (Technical Risks)

The report is 10 pages long, including a front page of summary information, pages on the technical, managerial, and strategic risks, and prioritised sections of advice.

The RECOMS item on the top-level menu allows inspection of the advice proposed by the system as a result of the current set of user-responses. These pieces of advice are in the form of recommendations. These can be inspected on-line, and annotated by the user. These user comments then appear in the report, attached to the recommendation. This is how the user can override or comment on recommendations which are not valid in a particular case

The EXPLAIN item guides the user through the reasons why a particular recommendation is currently true.

6 Knowledge Representation

The RAD system was to be used across Europe, and business practices can be slightly different in different countries, so the system had to be designed in such a way that the knowledge could be modified easily. The system was also designed in order to ease the creation of local language versions.

```
RAD test_proj 27-jan-1989 run by GMCG



7   URGENT


test_proj 27-jan-1989 RAD REPORT
----------------------------
*** URGENT ***

You must deal with these problems immediately
----------------------------


Find out what the competition are doing


Get a formal quote from an Applications Centre (depending on the
size of the country) as soon as possible


Check the availability of the proposed DEC project manager as
soon as possible


Check the performance penalty/guarantee or warranty with an
expert It could mean extra provisioning of machine power or even
money
```

Figure 3 : RAD Report Fragment (Urgent Advice)

Because of the modifiability requirements, and the absence of a suitable tool, it was decided to develop in parallel a tool specifically designed to implement advisory systems. This would be simpler to use by non-technical people than a general-purpose tool since it would be oriented specifically towards the advisory type of problem. This tool, AISE, has been used in a number of other projects, and is described in [GUIM89]. AISE is implemented in Prolog and C.

The knowledge used by the experts is heuristic knowledge. This meant that AISE had to be designed to represent knowledge explicitly, and allow it to be easily modified as development proceeded.

AISE consists of two parts, a sophisticated knowledge editor for the system developer, and a run-time system which interprets the knowledge-base defined by the first part.

It was decided to create a system which matched the way the experts represented their knowledge, and this led to a design which uses some of the techniques of object-oriented systems, giving advantages of modularity inherent in such systems [LIEB87].

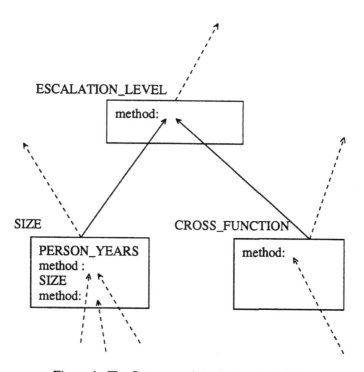

Figure 4 : The Structure of the Objects in AISE

The knowledge in RAD is represented as a network of objects which are linked together by "methods" which describe how the attributes of an object derive their value. There are objects which use a special method which asks the user a question in order to derive their value, and there are others which derive their values by using the values of other objects combined using arithmetic or logical expressions. An example of the latter type of method from the RAD knowledge-base is given below:

METHOD:
    if KNOWN(SIZE) then
                  (if SIZE: PERSON_YEARS < 1 and SIZE:MDOLLARS < 0.3
                  and CROSS_FUNCTION = NO then LOCAL
        else (if SIZE:PERSON_YEARS < 2 and SIZE:MDOLLARS >= 0.3
        then DISTRICT else REGION))
    else NOT_KNOWN

This is the method of an object called ESCALATION_LEVEL which acquires the value LOCAL, DISTRICT, REGION, or NOT_KNOWN, depending on the values of the objects SIZE (two attributes PERSON_YEARS and MDOLLARS) and CROSS_FUNCTION (only one attribute). These other objects may be dependent on other objects, or may directly prompt the user.

AISE is a data-flow system , since each objects value is only derived if, and when it is required. The similarity of this approach to how spreadsheet languages work makes it a very natural way to express knowledge for people who have had exposure to spreadsheets [DUDA87, ACKE82].

AISE builds up a tree (actually a directed-acyclic graph) as objects are defined by the user. The user does not directly edit the tree; it is defined implicitly by the methods describing how the values of objects are derived. Figure 4 shows a fragment of the knowledge-base for RAD, created for the ESCALATION_LEVEL method as defined above. The solid lines show the links defined by the method, the dashed lines indicate how the objects might be related to other objects in the system. At run-time, this network maintains consistency by propagation. For example, a request for the value of ESCALATION_LEVEL (by a request for a report, say) will kick-off evaluation of the SIZE and CROSS_FUNCTION objects, and this may in turn kick off further object evaluation until bottom-level objects are reached (user-queries, or data-access methods). On the other hand, if the user changes the value of SIZE, say, the system uses the stored links to decide which objects need their values to be updated, and propagates the change through the network.

Finally there are special recommendation objects which are either true or false depending on the truth or falsity of their methods. Again, these methods can depend on the values of other objects in the network. If during the run of the system a recommendation becomes true, then it becomes visible both on-line, and in the report. Recommendations have pieces of text in which object values may be embedded at run-time. AISE provides a report writing facility which allows the user to define how the recommendation texts are presented in the report (if they are valid). The format of the report shown in Figures 2 and 3 was defined in this way.

Each object has PRE- and POST- evaluation slots where the user can enter expressions. The former is evaluated before the objects method(s) and the latter after. This is where the consistency functions which were described in section 4 are implemented. For example objects can enable, disable, or reset other values from their POST-evaluation field, depending on the values acquired by their attributes during evaluation.

AISE provides a sophisticated VAXstation[1] based editor which allows the entry of such objects, allows the user to observe graphically, check and manage the links between the objects. After the knowledge has been entered in this way, the knowledge-base is used to create the run-time system. It is this run-time system which constitutes RAD as seen by the final user.

In RAD there are 230 recommendation objects, and 135 other objects, including 84 questions.

This section has hopefully given a feel for the knowledge-representation method. More about the design of AISE will be found in [GUIM89]

7 Features of the Development Process

The following sections describe some of the interesting aspects of the development process.

The development took place over a period of two years, involving about 4 person-years of effort. Initially prototype versions of the Knowledge Editor and RAD were created in OPS5 and Pascal. When it was clear what the representation requirements were, and after feedback on the various interfaces, these systems were scrapped, and a production version of AISE was built in Prolog and 'C'. The production RAD was then built on top of the new AISE.

[1]VAX and VAXstation are trademarks of Digital Equipment Corporation

The knowledge elicitation activities consisted of workshops involving 3 experts from France, Germany and the UK. These were videotaped. The experts had constant access to RAD during the development period, and an on-line conference was created to encourage feedback via the network.

Some of the most important features of the process were as follows:

- Multiple Experts:
  There were in all 6 experts involved in the project. This would be considered by some to be unmanageable. There is much in the literature about the problems of having multiple experts, e.g. [WALT88]. In fact it was very useful, because discussion between experts often revealed knowledge which may not have been uncovered otherwise. Any disagreements could be seen to be due to local variations, and were therefore to be integrated in local versions. In general if there is a sufficiently large core of shared expertise, having multiple experts does not pose a problem.

- Development of a Tool/Methodology:
  It was apparent from the start that there would be many other applications for an "Advisory Expert System Shell". The development of AISE in parallel with RAD proved to be a very good decision. This tool has been used in three other substantial expert system projects. Once the "recommendations" representation was arrived at, knowledge acquisition went very rapidly because experts, knowledge engineer and RAD shared a common representation language.

- Acceptance Testing
  There are certain problems posed by the acceptance of this type of system. This is because exhaustive testing is impossible. These problems were resolved by having two acceptance tests; one for the core knowledge in the system and one demonstrating the modifiability of the knowledge. The first test showed that the system's advice corresponded to the advice given by experienced project-managers for a number of test-cases. This showed that the core knowledge had reached a satisfactory level of sophistication. The second test showed formally that the knowledge could be modified by someone other than the developer. Two RAD knowledge-bases were modified independently from a change request in English, and the advice of the two systems was demonstrated to be the same.

- Maintenance
  The underlying system AISE is supported and maintained centrally, but after central acceptance, the maintenance of the knowledge-base was delegated to each individual country. This makes sense because of the local modifications which are necessary. One

of the important points about this is that there is no extra maintenance overhead, because there are methodology groups in each country which look after the way in which the projects business is carried out. These groups take over the maintenance of RAD as a method of distributing their rules and standards (which can be encapsulated in the knowledge-base)

8 Summary

There are three ways in which RAD helps Digital staff perform better their roles:

- It always remembers to ask the right questions at the right time.
- It assesses
- It advises

There are many applications where this type of system would be of use. The situation where there is a process to follow, or a check-list exists already could be immediate candidates for this type of advisory system. The key point is that such systems are not making the decisions, but are helping to present the situation in a way that intelligent decisions can be taken.

References

[ACKE82]: Ackerman W.B., "Data-Flow Languages", COMPUTER February 1982 , pp. 15-25

[DUDA87]: Duda R.O., Hart P.E., Reboh R., Reiter J., Risch T., "Using a Functional Language for Financial Risk Assessment", IEEE Expert, FALL 1987 pp.18-31

[GUIM89]: Guimbal B., McGregor G.C. and Wild, C., "The AISE Knowledge Representation Paradigm for Advisory Expert Systems", To be published

[LIEB87]: Lieberman H., "Object-Oriented Systems" in Shapiro S.C. (editor), "Encyclopaedia of Artificial Intelligence" Wiley 1987 pp. 452-453

[WALT88]: Walters J.R., Neilsen N.R., "Crafting Knowledge-Based Systems", Wiley 1988 pg. 39

Run-Through Algorithms for Applications of Autonomous Mobile Robots

Weiqing Tian

Department of Data Processing, Ruhr-University Bochum
D-4630 Bochum, West Germany

Abstract

This paper introduces algorithms for an autonomous mobile robot (AMR) that play a big role for AMRs in learning an unknown world. The knowledge to describe the world can be completely acquired by algorithms. By virtue of the algorithms it is possible to generate different world models. On the other side the algorithms also have practical applications.

Key words

Run-Through, World Models, Knowledge Acquisition, Route Problems, Learning, Knowledge Based System.

1. Introduction

The basic problems for an AMR to move can be divided into two categories: the planning problems and the navigation problems. In the second category the AMR moves in an unknown real world and should avoid any collision with obstacles. In the first category, however, the AMR has a map of the world so that it can plan a route at first and then move with a plan.

The majority of previous researches dealt with the problem of identifying the most direct path between a point of departure and of destination. If the world is unknown, then a route must be found according to a definite strategy (called route finding) /1/, /2/, /3, /4/, /5/. If the world is well-known, then a route can be planned (called route planning) /6/, /7/, /9/, however an AMR's capacity to learn an unfamiliar world has as yet been largely neglected.

The other class of route problem is encountered if one assumes a traversable surface in a closed space and intends to move over each traversable point at least once. This kind of route problem is refered to as "run-through" /10/, /11/. With an unknown world a suitable run-through must be found (run-through finding or first run-through), and with a known world a run-through can be planned (run-through planning or second run-through).

Run-through finding algorithms support the AMR to gain complete knowledge of an unknown world /10/, /11/. Especially, they are very useful for a knowledge-based system, if they can generate different world models during the performance of the first run-through. In this paper there will be introduced first run-through algorithms that immediately generate grid, quadtree and free space world models. Several kinds of world models were investigated by Tian and Weber /10/, /11/, those world models are saved in a knowledge-based system and can be transformed into each other. In this paper examples of second run-throughs will also be demonstrated.

2. First Run-Through to Generate Grid World Model

The most known world model is the grid structure in which every grid defines the smallest unit of the represented world. This type of structure is based on the cartesian coordinate system so that many mathematical tools can be used immediately. This structure is however a fundamental world model by reason of its simplicity and flexibility of implementation. Every grid represents the state of the space unit whether it is an obstacle or a free space. This world model represents the world with the finest resolution, but it gives few global declaration about the world. In other words it can provide little planning information to describe a subspace.

For the run-through every point of the space should be moved over at least once. It is therefore important that the run-through is systematically performed. The systematic run-through can be guaranteed by strategies which consist of rules. They are called as 'run-through strategies'. The rules decide the matching between the priorities and the motion directions. For the reason of the systematic run-through the motion directions are limited in four directions which are marked with $D = \{N, E, S, W\}$ (north, east, south and west). The priority set can be written with

$$P = \{(x_1, x_2, x_3, x_4) \mid x_i \in \{1, 2, 3, 4\}, 1 \leq i \leq 4\}$$

in which number 4 has highest priority and number 1 the lowest priority. In this way a run-through strategy is a triple (P, D, R_e) in which R_e is a rule set to define the relation between the sets D and P.

Here the number of possible run-through strategies can be calculated with consideration to the following cases:

Case 1: the priorities of motion directions are different to each other. In this case one yields $\frac{4!}{1!} = 24$ possible strategies.

Case 2: with the definition of R_e only two motion directions have the same priority and the other directions are different. The number of possible run-through strategies results $\frac{4!}{2!} \times 3 = 36$.

Case 3: the rules define the priorities of the motion directions in such a way that they are the same by pairs. One has now $\frac{4!}{2!2!} = 6$ strategies.

Case 4: three motion directions have the same priority. In this case there are $\frac{4!}{3!} \times 2 = 8$ run-through strategies.

Case 5: all motion directions possess the same priority. This kind of strategy has a spiral property. It differs from the spiral directions if in the clockwise direction or not. One yields here four different run-through strategies, if the spiral direction is always from outside to inside.

Together there are 78 elemental run-through strategies and every strategy can be described with the formula

$$s = \{(p(N), p(E), p(S), p(W)) \mid p(N), p(E), p(S), p(W) \in \{1, 2, 3, 4\}\}.$$

All run-through strategies are listed in table 1 (see appendix) and by reason of the structure of strategies they are divided into 15 categories.

Two definitions of operations of strategies are now introduced that are named 'rotation' and 'reflection'.

Definition 1 The operation 'rotation' ro and 'reflection' re of a run-through strategy are defined respectively by

$$ro(p(N) = x_1, p(E) = x_2, p(S) = x_3, p(W) = x_4) = (p(N) = x_4, p(E) = x_1, p(S) = x_2, p(W) = x_3),$$

$$re(p(N) = x_1, p(E) = x_2, p(S) = x_3, p(W) = x_4) = (p(N) = x_3, p(E) = x_2, p(S) = x_1, p(W) = x_4),$$

whereby x_i $(i = 1, .., 4)$ is the priority.

It is obvious that a strategy can be transformed to another one in the same category by those operations. That is, one can abstract all strategies in one category to only one strategy. Then there are only 15 typical strategies to investigate instead of 78 strategies. The first strategy in every category here is chosen as the typical strategy of this category. As examples several run-through strategies (2, 6, 9, 10, 13, 15) are demonstrated in figure 1.

The investigation of the strategies has the goal to determine the properties of strategies under the influence of different obstacles. The typical influences of an obstacle are the obstacle's form, size and position.

To assess the strategies a cost function is introduced consisting mainly of energy and time costs. The more the cost of a run-through in a scenario, the worse the quality of the strategy in this scenario. The cost of run-through here is sorted into seven levels and numerous scenarios were investigated. To obtain a correct assessment of strategies, every scenario to be observed contains only one obstacle at first . The assessments of strategies are ascertained by the middle values of the numerous results. Figure 2 presents the results of all the investigated scenarios for the 15 elemental strategies. Strategy 10 has the best results and strategy 8 the worst.

After the investigation of the different strategies one chooses suitable strategies for a scenario to be run, if the scenario is well-known. During the first run-through it is also possible to use different strategies for a scenario by way of using the rules system in which human knowledge is implemented.

Generating the grid-structure world model is clearly dependent on the quality and kind of sensors installed. Some sensors can see a big range of distance so that the run-through for learning the unknown world can be demonstrated in figure 3 whereby the distance between lines of two ways corresponds to the sensor range. By first run-through algorithms an unknown world can be learnt completely and the world model 'grid structure' is generated which is the elemental world model and most often used.

3. First Run-Through to Generate a Quadtree World Model

The quadtree is already well-known to represent a two-dimensional world /6/, /8/. The concept of 2^2-trees can be easily demonstrated in figure 4 in which the white leaves are free areas, the black leaves show the areas that are covered by obstacles and the grey knots point to the areas where there are both free areas and obstacles.

Although the algorithms to generate a quadtree are relatively complicated /8/, on account of the hierarchical tree structure it is possible that a quadtree grows. The quadtree world model is well-known for route planning /6/, /10/, /11/. For this reason it is meaningful to directly generate a quadtree world model.

A quadtree can grow by increasing the order of the quadtree as shown in figure 5. The expanding directions of a quadtree can be illustrated in figure 6 which present the expanding rules. By means of the rules an AMR can expand a quadtree as a world model to learn an unknown world.

To explain the algorithm simply, an example can be given. Figure 7 shows the unknown world and the line which the AMR should run. At the beginning the AMR knows only the surroundings as shown in figure 8 (a) and the corresponding quadtree is generated (see figure 8 (b)). By the run-through algorithm the AMR runs one step forward and discovers new areas (figure 9 (a)). At this time the quadtree is expanded from order 3 to order 4. After the run-through the unknown world is completely learnt (see figure 9 (b)). Then the learnt world is represented in a quadtree world model (see figure 10).

The advantages of generating on first run-through are the facts that one gains the quadtree world model immediatley after learning the unknown world and the quadtree provides directly global descriptions of the world which are suitable for 'top-down' route planning. On the other hand the quadtree world model saves much computer memory with a simple scenario.

4. First Run-Through to Generate a 'Free Space' World Model

The free space structure possesses graph representations in which nodes identify free spaces and edges describe the connections between free spaces. Due to proper separation of free spaces and obstacles the world model has many important advantages. In particular it is uncomplex and the most important knowledge about the world is clearly elicited so that it can be immediately used for route and run-through planning. Additionally the safety problems in path planning can be very easily solved. Figure 11 shows an example of a free space structure. The edge lines of an obstacle represent the boundaries of a free space. In other words the edge lines of obstacles play a very important role in generating a free-space world model.

To generate the free space, however, one uses only two run-through strategies $s_{2.1}$ and $s_{2.2}$. In contrast to the first run-through in a grid structure the run-through algorithm here limits the running of the AMR only within the bounds of the discovered edge lines of obstacles. In this way the free spaces can be generated one by one. At the same time the connections between free spaces are also defined. Figure 12 gives an example. However the free-space structure generated by the first run-through is not optimized for a second run-through and has possibly remaining free spaces. The optimizing algorithms for free-space structures can be found in /11/ which can be immediately used after the generating of a free space.

5. World Models and Applications

A new concept of knowledge-based system to run several world models was introduced in /10/ and /11/. In the data base of the knowledge-based system different kinds of world models are involved. These are: 'grid structure', 'quadtree', '4_2-tree', 'quadregion structure', 'free space structure' and 'simple space structure'. They can be transformed into each other by transformation algorithms that are saved in the component 'knowledge base'. The transformation connections of the world models are illustrated in figure 13. After the first run-through the AMR has learnt the world compeletely and one world model is generated. It is clear that different route problems need corresponding world models. By use of transformations one can perform route planning and second run-through planning with different world models.

As an example figure 14 shows a transformation from grid structure to free space structure. One extends at first the edge lines of obstacles as boundaries of free spaces. The small free spaces separated are concentrated if it is possible. In the algorithm the optimizing of free spaces for the run-through planning is integrated so that every transformed free space is suitable for the second run-through.

Figures 15, 16 and 17 show three examples of route planning on a quadtree, free space structure and quadregion structure respectively. The algorithm for route planning on a quadtree is different to /6/ because of its strict 'top-down' property. The algorithms for second run-through can be performed on whole world models in the data base. Of course thanks to the first run-through the run-through planning has better results. Run-through algorithms just like route finding and planning have many applications, e.g., the AMR can be applied as a vacuum cleaner or cleaner in a swimming-pool and so on. Now follow two examples for second run-through on a free space structure and on a simple space structure (see figure 18).

6. Conclusion

The concept of first run-through to learn an unknown world is discussed in this paper. The important properties of the concept and the algorithms are the facts that the AMR can generate different world models on a first run-through. The knowledge learnt on the first run-through is saved in the data base of the knowledge-based system and can be transformed to another world model or can be immediately used for route planning and second run-through. The further discussion of the structure of this knowledge-based system, the transformations between world models, algorithms for solving route problems on those world models and so on, is described in detail in /11/.

References

/1/ R.Chattergy, "Some Heuristics for the Navigation of a Robot", Int. Jour. of Robotics Research, vol. 4, No.1 1985

/2/ F.Freyberger, P.Kampmann und G.Schmitt, "Ein wissensgestütztes Navigationsverfahren für autonome mobile Roboter", Robotersysteme, 1986 2, pp 149-161

/3/ G.Giralt,R.Chatila,M.Vaisset, "An Integrated Navigation and Motion Control System for Autonomous Multisensory Mobile Robots",1st. Int. Symp. of Robotics Research, 1983

/4/ C.Isik, "Knowledge-based Motion Control of an Intelligent Mobile Autonomous System", Ph.D. dissertation, Uni. Florida. Gainesville, 1985

/5/ S.S Iyengar,C.C.Jorgensen,S.V.N.Rao,C.R.Weisbin, "Robot Navigation Algorithms Using Learned Spatial Graphs", Robotica, 1986 volume 4, pp 93-100

/6/ S.Kambhampati,L.S.Davis, "Multiresolution Path Planning for Mobile Robots", IEEE Jour. Robot. Auto. vol. 2, No.3, Sep. 1986

/7/ C.Y.Lee,"An algorithm for path connections and its applications", IRE Trans. Elec. Comput. Sept. 1961

/8/ H.Samet,"An Algorithm for Converting Rasters to Quadtrees",IEEE Trans. Patt. Analy. Mach. Intell., vol. 3, 1981

/9/ W.Tian,W.Weber,"Wegefindungsalgorithmen bei einem autonomen Mobil-Roboter", FACTA UNIVERSITATIS, Universität Nis, Jugoslawien, 1989

/10/ W.Tian,W,Weber,"Ein neues Konzept wissensbasierter Systeme zur Lösung der Wegeprobleme für Autonome Mobile Roboter", 5. Österreiche AI-Tagung, Innsbruck, Austria, 1989

/11/ W.Tian,"Ein wissensbasiertes System zur Fahrtplanung und -kontrolle eines autonomen mobilen Roboters", Dissertation, Ruhr-Uni Bochum, Bochum, West Germany, 1989

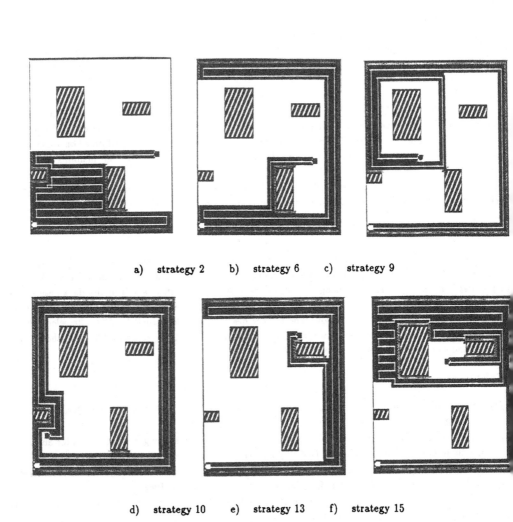

a)   strategy 2   b)   strategy 6   c)   strategy 9

d)   strategy 10   e)   strategy 13   f)   strategy 15

Figure 1   Examples of the first run-through with diffenrent strategies

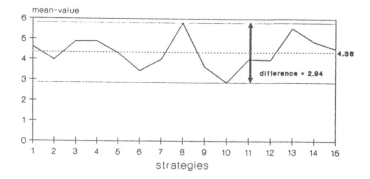

Figure 2   Entire quality of 15 elemental run-through strategies

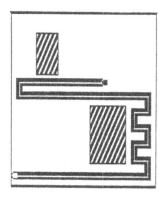

Figure 3   An example of the first run-through with big sensor range

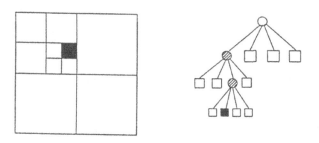

Figure 4   Representation of a quadtree

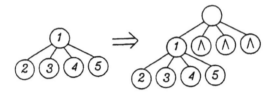

Figure 5   An example of quadtree expanding

a) Northern and eastern direction   b) Western and sorthern direction

Figure 6   Expanding rules

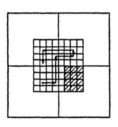

Figure 7   An unknown world

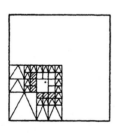 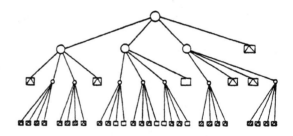

a) Surroundings of the AMR   b) Presentation of the corresponding quadtree

Figure 8   At beginning of the run-through

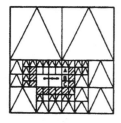

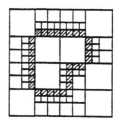

(a) Learning the new surrounding   (b) Completely learning

Figure 9   Learning the unknown world

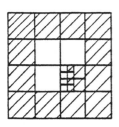

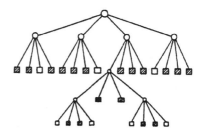

(a) The learnt world   (b) The corresponding quadtree

Figure 10   The generated quadtree

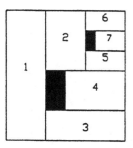

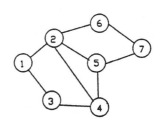

Figure 11   An example of a 'free space' structure

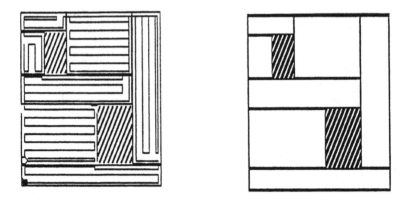

Figure 12   An example of the generating a 'free space'

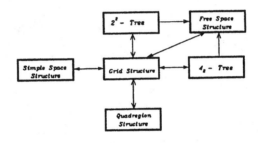

Figure 13   The relationship between world models

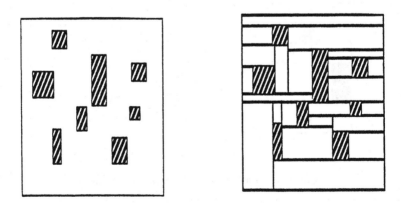

Figure 14   An example of transformation from grid structure to 'free space'

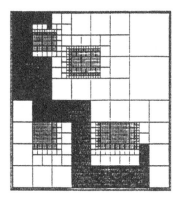

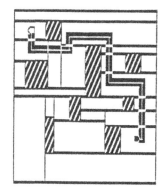

Figure 15   Route planning on a quadtree   Figure 16   Route planning on a 'free space'

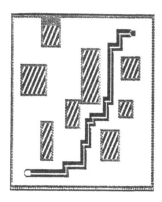

Figure 17   Route planning on a quadregion

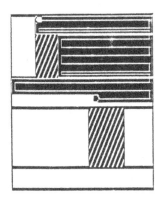

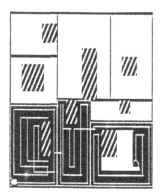

Figure 18   Two examples of 2. run-through on a 'free space' and a 'simple space'

Appendix

Table of Run-Through Strategies

Category 1

$s_{1.1}^* = \{N-3, O-4, S-1, W-2\}$ $s_{1.2} = \{N-4, O-1, S-2, W-3\}$
$s_{1.3} = \{N-1, O-2, S-3, W-4\}$ $s_{1.4} = \{N-2, O-3, S-4, W-1\}$
$s_{1.5} = \{N-1, O-4, S-3, W-2\}$ $s_{1.6} = \{N-4, O-3, S-2, W-1\}$
$s_{1.7} = \{N-3, O-2, S-1, W-4\}$ $s_{1.8} = \{N-2, O-1, S-4, W-3\}$

Category 2

$s_{2.1}^* = \{N-2, O-4, S-1, W-3\}$ $s_{2.2} = \{N-4, O-1, S-3, W-2\}$
$s_{2.3} = \{N-1, O-3, S-2, W-4\}$ $s_{2.4} = \{N-3, O-2, S-4, W-1\}$
$s_{2.5} = \{N-1, O-4, S-2, W-3\}$ $s_{2.6} = \{N-4, O-2, S-3, W-1\}$
$s_{2.7} = \{N-2, O-3, S-1, W-4\}$ $s_{2.8} = \{N-3, O-1, S-4, W-2\}$

Category 3

$s_{3.1}^* = \{N-3, O-4, S-2, W-1\}$ $s_{3.2} = \{N-4, O-2, S-1, W-3\}$
$s_{3.3} = \{N-2, O-1, S-3, W-4\}$ $s_{3.4} = \{N-1, O-3, S-4, W-2\}$
$s_{3.5} = \{N-2, O-4, S-3, W-1\}$ $s_{3.6} = \{N-4, O-3, S-1, W-2\}$
$s_{3.7} = \{N-3, O-1, S-2, W-4\}$ $s_{3.8} = \{N-1, O-2, S-4, W-3\}$

Category 4

$s_{4.1}^* = \{N-2, O-4, S-2, W-1\}$ $s_{4.2} = \{N-4, O-2, S-1, W-2\}$
$s_{4.3} = \{N-2, O-1, S-2, W-4\}$ $s_{4.4} = \{N-1, O-2, S-4, W-2\}$

Category 5

$s_{5.1}^* = \{N-2, O-4, S-1, W-2\}$ $s_{5.2} = \{N-4, O-1, S-2, W-2\}$
$s_{5.3} = \{N-1, O-2, S-2, W-4\}$ $s_{5.4} = \{N-2, O-2, S-4, W-1\}$
$s_{5.5} = \{N-1, O-4, S-2, W-2\}$ $s_{5.6} = \{N-4, O-2, S-2, W-1\}$
$s_{5.7} = \{N-2, O-2, S-1, W-4\}$ $s_{5.8} = \{N-2, O-1, S-4, W-2\}$

Category 6

$s_{6.1}^* = \{N-1, O-4, S-1, W-1\}$ $s_{6.2} = \{N-4, O-1, S-1, W-1\}$
$s_{6.3} = \{N-1, O-1, S-1, W-4\}$ $s_{6.4} = \{N-1, O-1, S-4, W-1\}$

Category 7

$s_{7.1}^* = \{N-1, O-2, S-1, W-2\}$ $s_{7.2} = \{N-2, O-1, S-2, W-1\}$

Category 8

$s_{8.1}^* = \{N-1, O-2, S-2, W-1\}$ $s_{8.2} = \{N-2, O-2, S-1, W-1\}$
$s_{8.3} = \{N-2, O-1, S-1, W-2\}$ $s_{8.4} = \{N-1, O-1, S-2, W-2\}$

Appendix

Category 9

$$s_{9.1}^* = \{N-1, O-1, S-1, W-1\}$$
(counterclockwise)

$$s_{9.2} = \{N-1, O-1, S-1, W-1\}$$
(clockwise)

Category 10

$$s_{10.1}^* = \{N-1, O-1, S-1, W-1\}$$
(counterclockwise)

$$s_{10.2} = \{N-1, O-1, S-1, W-1\}$$
(clockwise)

Category 11

$$s_{11.1}^* = \{N-1, O-4, S-1, W-2\}$$
$$s_{11.3} = \{N-1, O-2, S-1, W-4\}$$

$$s_{11.2} = \{N-4, O-1, S-2, W-1\}$$
$$s_{11.4} = \{N-2, O-1, S-4, W-1\}$$

Category 12

$$s_{12.1}^* = \{N-1, O-4, S-2, W-4\}$$
$$s_{12.3} = \{N-2, O-4, S-1, W-4\}$$

$$s_{12.2} = \{N-4, O-2, S-4, W-1\}$$
$$s_{12.4} = \{N-4, O-1, S-4, W-2\}$$

Category 13

$$s_{13.1}^* = \{N-1, O-4, S-2, W-1\}$$
$$s_{13.3} = \{N-2, O-1, S-1, W-4\}$$
$$s_{13.5} = \{N-2, O-4, S-1, W-1\}$$
$$s_{13.7} = \{N-1, O-1, S-2, W-4\}$$

$$s_{13.2} = \{N-4, O-2, S-1, W-1\}$$
$$s_{13.4} = \{N-1, O-1, S-4, W-2\}$$
$$s_{13.6} = \{N-4, O-1, S-1, W-2\}$$
$$s_{13.8} = \{N-2, O-1, S-4, W-1\}$$

Category 14

$$s_{14.1}^* = \{N-4, O-4, S-1, W-2\}$$
$$s_{14.3} = \{N-1, O-2, S-4, W-4\}$$
$$s_{14.5} = \{N-4, O-4, S-1, W-2\}$$
$$s_{14.7} = \{N-1, O-2, S-4, W-4\}$$

$$s_{14.2} = \{N-4, O-1, S-2, W-4\}$$
$$s_{14.4} = \{N-2, O-4, S-4, W-1\}$$
$$s_{14.6} = \{N-4, O-1, S-2, W-4\}$$
$$s_{14.8} = \{N-2, O-4, S-4, W-1\}$$

Category 15

$$s_{15.1}^* = \{N-4, O-4, S-1, W-4\}$$
$$s_{15.3} = \{N-1, O-4, S-4, W-4\}$$

$$s_{15.2} = \{N-4, O-1, S-4, W-4\}$$
$$s_{15.4} = \{N-4, O-4, S-4, W-1\}$$

Events, Situations, and Adverbs

Robert C. Moore
Artificial Intelligence Center, SRI International
333 Ravenswood Ave., Menlo Park, California 94025, USA

1   Introduction

This paper concerns a dispute about the relationship of sentences to the events they describe, and how that relationship is manifested in sentences with adverbial modifiers. The two sides to the argument might be called the "Davidsonian position" and the "situation semantics position"; the former being chiefly represented by Donald Davidson's well-known paper "The Logical Form of Action Sentences" [1] and the latter by John Perry's critique of Davidson's view, "Situations in Action" [2]. (This dispute is really just a special case of a much deeper disagreement about semantics that is treated in depth by Barwise and Perry in *Situations and Attitudes* [3].)

The issue turns on Davidson's analysis of how a sentence like (1) is related to a similar sentence with an adverbial modifier, such as (2).

(1) Jones buttered the toast.

(2) Jones buttered the toast in the bathroom.

Stated very informally, Davidson's position is this: (1) claims that an event of a certain type took place, to wit, a buttering of toast by Jones, and that (2) makes a similar claim but adds that the event took place in the bathroom. Put this way, an advocate of situation semantics could find little to complain about. Perry and Barwise themselves say rather similar things. The dispute is over the way that (1) and (2) claim that certain events took place. Davidson suggests that the event in question is, in effect, a hidden argument to the verb "butter". As he would put it, the logical form of (1) is not

(3) Buttered(Jones, the toast)

but rather

(4) ∃x(Buttered(Jones, the toast, x)),

where the variable x in (4) ranges over events. (This analysis obviously makes no attempt to analyze the tense of the verb or the structure of the noun phrase "the toast".) Adding the adverbial modifier is then quite straightforward; it is simply an additional predication of the event:

(5) ∃x(Buttered(Jones, the toast, x) ∧ In(the bathroom, x))

Perry objects strenuously to making the event described by the sentence an explicit argument to the relation expressed by the verb. He says:

> If we ask what about the statement tells us that there was an event of that type, the only reasonable answer is that the whole statement does. It is not that part of the statement refers to an event, and the other part tells us what it was like. Part of the statement refers to Jones and the other part tells us what he did. Both parts working together tell us that an event of a certain sort occurred. The simple parts of the sentence refer to basic uniformities across events: Jones, buttering, and the toast. The way the simple parts are put together in the sentence describes the event. [2, p. 2]

Now it happens that Davidson considers but rejects an analysis derived from Reichenbach [4, pp. 266–274] that is in the spirit of Perry's objection. On this analysis, (1) and (2) would be rendered by (6) and (7), respectively:

(6) ∃x(x consists in the fact that Jones buttered the toast)

(7) ∃x(x consists in the fact that Jones buttered the toast and x took place in the bathroom)

This seems to meet Perry's objection in that it is the whole statement "Jones buttered the toast" that gives rise to the reference to the event, rather than a hidden argument to the verb. Davidson rejects the analysis, however, on the grounds that its logical properties are problematical. Davidson notes that, from the identity of the Morning Star and Evening Star, we would want to be able to infer that, if I flew my spaceship to the Morning Star, I flew my spaceship to the Evening Star. On the analysis under consideration, this requires being able to infer (9) from (8).

(8) ∃x(x consists in the fact that I flew my spaceship to the Morning Star)

(9) ∃x(x consists in the fact that I flew my spaceship to the Evening Star)

Davidson argues that the only reasonable logical principles that would permit this inference to go through would entail the identity of *all* actually occuring events, which would be absurd. Barwise and Perry's [3, pp. 24–26] rejoinder to this is that Davidson makes the unwarranted assumption that logically equivalent sentences would have to be taken to describe the same event, an idea they reject. Perry [2] goes on to develop, within the framework of situation semantics, an analysis of event sentences and adverbial modification that is faithful to the idea that, in general, it is an entire sentence that describes an event. (We omit the details of Perry's own analysis of adverbial modification, as it would require a far more extensive presentation of Perry and Barwise's theory of semantics than is really appropriate for this paper, and it is not really needed for the points we wish to make.)

To summarize the state of the argument: Davidson and Perry agree that sentences describe events, but Davidson thinks that it virtually incoherent to view the event as being described, as it were, "holistically" by the entire sentence, whereas Perry views it as "the only reasonable answer." Barwise and Perry pinpoint where they think Davidson's argument goes wrong, and Perry provides an analysis of adverbial modification consistent with the holistic view.

2   Some Facts about Adverbs and Event Sentences

One of the things that Perry's and Davidson's analyses have in common is that neither is based on a very extensive survey of the *linguistic* data to be accounted for by a theory of adverbial modification. The strongest considerations in motivating their analyses are more general logical and metaphysical concerns. A more careful examination of the relevant linguistic phenomena, however, shows that neither Davidson nor Perry have the story quite right, and that a more complete account of adverbial modification has to make room for at least two views of the relation between sentences and events, one close to Davidson's and the other close to Perry's.

The key set of data we will try to account for is that there is a significant class of adverbs that can be used to modify event sentences in two quite distinct ways:

(10) (a) John spoke to Bill rudely.

    (b) Rudely, John spoke to Bill.

(11) (a) John stood on his head foolishly.

    (b) Foolishly, John stood on his head.

(12) (a) John sang strangely.

    (b) Strangely, John sang.

The difference between the first and second member of each pair should be clear. For instance, (10a) suggests that it was the way that John spoke to Bill was rude, while (10b) says that the very fact that John spoke to Bill was rude. Thus (10a) leaves open the possibility that John could have spoken to Bill without being rude, but (10b) does not. Similar remarks apply to the other pairs. With this class of adverbs, in general, "X did Y Adj-ly" means that the way X did Y was Adj, and "Adj-ly, X did Y" means that the fact that X did Y was Adj. We will therefore say that the (a) sentences involve a "manner" use of the adverb and that the (b) sentences involve a "fact" use.

One notable observation about the fact use of these adverbs is that they are indeed "factive" in the sense that the truth of the sentence with the adverb entails the truth of the sentence without the adverb. This is in contrast to other "sentential" adverbs like "allegedly" or "probably":

(13) Probably John likes Mary.

(14) John likes Mary

The truth of (13) would not necessarily imply the truth of (14). This factivity extends to the adjective forms from which the adverbs derive:

(15) It was rude for John to speak to Bill.

(16) It was foolish for John to stand on his head.

(17) It was strange for John to sing a song.

Another significant fact is that with copular constructions, only the factive use is possible; the manner use doesn't exist:

(18) Strangely, John is tall.

(19) *John is tall strangely.

Copular constructions accept the fact use of adverbs, as is shown by (18). If we move the adverb to the end of the sentence to try to obtain a manner interpretation as in (19), the sentence is unacceptable.

Finally, perhaps the most important logical difference between the fact and manner uses of these adverbs is that the manner sentences are extensional with respect to the noun phrases in the sentence, whereas the fact sentences are not. That is, we may freely substitute coreferential singular terms in the manner sentences, but not the fact sentences. Suppose it is considered rude to speak to the Queen (unless, say, she speaks to you first), and suppose John is seated next to the Queen. Then it could well be that (20) is true, while (21) is false, although the differ only in having substituted one singular term for a coreferring one.

(20) Rudely, John spoke to the Queen.

(21) Rudely, John spoke to the woman next to him.

(21) can differ in truth-value from (20) because—on at least one interpretation—it seems to entail that it was rude for John to speak to the woman next to him, *whoever* she was, i.e., even if she were not the Queen. The issue is somewhat complicated by the fact that these sentences also exhibit the sort of *de dicto/de re* ambiguity common to most nonextensional constructs. That is, (20) and (21) seem to be open to an an additional interpretation, whereby we might be saying that there is a certain woman, whom we may identify either as the Queen or the woman next to John, and that it was rude for John to speak to that particular woman.

On the other hand, it seems that (22) and (23) must have the same truth-value on *any* interpretation, so long as the Queen and the woman next to John are the same person. Moreover, no *de dicto/de re* distinction seems to obtain.

(22) John spoke to the Queen rudely.

(23) John spoke to the woman next to him rudely.

Note, however, that (22) and (23) are not completely extensional in the sense that first-order logic is extensional. That notion of extensionality requires, not only intersubstitutivity of coreferring singular terms, but also intersubstitutivity of sentences with the same truth-value. But even if (24) and (25) have the same truth-value, it does not follow that (26) and (27) do.

(24) John spoke to the Queen.

(25) John spoke to the Prince.

(26) John spoke to the Queen rudely.

(27) John spoke to the Prince rudely.

This sort of behavior is quite general with these adverbs. Examples similar to (20)-(27) can be constructed for "foolishly," "strangely," and all the other adverbs in this class.

3 Situations and Events

Before we can give a semantic analysis of event sentences that accounts for all these observations, we must develop the framework within which the analysis will be couched. Our analysis will require technical notions of situation and event, and this section is devoted to working those out.

A word of caution is in order before proceeding further. The goal of this exercise is semantical analysis of natural language, not the discovery of Deep Metaphysical Truths. If we postulate situations or events as entities in the world, it is not necessarily because we believe there are really and truly such things objectively out there, but because postulating them gives the most natural analysis of the meanings of the class of sentences we are trying to analyze. Our real concern is what metaphysics is embedded in the language, not whether that metaphysics is actually true.

A second word of warning concerns our use of the term "situation". This term is so closely identified with the work of Barwise and Perry, that one might be misled into assuming that the theory of situations assumed here is just Barwise and Perry's theory. That is emphatically not the case. Yet it seems so clear that both Barwise and Perry's theory and the theory presented here are attempts to formalize a single intuitive notion, that in the end it would probably be even more misleading to employ a different term.

3.1 Situations and Propositions

Relatively little in the way of a theory of situations is actually needed to construct an analysis of the linguistic data that we have presented. We really need to say little more than (1) that situations are part of the causal order of the world rather than an abstraction of it, and (2) that situations are in one-to-one correspondence with true propositions. To leave the theory of situations at this, however, would leave open so many questions about what sort of objects situations and propositions were that it might cast serious doubt over the application of the theory to the analysis of event sentences.

In our theory, situations are simpler entities than in Barwise and Perry's theory. For us, a situation is just a piece of reality that consists of an n-tuple of entities having an n-ary property or relation. (We might want to add "at a spatio-temporal location", but we will ignore this aspect of the problem, as there are various ways that it could be handled, and the issue seems independent of the others considered here.) Like Barwise and Perry, then, we take properties to be first-class entities. A proposition is simply an abstraction of a situation—a way that a situation could be. We will assume that for every n-ary property and every n-tuple of entities, there exists the proposition that those entities satisfy that property. That is, suppose we have an individual John and the property of being tall. If John is tall, then there is an actual situation of John being tall. Even if John is not tall, however, there is the abstract possibility of John being tall; i.e., there might have been a John-being-tall situation, but as things turned out, there wasn't. This abstract possibility is what we take a proposition to be. A true proposition is one that is the abstraction of an actual situation. We can ask what the individuation criteria for situations and for propositions in this theory would be, and while various answers are possible, the most natural one would be that identity of the properties and each pair of corresponding arguments are required for the identity of two situations or propositions.

The theory so far satisfies both of the requirements that we placed on situations above. They are part of the causal order of the world, because they are taken to be pieces of reality (just as Barwise and Perry take real situations to be). They are in one-to-one correspondence with the true propositions, because they have been individuated in such a way that there is exactly one situation for every proposition that accords with reality. What may be in doubt, however, is that there will be enough propositions to do the work that notion normally has to do in semantics. Elsewhere [5], we show how the theory can be extended to handle first-order quantification, propositional connectives, and propositional attitude attributions, by admitting propositions and propositional functions among the entities that properties and relations can be applied to.

To summarize the extensions briefly: Propositional connectives become properties of propositions. Negation, for example, would be a unary property of propositions. A proposition has the negation property just in case it is false. For every false proposition, there is an actual situation of it being false, and for every proposition there is the additional proposition that it is false. Conjunction, disjunction, etc., would be binary relations between propositions. First-order quantifiers become properties of functions from individuals to propositions. (A generalized quantifier treatment where quantifiers are considered to be binary relations on pairs of properties is probably preferable, but we present the simpler treatment in this paper to be consistent with standard logic and with Davidson.) For example, in standard logic "All men are mortal" is rendered as "Everything is such that, if it is a man, then it is mortal." In our framework this would be analyzed as the proposition that every individual is mapped into a true proposition by the function that maps an entity into the proposition that, if the entity is a man, then it is mortal.

Within this theory there is a natural semantics for first-order logic with formulas taken to denote propositions—distinct formulas denoting distinct propositions unless they can be made identical by renaming of variables. We will therefore use the notation of standard logic freely in the rest of this paper, but with the semantics sketched here intended rather than the normal Tarskian semantics.

3.2 Situations and Events

The preceeding discussion makes an attempt to clarify the relation between situations and propositions, but what of events? Although we have claimed that situations are parts of the real world, they still may seem rather abstract. Events, on the other hand, may seem much more real and much more familiar. For instance, if a bomb goes off, there seems little doubt that there really is such a thing as the *explosion*. We can see it and feel it, and it has undoubted causal effects. We will maintain, however, that situations and events are intimately related; that, in fact, robust large-scale events such as explosions consist of nothing more than the sum of (literally) uncountably many simple situations.

Suppose an object moves from point P1 to point P2 between T1 and T2. Consider the situation of the object being at P1 at T1, the situation of it being at P2 at T2, and all of the situations of it being at some intermediate point at the corresponding intermediate time. We claim that the event of the object moving from P1 to P2 between T1 and T2 consists of nothing more than the sum of all these situations. The argument is really quite simple. If one has all these situations–that is, if the object is at P1 at T1 and at P2 at T2 and at all the intermediate points at the corresponding intermediate times–then the movement in question exists. Nothing more needs to be added to these states of affairs for the moving event to exist, therefore it is gratuitous to assert that the moving event consists in anything beyond these situations.

The only qualification that needs to be mentioned is that the verb "consist" is used quite deliberately here, instead of the "be" of identity. That is because, according to common sense, one and the same event could have consisted of slightly different smaller events, and hence of a slightly different set of situations. World War II would not have been a different war merely if one fewer soldier had been killed. But this is no different than the observation that changing one screw on a complex machine does not make it a different machine. Thus we will say that situations are the "stuff" out of which events are made, just as material substances are the stuff out of which objects are made. The exact identity criteria for events in terms of situations are likely to be just as hard to give as for objects in terms of their material. But by the same token, there is no reason to conclude that there is something to an event over and above the situations it includes any more than there is to conclude that there is something to an object over and above what it is made of.

4 The Analysis

With this framework laid out, let us look again at "Jones buttered the toast." Perry begins his analysis by saying

"Jones" refers to Jones, "the toast" refers to some piece of toast, and "buttered" refers to a relational activity, with the tense constraining the location.

[2, p. 2]

This certainly seems unobjectionable. We have two objects and a binary relation (ignoring tense, as we have done throughout this paper). If the objects in question actually satisfy the relation, then there is a corresponding situation. But how is this situation related to the commonsense event of Jones buttering the toast? The buttering is surely a complex moving event, so by the argument of the last section it must consist of countless situations of the butter, the toast, the knife, Jones's arm, etc. being in certain positions at certain times. According to the identity criterion we have given for situations, those situations and the event which is constituted by their sum are distinct from the single situation of the buttering relation holding between Jones and the toast.

Clearly the buttering situation and the buttering event are closely related, but according to the principles we have adopted, they cannot be one and the same. Davidson's analysis of event sentences turns out to provide a very attractive way of expressing the relation between them. If we analyze an event sentence as asserting the existence of an event, as he suggests, then according to our semantic framework, the sentence asserts of a certain property of events that it is instantiated. (Strictly speaking, the theory says the sentence asserts there is an event mapped into a true proposition by a certain propositional function, but for simplicity we will paraphrase this in terms of the corresponding property of events.) In the buttering toast example, the sentence says that the property of being a buttering of the toast by Jones is instantiated. The situation that the whole sentence describes, then, is the situation of the property of being a buttering of the toast by Jones being instantiated. On the one hand, then, we have a situation of a certain property of events being instantiated, and on the other hand we have the event that actually instantiates the property.

On first exposure, this may seem like an artificial distinction imposed to solve an artificial problem. In point of fact, however, this distinction seems to be just what is needed to explain the two types of adverbial modification discussed in Section 2. Moreover, all the data presented there can then be quite straightforwardly accounted for within the framework we have developed.

Let us look again at perhaps the simplest pair of sentences illustrating these two types of modification:

(12) (a) John sang strangely.

(b) Strangely, John sang.

The manner use of the adverb in (12a) seems to fit quite comfortably within the David-sonian pattern of treating adverbs as making additional predications of the event whose existence is asserted by the basic sentence. If John sang strangely, it seems most definitely to be the singing event itself that is strange. With (12b), though, the singing event itself may be quite ordinary as singing events go. It seems to be the fact that there is any singing by John at all that is strange. But this is precisely what we would be saying if we analyzed (12b) as predicating strangeness of the situation of the property of being-a-singing-by-John being instantiated.

We can represent this symbolically by making a minor extension to ordinary logic. (12a) will just be represented in the way Davidson has already suggested.

(28) $\exists x(Sang(John, x) \wedge Strange(x))$

The extension is required to represent the fact use of the adverb in (12b). That sentence attributes strangeness to a situation, and since we have decided to let formulas denote propositions, we do not yet have any notation for situations. One way of remedying this is to let situations be in the domain of individuals (as Davidson already assumes events to be) and introduce a relation "Fact" that holds between a situation and the corresponding true proposition. The name "Fact" is chosen because this relation quite plausibly provides the semantics of the locution "the fact that P". Note that while "Fact" denotes a relation between a situation and a proposition in our semantics, it will be an operator whose first argument is a singular term and whose second argument is a formula, rather than an ordinary relation symbol. (12b) would then be represented by

(29) $\exists y(Fact(y, \exists x(Sang(John, x))) \wedge Strange(y))$

This says literally that there exists a fact (or situation) of there being a singing-by-John event and that fact is strange, or more informally, the fact that John sang is strange.

If there is a distinct situation corresponding to every true proposition, it may be worrying to allow situations into the domain of individuals. There are various foundational approaches that could be used to justify this, but we will merely note that the logical principles needed for our use of situations are so weak that no inconsistency seems threatened. The only general principle that seems appropriate is the schema

(30) $\exists y(\text{Fact}(y,P)) \equiv P$

This schema can easily be shown to be consistent by giving "Fact" a simple syntactic interpretation that makes the schema true.

Under this analysis of event sentences and adverbial modification, all the other data are easily accounted for. The factivity of the fact use of adverbs and their related adjectives arises because the adverbs and adjectives express properties of situations, which are real pieces of the world that don't exist unless the corresponding propositions are true.

Copular sentences don't exhibit the fact/manner distinction in their adverbial modifiers, because they don't involve event variables; only the overall situation is available for the adverb to be predicated of. This provides one answer to Perry's objection to the Davidsonian treatment of event sentences: "The idea that 'Sarah was walking' gets a cosmically different treatment than "Sarah was agile' strikes me as not very plausible." [2, p. 3] The first of these can take manner adverbials, and the second cannot, a fact that seems to require *some* difference in analysis to explain.

The extensionality with respect to noun phrases of sentences with manner adverbials follows directly from Davidson's original proposal. The noun phrases do not occur within the ultimate scope of the adverbial, which ends up being only the event variable. Changing the entire sentence, as in (24)–(27), changes the event, though, so we do not get that sort of extensionality.

The nonextensionality of sentences with fact adverbials follows from the fact that changing a description of a participant in an event changes the property of the event that goes into determining what situation is being talked about, even though the event itself does not change. If we compare (20) and (21),

(20) Rudely, John spoke to the Queen.

(21) Rudely, John spoke to the woman next to him.

we see that the two sentences describe a single event, John's speaking to the Queen, who is also the woman next to him. They describe the event in two different ways, though, so they ascribe two different properties to it. (To make sure these two properties do come out nonidentical in our semantics, we need to treat "the" as a quantifier. There are many independent reasons for doing this, however.) If we leave out the adverb, the unmodified sentences assert that these two properties of events are instantiated. Since these properties are different, the situation of one of them being instantiated is a different situation from that of the other one being instantiated. Hence one of those situations might be rude (of John) without the other one being so.

5 Conclusions

Let us return to Davidson's and Perry's analyses of event sentences, to see how they fare in the light of the data and the theory presented here. We have adopted Davidson's analysis of manner adverbials wholesale, so we are in complete agreement with him on that point. We sharply disagree with him, however, on the possibility of associating event-like entities (i.e., situations) with whole sentences, and we find them absolutely necessary to account for the fact use of adverbs, a case Davidson fails to consider. Perry, on the other hand, rightly takes Davidson to task for his faulty argument against associating something like situations with whole sentences, but then fails to look closely enough at the data to see that something like Davidson's analysis is still needed to account for the detailed facts about manner adverbials.

References

[1] D. Davidson, *Essays on Actions and Events*, Essay 6, pp. 105–148 (Clarendon Press, Oxford, England, 1980).

[2] J. Perry, "Situations in Action," unpublished ms. of a lecture presented at the annual meeting of the Pacific Division of the American Philosophical Association, March 1983.

[3] J. Barwise and J. Perry, *Situations and Attitudes* (The MIT Press, Cambridge, Massachusetts, 1983).

[4] H. Reichenbach, *Elements of Symbolic Logic* (Macmillian Co., New York, New York, 1947).

[5] R. C. Moore, "Propositional Attitudes and Russellian Propositions," Report No. CSLI-88-119, Center for the Study of Language and Information, Stanford University, Stanford, California, February 1988.

LING2: A System for Induction

António G. Portela

Departamento de Engenharia Mecanica
Instituto Superior Técnico
Av. Rovisco Pais
1096 Lisboa Codex, Portugal

Abstract

F-LING is a formal language based on the concept of holonic sentence, a 4-word declaration where the first word symbolises the semantic environment.

The holonic sentence, preceded by 2 words (the symbols of the initial sentence and of the holonic sentence), is stored in a repository. The constancy of the number of words (2 + 4) in each sentence is very helpful.

The main purpose of this paper is to show how induction can be done in F-LING.

1   Introduction

F-LING is a formal language based on the concept of holonic sentence, (HOL), a 4-word declaration which is considered the simplest structure conveying some information. The general form of an holonic phrase is:

$$HOL_z \quad Wrd_0 \quad Wrd_1 \quad Wrd_2 \quad Wrd_3$$

The holonic sentence, HOL_z, informs:

- There is a nexus between the words Wrd_1 and Wrd_3;

- The "nexus" is named Wrd_2 and, in general, there are many other pairs having the same nexus;

- The triad Wrd_1, Wrd_2, Wrd_3 holds in the semantic context or referential, symbolised by Wrd_0.

For example:

$$HOL_z \text{ Jack Mary is-maried-to John}$$

- HOL_z is the symbol of the holonic sentence;

- Jack has made the declaration, "Mary is-maried-to John";

- "Jack" is the symbol given to the semantic context;

- There is a nexus between "Mary" and "John";

- ("Mary", "John") is an ordered pair;

- "is-maried-to" is the word that represents the nexus.

F-DIALOG [Portela 88] is an liguistic tool that enables the dialog with F-LING, using natural (idiomatic) language instead of a formal one. The main functions of F-DIALOG are:

1. *Elimination of ambiguities.* A dialog with the user takes place and only terminates when F-DIALOG considers an ambiguous sentence clarified. The dialog may not take place if the sentence is not ambiguous, from F-DIALOG's point of view.

2. *Separation of the unambiguous (clarified) sentence in one or more holonic sentences.* This operation is performed without loss of information and it is possible to reconstruct a sentence with the same "information content" of the original clarified sentence.

3. *Placing all the sentences in a repository (REP).* The standard form of an holonic sentences in the repository is:

$$Sent_z \quad Hol_z \quad Wrd_0 \quad Wrd_1 \quad Wrd_2 \quad Wrd_3$$

where $Sent_z$ is the symbol of the "clarified ideomatic sentence" and Hol_z is the symbol of one of the holonic sentences derived from $Sent_z$ by F-DIALOG.

4. *Creating a dictionary (DIC), with all the words given to or created by F-DIALOG.*

5. *Revise REP and DIC whenever necessary.* Both, REP and DIC are "infinitely" expansible.

6. *Definition of referent.* F-DIALOG "asks" how sure Wrd_0 is about the statement made and, if possible, a value in an appropriate credibility-scale is requested. F-DIALOG asks also a credibility-value regarding Wrd_0 (the semantic context).

1.1   Example 1

1. Suppose that one states that "the coordinates of point P are 235, 29, and 4"

   After clarification of this sentence by F-DIALOG one obtains:

   $Sent_A$: "the origin of the space is origin-0, 235, 29, and 4 correspond, in origin-0, to the second, third and first coordinates, respectively".

   After de-articulation of $Sent_A$, the following holonic sentences are obtained:

   $Sent_A \ Hol_1$ origin-0 4 is first-coordinate
   $Sent_A \ Hol_2$ origin-0 235 is second-coordinate
   $Sent_A \ Hol_3$ origin-0 29 is third-coordinate

2. Suppose that one states that "origin-0 is an origin for a 3 dimensional linear ortogonal space (3-D-Space) and all coordinates are given in meters".

The de-articulation of this sentence gives:

$Sent_B$ Hol_4 3-D-Space origin-0 is a-origin
$Sent_B$ Hol_5 origin-0 meter is 1-coordinate-unit
$Sent_B$ Hol_6 origin-0 meter is 2-coordinate-unit
$Sent_B$ Hol_7 origin-0 meter is 3-coordinate-unit

1.2 Example 2

$Sent_{J1}$ "John said that Peter is tall"
$Sent_{A4}$ "Don said that Peter is small"
$Sent_{Pl}$ "Anthropologist said that John is a pygmy"
$Sent_{Q3}$ "*Someone* said Don plays basketball"

Will be converted as follows:

$Sent_{J1}$ "John-point-of-view Peter is tall"
$Sent_{A4}$ "Don-point-of-view Peter is small"
$Sent_{Pl}$ "Antropologist-statement John is a pygmy"
$Sent_{Q3}$ "X? Don plays basketball

1.3 Example 3

$Sent_{X2}$ "Mary said if John is gambling then his spending is great"

Converts to:

$Sent_{X2}$ Hol_{24} Mary-statem. John is gambling
         80   0   0 0
$Sent_{X2}$ Hol_{25} Mary-statem. John-spend. is great
         80   0   0 0
$Sent_{X2}$ Hol_{26} Mary-statem. Hol_{24} implies Hol_{25}
         80   0   75 0

Obs.: "Mary" is highly credible (80). The implication (Hol_{26}) is judged by "Mary" as highly credible (75). But the credible-value of both Hol_{24} and Hol_{25} is not given by Mary in $Sent_{X2}$.

2 Repositories

All information, in holonic sentences is stored in the repository (REP) and all words employed are listed in the dictionary (DIC), both of them can increase and be revised indefinitely. Several types of sub-repositories can be extracted from REP, selecting in REP all the holonic sentences, HOLs, that possesse a given set of "words" in a given set of "places" in the HOL. The normal form of an holonic frase in REP is:

<Sent>   <Hol> <Word.C> <Word.D> <Word.V> <Word.R>

where:

- <Sent> is a reference to the original sentence;
- <Hol> is the symbol of the holonic sentence;
- <Word.C> is the semantic context;
- <Word.D> is an element of the domain of the "nexus";
- <Word.V> is the designation of the "nexus";
- <Word.R> is an element of the range of the "nexus".

There are four types of objects in a repository:

1. *Type REP-X*: There are 4 distinct cases, depending on the meaning of X (C, D, V, R):
   - REP-C: the semantic contexts <Word.C>;
   - REP-D: the domain elements <Word.D>;
   - REP-V: the verbs <Word.V>;
   - REP-R: the range elements <Word.R>.

2. *Type REP-X-Y*: There are 6 distinct cases: REP-C-D, REP-C-V, REP-C-R, REP-D-V, REP-D-R, REP-V-R. Note that REP-X-Y = REP-Y-X and REP-X-X are meaningless.

3. *Type REP-X-Y-Z*: REP-C-D-V, REP-C-D-R, REP-C-V-R, REP-D-V-R.

4. *Type REP-X-Y-Z-W*: There is at most one case that corresponds to a well defined HOL but this type of sub-repository may be an empty set.

Some sub-repositories are used often and should be "constructed" before the solution to a given problem begins, for example:

- REP-C (with C = C_1 ... C_n)

  This type is usefull in problems, where only the semantic contexts C_1 ... C_n are of interest. It may be more efficient to create, to start with, a sub-repository of the type REP-C.

- REP-C-V (with V = V_v and C = C_s, C_t)

  This type of sub-repository may be useful to study the verb V_v in the semantic contexts C_s and C_t.

- REP-C-V-R (with C = C_c, V = V_v and R = R_a ... R_q)

  To supply the set d_v (domain of V_v) with a topologic structure, this type of sub-repositories are well suited.

All these sub-repositories, may configurate a "list of addresses" of the holonic sentences stored in REP. The amount of memory used is much reduced but the access to REP is inderect.

3 Primitive and Derived Concepts

The primitive concepts in F-LING are the holonic sentences HOL and the words WORD, which are stored respectively in the repository and in the dictionary. Concepts like set, multiple, set element, etc. are derived concepts. A presentation of some typical derived concepts is appropriate:

1. *Sets.* All sub-repositories presented in Section 2 are subsets of REP, and REP is the "universal-set" of HOL. The empty set and REP are sets. The dictionary DIC is the "universal-set" of words (WORD) and there is a word "is-member-of" (a verb) from which a very important type of HOL can be created, namely

   $$Sent_f \ Hol_h \ D_x \ \text{is-a-member-of} \ C_c$$

   Building REP based on "D_x is-member-of C_c", all D_x retained constitute a set (eventualy an empty set) that is a subset of the dictionary DIC. The symbol for a set is "SET" and the above referenced set of words can be represented as

$$\text{SET } (C_c = \{D_z : D_n, ..., D_w\}$$
$$\text{or}$$
$$= \{D_z : Sent_f \ Hol_h \ D_z \text{ is-a-member-of } C_C\}$$

the first mode is a simple listing of words, the second is based on the operator "is-a-member-of" that enables the construction of the set.

2. *Relations.* A relation can be exhaustively represented by the set of all pairs (nexus between 2 words) that satisfy a certain verb V_v, (sub-repository of the type REP-V_v). The list may include nexus in various semantic-environments.

A problem arises when a relation REL has infinite nexus (see Section 5) and the exhaustive representation is not feasible. The strict-order-relation ($>=$) will be used as an example.

Let SET $= \{a, b, ..., n\}$ be a set and "$>=$" a verb. In REP there are the following holonic sentences:

H_{ab} b $>=$ a
H_{ac} c $>=$ a
......
H_{an} n $>=$ a
H_{bc} c $>=$ b
H_{bd} d $>=$ b
H_{bn} n $>=$ b
H_{mn} n $>=$ m

"Rules" are not explicitly declared.

3. *Multiples.* Let SET$>=$C be an ordered set of sets SET_z

$$\text{SET}>=\text{C} = \{SET_a ... SET_n\} >=]$$

We define MLT_z of SET$>=$C as any ordered set of elements of SET_z and x : $[\{a ... n\} >=]$. A multiple (MULT) is an element of the cartesean product of SET_z of SET$>=$C.

4. *Connectives.* The connective is the general designation of a class of relations used to introduce an algebraic structure in a set. In general a Cartesian product is formed between a set and another set and a relation is defined, as the Cartesian product being the domain and the set the range, for example, max, min, sup, inf, $+$, $*$, union, conjuction etc.

A very simple example, introducing the connective "max", follows: The given set is $\{0, 1\}$.

H_1 S-boole 0,0 is-an-ordered-pair-of Cart. Prod.
H_2 S-boole 0,1 is-an-ordered-pair-of Cart. Prod.
H_3 S-boole 1,0 is-an-ordered-pair-of Cart. Prod.
H_4 S-boole 1,1 is-an-ordered-pair-of Cart. Prod.
H_5 S-boole 0,0 Max 0
H_6 S-boole 0,1 Max 1
H_7 S-boole 1,0 Max 1
H_8 S-boole 1,1 Max 1

5. *Functional Relations.* The domain and or the range represent relations, for example:

   Functional: D=relation V=Funct. C=real
   Transform: D=relation V=Transf. C=relation
   Distribution: D=set V=Distr. C=relation

6. *Operators.* The standard form of a relation REL is a "table" of all the nexus which are members of REL (D-domain V-verb R-range). Another form of describing REL is by means of operators:

   direct: (OP-REL), OP-REL { D } >>> R
   converse: (OP-REL!), OP-REL { R } >>> D
   If these operators are given then the above referenced "table", is not needed. The inverse relations are usefull when introducing a topological structure in the domain set of REL.

4 Translation

The basic concept of HOL is described by an ordered set of four words (C D V R). The first element represents the semantic environment or context, the remaining triad (D V R) is a declaration. If the context or semantic environment C is substituted by c-, then the triad (D V R) is converted or "translated" into (d- v- r-), and conveys the same information:

$$(C\ D\ V\ R) == (c\ d\text{-}\ v\text{-}\ r\text{-})$$

A point P in a 2-D plane is spatialy described by two reals (coordinates of point P). Let P_0 be a point with coordinates 20 and 300. This information would be incomplete, without an explicit mention to the "origin" or referential used, for example,

H_1 S-originA 20 is-coordinate1-of P_0
H_2 S-originA 300 is-coordinate2-of P_0

Two types of translation are here presented:

- *Literal or word-to-word translation.*

  H_{11} S-originA translates-to S-originB
  H_{12} 20 translates-to 40
  H_{13} 300 translates-to 150

  H_1 and H_2 are "translated" as follows:

  H_{1-t} S-originB 40 is-coordinate1-of P
  H_{2-t} S-originB 150 is-coordinate2-of P

- *Semantic or sentence-to-sentence translation.*

  H_{s1} H_1 translates-to H_{1-t}
  H_{s2} H_2 translates-to H_{2-t}

In general, these two methods yield diferent results, but are equivalent, in formal languages. The inverse translation does not reproduce the initial holonic sentences, in general. Again the existence of an inverse operation in formal languages is important.

5   Infinite Sets (continuum)

Finite processors are unable to deal with the continuum and the usual method consists in the conversion of the continuum into a discrete form. A table of circular functions is a discrete image of the continuous functions it represents. The output of a program that computes a circular function is also discrete. The choice between using more memory or consuming more time in computation is a practical problem but not a conceptual one.

The "coarsenness" of a table can be reduced by interpolators. In the following, the method of obtaining a discrete image of the continuum will be considered adequate to the type of problem to be solved and this assumption is applicable both to tables and operators (hard or soft).

6 Credibility

Credibility is fundamental in F-LING. This is discussed in [Bourbaki 57]. Here we will just give a sumarised reference.

To a tetrad of words corresponds a tetrad of reals belonging to the set [-1, 1]. The absolute meassures the credibility are 0 (no crebility); 1 (total credibility). Negative numbers stand for "negation", for example, -1 means totaly false. A set of functions over the set of tetrads yields the credibility of the set.

7 Deduction and Induction

7.1 First example

- *Deduction.* The verb "is-maried-to" is declared as a symmetrical relation i.e. if (X is-maried-to Y) then (Y is-maried-to X) or from H_1 X is-maried-to Y we may infer H_2 Y is-maried-to X. Thus, the declaration: (A is-maried-to B) and the symmetry of the "is-maried-to" relation, permits to infer: (B is-maried-to A). This is a typical deduction, after it is completed, the total information in REP has not increased.

- *Induction.* A process of induction applied to the study of properties of the verb "is-maried-to" may be described by the following steps:

  1. *Data retrieval regarding "is-maried-to".* Find in REP, all the HOLs where "is-maried-to" is the verb. Suppose the following list, was obtained:
     A_1 is-maried-to B_6,
     A_2 is-maried-to B_5,
     A_4 is-maried-to B_3,
     B_5 is-maried-to A_2,
     B_7 is-maried-to A_3,
     B_3 is-maried-to A_4.

  2. *Looking for symmetries in list.* The program having the capability, and the initiative, to test various concepts, namely the symmetry of relations, produces a list of all pairs of symmetric HOLs contained in the previous list:
     ((A_2 is-maried-to B_5) and (B_5 is-maried-to A_2)),
     ((A_4 is-maried-to B_3) and (B_3 is-maried-to A_4)).

3. *Conjecture formation.* The 2 cases of symmetry observed and the lack of existence of counter-examples, may be considered enough to form the following conjecture: *"is-maried-to" is symmetric.*

4. *Testing the conjecture.* From now on, every new HOL containing "is-maried-to" as a verb will be tested for symmetry. If some new cases are detected and no counter-examples were found, then the conjecture is converted in a "finding" and "is-maried-to" is declared a symmetrical verb and a new rule is included in REP.

5. *Consolidation.* After step 4, the symmetry of "is-maried-to" is now a rule and this rule can be used in deductive processes whenever needed.

Eventualy, new findings may imply the revision of the rule. The development of the theme, inductive processes, follows.

7.2 Endowment of capabilities

All living things (agents) inherit and or aquire "capabilities" essencial to perform tasks. The construction of a computer language adapted to a certain species of agents must take in account these capabilities.

It would be senseless to provide the computer language with means to describe 3-dimensional objects, if the agents of the species we are trying to simulate are blind and deaf. But if a given species is endowed with the faculty of sensing the magnetic inclination, the language should provide concepts like: "up and down", "distance and velocity" and the necessary rules to process the information aquired and appropriate to an one-dimensional linear space, with the usual topology and the usual operators: order-relation, connectives $(+, *)$, scalar derivatives, etc.

Humans are endowed with so many innate capabilities and further developed by learning, that even a modern natural language and all formal languages so far developed are insufficient to adequately simulate a human being. The method usualy adopted is to provide a basic set of formal procedures and functions, for example,

- A finite set of characteres with a strict order relation and two connectives;

- A finite set of numbers and two not closed connectives $(+, *)$, a mimic of the integer numbers;

- A set of numbers, emulating imperfectly the reals;

- A set of pre-defined functions, on the reals;

- Input and output devices.

The basic set of procedures and rules can be increased, including other specialised functions and or structured sets. This final set (basic and specialised) represents the "inherited capabilities" of the artifact (processor) and emulates a certain "species" real or imagined.

7.3 Paradigms and Reconnoitre

Formal algebic and topological structures and concepts were developed mostly because they serve as models or paradigms. Natural and formal languages are essentially an antropomorphic artifact, adjusted to and inspired in the capabilities and atributes of the human species.

Paradigms can be confronted or compared with the atributes of the real or imaginary objects and beings. For example,

- counting == cardinal of set ; natural numbers;

- precedence (in a tribe or table) == order-relation;

- stereocopic vision == distance, proximity;

- cup to contain a liquid == concave (convex);

- straight line, vertical, horizontal == linear spaces;

- biologic clocks, sideral time == time.

The atributes of a paradigm are invariant and all theorems and inferences are also invariably valid. If an "object" conforms well with a paradigm then "all" atributes of the paradigm can be applied to the "object". The pair (paradigm, to-reconnoitre-it) represents a faculty, inherited or learned, by the artifact and the two are usefull only as a pair.

When we discussed induction, step 2, looking for symmetries, is only feasable if the processor is endowed with the pair (paradigm symmetry, procedure to reconnoitre symmetry).

7.4 Conjectures propounding

The artifact (processor), at each stage of evolution, possesses a set of pairs (Pairset), of the form:

$$(Paradigm, Reconnoitre procedure)$$
$$or$$
$$(P, RP)$$

In REP, there are holonic sentences that can be compared with a Paradigm (P_k) by means of a Reconnoitre procedure (RP_k), the result is given by an element of the range of (RP_k). Usualy the range (RP_k) is the set {Yes, No}, but other sets can be considered, for example, {Yes, Undecided, No}. Systhematicaly or randomly, the processor takes the iniciative to proceed with a reconnaissance of a pair (P_k, RP_k), belonging to the set (Pairset).

The successes and failures are remembered and a decision function (FC) is provided, to enable the processor to propound the paradigm P_k as a conjecture.

7.5 Conjectures testing

This is mainly designed to test the conjecture, giving time to confirm or refute the conjecture. A functor (FT) is provided to perform this function.

7.6 Another example

This example presents another aspect of induction and is based on simple generalization or exsention of the domain of application of a rule. Suppose that John sees a dog (B) bite Jack and declares:

$$H_{23} \text{ John dog (B) bites Jack.}$$

The functor (FCT) may suggest "rules", like: "dog (B) bites humans", or "all dogs bite Jack", or "all dogs bite all humans", etc.

The generalisation is a "risk avoider" posture, that has saved many human lives. The functor declares universally what as been observed once. Eventualy, later, the rule may be disproved so many times, that dogs have to be classified in bad and good dogs and the domain of the rule is reduced to bad dogs.

7.7 Concluding remarks

The final result of the induction is the proclamation of a "new rule" by the artifact (processor). This rule was not given by an external source, namely by the human operator.

A regular application of the inductive method, using all the pairs (P_k, RP_k) members of Srpr, will generate eventualy more "rules", following the introduction of new holonic sentences in the repository. If the repository is "frosen", that is no "new HOLs" are intruced in REP, then, after some time, the production of "new rules" stops.

Human progress is a long story of disproved conjectures: "The Earth is flat and is in the center of the world", "the space dimension is 3", "later 4", "now more then 4", "the atom is indivisible", etc. The statement "all rules are true" is acceptable, provided, the domain of the rule may be an empty set!

8 Conclusion

Humans do not create "ab nihil", the same applies to human artifacts and to F-LING in particular.

- F-LING starts with a Repository REP-0, a Diccionary DIC-0, a set of hardware capacities HW_0.

  In REP-0 are stored the initial holonic sentences (HOLs):

  - HOLs describing Pairset-0, a set of pairs (Paradigm, Reconnoitre-procedures)
  - HOLs describing rules (functions, procedures etc.).

  DIC-0 contains some initial words.

- The development of F-LING results of the contact with the "outside world", by means of the input/output devices. The information received, after interpretation, is stored in REP. By induction, new rules are created, increasing the available information. If needed, declarations not contained explicitly in REP can be deducted from the avaiable data, using the rules thar are in force. F-LING can also be developed by introducing in Pairset-0 new pairs (P-, RP-), that will increase the induction capacity of the processor and new rules will be uncovered.

9 Acknowledgements

I am gratefull to João P. Martins, Ernesto Morgado and Helder Coelho for their comments but the responsibility for all errors and misconceptions the paper may contain is mine.

10 References

Bourbaki N., *Actualites Scientifiques et Industrielles*, 1957.

Eytan M., "Fuzzy Sets: A Topos-Logical Point of View", *Fuzzy Sets and Systems, 5*, 47-67, 1981.

Portela A.G., Dialogos, *Inteligencia Artificial 0*, No.2, 1988.

Russell B., *Introduction to Mathematical Philosophy*, George Allen & Unwin, Ltd., 1930.

Zadeh L., "Fuzzy Sets", *Information and Control, 8*, 338 - 353, 1965.

Logical Foundations of
Nonmonotonic Truth Maintenance

Michael Reinfrank

ZFE F 2 INF 22

Siemens AG

8000 Munich 83, FRG

Abstract

Nonmonotonic truth maintenance systems and nonmonotonic logics have now been coexisting for more than a decade. I survey some recent results on the relationships between these two fields. I discuss what has been achieved so far and suggest some problems that demand further investigation.

1 Introduction and Overview

Nonmonotonic truth maintenance systems (TMSs) and nonmonotonic logics (NMLs) have now been coexisting for more than a decade. [Doyle, 1979] and the papers in [Bobrow, 1980] are commonly considered as *the* landmark publications in these areas, though some earlier publications and, in particular, technical reports are available. As early as 1980, McDermott and Doyle [1980] suggested that there is a close relationship between their NML I and Doyle's TMS, but they did not provide a systematic translation and corresponding equivalence results. Since then, considerable progress was made in both fields, but the relationship between nonmonotonic truth maintenance and logic remained obscure.

Meanwhile, some monotonic TMSs were developed, for which there is a characterization in terms of some incomplete, monotonic logic available. The two best-known systems of this kind are McAllester's TMS [1980], which performs unit clause resolution, and de Kleer's assumption-based TMS [de Kleer, 1986a], which is an instance of a more general "clause management system" [Reiter and de Kleer, 1988]. Another approach was taken by Martins and Shapiro [1988]. They first designed a new logic for belief revision and then implemented a novel TMS based on this logic.

Nevertheless, nonmonotonicity persists to be an important feature in truth maintenance, and several authors suggested using genuinely nonmonotonic TMSs [Goodwin, 1987; Petrie, 1987; Freitag and Reinfrank, 1988], or reintroducing nonmonotonicity into the essentially monotonic systems of McAllester or de Kleer [de Kleer, 1986b; Dressler, 1988; McDermott, 1989]. In each case, this was motivated by the need for nonmonotonicity to address particular application problems. So the study of the logical foundations of nonmonotonic truth maintenance remains as an important issue.

It was not until recently that one-to-one relationships between nonmonotonic TMSs and a descendant of Nonmonotonic Logic I, Konolige's version of Autoepistemic Logic (AEL) [Konolige, 1988a] have been established, [Fujiwara and Honiden, 1989; Elkan, 1989; Li and You, 1989; Reinfrank and Dressler, 1988; Reinfrank et al, 1989].

In the first part of this paper, we sketch these results from a technical perspective. Roughly speaking, a justification corresponds to an AEL-formula of the form $La \land \neg Lb \supset c$. Different versions of AEL-extensions then correspond to different restrictions on TMS-labelings. The main distinctive feature of these versions is the degree to which the belief states in consideration are *grounded*. Groundedness is identified as a crucial issue in truth maintenance, and we discuss how it can be reflected in the model theory. Using the semantical framework of preferential entailment [Shoham, 1987], we suggest that truth maintenance requires both the consideration of preferences between partial states and the application of an additional stability filter to models in order to guarantee groundedness.

Based on these results, nonmonotonic truth maintenance can be regarded as inference in some propositional NML, similar to the approaches used for monotonic systems. This yields a hitherto missing link between the two main subareas in nonmontonic reasoning and thus contributes to closing an important theory implementation gap.

In the second part of the paper, however, we argue that this is only a first, though important, step towards a complete logical characterization of truth maintenance. The networks a TMS works with evolve over time, and little is known about how one belief state should depend on its predecessor or even on the whole history preceding this state. Dependency-directed backtracking [Stallman and Sussman, 1977; Petrie, 1987] and incoherence handling [Morris, 1988] are related topics .Work on theory revision, e.g., in the sense of [Gaerdenfors, 1988], will certainly become relevant for TMSs.

In the long run, the real challenge will be to design reasonable principles that govern the *process* of evolving networks. Since these principles can hardly be domain independent, we will need more and better models of how to use TMSs to solve particular problems, e.g., in the spirit of GDE [de Kleer and Williams, 1987] and related logical theories [Reiter, 1987].

2 Truth Maintenance

2.1 Truth Maintenance Systems for Problem Solving

In the present paper, we consider nonmonotonic TMSs with explicit justifications. (There are other choices such as MBR [Martins and Shapiro, 1988] and McAllester's TMS, which automatically generate monotonic justifications from other information). Figure 1 shows the usual architecture and working cycle of a system based on such a TMS. The TMS maintains the problem solver's belief states in a network of justifications and nodes. The problem solver examines this network, makes some inferences, and then returns as a result a new conclusion along with a corresponding justification. The TMS integrates this justification in the network and updates the belief state.

Suppose that *closed(switch)* is a current belief and that the system has a rule such as **if *closed(switch)* unless *broken(bulb)* then *light*.** If there is no reason to believe *broken(bulb)*, the system will conclude *light* and tell the TMS that belief in *closed(switch)* and disbelief in *broken(bulb)* supports belief in *light*, by means of the justification shown in figure 2. Given a network of nodes, representing beliefs, and justifications, the TMS determines the set of nodes which can and should be believed given this information and marks the believed nodes as *IN* and the others as *OUT*. (Assumption-based TMSs work with a distinguished set of assumption nodes. They determine belief relative to assumption sets and label a node with those sets that provide sufficient support to believe it. Reinfrank and Dressler [1988] discuss transformations between assumption-based TMSs and others .)

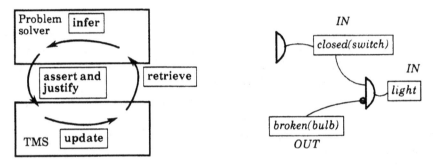

Figure 1 (left): Working cycle of a TMS-based system
Figure 2 (right): A justification for believing *light*

Note that *closed(switch)* is a premise, i.e., it has a justification without any supporting nodes and can be believed unconditionally. For any other node to be *IN*, a noncircular argument composed of valid justifications is required, where a justification is valid if all of its monotonic supporters, such as *closed(switch)*, are *IN* and none of its nonmonotonic supporters, such as *broken(bulb)*, is *IN*. It is important to note that a TMS only uses dependency information between beliefs but not the internal structure of the beliefs themselves, i.e., it is an inherently propositional system. A TMS mainly supports solutions to the following problems:

(1) Nonmonotonic inference: if, at some later time, *broken(bulb)* is inferred or, say, directly observed, the TMS can retract the conclusion *light* and selectively update all further conclusions depending on *light* by simple marker propagation.

(2) Caching: suppose that the switch is first opened and then closed again, i.e., the premise *closed(switch)* is retracted and reasserted. Its consequences then have to be computed only once and can be easily retrieved later. This is an important feature if exploring the consequences involves costly computations.

(3) Contradiction handling: if it is observed that $\neg light$, there is an obvious contradiction. The TMS then can identify the source of the contradiction and try to resolve it. Dependency-directed backtracking, e.g., creates a new justification for $broken(bulb)$.

For conceptual clarity, we consider contradiction handling to be located at an intermediate level between the problem solver and the basic TMS. Seen from the problem solver, there is a TMS which maintains contradiction-free belief states. Seen from the TMS, contradiction handling behaves like a problem solver: it examines in the network, performs some computations, and adds justifications.

2.2 Consistent and Well-founded Labelings

Formally, a dependency network consists of a set N of nodes and a set J of justifications of the form $<A|B{\rightarrow}c>$, where $A{\subseteq}N$ and $B{\subseteq}N$ are the monotonic and nonmonotonic supporters, respectively, for the conclusion $c{\in}N$. A TMS computes belief states, i.e., subsets $INS{\subseteq}N$ with the following properties (since such states are usually represented by IN/OUT-labelings, we call them simply labelings). Firstly, INS is said to be consistent if

$$\forall c{\in}N: \quad c{\in}INS \quad \Leftrightarrow \quad \exists <A|B{\rightarrow}c>{\in}J: A{\subseteq}INS \wedge B{\cap}INS=\varnothing$$

Consistent labelings still may contain nodes for circular reasons. $\{p\}$ is consistent given the justification $<\{p\}|\varnothing{\rightarrow}p>$. Therefore, INS is required to be well-founded in the following sense. For each $c{\in}INS$ there is a sequence of nodes $(c_1,c_2,...,c_n=c)$ such that:

- $\forall i: c_i{\in}INS$
- $\forall i \; \exists <A|B{\rightarrow}c_i>: A{\subseteq}\{c_1,c_2,...,c_{i-1}\} \wedge B{\cap}INS=\varnothing$

Drawing an analogy to logical proof theory, we can regard justifications as nonmonotonic rules of inference and require that every node $c{\in}INS$ has a non-circular proof, where the validity of the proof depends on INS itself, due to the nonmonotonic antecedents of the rules. In our example, $(closed(switch), light)$ is such a proof for $light$ in $INS=\{closed(switch), light\}$. So $\{closed(switch), light\}$ is consistent and well-founded using the justifications shown in figure 2.

This definition of well-foundedness is very strong. In particular, it is not reducible to minimal consistency, i.e., there are minimal consistent labelings which are not well-founded. The set of two justifications $<\{p\}|\varnothing{\rightarrow} p>$ and $<\varnothing|\{p\}{\rightarrow} q>$ only has $\{q\}$ as a consistent and well-founded labeling. $\{p\}$ is minimal consistent but not well-founded.

TMSs with a contradiction handling routine work with a distinguished node $False$. The TMS then is looking for consistent and well-founded labelings that mark $False\ OUT$. Since this is often not possible, it will create new justifications so that the resulting network has contradiction-free consistent and well-founded labelings. There are of course cases in which no additive changes can resolve all contradictions. The most simple example is $<\varnothing|\varnothing{\rightarrow} False>$.

3 Truth Maintenance and Logic

3.1 Motivation and Approach

Before summarizing some results on the relation between TMSs and NMLs, it is useful to consider some hypotheses and choices involved. To begin with, why should we care about such a relation? There are several important reasons. Firstly, truth maintenance and nonmonotonic logic are two main streams of the research into nonmonotonic reasoning in general, and to understand the relationships between different subareas is important to a field. Secondly, it is clear that any system based on some NML will need truth maintenance. It will be making assumptions that may later turn out to be wrong, due to further inferences or new information. Finally, many descriptions of TMSs are very informal. Bringing TMSs to bear on practical applications will require a better and more systematic understanding of truth maintenance. Hopefully, a logical analysis will contribute to such an understanding.

Being convinced that a relation between TMSs and NMLs is a worthwhile subject to be studied, there are several options on how to proceed. The approach taken in [Fujiwara and Honiden, 1989; Elkan, 1989; Li and You, 1989; Reinfrank and Dressler, 1988; Reinfrank et al, 1989] - and followed in this paper - is to accept TMSs as they are, however different they may seem to be from any logic, and to work bottom-up towards a "standard" NML. By standard NMLe we mean a member of one of the three main families Circumscription [McCarthy, 1986], Autoepistemic Logic [Moore, 1985], and Default Logic [Reiter, 1980].

There are of course other choices, some of which have been tried. To mention any two, Brown [Brown, 1988; Brown and Shoham, 1988] developed a new logic of "justified belief" to describe Doyle's TMS. Martins and Shapiro [1988] invented a new logic of belief revision and proceeded top-down to an implementation, which corresponds roughly to a variant of a monotonic assumption-based TMS without justifications.

Finally, we should realize that a translation from TMSs to NMLs will have to manage a couple of problems, including the following:

(1) Truth maintenance systems are inherently finite and hence logically incomplete, whatever the translation is.

(2) Justifications are asymmetric. $\{q\}$ is the only consistent and well-founded labeling for the single justification $<\emptyset|\{p\}\rightarrow q>$. There is nothing like a "justification contraposition", which would yield $\{p\}$ as a solution, p being justified by disbelief in q.

(3) Well-foundedness is an inherently global property. We have already discussed that it is, in particular, not reducible to minimal consistency.

(4) TMSs support so-called "brave reasoning" in the sense that there are networks with more than one consistent and well-founded labeling. A simple example is $<\emptyset|\{p\}\rightarrow q>$ together with $<\emptyset|\{q\}\rightarrow p>$, which has two labelings $INS_1 = \{p\}$ and $INS_2 = \{q\}$.

3.2 A Translation into Autoepistemic Logic

3.2.1 Choosing a Logic

The fourth problem above suggests that Circumscription is not a good target level for a translation, since it does not allow for multiple extensions. AEL does, and it is a logic designed to specify belief sets of an ideal reasoner. Furthermore, it is essentially equivalent to Default Logic [Konolige, 1988], so it is a promising candidate. Propositional AEL augments an ordinary propositional logic by a modal operator L, where Lp is interpreted as "p is believed". The meaning of the L-operator then is defined by fixed point equations, where an AEL-extension is a solution to such an equation. Let $\models$ be tautological entailment, and let A be a set of AEL-formulae. An AEL-extension of A is a set T such that

$$T = \{\rho | \, A \cup LT \cup \neg LT' \models \rho\}$$

LT here stands for $\{L\rho | \, \rho \in T\}$ and $\neg LT'$ for $\{\neg L\rho | \, \rho \notin T\}$. Conceptually, this fixed point equation describes a reconstruction procedure that takes a candiate extension T as input and tests if it is in fact an extension. Starting with a base set A, we can not know if it is safe to assume Lp or $\neg Lp$. Suppose however that we already know an extension T. We can then re-construct T by adopting assumptions such as Lp or $\neg Lp$ just in case of $p \in T$ or $p \notin T$, respectively, and by enumerating the consequences of $\models$, see figure 3. The fixed point equation then says that T is an extension if and only if the reconstruction succeeds.

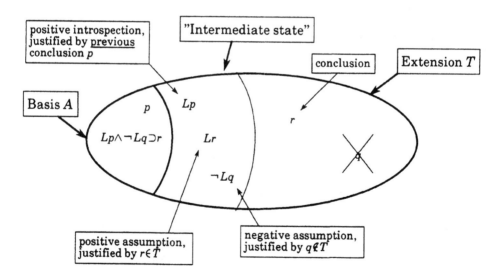

Figure 3: AEL extensions T are fixed points of reconstruction operators. Moderately grounded extensions only permit negative assumptions such as $\neg Lq$

Such extensions are only in a very weak sense grounded in A. An assumption Lp can be adopted and then be used to infer p, which in turn justifies the assumption "in retrospect". To see this, consider $A = \{Lp \supset p\}$. It has two AEL-extensions, one containing both p and Lp, and one containing $\neg Lp$ but neither p nor $\neg p$.

Other versions of AEL impose stronger groundedness conditions. Intuitively speaking, an AEL-extension is said to be moderately grounded if it uses only negative assumptions $\neg Lp$ when deriving conclusions. This restriction coincides with the requirement that the extension be minimal w.r.t. to the non-modal formulae it contains. As Konolige discusses in [Konolige, 1988], this still allows cases in which Lp may be inferred independently of p, and in which p is then concluded from Lp. As an example, take $A = \{Lp \supset p, \neg Lp \supset q\}$. Assuming $\neg Lq$, Lp follows using basic AEL-inferences and hence also p. I.e., moderate groundedness is not strong enough to formalize a strong notion of justified belief. Konolige therefore defines yet another fixed point equation. It relies on the formulae in A being in a particular normal form (this is a slightly modified version of Konolige's normal form which can be achieved by very simple rewriting):

$$L a_1 \wedge L a_2 \wedge ... \wedge L a_m \wedge \neg L\beta_1 \wedge \neg L\beta_2 \wedge ... \wedge \neg L\beta_n \supset \gamma$$

All of a_i, β_j, and γ here are nonmodal. Every AEL-formula can be transformed into this form. Now let T be an AEL-extension of A, and let A^* be the set of all formulae in A such that none of the β_j is in T. T is called strongly grounded if

$$T = \{\rho \mid A^* \cup LA^* \cup \neg LT_0' \vDash_{ss} \rho\}$$

T_0 here stands for the nonmodal formulae in T. The $\vDash_{ss}$-sign restricts the interpretations considered to some particular subset. For the technical details, see [Konolige, 1988]. The rationale behind this definition is that it guarantees that every conclusion is based on formulae whose modal parts, in particular the $\neg L\beta$'s, are still justified in the extension, and a belief $L\rho$ can only be inferred from ρ itself (and in fact is always, since $\rho/L\rho$ is a valid rule in AEL).

3.2.2 Choosing a Translation

From the previous discussion, strongly grounded AEL-extensions are a promising candidate for describing TMS labelings. The exact translation of justifications remains to be chosen. For the sake of simplicity, we consider only justifications with at most one monotonic and at most one nonmontonic supporter, such as $<\{p\}|\{q\} \to r>$.

The asymmetry of justifications requires the supporters to be on a different modal level than the conclusion. Otherwise, justifications would contrapose. I.e., using e.g. $Lp \wedge \neg Lq \supset Lr$, would permit backward conclusions about Lq from $\neg Lr$. The translation we use exploits the structural similarity between justifications and AEL normal forms:

$$<\{p\}|\{q\} \to r> \quad \Leftrightarrow \quad Lp \wedge \neg Lq \supset r \qquad\qquad (*)$$

Given their finiteness and logical incompleteness, TMSs of course do not label all formulae in a strongly grounded extension *IN*. They fail e.g. to make the logical deduction $p \lor q$ from p, and hence would label p and q *IN* if given $< \varnothing | \varnothing \rightarrow p >$ and $< \{p\} | \{p \lor q\} \rightarrow q >$. TMSs only work with atomic nodes and do not consider the internal structure of beliefs. I.e., we must restrict the AEL-sentences such that p, q, and r are propositional atoms. In this case, then, a TMS labels exactly the nonmodal atoms of a strongly grounded AEL-extension *IN*. AEL-extensions have the property that they contain a modal formula Lp if and only if they contain p. Identifying *IN* with L and *OUT* with $\neg L$, truth maintenance or, rather the labeling algorithms, perform inference in AEL.

The complete picture is the following. If J is a set of justifications and A a set of AEL-sentences, which stand in the relation (*), then there is a one-to-one corresponding between TMS labelings and (the nonmodal atoms contained in) AEL-extensions as follows:

Labelings	AEL-extensions
consistent	weakly grounded
minimal consistent	moderately grounded
well-founded consistent	strongly grounded

In principle, there are two ways to address the logical incompleteness of TMSs. One can base AEL on a weaker logic $\models^*$, or "compile" complex formulae into sets of justifications. A simple example is $Lp \lor Lq \supset r$ replaced by $Lp \supset r$ and $Lq \supset r$. Since this compilation does not provide a complete treatment of disjunction, both methods have to be combined.

Elkan [1989] proposes a different translation. He drops the modal operators in front of the monotonic supporters, i.e., he translates $< \{p\} | \{q\} \rightarrow r >$ into $p \land \neg Lq \supset r$. He shows that for the restricted, simple theories in consideration, the weakly grounded AEL-extensions of a set A of AEL formulae of the form $p \land \neg Lq \supset r$ coincide with the strongly grounded AEL-extensions of a set $A^{\#}$ which results from replacing every formula in A by $Lp \land \neg Lq \supset r$. I.e., the two translation schemata are in a sense equivalent, provided that we do not consider non-atomic nodes including disjunction or negation [Konolige, personal communication]. One can of course not replace $\neg Lq$ by $\neg q$ and still obtain the same results.

3.2.3 Backtracking

The discussion so far leaves one important problem unaddressed. Contradiction handling is a crucial TMS-feature for many applications. E.g., the conclusion *broken(bulb)* in our initial example is a diagnosis that explains the observation that there is no *light*. The method of "diagnosis by violation of expectation" is the basis of model-based diagnosis which is one of the most important contemporary applications of TMSs [de Kleer and Williams, 1987; Struss, 1989].

Thus far, the problem of a complete AEL characterization of dependency-directed backtracking (DDB) and other contradiction handling routines has not yet been solved. At least in principle, however, DDB is a justification-generating inference rule of the following form, with appropriate control restrictions:

from $\rho \land \neg L\beta \supset False$ infer $\rho \supset \beta$

where $\rho \equiv L\alpha_1 \land ... \land L\alpha_m \land \neg L\beta_1 ... \land \neg L\beta_n$, for some α and β. Note that $L\beta$ follows by mere propositional deduction, but is not grounded in the base set. This supports our view that DDB is located on top of a basic TMS.

4 Model Theory and "Groundedness"

4.1 Preferential Entailment

One benefit we expect from the translation is a logical semantics for truth maintenance. The equation for strongly grounded AEL-extensions provides a fixed point semantics. By semantics, however, we first of all mean model theory. AEL, at least the original version, has a model theory in terms of Kripke structures [Moore, 1984], and in terms of so-called autoepistemic interpretations [Konolige, 1988]. The now predominant approach to a model theory for NMLs is to define nonmontonic entailment as A entails p if p is true in all "best" models of A, according to some suitable preference relation [Shoham, 1987]. Exploiting the results on the relation between AEL and DL, we can adopt Etherington's semantics [Etherington, 1988].

Roughly speaking, a justification $Lp \land \neg Lq \supset r$ - Etherington of course talks about default rules - expresses a conditional preference for believing r rather than q, provided that p is already believed and $\neg q$ is consistent with what is believed. While we can talk about consistency in terms of one model, the condition that p be believed suggests considering preferences between sets of models. Let A be a set of justifications. Consider the set P of premises - in this case nonmodal atoms - contained in A. They define the hard constraints on our interpretations, so the preferences are between elements of $2^{Mod(P)}$, where $Mod(P)$ is the set of models of P. Let $\Phi, \Psi \in 2^{Mod(P)}$. Following Etherington, a single justification $Lp \land \neg Lq \supset r$ prefers Ψ to Φ if

(1) $\forall \phi \in \Phi: \phi \models p$
(2) $\exists \phi \in \Phi: \phi \models \neg q$
(3) $\Psi = \Phi \setminus \{\phi | \phi \models \neg r\}$

The preference relation induced by A then is the reflexive and transitive closure of the relations corresponding to the justifications contained in A. Maximality of model sets w.r.t. to this preference relation is however insufficient. Consider the two sets $\{Lp \supset p\}$ and $\{\neg Lp \supset p\}$. In both cases there is no premise involved. It is easy to see that $\{\phi | \phi \models p\}$ is a maximal element in $2^{Mod(\varnothing)}$ for both examples. A TMS would label p OUT in the first example, while the second example has no consistent and well-founded labeling at all.

Etherington proposes an additional stability condition for maximally preferred model sets. Let $\leq$ be the preference relation corresponding to a set of justifications A, where P are the premises contained in A. Let Ψ be $\leq$-maximal in $2^{Mod(P)}$. Ψ is said to be stable if

(1) $Mod(P) \leq \Psi$

(2) There exists a subset $A^* \subseteq A$ such that

    (2.1) Ψ is $\leq^*$-maximal, where $\leq^*$ is the preference given by A^*

    (2.2) $\forall\, Lp \wedge \neg Lq \supset r \in A^*\ \exists\psi \in \Psi\colon \psi \models \neg q$

Condition (1) guarantees that Ψ is in a sense grounded in $Mod(P)$, and (2) ensures that every single preference used in eventually preferring Ψ as a best model set is still tenable in Ψ.

Stability of best model sets is an additional filter that is needed to capture well-foundedness in the model theory. It is closely related to stable set semantics for logic programs with negation and, in fact, Elkan [1989] provides another equivalence result between TMSs and a particular class of logic programs with negation. This allows to inherit the results on stratified logics [Minker, 1988], which provides sufficient conditions for the existence of unique extensions.

4.2 Multivalued Logics

Preferences between sets of models come close to preferences between partial valuations. Sandewall [1987] suggests so-called semantic states, which map formulae of a logic to one of the four truth values *True*, *False*, *Unknown*, or *Contradiction*. A semantic state σ results from condensing a set Ψ of ordinary interpretations as follows. Let p be a formula, then

$$
\begin{aligned}
\sigma(p) \ &= \ True &\Leftrightarrow \forall\psi \in \Psi\colon \psi \models p\\
&= \ False &\Leftrightarrow \forall\psi \in \Psi\colon \psi \models \neg p\\
&= \ Unknown &\Leftrightarrow \exists\psi \in \Psi\colon \psi \models p \wedge \exists\psi \in \Psi\colon \psi \models \neg p\\
&= \ Contradiction &\Leftrightarrow \Psi = \varnothing
\end{aligned}
$$

It is easy to see than one can reformulate Etherington's semantics in terms of preferences between semantic states [Reinfrank, 1988]. Considering partial valuations that are not necessarily the condensation of a set of ordinary interpretations could possibly provide a technical tool to discuss the incompleteness of TMSs in the case of non-atomic nodes. Such a valuation then could, e.g., map p to *True* but $p \vee q$ to *Unknown*.

Przymusinski's [1989] recent results on the relations between "well-founded semantics" for logic programs and three-valued reformulations of some NMLs suggest that the issues of well-foundedness and multivalued or partial logics are closely connected to each other.

5 What Has Been Achieved?

After some 10 years of mere coexistence, the relationship between nonmonotonic TMSs and nonmonotonic logics has been put on a sound technical basis. This closes a major gap between theory and implementation in nonmonotonic reasoning.

From the perspective of TMSs, this allows a logical analysis of problems such as incoherence, i.e., nonexistence of any labeling, or the difference between negated assumptions [de Kleer, 1988] and OUT-assumptions [Dressler 1988]. The latter amounts to a proper distinction between p $\neg p$ and $\neg Lp$. Though this work is just being started, the expectation is that it will provide deeper insights into the nature of these problems, and that some wisdom from the field of NML can be inherited. E.g., some results on stratified logics can be directly imported into truth maintenance. Though backtracking is not yet completely understood, it can in principle be introduced as a new inference rule or as a theory transformation operator.

From the perspective of NML, the feedback gained through using NMLs to formalize real systems provides a testbed for the utility of NMLs and also suggests some new directions of research. E.g., well-foundedness is identified as an important issue to the whole field, and recent work on argument systems [Konolige, 1988b; Lin and Shoham, 1989] is partly inspired by similar ideas in truth maintenance. The formalization of inheritance systems is another major source behind this development. Actually, inheritance systems and TMSs share many common properties. Among others, they both started as purely procedural systems, with network-based conceptualizations and a very strong notion of a conclusion being grounded in the available information. Both fields contribute to a growing interest in multivalued logics [Ginsberg, 1988; Przymusinski, 1989].

6 Conclusions: Truth Maintenance as a Nonmonotonic Process

In spite of all the merits obtained or expected, much more work remains to be done than has been completed. The results presented in section 3 only address one aspect of truth maintenance. Given a fixed set of justifications, what nodes should the TMS label IN? Nothing is said about the relationship between a labelled network and the labeling of a new, extended network. There would be a simple answer to this question if labelings were unique, but they are not. Doyle [1983] suggests a principle of minimal change, i.e., choosing the labeling which is "closest" to the old one. Whether or not the symmetric set difference he proposes is a useful distance measure remains an open issue.

Related problems arise when a network is contradictory or incoherent. What changes should be made to the network? Should the changes be additive? Only little work has been done in this respect, see e.g. [Morris, 1988]. I suggest that work on theory revision

[Gaerdenfors and Makinson, 1988], [Rott, 1988], [Gaerdenfors, 1988] will become relevant for TMSs.

Considering the working cycle of a TMS-based problem solver, we see that a TMS works with networks that evolve over time. The translation into AEL specifies a correctness condition for the final results of an ideal TMS, assuming static information. The real challenge concerning the logical foundations of TMSs will be to come up with a set of reasonable principles that govern the process of reaching and managing reasonable conclusions in the context of a dynmaic information environment. From the TMSs perspective, this means deciding how to react in a principled way to a series of network modifications. This problem will be particularly hard if internal inferences interleave with network modifications. From the problem solvers perspective, this amounts to representing and using knowledge about when to introduce what assumptions, etc., to appropriately guide this process. This involves elaborate ways of formulating and executing "reasoned control of reasoning" [Goodwin, 1987], see also [Forbus and de Kleer, 1988; Dressler and Farquhar, 1989]. Since a substantial part of this knowledge will vary for different application domains, we need more and better models of how to use TMSs for particular application tasks.

Such models will require more than describing a TMS itself. We must consider the problem solver, too, and in particular the way in which it interacts with the TMS. Logical theories of this kind will be a much more demanding testbed for the utility of NMLs.

Acknowledgements

Some of the technical results presented in this paper were developed by different groups of researchers, independently of each other. In particular, Gerd Brewka, Oskar Dressler, Charles Elkan, Yasushi Fujiwara, Shinichi Honiden, Liwu Li, and Jia-Huai You have also worked on the relation between TMSs and AEL. Hartmut Freitag and Adam Farquhar commented on earlier drafts of this paper. I am also indebted to Peter Struss. His work on the application of TMSs to model-based diagnosis sharpened my views on the nature of truth maintenance, and his attitude towards logic is a constant source of motivation for investigating the logical foundations of truth maintenance and showing that it really pays off.

References

[Bobrow, 1980] Daniel G. Bobrow (ed.): Special Issue on Nonmonotonic Logic. *Artificial Intelligence 13*, pp. 1-172, 1980.

[Brown, 1988] Allen L. Brown, Jr.: Logics of Justified Belief. *Proceedings ECAI-88*, pp. 507-512, 1988.

[Brown and Shoham, 1988] Allen L. Brown, jr., and Yoav Shoham: New Results on Semantical Nonmonotonic Reasoning. *Proceedings of the 2nd Intl. Workshop on Non-Monotonic Reasoning.* Springer LNCS 346, pp.19-26, 1988.

[de Kleer, 1986a] Johan de Kleer: An Assumption-Based TMS. *Artificial Intelligence 28,* pp. 127-162, 1986.

[de Kleer, 1986b] Johan de Kleer: Extending the ATMS. *Artificial Intelligence 28,* pp. 163-196, 1986.

[de Kleer, 1988] Johan de Kleer: A General Labeling Algorithm for the ATMS. *Proceedings AAAI-88,* pp. 188-192, 1988.

[de Kleer and Williams, 1987] Johan de Kleer and Brian C. Williams: Diagnosing Multiple Faults. *Artificial Intelligence 32,* pp. 97-130, 1987.

[Doyle, 1979] Jon Doyle: A Truth Maintenance System. *Artificial Intelligence 12,* pp. 231-272, 1979.

[Doyle, 1983] Jon Doyle: Some Theories of Reasoned Assumptions. Tech report CMU-CS-83-125, 1983.

[Dressler, 1988] Oskar Dressler: An Extended Basic ATMS. *Proceedings of the 2nd Intl. Workshop on Non-Monotonic Reasoning.* Springer LNCS 346, pp.143-163, 1988.

[Dressler and Farquhar, 1989] Problem Solver Control over the ATMS. Siemens Report INF 2 ARM-13-89, 1989.

[Elkan, 1989] Charles Elkan: A Rational Reconstruction of Nonmonotonic TMSs. Submitted for publication.

[Etherington, 1988] David Etherington: *Reasoning with Incomplete Information.* Pitman 1988.

[Freitag and Reinfrank, 1988] Hartmut Freitag and Michael Reinfrank: A Nonmonotonic Deduction System Based on (A)TMS. *Proceedings ECAI-88,* pp. 601-606, 1988.

[Forbus and de Kleer, 1988] Kenneth D. Forbus and Johan de Kleer: Focusing the ATMS. *Proceedings AAAI-88,* pp. 193-198, 1988.

[Fujiwara and Honiden, 1989] Yasushi Fujiwara and Shinichi Honiden: Relating the TMS to Autoepistemic Logic. *Proceedings IJCAI-89,* this volume, 1989.

[Gaerdenfors, 1988] Peter Gaerdenfors: *Knowledge in Flux.* MIT Press, 1988.

[Gaerdenfors and Makinson, 1988] Peter Gaerdenfors and David Makinson: Revisions of Knowledge Systems Using Epistemic Entrenchment. *Proccedings 2nd Conf. on Theoretical Aspects of Reasoning about Knowledge.* Morgan Kaufmann, 1988.

[Ginsberg, 1988] Matthew L. Ginsberg: Multivalued Logics. Tech report, Stanford University, 1988 (abridged version to appear in *Computational Intelligence).*

[Goodwin, 1987] James W. Goodwin: A Theory and System for Non-Monotonic Reasoning. PhD Dissertation, University of Linköping.

[Konolige, 1988a] Kurt Konolige: On the Relation between Default and Autoepistemic Logic. *Artificial Intelligence 35,* pp. 343-382, 1988.

[Konolige, 1988b] Kurt Konolige: Defeasible Argumentation in Reasoning about Events. *Proccedings ISMIS-88,* pp. 380-390, 1988.

[Li and You, 1989] Liwu Li and Jia-Huai You: An Epistemic Analysis for the TMS. In submission.

[Lin and Shoham, 1989] Fangzen Lin and Yoav Shoham: Argument Systems, a Uniform Basis for Nonmonotonic Reasoning. *Proceedings of the 1st Intl. Conf. on Principles of Knowledge Representation and Reasoning.* To appear.

[Martins and Shapiro, 1988] Joao P. Martins and Stuart C. Shapiro: A Model for Belief Revision. *Artificial Intelligence 35,* pp. 25-80, 1988.

[McAllester, 1980] David McAllester: An Outlook on Truth Maintenance. MIT AI-Lab Memo 551.

[McCarthy, 1986] John McCarthy: Applications of Circumscription to Formalizing Commonsense Knowledge. *Artificial Intelligence 28*, pp. 89-116. 1986.

[McDermott and Doyle, 1980] Drew McDermott and Jon Doyle: Non-Monotonic Logic I. *Artificial Intelligence 13*, pp. 41-72, 1980.

[McDermott, 1989] Drew V. McDermott: A General Framework for Reason Maintenance. Tech Report YALEU/CSD/RR 691, Yale Unisevrsity, 1989.

[Minker, 1988] Jack Minker (ed.): *Foundations of Deductive Databases and Logic Programming*. (Part I: Negation and Stratification). Morgan Kaufmann, 1988.

[Moore, 1984] Robert C. Moore: Possible-World Semantics for Autoepistemic Logic. Tech Report 337, SRI, 1984.

[Moore, 1985] Robert Moore: Semantical Considerations on Non-Monotonic Logic. *Artificial Intelligence 25*, pp. 75-94, 1985.

[Morris, 1988] Paul H. Morris: Autoepistemic Stable Closures and Contradiction Resolution. *Proceedings of the 2nd Intl. Workshop on Non-Monotonic Reasoning*. Springer LNCS 346, pp. 60-73, 1988.

[Petrie, 1987] Charles J. Petrie, jr.:Revised Dependency-Directed Backtracking for Default Reasoning. *Proceedings AAAI-87*, pp. 167-172, 1987.

[Przymusinski, 1989] Teoder C. Przymusinksi: Three-Valued Formalizations of Nonmonotonic Resaoning and Logic Programming. *Proceedings of the 1st Intl. Conf. on Principles of Knowledge Representation and Reasoning*. To appear.

[Reinfrank, 1988] Michael Reinfrank: Defaults as Preferences between Partial Wolrds, Preliminary Report. *Proceedings European Workshop on Logical Methods in AI*, Univ. Paris VI, 1988.

[Reinfrank and Dressler, 1988] Michael Reinfrank and Oskar Dressler: On the Relation between Truth Maintenance and Nonmonotonic Logics. Siemens Report INF 2 ARM-11-88, 1988.

[Reinfrank et al, 1989] Michael Reinfrank, Oskar Dressler, and Gerd Brewka: On the Relation between Truth Maintenance and Autoepistemic Logic. *Proceedings IJCAI-89, to appear*.

[Reiter, 1980] Raymund Reiter: A Logic for Default Reasoning. *Artificial Intelligence 13*, pp. 81-132, 1980.

[Reiter, 1987] Raymond Reiter: A Theory of Diagnosis from First Principles. *Artificial Intelligence 32*, 1987.

[Reiter and de Kleer, 1988] Raymund Reiter and Johan de Kleer: Foundations of Assumption-Based Truth Maintenance. *Proceedings AAAI-87*, pp. 183-188, 1988.

[Rott, 1989] Hans Rott: Two Methods of Constructing Contractions and Revisions of Knowledge Systems. In submission.

[Sandewall, 1987] Erik Sandewall: Semantic States and Non-Truth-Functional Logic. Tech report, Linkoeping University, 1987.

[Stallman and Sussman, 1977] Richaerd Stallman and Gerald Sussman: Forward Reasoning and Dependency-Directed Backtracking in a System for Computer-Aided Circuit Analysis. *Artificial Intelligence 9*, pp. 135-196, 1977.

[Struss, 1989] Peter Struss: Diagnosis as a Nonmonotonic Process. *Proceedings Workshop on Model-Based Diagnosis, Paris 1989*. To appear.

The CASSIE Projects:
An Approach to Natural Language
Competence*

Stuart C. Shapiro
Department of Computer Science
State University of New York at Buffalo
226 Bell Hall
Buffalo, NY 14260-7022
U. S. A.
(716) 636-3182
shapiro@cs.buffalo.edu

1   Introduction

For a number of years, the SNePS Research Group at the State University of New York at
Buffalo has been pursuing research on Knowledge Representation, Reasoning, and Natural
Language Competence[1] (NLC). Although a number of projects have been pursued, they
have shared a common view of Intelligent Systems and of NLC. In this paper, I will
present an overview of our approach to NLC, illustrated by some of the dialogues we have
had with our systems. The group members whose work I will discuss include: William J.
Rapaport, Janyce Wiebe, Sandra L. Peters, Naicong Li, Soon Ae Chun, and Syed Ali.

Our approach to the general goal of Artificial Intelligence (AI) research (which we take
to be the computational understanding of the processes needed to produce human-level
general intelligence) has been to pursue general NLC and the knowledge representation
and reasoning techniques needed to support it. We have been impressed by the amount
of knowledge and general competence people gain through instruction carried out in their

---

*This work was supported in part by the National Science Foundation under Grant IRI-8610517, and
in part by the Air Force Systems Command, Rome Air Development Center, Griffiss Air Force Base, New
York 13441-5700, and the Air Force Office of Scientific Research, Bolling AFB DC 20332 under Contract
No. F30602-85-C-0008, which supports the Northeast Artificial Intelligence Consortium (NAIC).

[1] William J. Rapaport has suggested this term as a cover term for Natural Language Understanding
and Generation, and I will use it in this paper.

native language and through reading. As a result, our approach to building intelligent systems has not been to figure out how to program a computer, in a programming language such as Lisp or Prolog, to perform some task or solve some problem in an intelligent way (other than the problem/task of general NLC or general reasoning), but rather how to produce a system that a person could instruct in NL how to perform the task or solve the problem. This is not to say that we feel that other approaches to AI are invalid, just that this is the approach we have decided to take.

Our work proceeds both theoretically and by building experimental NL interacting systems. These systems are all built on SNePS [19] as the knowledge representation system, SNIP [3, 6, 22] as the reasoning system, and a Generalized Augmented Transition Network (GATN) grammar [20] to specify the NL understanding and generation. As a result of the experiments and our developing theories, these underlying systems (which are implemented in Common Lisp) gradually change. To focus our thinking and our discussions, we have invented CASSIE, the Cognitive Agent of the SNePS System—an Intelligent Entity. CASSIE is the computational cognitive agent we interact with when we are interacting with one of these experimental NL systems. In a given system, a particular GATN parsing/generation grammar specifies the SNePS arc labels and other representational constructs, that, in turn, represent CASSIE's beliefs (see [23] for more details). Since at any given time there are several group members working on different research issues, we tend to have several slightly different CASSIEs existing at once. That is why the title of this paper is "The CASSIE Projects," plural. Nevertheless, they are united by common underlying systems, philosophy, and architecture.

2   The CASSIE Architecture

The CASSIE system architecture is shown in Figure 1. Boxes show subsystems; circles show data structures; arrows show data flow. The human interlocutor types input to the GATN grammar, which, using the morphological analyzer and the lexicon to analyze words, parses the input and builds or accesses the belief structures stored in the SNePS semantic network, using SNePS commands and, where needed, SNIP. Responses to the human are formulated by the generation part of the GATN grammar using SNePS commands and, where needed, SNIP, to access information, and the morphological synthesizer

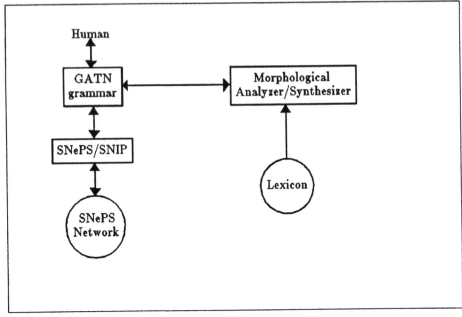

Figure 1: The CASSIE system architecture.

and the lexicon to formulate words.

Figure 2 is another view of the CASSIE architecture, focussing on a single interaction. An English statement or question is input; the GATN parser analyzes it in light of the current set of beliefs stored in SNePS; this may result in changes to the set of beliefs; and the SNePS structure that represents the main proposition of the statement or the answer to the question is given to the GATN generator, which outputs an English statement. Several points of this description are worth noting: although CASSIE produces an output sentence for each input sentence, and the GATN grammar has "sentence" as the highest-level syntactic structure, CASSIE is a discourse processor rather than a single-sentence processor, because each sentence is analyzed with respect to the belief structure built by previous sentences. The generator receives a proposition and uses the stored beliefs to help formulate the output sentence, especially to construct noun phrases. There is, as yet, minimal use of discourse or rhetorical structures in the planning and construction of output. These points will be illustrated further in the example interactions presented below.

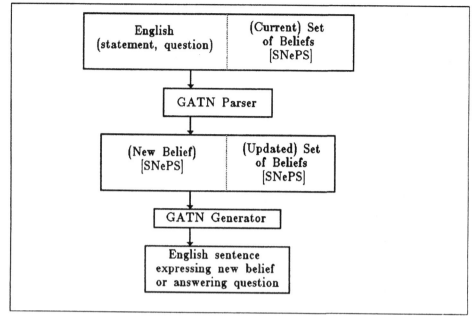

Figure 2: Processing of a CASSIE interaction.

3 Conversations with CASSIE

3.1 Basic Referring Exercises

The conversation of Figure 3 shows a basic interaction with CASSIE. The ":" character is CASSIE's prompt. The sentence after the prompt is input to CASSIE, and the following sentence is CASSIE's output. The number preceding the prompt has been added for this paper so we can refer to the interactions. This conversation is more fully discussed in [23], where the SNePS networks built as a result are also shown. SNePS networks will not be shown in this paper.

Before this conversation begins, the only thing in the SNePS network is a node representing the "current" time, indexed by the variable NOW, which is accessible to the GATN grammar. All words used in the conversation must already be in the lexicon, which includes the lexical categories noun, proper noun, pronoun, verb, auxiliary verb, adjective, determiner, and preposition. A lexical entry may have more than one lexical category—it will be disambiguated by the grammar. In particular, "pet" is stored as both a noun and a verb. The morphological analyzer determines that "petted" is the past tense of "pet".

As a result of analyzing sentence (1), CASSIE builds into the SNePS network structures representing the propositions: Act(b1, pet, b2, t1, t2), Before(t1, t2),

```
1: Young Lucy petted a yellow dog.
 I understand that young Lucy petted a yellow dog

2: What is yellow?
 a dog is yellow

3: Dogs are animals.
 I understand that dogs are animals

4: Who petted an animal?
 young Lucy petted a yellow dog

5: Lucy is sweet.
 I understand that young Lucy is sweet

6: Lucy is a girl.
 I understand that sweet young Lucy is a girl

7: Girls are people.
 I understand that girls are people

8: What was petted by a person?
 a yellow dog was petted by sweet young Lucy

9: The dog is named Rover.
 I understand that Rover is a yellow dog

10: What was petted by a person?
 yellow Rover was petted by sweet young Lucy
```

Figure 3: Conversation showing reference to previously introduced entities.

Before(t2, NOW), Property(b1, young), Name(b1, Lucy), Property(b2, yellow), Member(b2, dog).[2] The proposition Act(b1, pet, b2, t1, t2) is passed to the generation part of the grammar as the main proposition of the input statement. The grammar outputs the canned phrase "I understand that" at the beginning of the response to every statement, then generates a statement that expresses the proposition it was given. Past tense is chosen for "pet" because the network contains the information that t2, the ending time of the event, is before NOW. The noun phrase generation sub-network retrieves

---

[2]Representations will be discussed in this paper only informally. These propositions may be read as : "b1 performs the act of petting on b2, starting at time t1, and ending at time t2;" "t1 is before t2;" "t2 is before NOW," " b1 is young;" b1 is named 'Lucy';" "b2 is yellow;" and b2 is a dog". See [23] for a formal presentation of the representations built as a result of this conversation.

all properties in the network that apply to the entity being described, and makes adjectives of them. It describes an entity by using its name if it has one; otherwise, it uses a class the entity is a member of. For a more detailed walk-through of a CASSIE grammar operating on a conversation very like that of Figure 3, see [20]. A shorter walk-through of sentence (1), explaining the SNePS network it results in is presented in [16].

Interaction (2) shows CASSIE using the beliefs built in interaction (1) to answer a question. CASSIE says "a dog" rather than "the dog", because we have not yet implemented a facility for the proper creation of definite noun phrases.

Statement (3) is recognized by CASSIE as being an instance of a "bare-plural be bare-plural" sentence, and therefore it is understood as expressing the proposition Subclass(dog, animal). We believe that classification hierarchies can also be learned by intelligent systems through NL interaction, so such information is not pre-stored, but is built into CASSIE's belief structures as a result of such input.

Interaction (4) shows CASSIE answering a question based on the information of statement (1) and the class hierarchy learned in interaction (3). In this interaction, "dog" is used instead of "animal", because b2 is directly connected to dog in the network, but only indirectly connected to animal. A project that gets CASSIE to make the same choice for a better reason is described in [12] and [13].

With input (5), CASSIE learns an additional property that applies to Lucy. Although we realize that more than one person can have a particular proper name, and the representation used for CASSIE's beliefs are capable of storing a name as the proper name of more than one individual, CASSIE currently assumes that only one individual has a particular proper name (except for the case of nested beliefs—see Section 3.5). Therefore, CASSIE takes "Lucy" in statement (5) to refer to b1, the Lucy of statement (1). According to the noun phrase rules mentioned above, CASSIE would now describe b1 as "sweet young Lucy," as she does in output (6). However, that would make output (5) be "I understand that sweet young Lucy is sweet." This points out the necessity of keeping track of the clause-level proposition when noun phrases within the clause are being generated, so that the information of the clause is not also incorporated into the phrase.

Inputs (6) and (7) add a small class hierarchy above b1, which is tested by question (8). The topic-comment structure of question (8) was reflected in the answer by using the same voice (active *vs.* passive) in the answer as was used in the question. (The lexicon explicitly lists "people" as the plural of "person".)

In analyzing input (9), CASSIE examines her beliefs for dogs, and, finding exactly one, takes "the dog" to refer to b2. We do not yet handle the case where there are multiple possible referents for a definite noun phrase. The case where there is no referent for a definite noun phrase is illustrated in Section 3.3. Input (9) results in a node representing the proposition Name(b2, Rover) being added to the SNePS network. The CASSIE grammar is written so that a Name(x, n) proposition is expressed by a sentence of the form "n is _____," where the blank is filled with a description of x that does not use the name n.

Interaction (10) demonstrates the noun phrase formation rule that prefers to use the name of an individual whenever one is available. Notice that outputs (1), (4), (8), and (10) were all generated from exactly the same SNePS node—the one representing the proposition, Act(b1, pet, b2, t1, t2). The differences in the surface forms were caused by: whether the sentence was generated as the response to a statement or the answer to a question; the voice of the question being answered; and the information in the SNePS network at the time the sentence was generated. (Thus demonstrating that CASSIE is a discourse processor.)

3.2 Pronouns

Figure 4 shows CASSIE resolving pronouns. Additional examples are in subsequent figures. The pronoun resolution strategy, designed and implemented by Naicong Li [5], depends on an ordered focus list, based on but different from Sidner's [24]. Each component of our focus list consists of: a SNePS node that represents the referent; the gender of the referent, as far as currently known (male, female, either, or neither), initialized from the lexicon; the number of the referent (singular or plural); a grammatical/semantic category (see below); and a weight. The grammatical/semantic category codes the previous occurrence of a mention of the referent in the discourse. In decreasing order of initial weight, these categories include: subject of an active clause; non-reflexive direct object; non-reflexive indirect object; agent of a passive clause; reflexive object; possessor in subject noun phrase; possessor in object noun phrase. The weight of a component starts out at the initial weight for the grammatical/semantic category of its first mention. It is

```
1: Bill is clever.
 I understand that Bill is clever.

2: He dislikes John.
 I understand that clever Bill dislikes John

3: He hates him.
 I understand that clever Bill hates John

4: Bill saw a professor.
 I understand that clever Bill saw a professor

5: She is smart.
 I understand that a professor is smart

6: She likes him.
 I understand that a smart professor likes clever Bill
```

Figure 4: Resolving pronouns

decreased as CASSIE reads subsequent sentences, and may be incremented at subsequent mentions. A component is removed from the focus list when its weight drops below a certain threshhold.

When a pronoun is encountered, its gender and number are compared with components of the focus list according to the syntactic case of the pronoun. If the pronoun is nominative, it is compared with all components in the focus list. If it is reflexive, it is compared only with the subject of the current clause. If it is accusative, it is compared with the components in the focus list except for the subject of the current clause. If it is possessive, it is compared with the components in the focus list plus those in the current clause. The matching component with the highest weight is chosen.

In sentence (3) of Figure 4, Bill is chosen as the referent of "he" because, as a past subject he had a higher weight than John, a past object. Then John is chosen as the referent of "him" because, as an accusitive pronoun, it cannot match the subject of the current clause.

The lexicon lists "professor" as either male or female, and "she" in sentence (5) cannot match Bill or John because they are male, so it matches the professor, whose component is then changed to female only. Thus, in sentence (6), "she" must match the professor, and "him" matches the higher weighted of Bill and John, which, by now, is Bill.

```
1: John petted a yellow cat.
 I understand that John petted a yellow cat

2: The cat is a manx.
 I understand that a yellow cat is a manx

3: What did John pet?
 John petted a yellow manx

4: The dog is a mammal.
 I understand that dogs are mammals

5: For every d if d is a dog
       then there is a b such that b is a boy and b owns d.
 I understand that for every d, if d is a dog
   then there exists a b such that b is a boy
 and
  b owns d

6: Young Lucy petted a yellow dog.
 I understand that young Lucy petted a yellow dog

7: The boy saw her.
 I understand that a boy saw young Lucy

8: The boy is named Bill.
 I understand that Bill is a boy

9: The dog is named Rover.
 I understand that Rover is a yellow dog

10: Who owns Rover?
  Bill owns yellow Rover
```

Figure 5: Interpretation of definite noun phrases depends on current beliefs.

3.3 Varying Analyses of Definite Noun Phrases

Figure 5, based on the work of Sandra L. Peters, shows CASSIE interpreting definite noun phrases differently depending on the state of her beliefs. Input statements (2), (4), and (7) each contain a definite noun phrase, and each is interpreted differently because of the state of CASSIE's beliefs. Inputs (8) and (9) also contain definite noun phrases, but these are handled the same way as that of input (2).

When CASSIE reads a definite noun phrase, such as "the cat," "the dog," or "the boy," she tries to retrieve an appropriate referent from memory. At input (2), this retrieval is successful, and "the cat" is taken to be the yellow cat from input (1) that John petted. At input (4), the retrieval is unsuccessful. Because of this, "the dog" is taken to be a generic reference, and the statement is interpreted as expressing the proposition Subclass(dog, mammal). The explanation of CASSIE's interpretation of statement (7) is a bit more involved, and depends on inputs (5) and (6).

Statement (5) expresses the rule that every dog is owned by a boy. We are currently working on more natural ways of expressing rules, but, as a temporary expedient, we have implemented parsing and generation grammars so that every rule that can be represented in SNePS can be expressed in a "formalized" English. It is a significant part of our approach to the general AI problem that we can use NL to give CASSIE rules that she can later use in reasoning.

Once CASSIE inputs statement (6), she has a dog "in mind," and the rule expressed by statement (5) implies that that dog is owned by a boy. When CASSIE tries to retrieve a referent for "the boy" in statement (7), backward inference activates the rule, which successfully fires, inferring a boy who owns the dog, and who is taken as the referent of "the boy." No special operation is needed for this. The same retrieval operation was performed to find a referent in inputs (2), (4), and (7). The difference is that in (2), an explicit referent (and no rule) was found, in (7) no explicit referent was found, but a rule was found that produced one, and in (4) neither an explicit referent nor a relevant rule was found.

Notice that inference is performed during the parse of the input, and that the interpretation of the sentence (whether specific or generic) can depend on the results of the inference.

Inputs (8) and (9) were given just to make interaction (10) more comprehensible to humans. Interaction (10) shows that CASSIE knows that the boy who saw Lucy is the owner of the dog Lucy petted. This information, the proposition that Bill owns Rover, was inferred during the analysis of sentence (7) (although CASSIE didn't know their names until sentences (8) and (9)); it only had to be retrieved to answer question (10).

```
1: John owns a cat.
 I understand that John owns a cat

2: He bought a canary.
 I understand that John bought a canary

3: The canary is named Tweety.
 I understand that Tweety is the canary

4: The cat stalks Tweety.
 I understand that the cat is stalking Tweety

5: His tail is swishing.
 I understand that the tail of the cat is swishing

6: His chirp alerted John.
 I understand that the chirp of Tweety alerted John

7: Lucy walked the dog.
 I understand that Lucy walked the dog.

8: The leash became tangled.
 I understand that the leash of the dog became tangled.
```

Figure 6: Implicitly introduced referents based on basic-level categories

3.4 Implicitly Introduced Referents

In the previous section, CASSIE reads a rule that every dog is owned by a boy, and uses this rule to infer the existence of a boy when a dog is mentioned. A more thorough treatment of implicitly introduced referents is reported in [14], from which Figure 6 is taken.

This figure is the only one in this paper that begins with a non-empty SNePS network. Instead, the network already has representations of basic-level categories, presumably acquired by children during perceptual interaction with members of the category. This information is represented as a large collection of SNePS default rules giving basic, general, default information about members of the category such as its normal parts, functional attributes, and thematic attributes. Because of the standard structure of these default rules, these parts and attributes can be retrieved from the node representing the basic-level category by following certain pre-specified paths in the SNePS network.

Whenever a basic-level category, or a member of a basic-level category is mentioned in CASSIE's inputs, the associated parts and attributes are placed in a secondary, potential focus list (secondary to the focus list used for pronoun resolution discussed in Section 3.2), along with the primary referent that activated them. If a subordinate-level category is encountered, the parts and attributes of its basic-level supercategory are used. We will say that a concept is *activated* when it is placed in the secondary focus list.

Whenever a definite noun phrase is encountered by CASSIE, the primary and secondary focus lists are searched before the general retrieval discussed in the previous section is carried out. If a match is found in the primary focus list, it is chosen as the referent of the definite noun phrase. If none is found there, but one is found in the secondary focus list, the definite noun phrase is taken to refer to a part or attribute of the basic-level referent stored with it in the secondary focus list.

When CASSIE reads "a cat" in sentence (1) of Figure 6, associated parts and attributes, including tail, are activated. When she reads "a canary" in sentence (2), the associated parts and attributes of bird, including chirp, are activated. Thus, "his tail" in sentence (5) is taken to be the tail of the cat, whereas "his chirp" in sentence (6) is taken to be the chirp of the canary.

Some concepts are activated by a combination of a basic-level category along with a particular context or event-type. The general parts and attributes of dogs are activated when CASSIE reads "dog" in sentence (7). Additional ones are activated by the event of walking the dog. These latter include leash, which enables "the leash" of sentence (8) to be recognized as the leash of the dog.

3.5 Nested Beliefs

Figure 7 shows a conversation with CASSIE involving nested beliefs. That is, at the end of the conversation, CASSIE has beliefs about other agents' beliefs. This conversation is based on work reported in [15, 17, 18], and [25].

Inputs (1), (2), and (3) introduce the characters sweet young Lucy and clever Bill. Sentence (4) is a report to CASSIE of a belief of John's. Interaction (5) makes it clear that CASSIE doesn't necessarily believe what she believes others to believe, while interaction (6) shows that she can answer "Who is *property?*" questions.

```
1: Young Lucy is a girl.
 I understand that young Lucy is a girl

2: She is sweet.
 I understand that young Lucy is sweet

3: Bill is clever.
 I understand that Bill is clever

4: John believes that Lucy is rich.
 I understand that John believes that Lucy is rich

5: Who is rich?
 I don't know

6: Who is sweet?
 young Lucy is sweet

7: John believes that Lucy is old.
 I understand that John believes that rich Lucy is old

8: Lucy believes of Bill that he is stupid.
 I understand that
    sweet young Lucy believes of clever Bill that he is stupid.

9: Lucy believes that she is rich.
 I understand that sweet young Lucy believes that she* is rich
```

Figure 7: A conversation involving nested beliefs.

Output (7) shows that when constructing a noun phrase within a nested belief, CASSIE mentions properties she believes the believer (John in this case) believes to hold of the entity being described.[3]

It may not be as clear from the interactions, but CASSIE actually takes the Lucy of statements (4) and (7) to be a different Lucy from the one she believes to be sweet and young. This is at least a possible reading of them, so we are distinguishing the syntax of sentences like (4) and (7) from that of (8), where CASSIE takes "Bill" to refer to the Bill she already believes to be clever. Notice that "Lucy" in sentences (8) and (9) are taken to refer to sweet young Lucy.

---

[3] It is at least arguable that output (7) is standardly read to pragmatically imply that CASSIE believes Lucy to be rich. This needs to be pursued further.

```
1: Bill is Lucy's brother.
   I understand that Bill is Lucy's brother

2: He is a professor.
   I understand that Bill is a professor

3: Mary is his favorite student.
   I understand that Mary is Bill's favorite student

4: Her dog is named Rover.
   I understand that Rover is Mary's dog

5: John dislikes her dog.
   I understand that John dislikes Rover

6: He said "her dog is ugly".
   I understand that John said " her dog is ugly ", meaning Rover is ugly

7: That John is narrowminded is Bill's favorite proposition.
   I understand that that John is narrowminded is Bill's favorite proposition

8: Mary believes Bill's favorite proposition.
   I understand that Mary believes of John that he is narrowminded
```

Figure 8: A conversation about a sentence and a proposition

The "she" of sentence (9) is interpreted by CASSIE to be a quasi-indicator (see [15]), referring to Lucy, herself. That is the significance of the "*" in output (9).

In SNePS, propositions are represented as reified entities, and can serve as terms in other propositions. In particular, a nested belief is represented as a proposition that some agent believes another proposition. Propositions can be nested in this way arbitrarily deeply. CASSIE can also believe propositions to have properties. This is illustrated further in the next section.

3.6   Discussing Sentences and Propositions

Figure 8 illustrates that CASSIE can discuss propositions in other ways than as nested beliefs. It also shows that CASSIE can discuss sentences, and that it is important to retain a distinction between propositions and sentences. Soon Ae Chun wrote the sections of the CASSIE grammar illustrated in this conversation.

Sentences (1)–(5) introduce the characters Bill, Mary, Rover, and John. In input (6), CASSIE is informed that John uttered a particular sentence, namely "**her dog is ugly.**" Just as people do, CASSIE recognizes the occurrence of a sentence being mentioned by the surrounding quote marks. The sentence is represented in SNePS as a sequential (cons-cell–like) structure of word nodes, as was described in [9]. A sentence for CASSIE is just another kind of entity, so there is nothing peculiar about believing that it is the object of an act (*i.e.*, John said it). However, CASSIE does more with sentences. After representing the sentence and the proposition that John said it, CASSIE analyzes the sentence as if it had just been uttered to her. The main proposition that CASSIE understands the sentence to be expressing is also stored in SNePS, along with the proposition that the sentence expresses that proposition. All this is then output, as illustrated in output (6).

Of course, it is incorrect, in general, to analyze a mentioned sentence as if it had just been used. It should be analyzed in the context in which it was actually used, if it was used at all. This requires further work. We have constructed CASSIE to do this in order to point out a direction for further research, and to illustrate the difference between beliefs about sentences and beliefs about propositions.

Inputs (7) and (8) state beliefs about a proposition, namely that John is narrowminded. Sentence (7) gives a property of the proposition—that it is Bill's favorite proposition. Sentence (8) asserts that Mary believes it, but refers to the proposition indirectly, by the property it was given in sentence (7). It was claimed in [1] that the interaction pair (7), (8) could not be carried out in SNePS in a semantically consistent way; however, this interaction shows that it can.

3.7 Acting Instructions

A general AI system should not only interact in NL, and reason, it should also perform actions. (Actually, NL generation and reasoning are forms of acting.) Therefore, following our philosophy, we should be able to use NL to instruct an AI system how to act. Figure 9 shows part of a session in which CASSIE is instructed about the rules for action in a blocks-world. These inputs are shown in paragraph form, without CASSIE's output, but the actual session was run like the other CASSIE sessions, with CASSIE outputting a sentence after each input sentence.

There is a table. The table is a support. Blocks are supports.

Before picking up a block the block must be clear. After picking up a block the block is not clear. If a block is on a support then after picking up the block the block is not on the support. If a block is on a support then after picking up the block the support is clear. After picking up a block the block is held.

Before putting a block on a support the block must be held. Before putting a block on a support the support must be clear. After putting a block on a support the block is not held. After putting a block on a support the block is clear. After putting a block on a support the block is on the support. After putting a block on another block the latter block is not clear.

A plan to achieve that a block is held is to pick up the block. A plan to achieve that a block is on a support is to put the block on the support. If a block is on a support then a plan to achieve that the support is clear is to pick up the block and then put the block on the table.

A plan to pile a block on another block on a third block is to put the third block on the table and then put the second block on the third block and then put the first block on the second block.

Figure 9: Blocks-world acting instructions.

After this instruction, CASSIE can be asked to perform various tasks in the blocks-world (which is simulated on a graphics screen). She uses these instructions to decide how to carry out the tasks, and to know what the state of the world is after each action.

The first paragraph of Figure 9 establishes the table, which is mentioned repeatedly in the instructions, and tells CASSIE what sorts of things are supports. The second paragraph gives effects and preconditions of picking up blocks. The third paragraph gives effects and preconditions of putting blocks on supports. The fourth paragraph gives some small plans, including one conditional plan. The last paragraph gives a longer plan for making a stack of three blocks. Notice that the plan is still sketchy—it must be filled in with clearing blocks, picking blocks, etc. from the preconditions of putting and the situation CASSIE finds herself in when she is asked to make a particular pile of three blocks.

Every sentence of Figure 9 except those in the first paragraph is interpreted as a rule to be stored in the SNePS network. These are examples of naturally expressed rules mentioned in Section 3.3. Notice that the variables of a rule are first introduced with an indefinite noun phrase that provides the restrictions on the variables. Later occurrences of a variable are in definite noun phrases, and may include discourse adjectives such as "latter" or "second."

More information on the project discussed in this section may be found in [4] and [21].

4   Beyond Text

Several CASSIE projects have moved beyond interacting solely in printed text, to graphics, gestures, and speech. James Geller [2] describes a system that combines NL text and graphics. A user can specify the graphical form of an object or a class of objects using a graphical editor, can relate properties of the object to modifications of the form, can design complicated objects by using NL to give the part hierarchy and by specifying the forms of each of the parts (or classes of parts) using the graphical editor, and can direct the system to display objects on the screen at varying levels of detail, and with asserted or with hypothetical properties.

Jeannette G. Neal and co-workers [7, 8, 10, 11] have developed CUBRICON, a multi-media/multi-modal interface that can accept NL speech, NL text, and pointing (with a mouse) as input, and uses NL speech, NL text, tables and forms (presented on a graphics screen), maps and icons (presented on a color graphics screen), and pointing (by blinking, highlighting, drawing arrows, etc.) for output. CUBRICON is based on the CASSIE architecture, underlying systems, and techniques, and on some of the representational techniques of Geller's, and incorporates much new material.

Geller's work and the CUBRICON project bring AI systems past the mere Natural Language Comprehension stage into what we might call Natural Communication, since they combine language with drawing and pointing gestures.

5 Conclusions

The CASSIE projects are united not only by shared computer systems and techniques, but by the philosophy that one powerful way to create intelligent systems is to create systems that can be instructed *via* natural language (and NL extended with graphics and gestures) what to believe, how to reason, and how to behave. All the versions of CASSIE analyze inputs with respect to stored beliefs that are modified by the inputs, and generate output based on current beliefs.

The dialogues illustrated and discussed in this paper should give the reader a feel for the CASSIE projects, and an idea of some of the NLC techniques we are using. More details may be found in the cited papers.

References

[1] J. A. Barnden. A viewpoint distinction in the representation of propositional attitudes. In *Proceedings of the Fifth National Conference on Artificial Intelligence*, pages 411–415, San Mateo, CA, 1986. Morgan Kaufmann.

[2] J. Geller. *A Knowledge Representation Theory for Natural Language Graphics*. PhD thesis, Department of Computer Science, SUNY at Buffalo, Buffalo, NY, 1988.

[3] R. G. Hull. A new design for SNIP the SNePS inference package. SNeRG Technical Note 14, Department of Computer Science, SUNY at Buffalo, 1986.

[4] D. Kumar, S. Ali, and S. C. Shapiro. Discussing, using and recognizing plans in SNePS preliminary report—SNACTor: An acting system. In P. V. S. Rao and P. Sadanandan, editors, *Modern Trends in Information Technology: Proceedings of the Seventh Biennial Convention of South East Asia Regional Computer Confederation*, pages 177–182. Tata McGraw-Hill, New Delhi, India, 1988.

[5] N. Li. Pronoun resolution in SNePS. SNeRG Technical Note 18, Department of Computer Science, SUNY at Buffalo, 1987.

[6] D. P. McKay and S. C. Shapiro. Using active connection graphs for reasoning with recursive rules. In *Proceedings of the Seventh International Joint Conference on Artificial Intelligence*, pages 368–374, San Mateo, CA, 1981. Morgan Kaufmann.

[7] J. G. Neal, K. E. Bettinger, J. S. Byoun, Z. Dobes, and C. Y. Thielman. An intelligent multi-media human-computer dialogue system. In *Proceedings of the Workshop on Space, Operations, Automation, and Robotics*, Dayton, OH, July 1988. USAF, NASA, and Wright State University.

[8] J. G. Neal, Z. Dobes, K. E. Bettinger, and J. S. Byoun. Multi-modal references in human-computer dialogue. In *Proceedings of the Seventh National Conference on Artificial Intelligence*, pages 819–823, San Mateo, CA, 1988. Morgan Kaufmann.

[9] J. G. Neal and S. C. Shapiro. Knowledge-based parsing. In L. Bolc, editor, *Natural Language Parsing Systems*, pages 49–92. Springer-Verlag, Berlin, 1987.

[10] J. G. Neal and S. C. Shapiro. Intelligent multi-media interface technology. In J. W. Sullivan and S. W. Tyler, editors, *Architectures for Intelligent Interfaces: Elements and Prototypes*. Addison-Wesley, 1989.

[11] J. G. Neal, C. Y. Thielman, D. J. Funke, and J. S. Byoun. Multi-modal output composition for human-computer dialogues. In *Proceedings of the 1989 AI Systems in Government Conference*, pages 250–257, Washington, D.C., March 1989.

[12] S. L. Peters and S. C. Shapiro. A representation for natural category systems. In *Proceedings of the Ninth Annual Conference of the Cognitive Science Society*, pages 379–390, Hillsdale, NJ, 1987. Lawrence Erlbaum Associates.

[13] S. L. Peters and S. C. Shapiro. A representation for natural category systems. In *Proceedings of the Tenth International Joint Conference on Artificial Intelligence*, pages 140–146, San Mateo, CA, 1987. Morgan Kaufmann.

[14] S. L. Peters, S. C. Shapiro, and W. J. Rapaport. Flexible natural language processing and Roschian category theory. In *Proceedings of the Tenth Annual Conference of the Cognitive Science Society*, pages 125–131, Hillsdale, NJ, 1988. Lawrence Erlbaum Associates.

[15] W. J. Rapaport. Logical foundations for belief representation. *Cognitive Science*, 10:371–422, 1986.

[16] W. J. Rapaport. Syntactic semantics: Foundations of computational natural-language understanding. In J. H. Fetzer, editor, *Aspects of Artificial Intelligence*, pages 81–131. Kluwer, Holland, 1988.

[17] W. J. Rapaport and S. C. Shapiro. Quasi-indexical reference in propositional semantic networks. In *Proceedings of Coling-84*, pages 65–70. The Association for Computational Linguistics, 1984.

[18] W. J. Rapaport, S. C. Shapiro, and J. M. Wiebe. Quasi-indicators, knowledge reports, and discourse. Technical Report 86–15, Department Of Computer Science, SUNY at Buffalo, 1986.

[19] S. C. Shapiro. The SNePS semantic network processing system. In N. V. Findler, editor, *Associative Networks: The Representation and Use of Knowledge by Computers*, pages 179–203. Academic Press, New York, 1979.

[20] S. C. Shapiro. Generalized augmented transition network grammars for generation from semantic networks. *The American Journal of Computational Linguistics*, 8(1):12–25, January—March 1982.

[21] S. C. Shapiro, D. Kumar, and S. Ali. A propositional network approach to plans and plan recognition. In *Proceedings of the 1988 Workshop on Plan Recognition*, San Mateo, CA, 1989. Morgan Kaufmann.

[22] S. C. Shapiro, J. Martins, and D. McKay. Bi-directional inference. In *Proceedings of the Fourth Annual Meeting of the Cognitive Science Society*, pages 90–93, Ann Arbor, MI, 1982.

[23] S. C. Shapiro and W. J. Rapaport. SNePS considered as a fully intensional propositional semantic network. In N. Cercone and G. McCalla, editors, *The Knowledge Frontier*, pages 263–315. Springer-Verlag, New York, 1987.

[24] C. L. Sidner. Focusing in the comprehension of definite anaphora. In M. Grady and R. C. Berwich, editors, *Computational Models of Discourse*. MIT Press, Cambridge, MA, 1983.

[25] J. M. Wiebe and W. J. Rapaport. Representing *de re* and *de dicto* belief reports in discourse and narrative. *Proceedings of the IEEE*, 74(10):1405–1413, October 1986.

Knowledge Acquisition by Teachable Systems

John F. Sowa
IBM Systems Research
500 Columbus Avenue
Thornwood, NY 10594

Abstract: Knowledge acquisition for expert systems is a time-consuming, error-prone task that depends on knowledge engineers who are highly sensitive to the nuances of language and logic. Teachable systems can automate much of the knowledge acquisition process by enabling experts to build a knowledge base through a dialog in natural language. This paper surveys three prototypes of teachable systems and compares them to the more traditional representations used in hand-coding large volumes of knowledge. It uses conceptual graphs to illustrate the knowledge representation issues and shows that the kinds of representations typically encoded by hand can also be generated through a dialog. A by-product of the dialog is a more precise set of specifications in a humanly readable form as well as better facilities for an expert system to generate automatic help and explanations.

Knowledge Acquisition

Fully automated knowledge acquisition is as difficult as unrestricted natural language understanding. The two problems, in fact, are different aspects of exactly the same problem: the task of building a formal model for some real world system on the basis of informal descriptions in ordinary language. Alan Perlis once made a remark that characterizes that difficulty: *You can't translate informal specifications into formal specifications by any formal algorithm.* Knowledge acquisition cannot be completely automated, at least not with the techniques known today or even with ones that might be developed before the end of this century. Yet research within the past decade has led to the promise of *teachable systems* that could make the task of knowledge acquisition easier and more systematic.

The ideal knowledge acquisition tool would be a computer that is easy to teach. It wouldn't have to understand everything that it was told. Instead, it would have to recognize when it did not understand something and be able ask a question that could lead to a better understanding. It might not discover new knowledge automatically, but it should build its knowledge base in a semi-automated way with the help of a tutor. Once it acquired knowledge in one form, it could translate it into other forms:

- Rules, frames, and type hierarchy for expert systems;
- Relations and integrity constraints for database systems;

- Object hierarchy and declarations for object-oriented systems.

Critics often complain that computers can't handle ambiguities. That complaint is not completely true. Natural language systems, in fact, are far superior to human beings in *detecting* ambiguities. But once they find an ambiguity, they are much worse at deciding what to do about it. With the help of a tutor, however, a teachable system would not have to decide everything by itself. It would not compete with a brilliant student who could learn almost anything by self-study. Instead, it would be like a plodding student who would need a lot of help and would continually ask seemingly "dumb" questions. But even such a system would make a major advance over current methods of knowledge engineering. Dumb questions are often the most penetrating ones that a knowledge engineer can ask to ferret out the fundamental, usually unstated assumptions.

A teachable system would acquire knowledge through dialog, which has always been one of the best ways of teaching people. Knowledge about an application would be entered in natural language, not in a computer-oriented jargon. But natural language should not be the only interface. For spatial information, graphics are far more efficient. For making a selection from a small number of options, menus are best. But a dialog is best for clarifying misunderstandings and for asking about ambiguities, contradictions, and missing information. After the dialog, the traditional AI notations of frames, rules, predicates, or graphs could be generated automatically by the computer, not by the human.

Examples of Teachable Systems

During the past decade, several prototypes of teachable systems have been implemented. The following three illustrate the techniques:

- Nanoklaus by Haas and Hendrix (1980, 1983);
- Unix Consultant by Wilensky et al. (1984, 1988);
- Kalipsos by Fargues et al. (1986).

A brief discussion of these three systems may clarify the issues and lead to a better understanding of how teachable systems should be designed.

Nanoklaus is a classic example of a system that is easy to teach. Most of the later developers cite it as one of their inspirations. As a result of a dialog, Nanoklaus builds up a type hierarchy of concepts, constraints on quantifiers and functional dependencies, and simple word definitions. Following is a dialog with Nanoklaus, annotated with comments about the knowledge it is acquiring:

```
Tutor:  What do you know about?

NK:     I know about physical objects, people, men, women,
        measures, and things.
```

These are the most general types in its hierarchy. To avoid a tedious dialog, the most common types should be available for all applications. The tutor now introduces LENGTH as a subtype of MEASURE and FOOT as a unit of length:

```
Tutor:   A length is a measure.

NK:      You're saying that anything that is a length is also
         a measure.
         OK.  Now I understand length.

Tutor:   A foot is a unit of length.

NK:      Foots are the first units of length you've defined.

Tutor:   The plural of foot is feet.

NK:      Feet.  Got it.  Thanks.
```

This dialog illustrates the *echo* where Nanoklaus repeats what it has learned in its own words. The echo lets the tutor know whether the input has been understood; if not, the tutor can immediately correct it. The details about plurals and parts of speech were necessary for Nanoklaus, but more recent systems usually include large dictionaries that make such detail unnecessary.

```
Tutor:   A meter is a unit of length.

NK:      How is it related to foot?

Tutor:   There are 3.3 feet in a meter.

NK:      Now I understand meter.
```

Whenever a new node is introduced in the type hierarchy, Nanoklaus always asks how the new type is related to any other subtypes of the same supertype. That is the kind of question that a human knowledge engineer should ask during an interview. To a large extent, a teachable system plays the role of a knowledge engineer. In the continuation of the dialog, Nanoklaus asks questions about constraints on quantifiers, functional dependencies, and set relations. Yet it asks those questions in a natural way that avoids computer jargon as far as possible:

```
Tutor:   A physical object has a length.

NK:      So physical objects have lengths.
         Must a physical object have exactly one length?

Tutor:   Yes
```

As a result of that question, Nanoklaus discovers the functional dependency from physical objects to lengths. In the continuation, it discovers that SHIP and PERSON are both subtypes of PHYSICAL-OBJECT, and it therefore asks how they might be related:

```
Tutor:   A ship is a physical object.

NK:      You're saying that anything that is a ship is also
         a physical object.
         Is person a proper subclass of ship?

Tutor:   No

NK:      Is person necessarily composed of entirely different
         members from ship?

Tutor:   Yes
```

NK: Do person and ship necessarily span the set of all physical objects.

Tutor: No

NK: OK. Now I understand ship.

Through such dialogs, Nanoklaus could build up a large part of the knowledge needed for database design or expert system design. Yet entering all knowledge through dialog could become tedious. There should be no need for the tutor to tell the system that *feet* is the plural of *foot*. To reduce the tedium, a teachable system should supplement the dialog with other sources of knowledge, including machine-readable dictionaries, predefined type hierarchies, and specification documents in ordinary language. The dialog is best suited to debugging and refining the knowledge base: checking for missing information, asking about inconsistencies, and explaining a line of reasoning.

The Unix Consultant (UC) is being developed as an intelligent help facility for teaching a Unix user about commands and their formats. It has two modes: a consultation mode where it explains Unix commands to a Unix user, and a teaching mode (UCT) where a Unix expert teaches new commands to UC. Following is an example where a user asks UC a question that it cannot answer:

User: How can I print a file?

UC: I'm sorry. I didn't understand what you said. Could you please rephrase that?

Since UC did not have that information, no rephrasing of the question would help to elicit the correct answer. Instead, a Unix expert can add that information through the UC teaching mode:

Tutor: There is a new command.

UCT: What is its name?

Tutor: lpr

UCT: What is it used for?

Tutor: It is used to print files.

UCT: Where does the output go?

Tutor: the lineprinter

UCT: You mean that typing 'lpr filename' will print the file on the lineprinter.

Tutor: Yes.

As in Nanoklaus, UCT responds with an echo that shows what it has learned. Given this new information, UC can now respond correctly to the Unix user:

User: How can I print a file?

UC: Use lpr. For example, to print the file named foo, type 'lpr foo'.

Originally, UC represented its knowledge in a frame-like form in a language called PEARL. But frames were not general enough to represent everything, and the UC teaching mode could not acquire all of the knowledge needed for specifying all Unix commands. UC now uses Kodiak, a more general network representation language. With Kodiak as the representation, the UC teaching mode can acquire more of the necessary knowledge about Unix through dialog. UCT is now an impressive example of a teachable system. Yet it is not powerful enough to serve as a general knowledge acquisition facility. Some of the limitations lie in the Kodiak language, which does not have a formal mapping to and from logic. For example, Kodiak cannot represent a quantified statement such as *All commands have names*. Any language that cannot express all of first-order logic has serious limitations for general knowledge representation.

Unlike Nanoklaus and UCT, Kalipsos was not designed to acquire all knowledge through dialog. Instead, it reads texts expressed in a natural language — in this case, French. As it reads a text, however, it may run into problems that it cannot resolve by itself:

- Missing word definitions,
- Insufficient background knowledge,
- Difficult linguistic constructions,
- Inconsistencies in the knowledge base.

Whenever it finds problems like these, Kalipsos asks a question. To reduce the total number of questions, Kalipsos starts with a vocabulary of 40,000 words, which is sufficient for the spelling, morphology, and parts of speech for all of the common words in French. By starting with a text, it is able to focus its questions on the topic and to use the dialog to build up a knowledge base specifically tailored to that subject. The result of the dialog is a disambiguated text mapped into conceptual graphs (Sowa 1984), which are general enough to represent all of logic. In addition to a disambiguated text, Kalipsos also acquires other information needed to understand the text, but not explicitly stated in it: extensions to the type hierarchy and canonical graphs that show implicit relationships (Sowa 1988).

Since Kalipsos is designed to handle unrestricted texts on any subject, it has a rich grammar with the ability to handle complex, nested constructions and context-sensitive dependencies on pronoun references (Berard-Dugourd et al. 1988, 1989). As an example, consider the sentence *Jean a mangé un steak au dîner* [Jean ate a steak at dinner]. That sentence has three masculine nouns, and the following possible continuations have three masculine pronouns, any of which could refer to any of the nouns:

```
Il l'a apprécié bien qu'il ait été dur.
Il l'a apprécié bien qu'il ait été lent.
Il l'a apprécié bien qu'il ait été long.
Il l'a apprécié bien qu'il ait été malade.
```

Kalipsos correctly resolves all of these pronouns. In the first sentence [He appreciated it even though it was tough], the verb *apprécier* requires a human subject, and the first *Il* must therefore refer to Jean. The second pronoun *l'* must refer to either the steak or the dinner; it cannot refer to Jean, since only the reflexive pronoun *se* could refer to the same individual as the subject. The pronoun *l'* probably refers to the same thing as the *il* in the second clause, which in this case must be the steak, since that is the most likely thing to be tough [dur]. Similarly, Kalipsos determines that *lent* [slow] refers to the dinner; *long* [long] most likely refers to the dinner; and *malade* [ill] must refer to Jean. Since some of these interpretations are likelihoods rather than absolute certainties, the system could respond with an echo that would allow the tutor to correct possible misunderstandings:

```
So Jean liked the steak even though it was tough.
```

As an example of a complex syntactic structure, the following sentence has four infinitives:

```
Jean pense pouvoir être capable de faire faire
son travail par Paul.
[Jean thinks to be able to be capable of causing to do
his work by Paul.]
```

For the sentence, Kalipsos correctly recognizes that *son* [his] refers back to Jean, that Jean is the subject of *pouvoir, être*, and the first *faire*, and that Paul is the subject of the second *faire*. The following sentence has three relative clauses:

```
Le Prix Goncourt est une institution qui comprend
un ensemble de jurés qui décernent chaque année
un prix sous forme d'argent à un auteur qui a publié
un roman remarquable.
```

In English, this sentence says "The Prix Goncourt is an institution that comprises a set of judges who each year award a prize in the form of money to an author who had published a remarkable novel." The Kalipsos dictionary contains the parts of speech and morphology for all the words in that sentence except for the name Goncourt. But to generate a conceptual graph, Kalipsos needs further semantic information about the type hierarchy and the canonical graphs, which specify constraints on the possible links between concepts and conceptual relations. Before Kalipsos can generate a conceptual graph, it must extend the type hierarchy for new words and add canonical graphs for the verb *décerner* [award] and the preposition *sous forme de* [in the form of]. To extend the type hierarchy, Kalipsos asks the tutor where new concepts should be placed. The following interchange defines ARGENT as a subtype of MATIERE:

```
K:       Quel est le type de concept associé à "argent"?
         [What is the concept type associated with "money"?]

Tutor:   matière
         [material]
```

For *sous forme de*, the tutor must specify the most general types of the two concepts that would be linked (e.g. *entité* and *matière*) and the conceptual relation that links them (e.g. MATR for material). Given that information, Kalipsos could associate the following canonical graph with *sous forme de*:

```
[ENTITE]→(MATR)→[MATIERE].
```

With this graph and the information about the type hierarchy, Kalipsos can interpret the phrase *prix sous forme d'argent*. For verbs, the canonical graph must specify the implicit relations and the expected concept types linked to them. For the verb *donner*

[give], the agent, patient, and recipient can be specified with the sentence *Le verbe donner a pour agent une personne, a pour récepteur une personne et a pour patient une entité* From this sentence, Kalipsos can construct the following canonical graph:

```
[DONNER]-
    (AGNT)→[PERSONNE]
    (RCPT)→[PERSONNE]
    (PTNT)→[ENTITE].
```

For the verb *décerner* [award], the tutor could say that it has the same pattern as *donner*.

Of the three teachable systems described in this section, Kalipsos has the largest grammar, and it is able to generate conceptual graphs, which form a complete system of logic. Yet many kinds of semantic problems still remain as research issues. Neither Kalipsos nor any other natural language processor will be able to translate unrestricted language into logic for a long, long time. Yet theses systems show that natural language processors today have the potential to simplify and improve the knowledge acquisition process. Such systems should be able to perform the following operations:

- Search for missing relationships and ask specific questions to elicit the information from the tutor.

- Rephrase and echo new information in order to confirm that the point was understood or to expose misunderstandings.

- Clarify and sharpen distinctions, especially those that involve quantifiers and constraints.

- Use machine-readable dictionaries and other reference sources in order to reduce the number of repetitive or tedious questions about "obvious" matters.

Each of these capabilities is implemented in one or more of the three systems discussed here. The result of processing specifications through these systems is not only a formal definition in a computer language, but a more complete and precise definition in the original natural language. In fact, even when the final specifications for a knowledge base are stated in natural language, they should not be written by a human. Instead, they should be generated automatically after a clarification and analysis dialog with a system like Nanoklaus, UCT, or Kalipsos.

As these examples illustrate, a teachable system does not directly translate language into logic. Instead, it begins by analyzing an informal statement that it does not fully understand. By means of a dialog, the tutor and the system jointly construct a formal specification that both can understand. Natural language is the medium of communication between the person and the machine. But as output, the system generates two equivalent specifications: one in natural language and the other in a formal language, suitable for compilation into other kinds of machine-processable forms. This approach eliminates the need to "prove" that some formal specification in logic is equivalent to some natural language statement. After the dialog, the original natural language specifications are no longer needed. The version stated in logic or other formal language should be considered the official specification, with more readable, natural language versions generated from it.

Knowledge Acquisition in Cyc

The Cyc project started by Doug Lenat at MCC is the most ambitious knowledge acquisition effort ever undertaken (Lenat et al. 1986, 1988). The name Cyc comes from the middle of the word *encyclopedia*, since his original goal was to encode knowledge from encyclopedia articles. The purpose was to provide a basic core of knowledge that other projects could use and adapt to build more specialized systems. Cyc is important to discuss here, since it represents the antithesis of a teachable system: instead of acquiring knowledge from natural language dialog, Lenat and his associates are entering it all by hand. They are using graphical tools and aids, but some person must encode each fact and formula in the knowledge base.

Knowledge in Cyc is encoded in two different, but related languages. The first is a frame language, and the second is a more general constraint language. The frames form a limited, but simple notation that is good for high-volume knowledge encoding. Following is a frame for a car owned by someone named Fred:

```
TheStructuredIndividualThatIsFredsCar
    instanceOf: Camaro
    allInstanceOf: Camaro, Chevy, AmericanCar,
        Automobile, Vehicle, Device,
        IndividualObject, Thing
    owner: Fred
    yearOfManufacture: 1988
    originalCostInUS$: 15000
    parts: FredsCarsSteeringWheel,
        FredsCarsLeftFrontTire,...
    setOfParts: TheSetOfPartsOfFredsCar
```

The first word *TheStructuredIndividualThatIsFredsCar* is the name of an entity. Its type is Camaro, and all its supertypes are listed on lines 3, 4, and 5 of the frame. The next three lines state its owner, year of manufacture, and original cost. Lines 9 and 10 list the names of the entities that are parts of the car, and the set of all parts has a separate name *TheSetOfPartsOfFredsCar*.

Frames can list simple information in a well-structured form. But Lenat himself admits that the frame language is unable to express many important logical relationships. Following are some of his examples of statements that cannot be expressed in Cyc's frames:

- Disjunctions: *Fred's middle name is either Bruce or Bertrand.*

- Negations: *Fred's middle name is not Bob.*

- Quantifications: *All of Fred's cars are expensive, and at least one of them is imported.*

- Relations with more than two arguments: *Fred received trains for Christmas in 1986.*

To supplement the frames, Cyc also has a constraint language, which is a version of predicate calculus written in a LISP-based notation. Following is a constraint statement for the sentence *All of Fred's friends who are artists live in the USA*:

```
(#%ForAll x
  (#%TheSetOf z
              (#%Fred #%friends)
              (#%allInstanceOf z #%Artist))
  (#%countryOfResidence x #%USA))
```

This statement places a constraint on the countryOfResidence slot of any frame for a person who happens to be both a friend of Fred's and an artist. It might be mapped into a quasi-English form like *For all x in the set of z in the set of Fred's friends where all instances of z are artists, the country of residence of x is USA.* But sentences like this, even though nominally English, are hardly more readable than the LISP notation. Neither the frame language nor the constraint language was designed to map smoothly to or from natural language. The lack of such a mapping would make them unsuitable as the primary knowledge representation for a teachable system. It would also make them hard to use for expert systems that would generate help and explanations in natural language.

Cyc is an important project that promises to contribute a great many interesting ideas to the AI literature. But hand-coding such a large amount of knowledge is expensive and risky. Much of it could become obsolete if there were changes to the type hierarchy, the underlying primitives, or the knowledge representation language. Instead of hand-coding the entire knowledge base, it would be better to build it up through a teachable system. There is now a natural language project at MCC that is starting to use the Cyc knowledge base for language understanding. But the timing seems wrong: the language project should have been started first so that the knowledge representation would have been designed for mapping to and from natural language. With the current Cyc formats, it would be difficult to design a teachable system that could express everything in the knowledge base in clear, unambiguous natural language.

Conceptual Graphs

Conceptual graphs are the primary representation used in Kalipsos. They are a version of semantic networks designed to meet two requirements: represent all of logic, including modal and higher-order forms; and support a direct mapping to and from natural languages. These criteria distinguish them from the Kodiak networks, which do not express all of logic, and from the Cyc languages, which were not designed for natural language semantics. As an example, Figure 1 shows a conceptual graph for the sentence *A cat chased a mouse.*

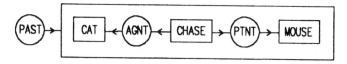

Figure 1. Conceptual graph for "A cat chased a mouse"

The boxes represent concepts, and the circles represent conceptual relations. The upper-case letters inside the boxes and circles are the labels of concept and relation types. For convenience, the box and circle graphs can also be written in a more compact linear form:

(PAST)→[[CAT]←(AGNT)←[CHASE]→(PTNT)→[MOUSE]].

The formula operator ϕ translates conceptual graphs into a formula in predicate calculus. In the corresponding formula, the concept types map into one-place predicates; the relation types map into predicates with as many arguments as there are arcs on the circle; and an existentially quantified variable is associated with each concept that does not have any other quantifier or constant as its referent.

past(($\exists$x)($\exists$y)($\exists$z)(cat(x) $\wedge$ chase(y) $\wedge$ mouse(z)
    $\wedge$ agnt(y,x) $\wedge$ ptnt(y,z))).

Note that this formula goes beyond first-order, since the *past* relation has a nested formula as its argument.

Since conceptual graphs are general enough to represent all of logic, they can also represent anything that may be written in Cyc frames or constraints. The mapping from frames to graphs is fairly direct. The slots in the frame become two-place relations, the constraints on the slots become type labels of concepts, and the values in the slots go into the referent field following the concept type label. The frame for Fred's car can be represented by the following graph:

```
[CAMARO: TheStructuredIndividualThatIsFredsCar]-
    (OWNR)→[PERSON: Fred]
    (WHEN-MANUFACTURED)→[YEAR: 1988]
    (ORIGINAL-COST)→[MONEY: @ $15,000 US]
    (PART)→[ENTITY: {FredsCarsSteeringWheel,
        FredsCarsLeftFrontTire, ...}]-
            (NAME)→[WORD: TheSetOfPartsOfFredsCar].
```

The first line has a concept of type CAMARO whose referent field contains the name TheStructuredIndividualThatIsFredsCar. The hyphen after that concept indicates that the relations attached to it are continued on subsequent lines. The @ symbol in the concept of type MONEY indicates that $15,000 is not the name of an individual instance of money, but a measure of some amount of money. The set of parts are enclosed in braces as the referent of a concept of type ENTITY, and the name of that set is a WORD with referent TheSetOfPartsOfFredsCar. The frame, but not the conceptual graph, also includes the branch of the type hierarchy. That could be shown in a separate statement:

```
CAMARO < CHEVY < AMERICANCAR < AUTOMOBILE
    < VEHICLE < DEVICE < INDIVIDUALOBJECT < THING.
```

Although both conceptual graphs and Cyc constraints can be mapped to predicate calculus, the mapping from Cyc to conceptual graphs is possible, but awkward. The reason for the awkwardness is that conceptual graphs are designed to map directly to natural language, but Cyc constraints are not. Therefore, the two languages have adopted rather different kinds of structures for representing similar information. Instead of mapping Cyc to conceptual graphs, it is easier to start with the original English. Following is a conceptual graph for the sentence *A friend of Fred's is an artist*:

```
[FRIEND: *x]←(POSS)←[PERSON: Fred]  [ARTIST: *x].
```

This graph says that a friend x possessed by person Fred is an artist. The variable *x shows a *coreference link* between the concept of type FRIEND and the concept of type ARTIST; it shows that the two concepts refer to the same individual. In the box and circle notation, variables are unnecessary, and the coreference link would be drawn as a dotted line connecting the two boxes.

In predicate calculus, quantifiers are bound to a variable, as in (∀x). The associated type for the variable x might be specified elsewhere in the formula or not at all. In English and other natural languages, variables are not needed, and the type is always associated with the quantifier, as in the phrase *every friend*. In the phrase *every friend of Fred's who is an artist*, the quantifier ranges over the subtype of friends who are possessed by Fred and who are also artists. In conceptual graphs, that subtype can be defined by starting with the previous conceptual graph and marking the concept [FRIEND] as a formal parameter. The Greek letter λ, which is the traditional notation for marking parameters, is used for that purpose:

```
(λx) [FRIEND: *x]←(POSS)←[PERSON: Fred]  [ARTIST: *x].
```

This λ-expression defines a type of friend of Fred's who is an artist. Since this expression defines a type, it may be inserted in a concept box in place of the type label. The following conceptual graph uses it to express the sentence *Every friend of Fred's who is an artist lives in the USA*:

```
[(λx) [FRIEND: *x]←(POSS)←[PERSON: Fred]  [ARTIST: *x]: ∀]-
    (STAT)→[LIVE]→(IN)→[COUNTRY: USA].
```

The operator φ transforms this graph into the following formula:

```
(∀x)((friend(x) ∧ person(Fred) ∧ artist(x) ∧ poss(Fred,x))
    ⊃ (∃y)(live(y) ∧ country(USA) ∧ stat(x,y) ∧ in(y,USA))).
```

The last graph expresses the singular *every*, but Lenat's original sentence used the plural *all*. In this case, the singular and the plural versions are logically equivalent, but the principle of keeping the graphs as close as possible to the original requires a separate notation for the plural. In conceptual graphs, plurals are represented by sets in the referent field. When the actual elements of the set are unknown, the generic set symbol {*} is used to represent them. Following are some examples of English noun phrases and their representation as concepts:

```
a friend          [FRIEND]
a friend Sam      [FRIEND: Sam]
the friend        [FRIEND: #]
every friend      [FRIEND: ∀]
some friends      [FRIEND: {*}]
five friends      [FRIEND: {*}@5]
all five friends  [FRIEND: {*}@5 ∀]
the friends       [FRIEND: {*}#]
all the friends   [FRIEND: {*}#∀]
```

With this notation, the sentence *All the friends of Fred's who are artists live in the USA* would be like the previous graph, but with {∗}#∀ in the referent field instead of ∀.

When two graphs are logically equivalent, each of them can be transformed into the other by means of rules of inference. One common transformation is to expand universal quantifiers into an if-then form. For example, the sentence *Every friend of Fred's who is an artist lives in the USA* is equivalent to the sentence *If a friend x of Fred's is an artist, then x lives in the USA*. The first sentence maps into the graph shown above. Then the rules for expanding the ∀ quantifier (Sowa 1984) allow the graph to be transformed into the following form:

```
IF      [FRIEND: *x]←(POSS)←[PERSON: Fred]  [ARTIST: *x]
THEN    [*x]→(STAT)→[LIVE]→(IN)→[COUNTRY: USA].
```

This expansion of ∀ quantifiers into an if-then form is useful for transforming statements expressed with quantifiers into expert system rules in an if-then form. The operator φ transforms it into the following formula, which is equivalent to the previous one:

```
~((∃x)(friend(x) ∧ person(Fred) ∧ artist(x) ∧ poss(Fred,x)
    ∧ ~(∃y)(live(y) ∧ country(USA) ∧ stat(x,y) ∧ in(y,USA)))).
```

Note that the conceptual graph "IF p THEN q" corresponds to $\sim(p \wedge \sim q)$ rather than $(p \supset q)$. The reason for this mapping is that the quantifiers in p must contain variables in q within their scope (Sowa 1984). It is closely related to Kamp's motivation for his choice of discourse representation structures (1981).

Defining High-Level Relations in Terms of Primitives

The slots in Cyc frames and the predicates in Cyc constraints tend to represent high-level relationships like yearOfManufacture or countryOfResidence. Most conceptual graphs, however, tend to use more primitive relations: AGNT (agent of some action); PTNT (patient or thing acted upon); RSLT (result); STAT (state); PART (have as part); PTIM (point in time); NAME (have name); POSS (have possession); IN (be located in). Both kinds of relations have advantages and disadvantages:

- High-level relations make the frames and constraints more concise by suppressing irrelevant detail, but they are harder to map to and from natural language.

- Low-level primitives map directly to the case relations and prepositions of natural languages, but they generate more nodes than necessary for a particular application.

High-level relations can be misleading since their names look meaningful to a human reader, but the computer knows nothing about their meaning. There is a fundamental principle of knowledge representation: *Whenever you see the word "of" buried inside a name, you know that somebody is sweeping something under the rug.* The word *of* usually links two words that are meaningful to a person (e.g. *country* and *residence*), but to the computer, the compound name appears to be a solid string with no associations to either country or residence. Sweeping details under the rug may be necessary to simplify the representation. But there should always be some way of recovering those details if they later become significant.

The definitional mechanisms of conceptual graphs provide a way of defining high-level relations in terms of more primitive ones. The definitions are like macros that can be expanded or contracted to show the details or to hide them. Even the primitives need not be ultimate atoms since it should always be possible to redefine them in terms of something even lower. A two-place relation like OWNR may be defined in terms of the concept OWN, which corresponds to the verb *own*:

```
OWNR = (λx,y)
    [ENTITY: *x]←(PTNT)←[OWN]←(STAT)←[PERSON: *y].
```

This graph says that the OWNR relation links an ENTITY x that is the patient of OWN to a PERSON y who is in the state of OWN. The COUNTRY-OF-RESIDENCE is another two-place relation, which may be defined in terms of the concept LIVE:

```
COUNTRY-OF-RESIDENCE = (λx,y)
    [PERSON: *x]→(STAT)→[LIVE]→(IN)→[COUNTRY: *y].
```

This definition links a PERSON x in the state of LIVE in a COUNTRY y.

Relations like WHEN-MANUFACTURED and ORIGINAL-COST involve an implicit point in time. At that time, there was a situation in which there was an act of manufacturing something. Situations occurring at points in time lead to conceptual graphs containing concepts with nested graphs in their referent fields. Following is the definition of the relation WHEN-MANUFACTURED:

```
WHEN-MANUFACTURED = (λx,y)
    [ENTITY: *x]
    [TIME: *y]←(PTIM)←[SITUATION:
        [MANUFACTURE]→(RSLT)→[*x] ].
```

This definition relates an ENTITY x to a TIME y, which is the point in time of a SITUATION, in which there existed a act of MANUFACTURE, which had a result x. Then the ORIGINAL-COST relation can be defined in terms of WHEN-MANUFACTURED:

```
ORIGINAL-COST = (λx,y)
    [ENTITY: *x]    [MONEY: @ *y]
    [*x]→(WHEN-MANUFACTURED)→[YEAR]←(PTIM)←[SITUATION:
        [*x]→(STAT)←[COST]→(PTNT)→[*y] ].
```

This definition relates an ENTITY x to an amount of MONEY y (where the symbol @ indicates amount rather than instance), and x is linked by WHEN-MANUFACTURED to a YEAR, which is the point in time of a SITUATION, in which x was in the state of COST with patient y. The rules for expanding λ-expressions (Sowa 1984) allow this definition to be expanded into more primitive relations:

```
ORIGINAL-COST = (λx,y)
   [ENTITY: *x]    [MONEY: @ *y]
   [YEAR]-
      (PTIM)←[SITUATION: [MANUFACTURE]→(RSLT)→[*x] ]
      (PTIM)←[SITUATION: [*x]→(STAT)←[COST]→(PTNT)→[*y] ].
```

This expanded definition relates the ENTITY x to an amount of MONEY y where there exists a year, which is the point in time of a SITUATION in which x is manufactured and the point in time of a SITUATION in which x cost y.

After these high-level relations have been defined, the conceptual graph for Fred's car can be expanded into a form that uses only primitive relations:

```
[CAMARO: TheStructuredIndividualThatIsFredsCar *x]-
      (PTNT)←[OWN]←(STAT)←[PERSON: Fred]
      (PART)→[ENTITY: {FredsCarsSteeringWheel,
         FredsCarsLeftFrontTire, ...}]-
            (NAME)→[WORD: TheSetOfPartsOfFredsCar];
[YEAR: 1988]-
      (PTIM)←[SITUATION: [MANUFACTURE]→(RSLT)→[*x] ]
      (PTIM)←[SITUATION: [*x]→(STAT)←[COST]-
            (PTNT)→[MONEY: @ $15,000 US] ].
```

Note that the original frame had a flat structure, but this graph contains nested structures. The nesting resulted from expanding the ORIGINAL-COST relation with its nested situations. High-level relations are a powerful mechanism for suppressing irrelevant detail. But that detail can often hide complexity that might have significant interactions with other entities in the domain. It is important to hide detail, but it is also important to recover it when needed. The λ-expressions provide a way of defining any relation in terms of an arbitrarily complex graph; all of that complexity, including highly nested structures, can be recovered when the definitions are expanded.

Cyc frames and constraints have no standard mapping into English, but conceptual graphs that contain only low-level relations do have a direct mapping into English. The expanded version of the frame can be translated line-for-line directly into English:

```
TheStructuredIndividualThatIsFredsCar is a Camaro;
it is owned by Fred;
it has as parts a set of entities consisting of
FredsCarsSteeringWheel, FredsCarsLeftFrontTire, ...;
and the set of parts is named TheSetOfPartsOfFredsCar.
In the year 1988, it was manufactured,
and it cost $15,000 US.
```

This kind of English is suitable for a specification document. It would also be suitable for a question answering system that could generate one or two lines at a time in order to answer a specific question. And for expert systems, the system could explain a line of reasoning by generating an English paraphrase from the sequence of rules and frames that were invoked. The ability to generate such explanations depends critically on the nature of the knowledge representation language. If it has a direct mapping to and from natural language, it can support teachable systems, and it can also support sophisticated explanations.

Building Expert Systems

This paper has concentrated on acquiring purely declarative knowledge. That is the kind of knowledge that the Cyc project has emphasized, that conceptual graphs can most easily represent, and that Nanoklaus, UCT, and Kalipsos can most easily acquire through dialog. But a practical expert system usually requires additional control information. The same declarative knowledge, when used for different purposes, may appear in very different forms in different expert systems. As an example, take the sentence *All the friends of Fred's who are artists live in the USA*, and consider how it might be represented for different purposes:

1. Answering questions about Fred's friends;

2. Verifying the accuracy of a database about friends and their professions;

3. Allocating and initializing a block of storage for a person who might be a friend of Fred's;

4. Predicting whether a particular individual might be a friend of Fred's;

5. Planning a party with compatible people.

With most expert systems shells, different kinds of rules would have to be written for each of these five uses. Each rule would contain a mixture of purely declarative knowledge about Fred and his friends together with procedural information about how to use that knowledge. Teachable systems can help to acquire the declarative knowledge, but practical expert systems will also require a considerable amount of procedural control. Application generators and specialized shells can provide the control for many routine applications. Techniques such as constraint logic programming may also help to reduce the dependence on procedural control. But the more complex systems will still require a lot of custom programming.

Acknowledgments

I would like to thank Jean Fargues and Norman Haas for their comments and suggestions on an earlier version of this paper. They have not had a chance to review the final version, and any errors or inaccuracies that remain are my own.

References

Berard-Dugourd, A., J. Fargues, & M-C. Landau (1988) "Natural language analysis using conceptual graphs," *Proc. International Computer Science Conference*, Hong Kong, 265-272.

Berard-Dugourd, A., J. Fargues, M-C. Landau, J. P. Rogala (1989) "Un système d'analyse de texte et de question/réponse basé sur les graphes conceptuels," in P. Degoulet, ed., *Informatique et gestion des unités de soins, Coll. Informatique et Santé*, vol. 1, Springer-Verlag.

Fargues, J., M-C. Landau, A. Duguord, & L. Catach (1986) "Conceptual graphs for semantics and knowledge processing," *IBM Journal of Research and Development* **30:1**, 70-79.

Guha, R. V., & D. Lenat (1988) "CycLing: Inferencing in Cyc," Technical Report ACA-AI-303-88, MCC, Austin.

Haas, N., & G. G. Hendrix (1980) "An approach to acquiring and applying knowledge," *Proc. of AAAI*, 235-239.

Haas, N., & G. G. Hendrix (1983) "Learning by being told," in R. S. Michalski, J. G. Carbonell, & T. M. Mitchell, eds., *Machine Learning*, Tioga Publishing Co., Palo Alto, 405-427.

Kamp, Hans (1981) "Events, discourse representations, and temporal references," *Langages* **64**, pp. 39-64.

Lenat, D., M. Prakash, M. Shepard (1986) "Cyc: Using common sense knowledge to overcome brittleness and knowledge acquisition bottlenecks," *AI Magazine* **6:4**, 65-85.

Lenat, D., & R. V. Guha (1988) "The world according to Cyc," Technical Report ACA-AI-300-88.

Sowa, J.F. (1984) *Conceptual Structures: Information Processing in Mind and Machine*, Addison-Wesley, Reading, MA.

Sowa, J.F. (1987) There's more to logic than the predicate calculus, talk presented at the U.S.-Japan AI Symposium, Tokyo, December 1987; paper to appear in a forthcoming volume edited by J. Carbonell and K. Fuchi.

Sowa, J.F. (1988) Using a lexicon of canonical graphs in a semantic interpreter, in M. Evens, ed., *Relational Models of the Lexicon*, Cambridge University Press, 113-137.

Sowa, J.F. (1989) Knowledge representation in databases, expert systems, and natural language, talk presented at the IFIP WG2.6 and WG8.1 Working Conference on the Role of Artificial Intelligence in Database and Information Systems, Guangzhou, China, July 1988; paper to appear in a volume edited by R. A. Meersman and C-H. Kung, North-Holland Publishing Co.

Sowa, J.F., & E. C. Way (1986) "Implementing a semantic interpreter using conceptual graphs," *IBM Journal of Research and Development* **30:1**, 57-69.

Wilensky, R., Y. Arens, & D. N. Chin (1984) "Talking to Unix in English," *Communications of the ACM* **27:6**.

Wilensky, R., D. N. Chin, M. Luria, J. Martin, J. Mayfield, & D. Wu (1988) "The Berkeley Unix Consultant Project," *Computational Linguistics* **14:4**, 35-84.

LIST OF CONTRIBUTORS

Joaquim Nunes Aparício, *Artificial Intelligence and Logical Programming Group, Universidade Nova de Lisboa, Lisbon, Portugal.*

Gerhard Barth, *DFKI, German Research Center for Artificial Intelligence, Kaiserslautern, West Germany.*

Pierre Berlandier, *INRIA, Sophia-Antipolis, Valbonne, France.*

Miguel Calejo, *Artificial Intelligence and Logical Programming Group, Universidade Nova de Lisboa, Lisbon, Portugal.*

Helder Coelho. *Laboratório Nacional de Engenharia Civil, Lisbon, Portugal.*

Maria R. Cravo, *Instituto Superior Técnico, Technical University of Lisbon, Lisbon, Portugal.*

John L. Cuadrado, *Computer and Software Engineering Division, Institute for Defense Analyses, Alexandria, VA, USA.*

Luís Damas, *Universidade do Porto, Porto, Portugal.*

Miguel Filgueiras, *Centro de Informática, Universidade do Porto, Porto, Portugal.*

Mireille Fornarino, *INRIA, Sophia-Antipolis, Valbonne, France.*

Dario Giuse, *The Robotics Institute, Carnegie Mellon University, Pittsburgh, PA, USA.*

Cheng-Seen Ho, *Department of Electronic Engineering, National Taiwan Institute of Technology, Taipei, Taiwan.*

Zhu Hong, *Computer Science Department, Nanjing University, Nanjing, P.R. China.*

Bassam Michel El-Khouri, *Department of Computer and Systems Sciences, University of Stockholm, Stockholm, Sweden.*

Harald Kjellin, *Department of Computer and Systems Sciences, University of Stockholm, Stockholm, Sweden.*

José Paulo Leal, *Centro de Informática da Universidade do Porto, Porto, Portugal.*

Jin Lingzi, *Computer Science Department, Nanjing University, Nanjing, P.R. China.*

Nuno J. Mamede, *Instituto Superior Técnico, Technical University of Lisbon, Lisbon, Portugal.*

Wiktor Marek, *Computer Science Department, University of Kentucky, Lexington, KY, USA.*

João P. Martins, *Instituto Superior Técnico, Technical University of Lisbon, Lisbon, Portugal.*

George C. McGregor, *European A.I. Technology Centre, Digital Equipment Corporation, Valbonne, France.*

Jacob L. Mey, *The Rasmus Rask Institute of Linguistics, Odense University, Odense, Denmark.*

Nelma Moreira, *Universidade do Porto, Porto, Portugal.*

Robert C. Moore, *Artificial Intelligence Center, SRI International, Menlo Park, CA, USA.*

Maria das Graças Volpe Nunes, *ICMSC, Universidade de São Paulo, São Carlos, SP, Brasil.*

Luis Moniz Pereira, *Artificial Intelligence and Logical Programming Group, Universidade Nova de Lisboa, Lisbon, Portugal.*

399

Stephen G. Pimentel, *Computer and Software Engineering Division, Institute for Defense Analyses, Alexandria, VA, USA.*

Anne-Marie Pinna, *INRIA, Sophia-Antipolis, Valbonne, France.*

Carlos Pinto-Ferreira, *Instituto Superior Técnico, Technical University of Lisbon, Lisbon, Portugal.*

António G. Portela, *Instituto Superior Técnico, Technical University of Lisbon, Lisbon, Portugal.*

Arkady Rabinov, *Computer Science Department, Stanford University, Stanford, CA, USA.*

Michael Reinfrank, *SIEMENS AG, Munich, West Germany.*

Donia R. Scott, *Philips Research Laboratories, Redhill, Surrey, UK.*

Stuart C. Shapiro, *Department of Computer Science, State University of New York at Buffalo, Buffalo, NY, USA.*

Clarisse Sieckenius de Souza, *Departamento de Informática, PUC/RJ, Rio de Janeiro, Brasil.*

John F. Sowa, *IBM Systems Research, Thornwood, NY, USA.*

Tomek Strzalkowski, *Courant Institute of Mathematical Sciences, New York University, New York, NY, USA.*

José Távora, *LNETI, Dept. Electrónica e Electromecânica, Lisbon, Portugal.*

Weiqing Tian, *Department of Data Processing, Ruhr-University, Bochum, West Germany.*

Ana Paula Tomás, *Centro de Informática, Universidade do Porto, Porto, Portugal.*

Brigitte Trousse, *INRIA, Sophia-Antipolis, Valbonne, France.*

Giovanni B. Varile, *CEC, Luxembourg, Luxembourg.*

Christoph Welsch, *Institut für Informatik, Universität Stuttgart, Stuttgart, West Germany.*

Gian Piero Zarri, *Centre National de la Recherche Scientifique, CERTAL-INALCO, Paris, France.*

Aidong Zhang, *Computer Science Department, University of Kentucky, Lexington, KY, USA.*

F. Zetzsche, *Battelle-Institut e.V., Frankfurt, West Germany.*

Lecture Notes in Computer Science

Vol. 340: G. Rozenberg (Ed.), Advances in Petri Nets 1988. VI, 439 pages. 1988.

Vol. 341: S. Bittanti (Ed.), Software Reliability Modelling and Identification. VII, 209 pages. 1988.

Vol. 342: G. Wolf, T. Legendi, U. Schendel (Eds.), Parcella '88. Proceedings, 1988. 380 pages. 1989.

Vol. 343: J. Grabowski, P. Lescanne, W. Wechler (Eds.), Algebraic and Logic Programming. Proceedings, 1988. 278 pages. 1988.

Vol. 344: J. van Leeuwen, Graph-Theoretic Concepts in Computer Science. Proceedings, 1988. VII, 459 pages. 1989.

Vol. 345: see inside front cover (LNAI).

Vol. 346: see inside front cover (LNAI).

Vol. 347: see inside front cover (LNAI).

Vol. 348: P. Deransart, B. Lorho, J. Maluszyński (Eds.), Programming Languages Implementation and Logic Programming. Proceedings, 1988. VI, 299 pages. 1989.

Vol. 349: B. Monien, R. Cori (Eds.), STACS 89. Proceedings, 1989. VIII, 544 pages. 1989.

Vol. 350: A. Törn, A. Žilinskas, Global Optimization. X, 255 pages. 1989.

Vol. 351: J. Díaz, F. Orejas (Eds.), TAPSOFT '89. Volume 1. Proceedings, 1989. X, 383 pages. 1989.

Vol. 352: J. Díaz, F. Orejas (Eds.), TAPSOFT '89. Volume 2. Proceedings, 1989. X, 389 pages. 1989.

Vol. 354: J.W. de Bakker, W.-P. de Roever, G. Rozenberg (Eds.), Linear Time, Branching Time and Partial Order in Logics and Models for Concurrency. VIII, 713 pages. 1989.

Vol. 355: N. Dershowitz (Ed.), Rewriting Techniques and Applications. Proceedings, 1989. VII, 579 pages. 1989.

Vol. 356: L. Huguet, A. Poli (Eds.), Applied Algebra, Algebraic Algorithms and Error-Correcting Codes. Proceedings, 1987. VI, 417 pages. 1989.

Vol. 357: T. Mora (Ed.), Applied Algebra, Algebraic Algorithms and Error-Correcting Codes. Proceedings, 1988. IX, 481 pages. 1989.

Vol. 358: P. Gianni (Ed.), Symbolic and Algebraic Computation. Proceedings, 1988. XI, 545 pages. 1989.

Vol. 359: D. Gawlick, M. Haynie, A. Reuter (Eds.), High Performance Transaction Systems. Proceedings, 1987. XII, 329 pages. 1989.

Vol. 360: H. Maurer (Ed.), Computer Assisted Learning – ICCAL '89. Proceedings, 1989. VII, 642 pages. 1989.

Vol. 361: S. Abiteboul, P.C. Fischer, H.-J. Schek (Eds.), Nested Relations and Complex Objects in Databases. VI, 323 pages. 1989.

Vol. 362: B. Lisper, Synthesizing Synchronous Systems by Static Scheduling in Space-Time. VI, 263 pages. 1989.

Vol. 363: A.R. Meyer, M.A. Taitslin (Eds.), Logic at Botik '89. Proceedings, 1989. X, 289 pages. 1989.

Vol. 364: J. Demetrovics, B. Thalheim (Eds.), MFDBS 89. Proceedings, 1989. VI, 428 pages. 1989.

Vol. 365: E. Odijk, M. Rem, J.-C. Syre (Eds.), PARLE '89. Parallel Architectures and Languages Europe. Volume I. Proceedings, 1989. XIII, 478 pages. 1989.

Vol. 366: E. Odijk, M. Rem, J.-C. Syre (Eds.), PARLE '89. Parallel Architectures and Languages Europe. Volume II. Proceedings, 1989. XIII, 442 pages. 1989.

Vol. 367: W. Litwin, H.-J. Schek (Eds.), Foundations of Data Organization and Algorithms. Proceedings, 1989. VIII, 531 pages. 1989.

Vol. 368: H. Boral, P. Faudemay (Eds.), IWDM '89, Database Machines. Proceedings, 1989. VI, 387 pages. 1989.

Vol. 369: D. Taubner, Finite Representations of CCS and TCSP Programs by Automata and Petri Nets. X, 168 pages. 1989.

Vol. 370: Ch. Meinel, Modified Branching Programs and Their Computational Power. VI, 132 pages. 1989.

Vol. 371: D. Hammer (Ed.), Compiler Compilers and High Speed Compilation. Proceedings, 1988. VI, 242 pages. 1989.

Vol. 372: G. Ausiello, M. Dezani-Ciancaglini, S. Ronchi Della Rocca (Eds.), Automata, Languages and Programming. Proceedings, 1989. XI, 788 pages. 1989.

Vol. 373: T. Theoharis, Algorithms for Parallel Polygon Rendering. VIII, 147 pages. 1989.

Vol. 374: K.A. Robbins, S. Robbins, The Cray X-MP/Model 24. VI, 165 pages. 1989.

Vol. 375: J.L.A. van de Snepscheut (Ed.), Mathematics of Program Construction. Proceedings, 1989. VI, 421 pages. 1989.

Vol. 376: N.E. Gibbs (Ed.), Software Engineering Education. Proceedings, 1989. VII, 312 pages. 1989.

Vol. 377: M. Gross, D. Perrin (Eds.), Electronic Dictionaries and Automata in Computational Linguistics. Proceedings, 1987. V, 110 pages. 1989.

Vol. 378: J.H. Davenport (Ed.), EUROCAL '87. Proceedings, 1987. VIII, 499 pages. 1989.

Vol. 379: A. Kreczmar, G. Mirkowska (Eds.), Mathematical Foundations of Computer Science 1989. Proceedings, 1989. VIII, 605 pages. 1989.

Vol. 380: J. Csirik, J. Demetrovics, F. Gécseg (Eds.), Fundamentals of Computation Theory. Proceedings, 1989. XI, 493 pages. 1989.

Vol. 381: J. Dassow, J. Kelemen (Eds.), Machines, Languages, and Complexity. Proceedings, 1988. VI, 244 pages. 1989.

Vol. 382: F. Dehne, J.-R. Sack, N. Santoro (Eds.), Algorithms and Data Structures. WADS '89. Proceedings, 1989. IX, 592 pages. 1989.

Vol. 383: see inside front cover (LNAI).

Vol. 384: G.A. van Zee, J.G.G. van de Vorst (Eds.), Parallel Computing 1988. Proceedings, 1988. V, 135 pages. 1989.

Vol. 385: E. Börger, H. Kleine Büning, M.M. Richter (Eds.), CSL '88. Proceedings, 1988. VI, 399 pages. 1989.

Vol. 386: J.E. Pin (Ed.), Formal Properties of Finite Automata and Applications. Proceedings, 1988. VIII, 260 pages. 1989.

Vol. 387: C. Ghezzi, J.A. McDermid (Eds.), ESEC '89. 2nd European Software Engineering Conference. Proceedings, 1989. VI, 496 pages. 1989.

Vol. 388: G. Cohen, J. Wolfmann (Eds.), Coding Theory and Applications. Proceedings, 1988. IX, 329 pages. 1989.

Vol. 389: D.H. Pitt, D.E. Rydeheard, P. Dybjer, A.M. Pitts, A. Poigné (Eds.), Category Theory and Computer Science. Proceedings, 1989. VI, 365 pages. 1989.

Vol. 390: see inside front cover (LNAI).